Becoming a ———— WIN-WIN TEACHER

To Marian Morris and Anne Marshall—intern program coordinators, resources, support people, and witnesses to my first year. With gratitude.

JANE BLUESTEIN

Becoming a ———

WIN-WIN TEACHER

SURVIVAL STRATEGIES FOR THE BEGINNING EDUCATOR

CORWIN

A SAGE Company

For information:

Corwin
A SAGE Company
2455 Teller Road
Thousand Oaks, California 91320
(800) 233-9936
Fax: (800) 417-2466
www.corwin.com

SAGE Ltd.
1 Oliver's Yard
55 City Road
London EC1Y 1SP
United Kingdom

SAGE India Pvt. Ltd.
B 1/I 1 Mohan Cooperative
    Industrial Area
Mathura Road, New Delhi 110 044
India

SAGE Asia-Pacific Pte. Ltd.
33 Pekin Street #02-01
Far East Square
Singapore 048763

Printed in the United States of America

Library of Congress Cataloging-in-Publication Data

Bluestein, Jane.
Becoming a win-win teacher : survival strategies for the beginning educator / Jane Bluestein.
    p. cm.
Includes bibliographical references and index.
ISBN 978-1-4129-6749-5 (pbk. : alk. paper)

   1. First year teachers—United States. 2. Mentoring in education—United States. 3. Successful teaching—United States. I. Title.

LB1731.4.B58 2010
371.1—dc22   2009054005

This book is printed on acid-free paper.

10   11   12   13   14   10 9 8 7 6 5 4 3 2 1

Acquisitions Editor:	Hudson Perigo
Associate Editor:	Julie McNall
Editorial Assistant:	Allison Scott
Production Editor:	Cassandra Margaret Seibel
Copy Editor:	Cynthia Long
Typesetter:	C&M Digitals (P) Ltd.
Proofreader:	Sarah J. Duffy
Indexer:	Sheila Bodell
Cover Designer:	Michael Dubowe

Contents

About the Author

A dynamic and entertaining speaker, **Dr. Jane Bluestein** has worked with thousands of educators, counselors, healthcare professionals, parents, childcare workers, and other community members worldwide. She has appeared internationally as a speaker and talk-show guest, including several appearances as a guest expert on *CNN, National Public Radio,* and *The Oprah Winfrey Show.*

Dr. Bluestein specializes in programs and resources geared to provide practical and meaningful information, training, and hope in areas related to relationship building, effective instruction and guidance, and personal development. Much of her work focuses on interactions between adults and children, especially children at risk. Her down-to-earth speaking style, practicality, sense of humor, and numerous stories and examples make her ideas clear and accessible to her audiences.

Dr. Bluestein is an award-winning author whose books include *Creating Emotionally Safe Schools; High School's Not Forever; 21st Century Discipline; Being a Successful Teacher; Parents, Teens, and Boundaries; The Parent's Little Book of Lists: Do's and Don'ts of Effective Parenting; Mentors, Masters, and Mrs. McGregor: Stories of Teachers Making a Difference;* and *Magic, Miracles & Synchronicity: A Journal of Gratitude and Awareness.* Dr. Bluestein's latest books include *The Win-Win Classroom* and a companion facilitator's guide.

Formerly a classroom teacher in inner-city Pittsburgh, Pennsylvania, crisis-intervention counselor, teacher training program coordinator, and volunteer with high-risk teens at a local day treatment program, Dr. Bluestein currently heads Instructional Support Services, Inc., a consulting and resource firm in Albuquerque, New Mexico.

Her words will touch your heart;
her ideas will change your life.

Prologue:
Why I Teach

If you had asked me back in the beginning to tell you why I teach, I don't know how I might have answered. It wasn't the money—back in my days as a teaching intern, I was bringing home a mere $318 a month, which wasn't much, even then. It wasn't the hours—between graduate school and losing the battle to stay one step ahead of my thirty-nine fifth-graders, I was putting in ridiculously long days. And it certainly wasn't the chance to exercise my genius as an instructor—I was lucky if I could get through one day without a fight breaking out.

No, there wasn't much glory in working with kids who greeted me with, "I don't do reading," before I'd had a chance to learn their names. Nor was it heartwarming to teach kids who saw me more as an annoyance than an inspiration, kids who couldn't care less that all I'd ever wanted my entire life was to be a teacher.

I cried a lot my first year. I cried the day my whole class failed what I thought was a simple pretest. I cried the day my kids wouldn't sit down and be quiet while my supervisor was in the room. I cried the day a parent said that maybe her son would do better with an "older" teacher. And I cried the day I visited the home of one of my most difficult students and found her mother falling-down drunk before lunchtime.

So what kept me in the game, especially that first year? Looking back, it took remarkably little to renew my sense of hope, or at least suggest that maybe all was not lost. I would come this close to throwing in the towel when a child would uncharacteristically come to class prepared, make a positive behavioral change, or help a classmate. I'd be sure I couldn't make it through the day when someone would suddenly *get* subtraction or appear excited about a subject we were about to discuss. And just as I was about to give up, they'd finally sit still for a story or laugh at one of my jokes.

For other teachers, perhaps it's the progress, imperceptible as it may seem at times, the little connections, a hug here and there, or the realization that we might well be the only source of encouragement some child is getting right now. Perhaps deep down there's the possibility that our excitement, or even our good intentions, somehow makes a dent, that our caring and commitment allow us, inevitably, to touch the future. But we give what we give because we can't not give, and we give in the best of faith, because the evidence of our devotion is sometimes long in coming. We are tested again and again, and sometimes we just keep coming back for no good reason besides the fact that, for better or worse, we are called to teach. Maybe this is something only another teacher can understand: It's not just what we do. It's who we are.[1]

NOTE

1. This piece originally appeared as the foreword I wrote for the book *Why I Teach*, by Esther Wright (Bluestein, 1999b, pp. vii–viii). Reprinted by permission.

Introduction

In retrospect, I was one of the lucky ones. I did my student teaching and first-year internship at two tough inner-city schools, the professional equivalent of learning to swim by jumping off a ship a mile from shore. As solid as my teacher training classes had been, I discovered a number of gaping holes in my preparation once I was actually facing my students for the first time. At the very least, I was surprised to discover that the majority of my students were *not* easily engaged, self-managing, traditional learners who wanted to be there and who wanted to learn—the very students I had been trained to teach. So much of what I had learned prior to my work with real live students wasn't as helpful as I would have liked.[1]

There were so many things about the profession that were never mentioned or discussed in my training. I knew a lot about teaching, but I didn't know anywhere near what I needed to know about the culture of the profession I was entering. Having a good grasp of curriculum, scope and sequence, or the effective use of instructional activities and materials was small comfort when up against the emotional defenses and apparent indifference of students whose previous school experiences were laced, to varying degrees, with discouragement and failure.

Likewise, my instructional skills didn't help prepare me for the challenges of becoming a part of the adult community at school. And I don't remember anything that would have helped me to develop the flexibility, resiliency, people skills, or sense of humor I'd need—or even to appreciate how important these qualities would be. As comprehensive as my training may have been, if there was *any* instruction that would have helped me deal with the politics of the workplace, recognize the hidden agendas of colleagues and administrators, anticipate the range of cognitive and social realities I would encounter in my students and their families, or even learn how to function as an adult and professional in a school, I was apparently absent that day.

My own failures and frustrations as a beginning teacher were reflected (and validated) years later when I started working with first-year interns, many of them struggling with similar gaps in their personal and professional development. In response, I put together a survival manual for these individuals, and like the resources and materials I had encountered in my own training a few years before, it addressed the immediate management issues they were facing. Among the original forty-four chapters were strategies for dealing with lesson plans, bulletin boards, and field trips—important information, to be sure—and back then, there were nowhere near the number of resources on these topics that are now available in books or online. But when the opportunity to revise that book arose, I found myself led in a somewhat different direction. This was more than a simple case of "been there, done that." Whatever guidance I received, whether an intuitive hit or a reaction to what I was hearing from beginning teachers around the country, it seemed far more appropriate for me to take on the challenge of addressing some of the less tangible issues and realities for which many new teachers are still unprepared.

In itself, this has proved to be no easy task. There continues to be a fair amount of black-and-white thinking around teacher preparation. But somewhere between the giddy exuberance of so many beginning teacher resources and the disquieting accounts from survivors of extremely negative (even dangerous) teaching situations, I believe there is a place for something that reflects the actual experience of working in a school, which for most of us is much closer to the center, somewhere between these two extremes. I certainly want to share the good stuff, because teaching can be incredibly satisfying and there are many positives in teaching that you are unlikely to find anywhere else. But I also believe that a balanced teacher-preparation resource needs to include a visit to the dark side, a glimpse of the negative aspects that can tank an otherwise promising career.

I have no intention of scaring anyone off or painting an unduly bleak picture of the teaching profession. (I certainly would not have devoted my entire adult life to this field were it not returning a great deal on my investments of time and energy or if I didn't believe in its potential.) But the stories of teachers who simply walked off the job—sometimes in the middle of the day—begs the question of what might have helped them prepare for whatever in their experience overwhelmed them.

I want this book to help you have a successful and satisfying experience, and a part of this book is about the ways you can create the support and protection you may need to do so. So let's take a look at education from a big-picture perspective, including some of the stuff you may not have heard about in your training—good and not-so-good—because teaching is hard enough without walking into a situation unaware of the things that can make it even harder.

NOTE

1. Although I doubt I could appreciate it at the time, this experience gave me an edge over the numerous people I've known who had a relatively easy placement initially and later encountered a far more challenging reality once assigned to their own classrooms, often in a very different sort of school. While I don't believe there is such a thing as an "easy" school, clearly some settings offer greater challenges than others, and if a teacher is going to feel shocked, betrayed, and unprepared, it's probably best to do so earlier rather than later, particularly during a time when a cooperating teacher and some university support might be available.

Win-Win Teaching

Start by doing what's necessary, then what's possible, and suddenly you are doing the impossible.

Saint Francis of Assisi[1]

School, as it was built, is an essential support system for a model of social engineering that condemns most people to be subordinate stones in a pyramid that narrows as it ascends to a terminal of control.

John Taylor Gatto[2]

Teachers have an opportunity to touch lives in ways that can make a difference in the futures of thousands of people. I believe that from the efforts of teachers all careers spring.

Don Quimby[3]

This is a book about becoming a win-win teacher. As an educator, I never heard this term. In none of my teacher training classes and inservice programs were those words ever mentioned, nor did any of the educational literature I encountered refer to the concept. It was only when I started to scour the business-management literature that I found what turned out to be the conceptual missing link, a structure for what I understood about how human beings interacted in organizations and relationships, and a framework for the ingredients that seemed to contribute to effective and successful teaching.

As it turns out, the concept was first proposed back in the 1920s by Mary Parker Follett, a visionary and pioneer in human relations, democratic organization, and management.[4] In the late 1980s and throughout the following decade, a number of well-known business leaders and management consultants[5] helped bring the term more into the mainstream. In business, the term *win-win* generally refers to strategies that allow "both, or all, parties involved in a negotiation or another activity to be successful to a degree."[6]

So how would the concept translate to a school setting, where negotiation is not a particularly common practice among adults, and even less so between adults and students? Win-win also presumes a certain degree of autonomy and respect for the wishes and preferences of everyone involved—something else we don't often see in educational settings, where we're more likely, especially as beginning teachers, to be directed to a particular classroom, given a certain set of supplies, assigned to a specific schedule, and handed a student roster, without our input or preferences ever being solicited. And how can win-win objectives, which prioritize allowing for each party to benefit in some way and which emphasize "the importance of cooperation, fun, sharing, caring, and overall group success,"[7] coexist in a system that has traditionally been characterized by things like top-down management, scarcity thinking, social cliques and hierarchies, bell curves, standardization, and competitive grading?

People who try to shape education around a business model have not met with much success. Nor have attempts to drive decisions down to point of greatest impact within that context been particularly effective. As one former school administrator observed, "The political structure of schools is different from the political structure of businesses. Superintendents are responsible by law for decisions and have to answer to a school board and local politicians." So, traditionally, decisions in school settings have been made at the top and passed down. Most often, staff opinions are given scant attention when it comes to making major changes in policies or procedures, if staff members are invited to the table at all. As this contributor noted, even the most sincere attempts to "involve staff in the decision-making process usually ends up relegated to making choices having to do with the lunchroom or playground."

Few educators in any position or level in the profession are trained in the skills necessary for creating a win-win classroom environment, and the lack of role models and cultural examples doesn't help. Although experience suggests that our schools are not particularly conducive to a strategy pulled from the world of business and commerce, it's important to note that win-win issues are not business issues—they are *people* issues, relationship issues, and issues involved in creating a sense of community, competence, and mutual respect, all of which lie at the heart of education and successful teaching. This makes the classroom the perfect place to implement a win-win philosophy along with the practices that go with it. Although there will always be factors beyond our immediate control, there are also many decisions individual teachers—including educators who are new to the profession—can make that can have a positive, win-win effect on the culture of the classroom.

If you're new to the profession or new to your school, you're understandably going to be more concerned with things like finding the supply closet or getting to know the curriculum than, say, constructing a philosophical context in your classroom that may not actually exist anywhere in the school district. Even if you're a well-established veteran who is simply new to the concept of win-win strategies and dynamics, the prospect of making these changes can be overwhelming. And be aware that even teachers who are committed to win-win goals are likely to run into opposition and restrictions designed to keep anything in education from ever actually changing.

But rest assured, this doesn't have to be hard and there are a lot of things you can do that don't require whole-school buy-in or administrative support. Whether your reasons are noble (creating an emotional environment in which kids are more likely to be academically and socially successful, more cooperative, more responsible, more committed, and more likely to become contributing members of society) or purely selfish (getting through the day with fewer headaches and less conflict), there is a potentially huge payoff for these intentions for everyone involved. Besides, everything you want to accomplish, all the dreams (I hope) you have of being an effective and successful teacher, will be realized in the context of the environment you create, and it will always be easier to accomplish your goals in a win-win structure than in an atmosphere of win-lose (not to mention no-win) interactions and relationships.

A win-win approach to teaching is really about being able to think, plan, and make decisions in ways that take the needs of others into consideration—your students, certainly, as well as other members of the school community. Win-win strategies can help you

- establish your authority without disempowering students (or making students *lose*);
- build students' independence, self-management, and accountability;
- defuse conflict and in-your-face challenges;
- avoid frustrating and self-defeating teacher behaviors;
- maintain high standards and consistent follow-through;
- focus on the positive aspects of students' behavior and work;
- match instruction to students' needs and learning styles;
- engage a wide range of kids, including defiant, defeated, and at-risk learners;
- accommodate students' needs for autonomy and the ability to influence their learning (topics, presentation, evaluation, and environment);
- accommodate students' needs for respect, acceptance, and belonging;
- accommodate students' needs for success and competence, as well as honest feedback and continual, appropriate challenge;
- consider students' needs and preference in making decisions with regard to instruction and activities, topics, and materials;
- create an emotionally safe classroom environment;
- encourage positive social interactions among students;
- build positive, supportive relationships with mentors, supervisors, administrators, and colleagues;
- generate support for implementing programs and ideas, obtaining materials or equipment, and securing repair services, for example;
- build positive, supportive relationships with parents; and
- reduce stress and burnout.

This challenge of becoming a win-win teacher is really about your priorities and sense of purpose, what brought you to education in the first place. While true that it's important to get your bulletin boards up (and changed on occasion), cover whatever is on page eighteen, and figure out the district's record-keeping requirements, I'm willing to bet that you didn't wake up wanting to be a teacher just so you could attend to these details. Teaching is, first and foremost, a people business. It may be easy to get distracted from all the people aspects of your work by data- and content-driven demands, but when things like classroom climate, connecting with kids, and appropriately challenging each individual student become the "important stuff," the data and content tend to fall much more easily into place.

So let's get our proverbial ducks in a row and look at some of the things you might want to know, learn, or do to get your career off to a great start (or if you've been at this a while, to tweak your skills and make your job more effective and enjoyable). If you're interested enough in the teaching profession to be reading this book, then here are some ideas to help you become (or continue to be) the kind of teacher who not only gets results in the classroom in terms of student commitment and academic performance but who also wakes up excited about going into work every day and being a part of the profession—not just tomorrow but down the road, years from now, as well.

ACTIVITY

Considering your personal experience (as a student, as an educator, and as an observer), answer the following questions:

1. Give an example of where you have seen or experienced a *win-lose* philosophy or approach in a noneducational arena such as advertising, media programming, management, or social relationships.

2. Give an example of where you have seen or experienced a *win-win* philosophy or approach in a noneducational arena such as advertising, media programming, management, or social relationships.

3. Give an example of strategies or approaches you have observed, experienced, or imagined that promote *win-lose* outcomes in the following educational arenas:

   a. Behavior management and power dynamics

   b. Academic achievement

   c. Social interactions and relationships

   d. Learning styles

4. Give an example of strategies or approaches you have observed, experienced, or imagined that promote *win-win* outcomes in the following educational arenas:

   a. Behavior management and power dynamics

   b. Academic achievement

   c. Social interactions and relationships

   d. Learning styles

5. Why do you think a win-win approach has traditionally been uncommon in a school setting?

6. What obstacles do you envision for a teacher attempting to establish a win-win approach in the classroom?

7. What supports do you believe exist for a teacher attempting to establish a win-win approach in the classroom?

NOTES

1. Thank you to Seta Khajarian for contributing this quote in an e-mail sent January 15, 2008.

2. Gatto (2005, p. 13).

3. Quimby (2003).

4. Mary Parker Follett Foundation (n.d.); Lantieri and Patti (1996, p. 19).

5. Including folks such as Stephen Covey, Peter Drucker, Charles Garfield, John Naisbitt, and Peter Senge.

6. Win-win strategy (n.d.).

7. Apple Dictionary Version 2.0.2 (51.4); Win-win games (n.d.).

PART I
Commitment

All who have meditated on the art of governing mankind have been convinced that the fate of empires depends on the education of youth.

Aristotle, philosopher[1]

Experience is not what happens to you. It's what you do with what happens to you.

Aldous Huxley, English novelist[2]

Let the wise guide beings away from darkness, give direction and advice. They will be treasured by the virtuous and dismissed by the foolish.

Dhammapada, verse 77[3]

Imagine this: One hundred people want to go to a place they've never been. They've each read the guidebooks, watched the travel shows, learned a bit about the culture and language, and packed exactly what they think they'll need. Even if they all head to the same place, at the same time, and on the same tour, chances are good that the end result will be one hundred very different experiences.

Teacher training isn't all that different. Send one hundred people into their own classrooms, and you'll see a wide variety of outcomes. Even with similar preparation, there are so many factors that can influence the experience—from the classrooms, combination of students, schedules assigned, or the resources or support available to differences in personalities, preferences, and needs—that each experience will be different. (I believe that this would be the case even if they all somehow ended up at the same school, teaching the same subject, grade level, and students.)

You probably know that armchair travel isn't even close to actually stepping off the plane in a foreign land, and there are people who will say that no amount of teacher preparation is as effective as what you learn by just doing it. To a certain degree, they would be correct, but forewarned is forearmed, as they say, and—back to my travel metaphor—I have discovered some real gems in doing my homework before I took off on a trip, from learning about a nearby village or restaurant I might never have discovered to anticipating problems I could avoid. I generally have more enjoyable and successful trips when I take the time to learn a bit of the language and familiarize myself with where I'm going ahead of time.

Again, teaching isn't much different, because in a lot of ways, walking into a classroom—or simply working in a school—is not unlike stepping down on foreign soil. Every educational system has its own unique culture, history, politics, and traditions, and there really is no good way to anticipate the full experience until you're there. (Indeed, even if you stay in the same school for a number of years, it's more likely than not that you will see changes over time and from one year to the next.) While I can't predict everything you might encounter in your teaching experience, I would like to share with you some of the possibilities that can exist, the educational equivalent of a freak cold spell or railroad strike. I want to relate some of the experiences that other teachers have shared with me and present some of the conditions and situations that are frankly unique to the culture of the profession, information you may not have encountered in your preservice experience.

Because whatever brought you to this profession—whether passion, curiosity, or the idea of having your summers off—I sincerely want you to defy the odds, to still be here years from now with your passion and commitment intact. You've put in a lot of time and effort to get where you are. It won't do anyone any good for you to give up before you've had a chance to get it right and be there long enough to truly make a difference. So let's journey together to explore the myths and realities of the teaching profession, along with some useful strategies and tools to make your trip successful, satisfying, and fun. Let your dreams and good intentions be your passport. And don't forget to pack the sunscreen.

NOTES

1. Aristotle (n.d., para. 1).

2. Huxley (n.d., para. 1).

3. *2008 Forest Sangha Calendar* (2007, p. 3).

Teaching as a Calling

When you find yourself lying awake at 3:00 in the morning, wondering what you can do to make yourself a better teacher, you have reached the point where you really do understand what teaching is all about.

David Friedli, secondary principal

This is not a profession—it is a passion! I send my students postcards when I am on vacation. I call them over holiday break and summer vacation. I am constantly creating new lessons. I cannot shop without finding something to share with them.

Carol Dinsdale, special education teacher

If you are glad to be teaching, your students will know.

Robert L. Wyatt and J. Elaine White[1]

We've probably all known teachers who were just putting in their time until retirement, either people who went into teaching for all the wrong reasons or individuals who simply burned out on the job. And while there may always be a handful of teachers who are just going through the motions, I believe that the majority of folks teaching today are dedicated professionals with good intentions, people who want to make a difference, people who really want to be there.

For most of us, teaching is more than just a job. A number of contributors to this book referred to their work as a *calling*—a term often associated with a religious or spiritual vocation—and surely many educators would classify their involvement with this profession in this way. Elementary gifted teacher Annette Dake noted that effective teachers simply "wouldn't be happy being anything else."

I've met many educators who came to teaching later in life. Some put off becoming a teacher to raise a family or to work in a field that would support them better financially. Others perhaps hadn't thought to become teachers earlier in their lives but picked up teaching as a second (or third) career after military service, for example, or working in other fields. One high school English teacher told me that she had come back to teaching after years in the jewelry business. Although she made less money when she left the business world, she went back into the classroom because "teaching is more rewarding." Elementary teacher Stacey Ferguson "wanted the personal, eyeball-to-eyeball contact with others" that she missed as a customer service representative. Eric Wright, an administrative intern, actually quit teaching after his first year to go into the business world. "I came back a year later and I've loved it ever since," he said.

Secondary math teacher Nancy Foote responded to a question asking if she thought that teaching had been a good career choice: "Of course I would do it again, only I would start sooner next time. I spent the first years of my professional career as a chemist, and I made a ton of money. But something was missing from my life." Once her children started school, Foote trained to become a teacher. "It was the best thing I ever did. Teaching is not only what I do, it is who I am. I could no sooner stop teaching than I could stop breathing."

I can relate, although I seemed to know this even before I'd actually gone to school. From my first episode of *Romper Room* at age three, I was hooked![2] By the end of my first week in kindergarten, my intentions were sealed for life. I get so excited about the first day of school each year that I don't think I've ever been able to sleep through the night, whether I was going in the next day as a student, a teacher, or more recently, as a teacher educator. This anticipation is part of a rhythm that has defined and informed my life for more than five decades.

Like many of the individuals I interviewed, I believe I was simply born with the desire to teach—and with the sense of mission that comes with a vocation or calling. I could not wait to get into my first classroom and went straight from college into a first-year teaching internship that started just weeks after finishing my undergraduate program. Observing a masterfully taught lesson can still take my breath away, and evidence of the impact we can have on a child's life can bring me to tears. Although my work in education has taken me down many different paths, I am among thousands of veterans who have hung in despite significant changes, challenges, and lots of crazy-making experiences over the years. This is undoubtedly what I came here to do.

Certainly, I am not alone. Educational consultant Aili Pogust found her calling early as well. Bilingual in Estonian and German at age six when her family immigrated to the United States, she began teaching her mother the English she was learning. "Picking up English was easier for me," she remembered. "I shared what I was learning with my mother so she could function in this new country. When she didn't understand something, I had to figure out another way to explain it to her. And so a teacher was born." Lindsay Shepheard, the executive assistant to her district's superintendent, suggested that becoming a teacher "is one of the decisions one makes without realizing it when, as a child, helping others is important, even in one's own family. Wanting to make a difference manifests itself in many ways, but those who truly want to teach know it long before they face their first class of students."

While this is probably true for most teachers, one of the best and most committed educators I know is a friend who never had any intention of going into the profession! Elementary language teacher Tuija Fagerlund ended up in the classroom because it was the only job she could find in her hometown, where her future husband had a job. But she stayed in the field and has been at the same school for over twenty-two years, admitting that teaching gets in your blood. "I've never done anything else, so imagining a life that doesn't include teaching is a bit hard," she observed. Although perhaps lacking the initial desire to go into teaching that many of us discovered early in life, I suspect that what makes this teacher so effective is a kind of dedication that allows her to care deeply for and about her students. Anne Morgan, a teacher of at-risk preschool children, noted similar sentiments. "I'm not a person who grew up knowing that I always wanted to be a teacher," she wrote. "I changed my mind about my major a few times, but now that I'm in a classroom, I couldn't imagine myself doing anything else."

Clearly, this journey varies from person to person—some starting early and with a great deal of certainty, others approaching the profession indirectly, even reluctantly. But regardless of how they arrived at their destination, the one thing all of the teachers I interviewed or surveyed had in common was a desire to make a difference in the lives of children. I have found this to be true of nearly all of the educators I have met throughout my life and career, including teachers who left the profession and those who stayed but regretted their choice of careers. (Indeed, the teachers who left because they felt unable to accomplish this objective were perhaps the most bitter and disappointed of all.) Calling or no, educator Don Quimby affirmed, "We became teachers because of one basic reason—we chose to become involved in a career in which we could directly impact the future through the feelings and attitudes we might be able to instill in our students."[3]

ACTIVITY

Think about what brought you to this profession and this place in your life. Was it just that inner knowledge, perhaps at a young age, that you were born to teach? Was it the need for a sense of purpose that may have been lacking in other jobs? Maybe teaching provided an avenue for expressing your passion for a particular subject or a place to make a difference. Or perhaps it was a teacher who touched your life and inspired you to give back in similar fashion. List or describe the factors that influenced your decision to become a teacher.

ACTIVITY

Think of a teacher who had a powerful, positive impact on you. (This person does not need to be a classroom teacher or someone you know from a school experience.) Describe the qualities you most admired or respected in this individual.

NOTES

1. Wyatt and White (2007, pp. 123–124).

2. *Romper Room* (n.d.) was a children's television series that ran in the United States, and in other countries around the world, from 1953 to 1994. The program was aimed at children five years of age or younger and included "games, exercises, songs and moral lessons" (para. 3).

3. Quimby (2005, para. 8).

Climate Advisory

Entering Win-Lose Territory

You will be told to inspire but be ridiculed for your enthusiasm. You will be told to make time for yourself but expected to stay late, serve on a bunch of committees, and devote your evenings and weekends to planning, calling parents, and grading papers. You will hear the merits of creativity and responding to students' needs but risk sanctions if you stray from curricular guides or district mandates. You will be encouraged to ensure that every child succeeds but be accused of being too easy if this actually occurs.

Veteran teacher

Our teachers are "helped" to death and are running screaming from the school because they cannot take working under such scrutiny and having to explain, report, reflect, discuss, and analyze everything we are asking them to do.

Former assistant superintendent

You have to jump through hoops just to get to the point where you are stifled again.

Jason McCord, teacher and therapeutic counselor

Considering the zeal and commitment of so many of the people drawn to this field—individuals who insist they were born to teach, who cannot imagine themselves doing anything else with their lives, and who genuinely want to have a positive impact on future generations—how do we reconcile statistics that consistently report that half of all teachers leave the profession within five years of their first assignment? Even if we only take into account the amount of time, effort, and financial resources that each of these individuals invested just to get into a classroom in the first place, how do we make sense of a trend that shows roughly 170,000 teachers leaving the profession each year for some reason other than retirement, putting the annual cost of teacher turnover in the neighborhood of seven billion dollars?[1]

While the research cites a number of reasons teachers leave the profession, I believe that *surprise* is a significant factor in attrition—or at the very least, in the kind of discouragement and frustration that can lead to attrition—in terms of the lack of preparation for the realities of teaching expressed by many of the professionals I've encountered. Authors Duane Inman and Leslie Marlow described what they call "classroom or reality shock,"[2] which was confirmed by quite a bit of the feedback I received from beginning teachers. Many of them, only a few weeks into their first teaching assignment, were already questioning their career choices. Although the majority of beginning teachers I interviewed were excited about what they were doing, many lamented, "This isn't at all what I was expecting."

Nobody enters this field hoping to fail, and I doubt many go through the preparation process planning to drop out of the profession within the first few years. I'm going to assume, regardless of where you are in your journey, that your goals include being a *good* teacher, enjoying your work, having a positive impact on your students, and maybe—be still my heart!—even having an impact on the system itself.

Now, it might be easy to assume that the system actually *wants* all teachers and students to succeed. (Isn't that what the brochures said?) But with very few exceptions, this is not the case. In fact, the teaching profession is structured on a number of principles and policies that pretty much guarantee a certain degree of failure—for teachers and students alike. Despite the good intentions behind many of these win-lose customs, most were forged in traditions that served the goals of a very different time. As schools catch up to the needs of current cultural, technological, and economic demands, it is my most fervent hope that the negative, anachronistic patterns that are so common—and which so often continue unquestioned—will come under greater scrutiny and eventually give way to more constructive priorities. In the meantime, let's take a look at some of the factors that contribute to the win-lose context in which you may find yourself working, characteristics of the profession that can erode the most passionate and dedicated educator. These are some of the reasons most often mentioned for teachers leaving or considering a change in career. Later in this book, I will explore many of these issues in greater detail and present some things you can do to avoid being sidelined—or surprised—by the most common of them.

FINANCIAL REALITIES

In my days in the classroom, it was rare that I wasn't also picking up a few extra dollars writing curriculum, waitressing, or working in my in-laws' bakery, at times holding more than one additional job to make ends meet—and I wasn't the only teacher on our staff who had at least one side job during the year. Years later, salary is still a concern for people in the profession, including a number of contributors to this book. Despite significant improvements in this area in past decades, a report by the National Education Association claimed, "New teachers are often unable to pay off their loans or afford houses in the communities where they teach. Teachers and education support professionals often work two and three jobs to make ends meet. The stress and exhaustion can become unbearable, forcing people out of the profession to more lucrative positions."[3]

Sixth-grade teacher Melissa Albright said she wished she had known that salary would always be an issue. "I grew up in a family of teachers and money was scarce; however, I never realized that my friends would double their salaries long before I would and that I would not get bonuses, tickets to games, or dinners out," she said. "With three college degrees in education, I still make less than half of what my friends do who only have one degree." One assistant superintendent responded, when asked if he had it to do over, would he choose teaching as his career, "After thirty-six years in this business . . . and seeing my sons, who are in private industry, receive [five-digit] end-of-year bonuses, I would say, no. Not in this day and age."[4] Jen Buttars, sixth-grade math teacher, regretted borrowing as much money as she did for school, because it has been hard to repay her loans on a teacher's salary. Another middle school teacher, Cheryl Converse-Rath, who was working as a substitute teacher "for daily pay and no benefits," left teaching because she could not afford to continue working under those conditions. "I have a master's degree," she said, "yet I felt like a beggar."

One report on teacher pay claimed that the "intrinsic rewards" of a career in education are "often used as a rationale for low salaries,"[5] although it makes no sense that education would be the only profession subjected to this reasoning. (Imagine expecting doctors, for example, to work for the satisfaction of making people feel better or saving lives.) High school teacher Ray Dagger cautioned against the myth of working for intrinsic rewards, noble though they may be. "We all do it for the money," he said. "If you don't believe that, check to see how many teachers return their paychecks each month."

Nonetheless, I doubt that many people go into teaching expecting to make a killing. And while some may ultimately find their paychecks less satisfying (or adequate) than anticipated, it is doubtful that many people prepare for a teaching career unaware of the financial aspects of the job. However, there is a tipping point where other issues and obstacles can overwhelm the satisfaction we take in a well-received lesson or a struggling student's sudden epiphany. Even teachers with tremendous support, materials, and freedom won't stay long in a job that doesn't pay the rent, and generous financial compensation—which we don't often see in education, especially for beginning classroom teachers—won't hold people if they are up against continually *unsatisfying* working conditions. While it may be easier to stay in a low-paying job when there *are* intrinsic rewards, when these positive experiences rarely occur or when the negative aspects of the job outweigh the good stuff, the financial issues and discrepancies become harder to ignore.

Although one report claimed that "thirty-seven percent of teachers who do not plan to continue teaching until retirement blame low pay for their decision to leave the profession," much of the research and personal feedback I've encountered suggest that job dissatisfaction claims even larger numbers.[6] University of Pennsylvania professor Richard Ingersol noted, "Novice teachers are much more likely to call it quits if they work in schools where they feel they have little input or support."[7] And author Cynthia Kopkowski noted, "The underlying issue on salary often comes down to [a lack of] respect."[8]

Interestingly, all of the survey respondents who mentioned teacher pay did so in the context of some negative aspect of their teaching experience. For example, my friend who mentioned his sons' bonuses also cited "seeing how the attitudes of the teachers, students and parents have changed" over the years. One fourth-grade teacher wrote, "If I had to do it over again, I would have become an attorney and made triple the money, and not have to deal with disrespectful children all day." A professional development project coordinator mentioned "too much responsibility for the pay" and the fact that "teachers do not get the respect they deserve from students and parents" or adequate support from administrators. And another longtime assistant superintendent mentioned "a bureaucracy that suffocates this field" in addition to "the lack of financial incentive to stay in this career path." It was never just about the money.

IT'S HARDER THAN IT LOOKS

Talk to some people outside of education and you'd swear we only work a few hours a day, basically babysitting or talking to kids, for a few months a year. Anyone who has actually worked as a teacher, however, would not be surprised at the number of contributors who mentioned the amount of time the job requires, the scope of responsibilities, or the degree to which teaching can take over our lives as stressful aspects of the job. This work involves a wide range of professional, instructional, and emotional demands, far beyond what people who are not in the field could possibly imagine. Although we no longer are required to fill lamps, light the fires to warm the rooms, or scrub the floors once a week,[9] the preparation, paperwork, and increases in accountability—along with concerns for our students' academic, social, and emotional well-being—can be overwhelming.

I certainly didn't see much of my family or friends my first year or two, unless they came over to help me cut out bulletin boards or laminate materials. A recent conversation with retired teacher Ken Bauer, who a long time ago co-interned with me in the same fifth-grade classroom, brought up memories of our first year in the profession: "Nobody had a dime and nobody got any sleep," he recalled. More recently, I had two new teachers, second careers for each of them, stumble into my seminar after having been in their respective classrooms well past midnight the day before. Although their schedules may not represent those of the majority of teachers, I doubt that there are many teachers who are not putting plenty of hours into their jobs, not only at home but in their classrooms as well, before school starts and long after their students have left for the day.

Kindergarten teacher Jill Snyderman noted, "I really wish someone would have told me how tiring teaching was and how much work you put into each day. By the time I leave school and get home, I am exhausted and all I want to do is relax, but I can't because I have work to do." She advises beginning teachers, "Tell your loved ones to hang in there for you. You will be busy and tired and, depending on your grade level, you may work all day and then come home and grade all night—not to mention going to your classroom or bringing home work on the weekends."

One fourth-grade teacher commented, "I really wish someone had told me about all the long hours, of my own time, to prepare and check student progress." Although as a matter of sanity and self-care, it is essential to carve out a little separation from work, I think that most teachers would chuckle at the notion of "my own time." Yes, you do get to leave the building, but be prepared to take the job home with you—in your heart and your head, as well as your briefcase or book bag. Guidance counselor Carrie Balent observed that "there is no down time," and several contributors wrote to discourage anyone from coming to teaching with the idea that it would be an eight-to-three job.

I always found it hard to disconnect from teaching. I often awoke in the middle of the night worried about the kids I couldn't seem to reach, stressed about an unhappy parent, or inspired with an idea for an activity or a game. Everything I did or saw, whether during the school year, on weekends, or even on vacation, tended to filter through the lens of how I could use the experience or item in my classroom. One contributor said, "It has taken over my life in many ways. I always think about my work, even when I'm trying to sleep or get a break on the weekend. I work every night and on weekends, too, to try and keep up and do a quality job." Or as principal Ales Zitnik wryly noted, "It is an all-day, all-week, all-month, all-year activity—working, thinking, exploring, acting—like a disease."

Although several teachers mentioned how much they enjoyed and appreciated having a break in the summer, a number found this time off to be a bit of a myth. Mandy Frantti, a secondary science teacher, wrote, "Many people, unfortunately, go into teaching because they see it as a way to get summers off. That's not teaching. Most states now have laws requiring continuing education, which means that after spending a long tiring school year teaching, you then turn around and put yourself in the student's spot for the summer. Not to mention the prep work good teachers do over the summer. There just isn't time during the year to do all the things that will mean the difference between a good teacher and a great teacher."

Third-grade teacher Jason Gehrke discovered, "You really don't get your summers off. There is always work to be done after the school year in preparation for the next year." High school English teacher Melody Aldrich agreed. She did not realize how consuming teaching would be. "Summers off?" she wrote. "You've got to be kidding. Working the same schedule as my kids? Think again. I stay late and come in early every day." People who are drawn to teaching by the prospect of short days and summers off are often the first to leave the profession. First-grade teacher Cindi Allen noted, "The teaching field is not for the weak. I had a student teacher one year who was getting her teaching degree only because of the holidays and summers off. I imagine she isn't in the field any longer."

Many respondents were surprised by how physically demanding teaching was. Even in my twenties, there were plenty of times when I practically collapsed just walking in the door after work, especially if my day had included afterschool home visits, meetings, conferences, or an inservice program or graduate class. Kindergarten teacher Jillian Tsoukalas recalled, "I was learning and the children were learning and I was so excited and the parents were happy and I was living my dream—and I was *exhausted!* I could hardly keep my eyes open to get through dinner each night." And the nonstop mental and emotional demands don't help. Author and educator Robin Fogarty reported, "It has been said that a classroom teacher makes 1500 decisions in a day."[10] No wonder we're tired!

Management and organization can be overwhelming and were frequently mentioned as issues astounding contributors. Although my undergraduate classes demanded a great deal of time and effort, nothing could have prepared me for the sheer number of hours I would need for planning, checking papers, developing materials, or communicating with parents—not to mention keeping up with professional literature or fulfilling the requirements of graduate classes I took during most of the years I was in the classroom. One high school English teacher wrote about how "the marking is insane and the planning is unending. Every time I teach a course, even if I've taught it before, I have to change and adapt to meet the needs of that particular group of students." Diane Callahan, middle school science teacher, also commented on the paperwork, "I don't mean grading papers—that's a given." But Callahan noted that many of her weekends were devoted to "doing reports or writing something that was of no value to my teaching or my students when I could have spent that time designing a new lesson or a new approach to a subject." Third-grade teacher Adrian Schaefer identified "the inundation of paperwork related to students who have special needs" as one area in which he felt least prepared. And staff development specialist Diane Laveglia wished she had learned more about ways to reduce the paper load and be more organized. "That was definitely not covered in my education classes," she said.

Effective teachers know that educating young people involves a whole lot more than simply getting up and talking about a particular subject. Many beginning teachers are surprised when they discover that their students lack prerequisite skills necessary for the content being presented, the auditory strengths and attention span to get much out of a lecture, or an inherent interest in the content area (or learning, for that matter).[11] Even veteran teachers may make certain assumptions about how people learn, and many of us enter the profession using the types of instructional techniques to which *we* responded best as students. One contributor noted, "I was least prepared in strategies to teach students math who did not learn in the way I did." Indeed, this topic has started to take over my seminars on working with challenging students, as differences in learning and modality preferences can be a huge source of frustration for students and teachers alike.

As far as experiences and interests, variations in cognitive abilities, developmental readiness, and learning styles, every group I've encountered—kids and adults—has been all over the map. It didn't take me long to discover that trying to teach to one style or one set of experiences disregarded the majority of my students. While I may have learned or heard about these differences in my preparation classes, there was a shocking difference between understanding this information intellectually and experiencing it up close and personal.

Many contributors were surprised by how much of their time would be devoted to activities *besides* teaching. Professional development coordinator Amy DesChane was assigned a paraeducator to supervise during her first year. She described how difficult it was "to be young and responsible for someone else's duties without any management experience." A special education coordinator commented, "I love teaching and working with children, when I actually get the chance to!" She was one of many professionals who commented about the degree to which paperwork, meetings, committee work, preparation for testing, and "a million other assigned duties" kept them from being able to just *teach*.[12] It's not hard to see how a love of teaching can quickly be eroded by so many demands and distractions.

LACK OF SUPPORT

Teachers have come under increased scrutiny in recent years. Unfortunately, this examination rarely focuses on the most important skills and talents, those that can have the greatest impact on children's confidence or love of learning. There is, instead, a tremendous pressure for teachers to "get it right," and in many settings, this has come to mean having their competence reflected in test scores or other measurable outcomes. I haven't met many people who were drawn to the profession so they could devote their time and expertise to giving (or preparing for) tests, and more and more I encounter people who are finding that the priorities that called them to the profession are significantly different from what receives the greatest emphasis in their district and community.[13] Any teacher will be challenged by the various—and often incompatible—expectations of colleagues, administrators, parents, and the students themselves, and holding onto ideals can be tough in an environment that does not actively support them.[14]

In addition, consider the fact that although "it takes at least two years to manage the basics of classroom management and six to seven years to become a fully proficient teacher," according to a report by Claudia Wallis,[15] teaching is the only profession in which beginners are expected to do the same things as twenty-five-year veterans and are generally held to the same performance criteria as experienced teachers.[16] It takes a tremendous amount of trust, especially for a beginning teacher, to be able to go to a colleague for advice, suggestions, or support and not risk being perceived as incompetent. (Ask anyone who's ever been told, "I didn't have a problem with them last year," how safe that person felt about requesting assistance after that—and how much energy was channeled into appearing capable and in control.)

And consider the incongruous, if fairly prevalent, practice of placing teachers with the least experience with the most challenging classes, often in schools with the greatest number of problems and fewest resources. "It would be ideal if every teacher taught in an environment that matched his or her skills and temperament," stated one report on teacher recruitment and retention.[17] But this is often not the case. Many new teachers end up at grade levels for which they are not best suited or teaching subjects for which their knowledge is not as strong or as adequate as it needs to be. Further, this report said that "schools with the largest percentages of poor and minority students tended to have the least-qualified teachers," and high-poverty schools have nearly double the percentages of teachers with three or fewer years' experience as their higher-income-area counterparts.[18]

There are good reasons that newcomers to other professions are not assigned the most difficult cases or the most complicated accounts. And yet, that is often exactly what happens with teachers. The absence of emotional safety and support can present significant challenges even for veteran teachers; for beginning teachers, the consequences can be devastating. I received a note from a first-year kindergarten teacher at the end of September saying, "My experience so far has not been very good. I started as a fourth-grade teacher. Last week I was moved to kindergarten. I was informed by the two other kindergarten teachers that they were each given five minutes to come up with a list of seven students who would go to my section. Guess who I ended up with?" Her note continued, "I'm starting to second-guess my career as an educator. I hope it gets better because I really love being with children." And in what may be one of the strangest conversations I've ever had, a teacher in a recent seminar I was presenting on the topic of dealing with difficult students told me that her colleague refused to attend the program because "she's afraid that if she takes this class, the principal will give her all the bad kids next year."

New teachers with the least seniority are also generally the most vulnerable to being subjected to last-minute grade changes. I often saw this happen to my first-year teaching interns who had spent the summer preparing and collecting the materials and resources they would need for one grade, only to be switched to another grade level at the last minute. In more than one instance, the individuals were notified the night before school started (although these individuals had a much easier time than those who were switched a month into the school year). That these practices—the professional equivalent of hazing—can easily lead to heartbreaking, no-win outcomes should surprise no one. Success builds confidence, and first-year teachers who don't get a chance to experience either are usually the first ones out the door.

I regularly hear from beginning teachers who are feeling completely defeated after continually hearing that they have to "do better" at their jobs. (I find it interesting that so many of these teachers use this same language, that so many report that the feedback they received focused on inadequacy, and that so few received specific suggestions about what they were doing wrong—or what they could do instead.) William Brock, the former Labor Secretary and head of the New Commission on the Skills of the American Workforce, noted the incongruity in assigning new teachers "to the toughest jobs in the most challenging schools with very low pay" and then, "when the results fall short, [telling] them, 'You just have to work harder . . . ' This is no way to treat professionals."[19]

I honestly believe that most veteran teachers sincerely *want* new teachers to succeed and that most are more than willing to provide information, materials, time, and encouragement. Still, a number of educators reported feeling very much alone and without support during their first year. Colleagues have their own issues and pressures, and even the best-meaning mentor or administrator can fail to appreciate certain procedures or resources that are unfamiliar to a new teacher, things a veteran would simply know about from experience. But a lack of sensitivity and awareness is one thing (and provides a good argument for beginning teachers becoming proactive about finding out what they're supposed to know or do); asking for help and not receiving it is quite another.[20] "With the lack of administrative support, it almost feels as if we are fighting a war on our own without the backing of our 'Commander in Chief,'" wrote one third-grade teacher. High school principal Aaron Trummer commented, "New teachers get beat up for their enthusiasm and their ideas—not just by their administrators, but also by colleagues who have no incentive to change or raise the bar." And several echoed the sentiments of a first-year elementary teacher who wrote, "I'm pretty sure the rest of the staff were making bets on which of us wouldn't last the year."

Even worse is the possibility of working with someone who will actually make the job more difficult than it already is. Newswriter Barry Ray noted that people are more likely to leave a job "if involved in an abusive relationship [with a colleague or superior] than if dissatisfied with pay."[21] Even if the interactions aren't overtly abusive, negative feedback, disappointment, impatience, derision, or contempt from colleagues or superiors can be especially corrosive to someone just learning the ropes. One elementary teacher told me about a principal she had in her second year who called her "a failure as a teacher" when large numbers of her students did poorly on a test. Although she admitted that she might approach her instruction and evaluation processes differently today, this feedback accomplished little more than to inspire self-doubt and mistrust, which took years to overcome. A veteran middle school teacher wrote, "I have been a teacher for seven years and the area where I needed most help was my confidence. The principal was an expert at making you feel like a failure." Despite receiving Teacher of the Year, this individual wrote that she "felt like the worst teacher in the world." (This contributor was fortunate enough to find a position in another district where, she reported, "I am finally treated with respect.")

How often do teachers get written up for trying new things or hassled for attempting to take advantage of professional development opportunities on their own? I recently received a correspondence from a teacher who attempted to notify the staff at her school that a national speaker would be making a rare appearance in her town. "I sent out an email to my colleagues and got busted for encouraging folks to take a day off!" she wrote.[22] Adding insult to injury, it's not unusual for me to hear from teachers who also had to reimburse the districts for the substitute teachers needed to work in their classrooms while they were off trying to improve their skill and effectiveness in their jobs, frequently at their own expense.[23] I have likewise heard from far too many teachers who had been sent to a conference or seminar (not infrequently because of a perceived weakness in their teaching) to learn the latest strategies and then received poor evaluations—generally from the person who had sent them to the training—when they were observed implementing the skills they learned there.

Inman and Marlow affirmed that teachers "are more likely to perceive themselves as isolated and even ridiculed when they are not supported by the individuals within their school."[24] One middle school English teacher stated, "I wish someone had warned me about the politics and negative attitudes I would encounter the first day of school." Anissa Emery, a high school counselor and English teacher, acknowledged, "I have known some phenomenal teachers in my career, who were generous and excited about working with students right up until the day that they retired." But she also wrote, "I was really unprepared for dealing with the pettiness and personalities of some of the other teachers on staff. It just never occurred to me that other teachers could be as vindictive and non-supportive as I have found some to be."

In an opposite scenario, there are some settings in which teachers actually get too *much* help. I received a long, plaintive e-mail from an assistant superintendent in a district where good intentions to provide support from a variety of sources had clearly gone awry. "These 'helpers' . . . all have their own agendas and assignments to improve the schools," she wrote. "They all demand another report, another look at one's lesson plans, another observation, another coaching session, another two meetings (preplan and debrief), and another idea of how to do it differently and by when. I'm sorry, but if in any job you had to jump through hoops for eleven different bosses while doing your job for the first time, you'd run away as well." She related a conversation she'd had with a talented new teacher who already had twenty-one hours toward her master's degree and successful student teaching and part-time teaching experiences before coming to this district. "I knew it would be hard," this teacher had said, "but . . . I can't teach these children, collaborate with my peer teachers, *and* please these other nine or ten adults who tell me something different every day!" Not surprisingly, this young lady left in the first two months of school, along with seven other beginning teachers in that district. On paper, this approach might look supportive, but in reality, it's placing excessive demand on new teachers and frankly chasing some of them headlong into other careers.

DIFFICULT STUDENTS, DIFFICULT PARENTS

Years ago, when I started presenting keynotes and training seminars to teachers, I offered a number of programs on a variety of topics. Not surprisingly, the programs most often requested have consistently been those that focused on behavior management, particularly with regard to difficult or challenging students. Discipline and motivation consistently register as huge concerns for teachers at all grade levels. Whether we're dealing with unmotivated students who perform below their capabilities, kids with weak social skills who have a hard time getting along with their peers, learners who struggle with the academic demands of the classroom, students who need a lot of attention, or kids with serious anger and self-control issues, student behavior can become a massive distraction from our instructional objectives. Dealing with defensive, disruptive, defeated, or indifferent behaviors is exhausting and after a while can wear down the most enthusiastic and committed teacher. The fact that so little training is generally offered to help new teachers address behavioral issues—with strategies that *are* suggested being, for the most part, superficial and ineffective—might explain the consistency with which discipline and behavior management topics in professional development conferences and training programs are requested by districts, schools, and the teachers themselves.

Dealing with parents can present special challenges as well. Nancy Gibbs reported on a study that found that "of all the challenges they face, new teachers rank handling parents at the top."[25] In a survey asking contributors to this book to identify the areas in which they felt least prepared when they entered the profession, the topic of "parents" was right up there with discipline and negative student behavior. Many veterans observed a deterioration not only in student behavior but also in parental support during their time in the profession. One primary teacher suspected that she had overstayed her time in the classroom after seeing "what was considered appropriate behavior being replaced with bad behavior and socially accepted excuses for that negativity." Likewise, high school math teacher Michelle Tillapaugh declared herself "very disgruntled with the lack of discipline" she sees in her work. Joanne Davidman, a family and consumer science teacher, observed, "I like the students, but I do feel they are changing in ways that I just do not want to deal with. Kids today can be very rude and at times I feel I need to be an entertainer instead of a facilitator of knowledge." And another high school teacher, Theresa Weidner, felt she was unprepared "to deal with all the needs these kids have today—whether they are self-imposed, parent-imposed, or biological."

In some cases, differences in teachers' expectations, values, and personal experiences made for some rude awakenings. Allen observed, "My college and student teaching experience had not prepared me for the real classroom. I expected students to listen, obey, and follow the rules." After all, she figured, she had raised three of her own children and had taught them to respect adults, listen, and cooperate with others. "I assumed all children were trained the same way. What bubble was I living in? I was surprised to see that five- and six-year-olds would lie, cheat, steal, physically hurt others, and much more. I had not seen anything like this in my college and student teaching experience." Middle school administrator Tammy Hanna reflected, "I really wish somebody had told me how it would be the parents that would challenge me the most! You just assume that they have the same educational goals for success for their kids that you have. Sadly, for some, education is not a priority. It is hard to convince students to value things their parents do not."

A number of the educators who contributed to this book felt that many parents had failed to teach their children any form of responsibility and that they were too quick to deny, defend, or make excuses for misbehavior. I continue to hear stories of parents who bring or fax their children's assignments to school when the kids forget and those who actually do the work for their children. (This really isn't anything new. Years ago, it was not uncommon for me to receive a note from a parent asking me to excuse the child for missing a homework or project deadline because the child "was up too late watching TV.") Well-meaning as these efforts may be, building accountability and responsibility in our students becomes especially challenging when faced with parents who insist on enabling them.

"I encountered many wonderful parents during my quarter century of teaching," remarked Aili Pogust. "However, those who were irrational and difficult could cast a pall on a school year. Teaching is extremely stressful with all the demands placed on a teacher's time. [Difficult] parents affect the dynamics of the whole class."[26] Indeed. During my first parent night, a woman I had never seen before walked into my classroom and started screaming at me. She soon realized that I was not her son's teacher and that she was in the wrong classroom, at which point she collected herself, walked out (without a word of apology), and started her harangue somewhere down the hall. I was twenty-two years old and had never been addressed with such belligerence and hostility. I was more shocked than upset or hurt, and totally unprepared for this type of encounter, which can, in some settings, actually be a normal part of the job.

VALUE AND STATUS

There's this joke about two former classmates who meet up at their high school reunion. One asks, "So, Bob, are you still a teacher?" The other replies, "Why, yes. Are you still a doctor?"

Teaching—such a worthwhile, righteous, and profoundly influential profession—is rarely distinguished by the authority or prestige it deserves. And with an increasingly large array of career options becoming available as information and technology explode, the value and attractiveness of teaching as a career choice may well decline. (How many educators have heard some version of this presumptuous inquiry: "Gee, you're so smart and creative. Why would you want to teach?") Even some lifelong educators interviewed for this book admitted trying to steer their own children onto different career paths, most often to protect their offspring from an overall scarcity consciousness, particularly with regard to resources, support, and income. (Public perception and an increasing emphasis on data-driven reforms also accounted for this negative attitude toward teaching among educators.)[27]

Nonetheless, Stephen Bongiovi, a high school English teacher, defended his pride in his profession: "There's no such thing as *just* a teacher. Never downplay or de-emphasize yourself or what you do," he advised. "Every successful venture—business, politics, publication, athletics, most any other field of endeavor—originates from the influence of a teacher." And while you'll get no argument here, I will concede that it can be pretty disheartening to be repeatedly exposed to a societal image in which teaching "is not worthy of the prestige of being a lawyer, doctor, or an engineer."[28]

To a certain degree, the profession perpetuates this perception. Inman and Marlow observed significant differences between teaching and other professions, financial discrepancies aside. "Professionals are usually distinguished by their specialty knowledge and skills, the unique contributions they make, the freedom afforded them to make decisions based on their best professional judgment, and the opportunity to organize their time and direct their own work," they wrote.[29] Yet how many educators would claim congruence between this description and their actual experiences *as* professionals? Lacking a private office, a secretary, access to telephones, time to confer with colleagues, or financial support for professional development—perks that professionals in other fields pretty much take for granted—doesn't help either. Add in other factors many teachers experience, things like having to schedule lunch and bathroom breaks, sign in and out of work, or supervise the hallways, buses, lunchrooms, and playgrounds, and the professional image erodes even further. "Research shows that dissatisfaction related to these aspects of teaching are ones that approximately two-thirds of teachers and former teachers cite as a reason for leaving the profession," claimed Inman and Marlow.[30]

Even basic supplies are not a given. While I've been in well-stocked schools where teachers wanted for nothing, this is not always the case. (A former fellow teaching intern and I recently reminisced about one of the most absurd moments of our first year as we attempted to maneuver a huge roll of brown paper towels through a ditto machine because we had run out of paper for that month![31]) "Too often our schools, especially in the urban core, rely on teacher martyrdom—teachers working sixty- or seventy-hour weeks, spending thousands of dollars of their own money on basic classroom supplies, or providing enrichment activities for underprivileged kids," cautioned high school teacher Karen Fernandez.

According to a recent study, "the average teacher spends at least $433" out of pocket for classroom supplies each year. About 8% spend $1,000.[32] New teachers often have to purchase what one first-year educator called "starter items." Even the "little things" add up quickly, and the students' parents can't always help. "The students I work with are living below poverty level," one new teacher wrote, "so asking for money from their parents to help with costs for a field trip or classroom supplies is always a touchy subject and generally avoided." This should not be an issue for so many teachers, but the fact is that many of us face additional challenges of trying to do our jobs without adequate books, furniture, equipment, and supplies. (In what other fields are professionals taught, as a regular part of their professional training, to go to garage sales, save egg cartons, or scrounge throwaway materials from businesses in order to perform their jobs?) It can be hard to feel like a valued professional without some of these very basic resources.

ISSUES OF AUTONOMY AND DISCRETION

One of the things that drew me to teaching was the creative outlet it offered. I loved being able to find different ways to teach different concepts, create instructional materials, and rearrange the schedule or student placements to better accommodate students' different academic needs and learning style preferences. I happened to start teaching in the early 1970s, and although at the time there certainly existed grade-level and content-area curricula—and the expectations, mandates, and standardized tests to go along with them—there was also a certain degree of flexibility and discretion that, for many teachers, has all but disappeared.

To some extent, teachers do have a certain degree of autonomy when they shut the door, although this can vary from one setting to another and will depend on factors ranging from the political climate in the district to the type of leadership in the school. Snyderman cited this factor as one of the reasons for going into teaching: "Your classroom is essentially your own domain. You can set it up how you wish, you can manage the students how you wish, you can basically be your own boss." But as many teachers face an increasingly scripted and politicized educational landscape, with rigid directives governing what, when, and how to present the content they are to teach,[33] they also see their professional and intuitive teaching skills discounted and dismissed.[34] Education professor Richard Biffle observed, "Linear, one-dimensional, myopic kinds of thinking is the product of the system that operates as a linear, one-dimensional, myopic organization." And longtime principal Marcella Jones said that where she used to look for "risk takers with new ideas" when she was interviewing prospective hires, "the standards movement has required everyone to rethink the job."

Educator and writer Glori Chaika reported that increases in the amount of curricula teachers are expected to cover along with a growing emphasis on standardized test scores result in less time for teachers to plan, create, and grow: "They have become technicians, implementing fragmented curriculum in a time frame that's frequently inadequate for the material required."[35] Many of the teachers I've met who left, or who thought about leaving, were frankly chafing under too many restrictions and a lack of respect for their professional instincts. One professional development project coordinator bluntly advised, "Find another profession. Until teachers are recognized for their ability, skills, and knowledge, they should go into another [field] where they will be respected."

Retired high school teacher, and longtime friend and colleague, Lynn Collins wrote, "I loved teaching and I loved the kids. I loved what went on in my classroom once I shut the door. But I hated the bureaucracy and limitations, which seem inherent in the system. I started working part time in adult settings outside the public schools and really liked the freedom and creativity that were available there." After fourteen years in the classroom, Collins decided, "I wanted to do more things my way and be able to adjust more readily and more deeply to the needs and expectations of the people I was teaching."

One fourth-grade teacher had gotten in the habit of developing lessons and activities according to needs she observed and documented for students who were years behind grade level and not being served by the materials she'd been given to teach them. "When my principal told me to simply follow the scripts in the teacher's manual and to leave my creativity and initiative at home, I didn't see any point in my being there," she said. Stifled and frustrated, she left the district at the end of the year. (Like Collins, this educator eventually found much more freedom and flexibility in working with adults in an instructional capacity.)

Fernandez acknowledged that "so many decisions are made for the convenience of adults, rather than to support the needs of children." At times, our priorities do seem pretty twisted. In the frantic days after 9/11, I called a friend, a history teacher in a high school about two hours north of New York City. After talking a bit about how she and her family were faring, I observed that this would have to be an amazing time to be a history teacher, with so much unfolding right on her students' doorsteps, so incredibly relevant and real to their world. "You're kidding, right?" she responded. "We have to get through ancient Egypt for the [standardized tests] this week."

"This is the most managed and bureaucratic system that I've ever experienced," Biffle noted. "It is, at times, an overwhelming series of managerial tasks, forms, and controls that paralyze creative and innovative thinking." Fernandez, a twenty-three-year veteran, shared a similar view. "I wouldn't go into teaching if I knew then what I know now," she claims. "When I began, I saw teaching as a creative endeavor, one focused on guiding students on their own personally meaningful paths to adulthood. Increasingly . . . teaching is all about one very limited path defined by standardized tests." And many of the teachers I meet complain about feeling set up to fail when pressured to follow the curriculum instead of "following the student," frustratingly distracted from responding to the academic and instructional needs of their charges.

But there is hope. In a recent conversation, high school department chair Don Garrett related, "I tell my teachers I don't care how they teach, as long as the students learn," and I have also known several administrators who encourage their staff to shut their doors and go about the business of teaching and connecting with kids, doing what they came to the profession to do. I have also witnessed courageous teachers who managed to challenge their students with cognitively and developmentally appropriate content, even within the constraints of a heavily managed and scripted environment. I've seen counterproductive policies and rules overturned, replaced by more brain-friendly, kid-friendly, and teacher-friendly alternatives. I believe that schools will eventually catch up with what we're learning about how people learn, the importance of classroom climate, and the needs of our twenty-first-century economy. And in the meantime, I believe that there are not only ways to avoid some of the win-lose obstacles currently built into the system but that there are also simple, practical ways to create elements of a win-win classroom environment—even in a win-lose system.

ACTIVITY

Looking at some of the negative factors or issues mentioned in this chapter, answer the following questions:

1. Which factors have you heard about, witnessed, or personally experienced?

2. Which factors were unfamiliar or surprising to you?

3. Which factors would be (or have been) most stressful to you?

4. Are there any other factors or experiences you have witnessed or experienced that you would add to this list?

5. In what ways has this information validated your experiences as a professional (or trainee)?

6. In what ways has this information better prepared you for your professional journey?

NOTES

1. Gibbs (2005, p. 42); Kopkowski (2008); National Education Association (n.d.); Skirble (2008), citing a report by the National Education Association (NEA); Wallis (2008, p. 31); and CNN (2003), which also notes that "about one-third quit during their first three years" and that "turnover is highest in poor, predominantly minority schools." According to Kopkowski (2008, p. 21), teacher attrition rose 50% in the past fifteen years. Finally, a report by Inman and Marlow (2004) noted that "most teachers who leave have fewer than ten years' teaching experience" (para. 2).

2. Inman and Marlow (2004).

3. NEA (n.d., para. 49). A 2004 report on teacher pay published by the Wisconsin Education Association Council noted that not only is pay for educators "considerably lower than for other workers with similar education and skills," but the pay gap is growing. "Over time, the wage gap between teachers and their peers becomes a gulf that can sabotage schools' best efforts to recruit the best teachers and keep them as their skills and experience grow." Economic Policy Institute (2004, para. 1, 3).

4. I know a very bright, self-taught IT (information technology) specialist with a high school diploma and a few courses toward an associate's degree whose end-of-the-year bonuses are bigger than my highest annual salary ever was working for a school district or college. Many people live very comfortably on a teacher's salary, depending on where they live and where they teach, but relative to compensation people in other fields receive, unless things change pretty significantly, "the growing salary gap between teachers and other college graduates" can be pretty discouraging and will continue to be a factor in teachers not only leaving the field but deciding on other career choices. Chaika (2000, para. 3).

5. NEA (n.d.).

6. Kopkowski (2008) reports 56% of teachers leaving because of job dissatisfaction in 2005 (p. 21); Skirble (2008) notes that NEA surveys also include poor working conditions among the "major factors in this exodus of teachers"; also NEA (n.d.); also Inman and Marlow (2004).

7. Wallis (2008, p. 31).

8. Kopkowski (2008, p. 24).

9. These items are on a number of lists of "Rules for Teachers," which I have seen in print and online many times over the years, attributed to various districts around the country. This most recent search turned up lists on numerous sites, including the Teaching Handwork (2008) blog and the Teacherworld site (Pastore, 2005). Although the Snopes (Mikkelson & Mikkelson, 2007) site suggests this list is little more than an urban myth that has been circulating for decades, the duties and restrictions listed are not that different from some of the stories I heard from older family members about their teachers (or teaching experiences) in the 1930s and 1940s.

10. Fogarty (2007, p. 9).

11. I hear this often from subject-area specialists and people coming to education as a second career after working in their field with adults.

12. Elementary teacher Lydia Aranda observed the challenges in balancing the demands of a teaching career and raising a family: "In many ways, teaching was much more conducive to a single lifestyle with no children of my own. Then again, in other ways, I am much 'wiser' now that I have my own children on which to base my understanding of my students." And high school biology teacher Sherry Annee commented about how the demands of teaching have affected her choices about expanding her family: "Although I would love to have more children, my husband and I have decided that my profession limits my ability to be attentive to more than one child at home. Teaching is a serious responsibility. . . . It's difficult to imagine that my teaching and students' learning would not suffer if I chose to have more than one child."

13. And while teachers who assume their primary role to be one of "raising test scores" may be a good match for some schools and districts, I would hope that along the way they are encouraged to value other, less measurable goals that their students can carry with them as learners for life, long after anyone has ever looked at the numbers.

14. Educator Roland Barth (2002) wrote, "By the time a beginning teacher waits the obligatory three years to speak in a faculty meeting, she, too, is likely to be so immersed in the culture that she will no longer be able to see with a beginner's clarity the school's cultural patterns of leadership, competition, fearfulness, self-interest, or lack of support" (para. 12).

15. Wallis (2008, p. 31).

16. I have paraphrased a comment by former NEA president Bob Chase, who was quoted in *Newsweek*. Kantrowitz and Wingert (2000). Since I first encountered this quote, numerous administrators, mentors, supervisors, and veteran teachers have validated Chase's observation.

17. Allen (2005, para. 4).

18. Allen (2005, para. 4).

19. Wallwork and Male (2008, p. 10).

20. Lack of support from parents and administrators is one of the chief complaints of teachers in my seminars. To some degree, I believe this reflects our approach to these individuals, as well as the things we're asking them to do. There are ways to effectively build collaborative and mutually supportive relationships with administrators, parents, and other staff, and strategies for doing so will be offered in later chapters in this book.

21. Ray (2004, para. 5).

22. I had a similar experience when I was in the classroom. Despite the fact that I would have to take a personal day and pay for my own attendance at a one-day conference featuring well-known, well-published national speakers addressing issues specifically pertinent to our community *and* come back and report on the latest research findings they were presenting to our staff, I was accused by my principal of "just trying to get out of work."

23. I marvel at friends whose companies send them across the country for professional development and absorb *all* costs, including travel and other relevant expenses, all the while compensating them for this time as regular work days! In fairness, as certification requirements increase, some school districts have improved the support they are able to offer, although this is certainly not uniformly the case. Relying on in-house training is an option, but staff development budgets are generally the most vulnerable to cutbacks and often the first to go any time money gets tight. Further, in-house programs are often devoted to district- or state-specific procedures and requirements and do not necessarily offer credit toward certification, salary increases, or graduate degrees. Some districts (particularly those with large turnover or rapidly increasing student populations) offer tuition toward advanced degrees as an incentive to attract new hires. Nonetheless, there is typically less financial and other support for professional development for teachers than in other fields.

24. Inman and Marlow (2004, p. 3).

25. Gibbs (2005, p. 42).

26. Similar concerns regarding inadequate preparation for dealing with discipline issues, mental health issues (students' and parents'), and parents in general were expressed by a large number of contributors.

27. Karen Fernandez, a high school English and language arts teacher, discovered, in her dissertation research, that many veteran teachers asked about beginning a teaching career would discourage new people from entering the field. Her interviews were framed in the context of the

impact of legislation (specifically No Child Left Behind). Fernandez noted that her interviewees usually modified their responses, "stipulating that prospective teachers needed to do a lot of soul searching and spend a good amount of time in schools prior to making a major career decision."

28. Ingersol, quoted in Kopkowski (2008, p. 25).

29. Inman and Marlow (2004, p. 4).

30. Inman and Marlow (2004, p. 4).

31. Copy machines were rare or nonexistent in schools when I started, so anything we needed to copy required a ditto machine, or "spirit duplicator," which used solvents to make purple imprints on paper that went through the machines. Thanks to Bonnie Milanak for validating this memory for me.

32. Kopkowski (2008, p. 24). A 2007 survey indicated that nearly half of respondents spend $500 or more, and one-third spend between $1,000 and $3,500 out of pocket for basic classroom supplies and necessities. Edutopia staff (2007).

33. Mandates, in some settings, also apply to the items teachers can bring in, arrange, or use in their classrooms. In the past year, I visited a number of kindergarten classrooms in several schools in which the play centers (sand tables, costumes, store, kitchen, etc.) had been removed in favor of a room full of "literacy centers." Despite incompatibilities with brain research regarding early developmental needs, there was no time allotted for any of the play and interactive activities you'd expect in a kindergarten, and teachers were given no discretion to vary their schedules or activities.

34. Particularly that inner antenna that picks up information about what's going on in the classroom and what a student needs, a teacher version of a "sixth sense," that many of us bring to the profession or develop with classroom experience.

35. Chaika (2000, para. 21).

4

Winning in a Win-Lose System

Why We Stay

Teachers are expected to reach unattainable goals with inadequate tools. The miracle is that at times they accomplish this impossible task.

Haim Ginott, teacher and child psychologist[1]

Experience helps so much. By the time I had taught five years, I had finally become comfortable in my role as a teacher. I knew what I was supposed to teach and how. I knew how to balance my time as a teacher and my time at home. I knew the school culture as a teacher and not just as a student. Just like with all things, practice makes things easier, and it does get easier after the first year.

Jolene Dockstader, seventh-grade English teacher

Sometimes in teaching, you don't get to see the fruits of the labor for many years, but it is so sweet when you do!

Gerri-Lynn Nicholls, special education teacher

I'll be honest with you. In the months of interviewing teachers and collecting data for this book, I encountered so many angry, frustrated, and unhappy educators that maintaining a balanced, big-picture perspective on the teaching profession proved a bit of a struggle.[2] My abiding love for (and faith in) this profession was routinely challenged by e-mails, conversations, and school visits that revealed priorities that seemed to be shifting away from students and from the very things we know to be most important in educating children. While many districts indeed promote the importance of win-win goals like connecting with kids (academically and emotionally), inspiring a passion for learning, and promoting a safe, positive school climate, many of these same districts, under pressure to boost measurable achievement, end up adopting policies and programs that are developmentally inappropriate, incompatible with current brain research, and disrespectful of the diversity of students' readiness, experience, and learning styles. Add to that the degree to which some districts have attempted to use threats and intimidation to motivate teachers to perform, and there were days I honestly wondered if it were even ethical to invite people to this field.

But something kept bringing me back to this project, and although I know all too well the corrosive negativity that can swallow creativity, dedication, and enthusiasm, the fact is, I'm still here—after thirty-six years in the profession—and so are millions of others, some at it longer than I. As close as I've come to throwing up my hands and renouncing my chosen path, at the core of my being is a place where I still get immensely excited about teaching in any form it might take—whether I'm in a classroom, up in front of hundreds of educators at a conference, or coaching my mom through a computer problem over the phone.[3]

So what keeps us coming back, year after year? Looking beneath the majority of complaints and grievances I received, I'd see some expression of how, somehow, it's still so worthwhile.[4] Among dozens of similar comments was a survey response from second-grade teacher Roxie Ahlbrecht, who noted that teaching "is time-consuming, heart-consuming, and yet so very, very rewarding." At the end of the day, enthusiasm and devotion endure in the majority of people working with kids—and this includes teachers having a tough year, teachers struggling with inadequate funding and support, and teachers disenchanted with the state of education in general. Perhaps we know, deep in our hearts, what this profession *could* be and that, regardless of what's going on outside of our classrooms, we never really lose our capacity to touch the heart of a student entrusted to our care.

We have plenty of research on why teachers leave this field, but I think it's even more important to take a look at some of the reasons we *stay*—because in spite of the negatives previously mentioned, there are still many strong selling points for choosing teaching as a career and also for choosing the kinds of teaching behaviors that will ensure that we're around long enough to enjoy these benefits.

THE GOOD NEWS

New teachers are the lifeblood of the profession. All schools need an infusion of new energy and fresh ideas from time to time, perhaps especially those schools with long-term, stable teaching populations. (Whether this infusion is always encouraged or appreciated, it *is* necessary.) Your enthusiasm, optimism, creativity, and fresh perspective can keep the spirit of the school alive. Though you may take a hit for bringing these qualities to your classroom, hang onto them for dear life. For my money, *naive* trumps *jaded* any day.

If you are a new teacher, you are not alone. The teacher workforce is growing, and in recent years, about 17% of all teachers were new hires at their school. Many of these teachers have some classroom experience under their belts, including those who have transferred from other schools or districts and those who have returned to teaching after taking some time off. But nearly a third of new hires have never worked in a classroom, so if you're just starting out, there's a good chance that you will find others in the same boat as you. (This possibility is even more likely if you are at a large urban school where turnover, on average, is even higher.)[5]

This is important, because some of the chief complaints from beginning teachers include feeling overwhelmed and isolated. While you'll certainly want to build relationships with veteran teachers who have more experience and familiarity with various aspects of the system, other new teachers can provide much-needed reality checks and validation for what you may be experiencing from a similar point of view. Further, the availability of current technologies gives you an edge that previous generations of new teachers could not have imagined. Whether or not you're finding it easy to connect with people in your building, you're only a mouse click away from a variety of online resources and communities specifically established for beginning teachers.

Another important factor to consider is that regardless of trends and changes in political climate that affect education, we have never known as much as we do now about what young bodies, brains, and hearts need when it comes to the kinds of classroom climate, interactions, and instructional strategies that promote learning in all its forms. These new discoveries are exciting and hold great promise for the future of education. Although schools can be notoriously slow to change, as this new information becomes more mainstream, subsequent innovations, accommodations, and effective strategies will likely make their way into classrooms and directly impact students in positive ways. (In many ways, the reported failures of our educational system may ultimately be blessings in disguise, particularly if these problems create an environment that is open to, if not desperate for, alternatives to doing things the way they've always been done—policies and priorities that are ineffective and anachronistic in a twenty-first-century global economy.)

There are other benefits as well, not the least of which is the beauty—and at times, relief—of a fresh start each fall. Even the most unpleasant classes or placements generally only last about ten months (although it may seem much longer). And there are fresh starts available throughout the year as you explore new topics, activities, and approaches with your students. We also get much-needed breaks that are typically not available in other professions. And while many (if not most) teachers use the summer to catch up on professional reading and coursework, supplement their income, or prepare for the coming year, this stretch at least offers a change of pace from the regular classroom teaching schedules and routines.

Further, consider the personal achievement component. "There is immense satisfaction knowing you are finally doing what you trained for," reflected elementary counselor and former junior high teacher Linda Keegan. Facing your first class of students validates a great deal of commitment and accomplishment on your part, as well as the intentions that have driven your efforts. It's so easy to become consumed with the enormous number of details in preparing for our work that we often forget to appreciate the journey and all that we have accomplished to reach this juncture. Take a moment to give yourself credit for all you have done to get where you are. Authors Robert Wyatt and J. Elaine White elaborated: "You have completed four years of training and proven yourself as a student, and you have passed certification tests that qualify you, in the eyes of the state department of education, to be in the classroom. You have survived application and interview processes and have become the district's choice to work with its children."[6]

Even if you came to teaching through less conventional certification avenues, it's clear that along the way, you secured somebody's faith in your expertise in your subject areas and in your ability to connect with your students. You are needed; good teachers are always needed.[7] You have been selected for one of the most important jobs in the world, and there is great honor in being handed the keys to the classroom.

TOUCHING THE FUTURE

Perhaps most important, your potential to make a difference is inestimable. Students of all ages need the warmth, skill, and passion you can bring to your classroom. Diane Callahan observed that teaching is about changing and affecting lives. "I have had students come back years later and tell me thanks for teaching them whatever they remembered," she said. "I have been blessed to be known as a teacher and to know that I have impacted many lives. At last count, I have touched over 3,000 lives. What other job lets you do that?"

"This is one career where you can really make a difference and turn lives around," said Ahlbrecht. Anissa Emery observed the importance of teachers and school for some students. "Even when their lives seem to be spinning out of control all around them, many children still manage to come to school and function," she noted. "The ones who are struggling the most academically, or who seem to be the most difficult to work with behaviorally, [may be] the ones who need us the most." She has also found that the most challenging students are often the ones who "come to school every single day, almost without fail. What that says to me is that they keep coming back for something, that there is some value in this shared experience for them, and that every day that they return to us is another opportunity for us to build the bridge between where they are and where we believe they can go."

Susan Bailey, a middle school reading specialist, commented, "The teaching profession is very difficult and demanding, but the satisfaction that I get from it is what I need. It's easy to get caught up in the politics, paperwork, committees, and constant research and education, but when I am in the classroom with students, I know that I am making a difference. I get to work directly with the people who benefit from my profession, the students. When I know that they have learned something, it is an amazing feeling to me, even though I have been teaching for eleven years." Special education teacher Gerri-Lynn Nicholls agreed. "There is no better feeling in the world than watching kids prosper and in knowing in some small way we had a hand in helping them," she wrote.

Educator Veronica de Andres congratulated people coming to this profession: "You can change and transform the lives of many students in the world!" Like so many successful people, she credited a teacher with having an enormous impact in her life: "After I met her, I started gaining confidence and believing in myself. That not only changed my life, but it gave me a sense of purpose." She asserted, "You are perhaps the most important person in a student's life! Do [your job] with passion and love." Julia Frascona, a teacher of students with emotional and behavioral disabilities, wrote, "It is a noble thing you are doing. Your job is so much more than teaching the basics. You are a child advocate now. Do it well and you will go to bed each night knowing you have made the world a better place."

For many years, I've heard powerful stories of how one teacher made a life-changing difference in someone's existence, even when that person didn't have much in the way of support or what we would call *protective factors* in his or her young life.[8] These reports continually confirm our ability to shape a young person's interests, achievements, and belief system, whether by a single innocent comment at just the right time or through a significant act of encouragement or faith. Sometimes by simply offering structure (which many students may not find elsewhere in their lives), providing opportunities for them to succeed, or being a stable, safe adult in their lives, for example, we become that one life-changing person for a number of our students every year. Of all the possible outcomes a teacher can experience, this potential for touching the future may be the most valuable, the most reinforcing, and the most likely to keep us in the game.

FEEDBACK AND SATISFACTION IN SERVICE

Many teachers express a great deal of satisfaction in knowing that they are making an important contribution to society. But even world-changers need a boost to keep them going from time to time, and fortunately, this profession offers opportunities to be truly touched and reassured by the impact our work can have. While you're not likely to make local news broadcasts when one of your kids spells *accommodate* correctly or finally gets a handle on nonlinear polynomials, there will be moments—signals, signs, and occasionally words—to let you know that your enthusiasm, clarity, persistence, and patience have helped your students create meaning, safety, or direction in their lives.

Sometimes, the feedback we receive can be rather dramatic. Imagine the high school teacher whose toughest student returned years later to thank her for a simple comment she had made, a seemingly inconsequential remark that resurfaced at just the right moment to interrupt a suicide attempt.[9] Or the middle school teacher who still has a note from a student, some twenty years later, that says, "I didn't know I liked math until your class." Mandy Frantti noted, "You are touching lives in a very real way. I have students come back on a regular basis to tell me how I changed the course of their lives. It's an awesome responsibility. It's an awesome legacy." Indeed—how many of us were inspired to a career in education by a special teacher *we* had at some point in our lives?

For most of us, however, it will be the little things that keep us going. Jillian Tsoukalas admitted, "There are days where I feel like I simply cannot answer another question, tie another shoe, break up another argument, pick up another pencil, zip another coat, dry another tear, smile one more smile, and then it happens. One of my students will walk right up to me and hug me, or thank me for something, or apologize to a friend for hurting her feelings, or ask me if I had a good day, or do something that makes it all worthwhile. My headache melts away and a smile appears on my face. . . . I cannot imagine having a more rewarding job." Older kids can offer similar benefits. Retired high school teacher Mel Alper recalled, "I loved the feeling of being needed that teaching gave me." Cindi Allen described the joy of seeing the students grow from her work with them, despite any difficulties her job may present: "On the flip side of all of the challenges are the rewards of teaching. They can be [the] greatest things that happen in your life. It is wonderful to watch kids grow and learn. . . . That's worth a million dollars!"

Dozens of the teachers I interviewed mentioned the power of witnessing these "light-bulb" moments, and I can attest to days when just one of these experiences was enough to keep me excited about teaching for weeks at a time. (This includes experiences with adult learners, as well as kids.) Lindsay Shepheard wrote about "the rush that you get when one of your students has an 'aha!' moment," and veteran teacher Marcia Rosen sees these instances as a very rewarding part of her thirty-five years in the field. "The feeling I get when I'm teaching, when the kids are with me and everything clicks, is indescribable!" she said. Elementary school counselor Holly Davis echoed Rosen's sentiments: "There is nothing like the light coming on in the eyes of a student who gets it—whatever *it* is."

VARIETY, JOY, AND CREATIVE EXPRESSION

If the structures, strategies, challenges, and demands of teaching are different from other professions, the potential rewards are similarly unlike any I've ever experienced in any other type of work. Educator Allan Ilagan reflected the feelings of many contributors when he shared, "There is so much joy and fulfillment in teaching." Stephen Bongiovi noted, "I have been rewarded in some small way or another every day of my teaching career." Michelle Erickson, a first-grade teacher, wrote, "I get excited just thinking about going back to school and hearing and seeing the excitement my students have when they come through the door—and their excitement for the next day when they leave!" Clearly there are powerful incentives to keep people in the field year after year.

Lifelong educator Gail Scott retired from public education the year before she contacted me and had already signed a contract to teach in a new private school in her town. "I feel like a first-year teacher again, but this time I have thirty-two years of experience to help me," she said. And my first-year coteacher, Ken Bauer, who has e-mailed me a dozen times about how much he misses teaching since he retired a few months ago, is about to jump on an opening where his wife teaches to fill in for someone going on maternity leave. "I just cannot stay away," he confessed.

One of the things I've loved most about my life as an educator is the variety of experiences and people I encounter, and how different one day can be from the next. This is certainly unlike other jobs I've had, and many educators cited the fact that "no two days are the same" as an important benefit of the job. I am continually challenged in this field, whether this involves polishing a lesson or presentation, developing new materials, keeping up with the literature, incorporating new content into my work, creating new content for my Web sites, or interacting with different groups and audiences around the world. There always seems to be something to engage my interests, curiosity, and creativity.

Erickson loves coming into school each morning for this very reason. "Each day is filled with so many new activities," she said. "I am never bored! Just when I think things are starting to slow down, something new comes along." High school science teacher Jeremy Freedman prefers teaching to being behind a desk: "Every day is different. Even though I might teach the same subject every year, there is always a different dynamic." The potential and opportunities for personal and professional growth in any aspect of the field of education are practically endless.

Educator, consultant, and trainer Glenn Capelli noted, "The more doors you open in teaching, the more you discover there is to learn, and that is exciting, challenging, and inspiring." Bruce Hammonds, an independent educational adviser, affirmed, "Teaching is potentially the most creative career one can have, even if it is hard to find the right conditions to be creative. Even in a less creative school environment there is plenty of room for an individual teacher to be creative and still comply with schoolwide expectations." The opportunity to express an interest or share a passion in something you value can be tremendously fulfilling as well. Administrator Stephen Vance believes that "teaching something that you excel in is the most enriching experience you can have. Whether [you are] teaching someone to ski, bowl, motorcycle ride, draw, or multiply numbers, sharing with someone else something you are passionate about is an amazing experience." A talented artist, Ales Zitnik sees teaching as an opportunity to merge his many interests and skills. And many professionals welcome the various challenges teaching presents, whether it involves attempting to reach every child or staying on top of changes in the curriculum.

THE POWER OF CONNECTION

We all know about the power a teacher has to influence and inspire a student. A number of contributors also mentioned the impact their students have had on *them*. "The students have inspired me and made me grow in directions that I would never have foreseen," remarked Callahan. Erin Beers, a sixth-grade teacher, also spoke of the opportunities her kids presented for her growth and development: "I am challenged by the students that I teach, which keeps me self-reflecting on my own best practices to be the best teacher that I can be for my students."

There are so many ways in which working with young people can enrich our lives, not least of which is sheer entertainment value. "I love working with young children because you never know what they will say or do," wrote Stacey Ferguson. "They are so full of life and wonder that it picks my spirits up each and every day." One primary teacher was surprised to discover how much fun her students could be: "My students are a riot. They do the silliest things and keep me laughing all day."[10] Adrian Schaefer noted that his students "always put things in perspective as soon as they walk through the door each morning. It's hard not to feel a sense of joy when the kids are smiling and upbeat, even on the days that I drive to school feeling a little stressed." Elementary principal Jacie Bejster Maslyk observed, "I can't think of many other careers that provide you with as much reinforcement and motivation."

Our students can so easily become a significant thread in the tapestry of our lives, and the connections we make can last long after they leave the classroom. Many contributors wrote about the sense of continuity they experience witnessing their students' growth over the years. Christie DeMello, eighth-grade teacher, noted, "I love seeing my former students years later, nearly grown up and well on their way to being successful." Ahlbrecht wrote, "I love having kids come back to work in my room as mentors. I love being invited to their graduations, recitals, and Christmas programs." This connection can occur at any age or grade level. Nancy Foote reflected, "After a few years, your kids will come back to visit you. They will tell you what you and your class meant to them. You really never will know where your influence ends."

I know teachers who have worked with generations of the same family, teachers who are a part of their students' lives and community, who routinely run into students and their families outside of school. I never had the pleasure. I lived across town from the school at which I could get a job and moved across the country after my years in the classroom. This was long before the days of the Internet, and although a few of my kids wrote after I left, it wasn't long before we lost touch. So it was especially meaningful when, not long ago, a former student tracked me down online and later brought her two kids to meet me when I was speaking in the town to which she had moved. I remembered her well after nearly three decades, and reconnecting as adults was one of the most gratifying experiences in my career.

Scott shared, "I never had any children of my own, but I've raised hundreds of them over the years and have had all of the joys and sorrows that parents have. My life has been richer and more marvelous than many people I know, and I feel blessed by my experiences with my students."

IT GETS EASIER

Perhaps the best news of all: It does get easier, and teachers who stick with it generally find that their effectiveness increases significantly over the course of the first several years.[11] Note that *easier* does not mean *easy*. I don't know that teaching is ever actually easy, and effective educators continue to challenge themselves to be knowledgeable and better at their jobs. Further, any teacher can run into an unexpectedly tough year from time to time, no matter how skilled or experienced. Changes in administration, policies, and priorities, or just a weird mix of kids (many of whom are fine individually but have no business being in the same city, much less the same classroom, as some of their class-mates), can throw the most seasoned and confident teachers off their game.

But so many of the things that are just so new and so different during the first years of teaching, things that are almost impossible to anticipate or prepare for, will be neither new or unanticipated after you've been in the classroom for a while. First-year teacher Suzanne Faas wrote, "I can't wait until next year! I will be more confident and have more of a background on our school and areas I can improve. There will be less of a surprise as to what is coming next. At the beginning of the year I was unfamiliar with a few things, like [our state's standardized] testing, reading assessments, parent teacher conferences, character education report cards and our school's unique grading system. Even now in the middle of the year I have fewer questions and feel much more confident." In other words, if you get a particularly challenging group of kids or have to adjust to a new administra-tor five or ten years into your career, you won't have to deal with it on top of having to get to know a bunch of new people and figure out the curriculum, district software, bell schedule, requisition procedures, or where the audiovisual equipment is stored as well.

Responding to a question about whether or not he would choose teaching again as his career, Josh Moberg, a high school career specialist, responded, "Had you asked me this question after my first two years of teaching, the answer would have been a definite no. Something changed the third year of my teaching profession." The difference, in Moberg's case, resulted from connecting with "a mentor who truly cared about whether or not I succeeded," someone who helped him appreciate "the enjoyable parts of our great profession." Several people identified year three as something of a turning point. "Your first year is really a juggling act, and your mission is to just get through the year," wrote fourth-grade teacher Sandy Goldman. "You begin to know the ropes after your first year, and by the third year, you really begin to feel like a veteran."

There are any number of influences and factors that can make your teaching life less complicated, less stressful, and more satisfying as you gain experience and confidence. Dozens of educators shared their ideas about how teaching gets easier,[12] and I want to share these "voices from the classroom," not only for the authenticity of their in-the-trenches experience but also for the promise that their comments offer. In general, their responses focused on issues of self-assurance, familiarity with the system, and general management. "Every new class is a new challenge, but with experience, confidence develops that gives you the ability to handle whatever comes along," said Hammonds.

Professional Identity

It can take some time to develop a sense of who we really are in the classroom and to get comfortable with our role as a professional in an authority relationship (in some cases, with students who are not much younger than we are). In general, behavior management gets easier with time and experience. "You learn where the line is between being friendly and being friends," claimed Foote. High school science teacher and consultant John Bickart said that he got used to being the authority figure in the classroom after the first year. "I realized that kids feel better when they know the teacher is in charge," he wrote.

Vance found that teachers "gain confidence and learn how to talk with [students] and build relationships with them. You learn how to react—or not react—to those behavior situations." Shelly Traver, a middle school science teacher, put it this way: "As with anything new, the experience builds your foundation, and each day, each encounter is a building block. You know more about the system and the logistics in the organization. You find your rhythm. You belong to the profession. You are part of a community. You know where and how to access the support system."

All of this is part of a larger evolutionary picture of developing as a professional. Cheryl Converse-Rath shared, "I found my voice and realized that no matter how unsure I feel on the inside, I still have the teacher title. . . . They don't know I am dying inside." And beginning teacher Sione Quaass found that she learned from the mistakes she made the first time round. Like many others, she noted that we become more comfortable in our role after we've been there for a while. "You feel less like an impostor and more like a real teacher," she said.

Maslyk wrote, "Not only do you begin to learn more about the profession, but you also learn more about yourself as a teacher." During your first year or two, you emerge from the shadow of your cooperating teacher or mentor into an ever-developing teaching self. For Carrie Balent, "the job got easier when I was able to figure out what works best for me and settle into my own style." Teddy Meckstroth, seventh-grade science teacher, agreed: "After the first year you start to find out how your personality can work for you. You find your teaching style and you learn what works and what doesn't."

It also takes a while to build your credibility and to prove yourself, as it were. Bonnie Milanak, who started out with me as a first-year intern and is still teaching thirty-six years later, noted that after a couple of years, experience allows us to get bolder and stronger in our beliefs. "Experience and courage go hand in hand," claimed veteran behavior specialist Marti Johnson, referring to "the ability to speak your mind and the courage to stand by your convictions." Your track record eventually establishes you as a professional and can add weight and legitimacy to your ideas and proposals, as well as whatever professional style you have developed.

Priorities

Priorities become clearer with experience as well. Jason Cushner, secondary math teacher, observed that becoming more comfortable with the variables that affect teaching allows us to "know what is important to focus on and what not to worry about." Joel Black, high school alternative teacher, shared, "Teaching gets easier as you find ways to avoid the irrelevant, streamline the grading, get to the real meat, and prepare materials that can be used again." Tuija Fagerlund was more specific: "You learn that it's not such a big deal if you skip the irregular past tense today because you have to clear up yet another mess in the classroom." Likewise, Elaine Anderson, attendance improvement facilitator, suggested that after the first year, "You have probably realized the significance of teaching beyond the academics." Rosen concurred, "Once you really know the material, you can focus more on what really matters—the kids." And one middle school teacher noticed that after the first year, you learn that you do not need to try to immediately conquer the world. "You can do it in small steps," she said.

Perspective and Connections

Perspective is another gift of time. Take some comfort in knowing that all teachers have bombed out at one time or another. Even lessons or activities that worked with one class can tank with another. "If something you tried wasn't as successful as you would have liked, then target those elements for a more improved lesson," advised Lois Romm, an elementary reading teacher. If the majority of my students failed a test or misunderstood an assignment or didn't get a joke, although initially devastating, at some point I realized that I needed to go back to the drawing board and adjust what I was doing so that my instruction, materials, or delivery were better matched to that group. "If you learn from your mistakes, I believe it does get easier. I believe teaching becomes harder when you try to make it easy," cautioned Darren Raichart, a junior high special education teacher and coach.

Further, after some time in the classroom, "your expectations about students hanging onto your every word and soaking up all your expertise are gone and reality takes its place," assured Melody Aldrich. "You are no longer as deeply disappointed spending hours planning the perfect lesson only to have your students not get it. Plus, it gets much easier to think on your feet and not panic when you have to change things around at the last minute." And author and educator Chick Moorman noted, "You learn to roll with the punches. You learn not to take it personally."

A part of your first year is devoted to building relationships with other staff members. Becoming a part of a school community is also a process, but the quality of the connections you make can become one of the most important factors in your success and longevity in the profession. "Once you begin establishing relationships with colleagues, you develop a support system for the days that you feel like you are losing your mind," advised reading specialist Michelle Mayrose. DeMello also noted that the first year or so involves building relationships with families in the community, "some of which send siblings or cousins year after year." As many others observed, "You find your niche in the school," she wrote.

Resources

The issue of materials and resources is usually less problematic after a year or two, especially if you stay at the same grade level or subject area for a while. Very few teachers start out with everything they need. For most of us, this is an ongoing process, and your life will certainly get easier as you build up your arsenal of materials, resources, furniture, and ideas. Even in well-stocked classrooms, there will always be items you will want to make, find, or buy to enhance your lessons and help you stay organized. "I am still in my first year, but I have already noticed how things seem a little easier," said Adrian Schaefer. When I visited Schaefer's classroom only a few months into his career, I saw that he had already gotten a good start establishing his collection of teaching aids. At the other end of the spectrum, after thirty-six years in the profession, Milanak is the go-to teacher for resources in her school. With her basement, garage, and attic stuffed with materials (some of them going back to our first year of teaching), "I have anything anyone needs," she said. Although Milanak continues to collect and save things for her classroom and puts as much time into her work now as she ever has, she is not plagued by a shortage of ideas or materials or by not having what she needs when she plans a lesson.

Familiarity and Fluency

High school biology teacher Sherry Annee was one of several teachers who described the first year as "living in survival mode." Callahan agreed. Although "the learning curve lessens a bit" during your second year, she noted that many teachers spend the first year scrambling to "stay pretty much one day ahead of the students." She outlined a progression during which "your first year is devoted entirely to learning the curriculum and trying to maintain what little control you have." In year two, "you know more about the curriculum and can now deal with discipline and all the things they don't teach you in college, such as all the paperwork, state testing, or what happens when kids smart off to you. The third year is when you can start to spread your wings and create new lessons and enjoy being a teacher." Beyond survival mode is a place where you can relax and enjoy your work in new ways. You also have the luxury of adding "some finesse to your lessons," said special education teacher Carol Dinsdale. "You remember what worked and repeat it. You [also] remember what did not work, and if you are smart, you reflect, and make changes for the better."

Bongiovi noted that although "teaching never gets easy," with time comes "the slow but steady accumulation of materials and activities, [an increasing] comfort level of ongoing classroom experience, and . . . [an] incremental assimilation into the life, culture, and history of the building." Likewise, Bill Funkhouser, middle school math teacher, cautioned that "dedicated teachers keep working just as hard as they did the first year. As your time is freed up by being prepared in one area, you see new needs that you hadn't seen or had the time to tackle previously." This is certainly true from my experience and observation. Fortunately, however, the "hard work" after the first couple of years tends to emphasize things like enhancing lessons and refining skills rather than simply getting through the day. As Jen Buttars explained, "To mix metaphors, you're not reinventing the wheel anymore, you're building a better mousetrap."

"Everything is new the first year," wrote Holly Davis. Quite true. As time goes on, organizational issues get easier and routines, policies, and logistics become more familiar. If you get to stay at the same school, after your first year, among other demands, you will already "know the staff, the rules, how to take the attendance [and] the lunch count, how to fill out forms and turn in money for field trips, how to do the reading evaluations and the county math assessment tests, and have been through a year of state testing," claimed preschool teacher Michelle Colbert. "You know the curriculum, have a database of lesson plans, a few tricks up your sleeve for classroom management, and have a better sense of what works and what does not." Moberg also mentioned, "After the first year, I was able to get a grip on the paperwork and lesson plans were easier."

Fifth-grade teacher Charla Bunker noted, "With experience, you expand your personal toolbox of effective strategies for instruction, assessment, classroom management, and fostering relationships with students, families, and staff members." But although you will discover that you have more answers than when you started, "the question of 'How can I do this better?' constantly creates a challenge," she added. Beers agreed: "I still drive home daily thinking about how I could have done something differently with my students." And even after decades at the same grade level, Milanak said she constantly asks herself, "How can I modify this activity or lesson?"

The actual process of teaching also becomes more familiar, and with this familiarity comes a greater understanding and fluency. "You can see the continuum of learning that your students will go through during their time with you," observed elementary teacher

Lydia Aranda, "and you are better equipped to teach each part of every concept. When you are learning content as you go, you have a hard time helping your students to see the 'big picture' because you haven't seen it yet for yourself." One third-grade teacher also noted how much it helps to be able to "anticipate how the children in your grade level grow, change, and mature over the course of a year." In addition, "having content down makes classroom management easier," said Eric Wright.

Elementary teacher April Keck DeGennaro identified "with-it-ness," another characteristic that develops with time and experience. "Something happens, almost like magic, that allows you to sense the climate in a classroom without specifically focusing on the individual events that are setting that climate," she wrote. "Some fields call it 'situational awareness,' but it is a type of awareness that is specific to a classroom. It has to do with the sound and the energy of the class. It is an abstraction, but a necessary skill for a successful teacher."

I think the same is true of time management. Academic adviser Seta Khajarian said, "You really get to gauge how long a minute is, and how many minutes are needed for certain activities and explanations." There seems to be a certain instinct that develops over time and with increased familiarity with the content. (In my seminars and presentations, I've gotten much better at estimating how long it will take to make a particular point or relate a particular example. Any time I change a program or develop a new one, it may take me a while to reestablish my rhythm, but the basic foundation is there.) And after her first year, Beth Zelfer, fourth-grade teacher, "didn't need to do everything from scratch each week." Having the plans from the previous year to use as a guide, along with notes about what had worked and what hadn't, helped her reduce the time needed for planning. Even as you enhance a lesson or unit you've taught before, "there is not as much prep work involved," said high school music teacher Eric Flowers.

So if you're having a tough time or feeling overwhelmed, this should all come as especially good news. (And if you're having a great year, so much the better.) Just know that it won't be long before you will be taking certain things for granted, and with experience, you'll develop a nose for what will work with a particular student or class and what is likely to go south well before it ever does.

Looking at some of the positive factors or issues mentioned in this chapter, answer the following questions:

1. Which factors have you heard about, witnessed, or personally experienced?

2. Which factors were ones you might not have expected or anticipated?

3. Which factors promise (or have been) the most relief for you?

4. Are there any other ways you would anticipate (or have experienced) your teaching life getting easier that you would add to this list?

5. If you have been teaching for a while, in what ways did this chapter help make you aware of ways in which your work has gotten easier (skills you have developed or knowledge you may now take for granted)?

6. In what ways has this information validated your experiences as a professional (or trainee)?

7. In what ways has this information better prepared you for your professional journey?

NOTES

1. A longtime fan of Dr. Ginott's work, I got this quote from a PowerPoint sent to me by my friend Dr. Jo Ann Freiberg (2007c) at the Connecticut State Department of Education.

2. People whose work focuses on discipline issues and dealing with difficult students will often have participants in their programs who are having a particularly stressful year or who are there because their supervisor or administrator lacked faith in their skills in the classroom and sent them there for help (or punishment). I am also called on to do observation and coaching in schools where problems have been noted by higher-ups. In either instance, while some teachers are very open to and appreciative of any help they can get, others are understandably angry, discouraged, and defensive. The preponderance of teachers I encounter in my work *because* they are having problems (or have been perceived as having problems) may have skewed the feedback I received in these circumstances. Nonetheless, the majority of contributors did not fit this profile. (Indeed, the contributors included a large number of individuals I had never met, people who found out about this project through e-mail forwards.)

3. This last example is undoubtedly the most difficult, for all sorts of reasons.

4. Visit www.janebluestein.com/forum/again.html to see the full list of responses or to add your own.

5. Kopkowski (2008, p. 21); National Center for Education Statistics (n.d.). These numbers are national averages in the United States. Turnover is higher in urban districts, where the percentage jumps to 20%. About 12% of new hires (more than 102,000 individuals) are recent college graduates with no teaching experience. Kopkowski (2008).

6. Wyatt and White (2007, pp. 123–124).

7. Teacher shortages are especially acute in large inner-city districts and in certain fields, notably math and science. Many school districts are so tight for teachers that, according to an online article by Glori Chaika (2000), some school districts are streamlining hiring procedures, interviewing over the phone or online, relaxing residency and certification requirements, providing low-cost housing or housing subsidies in high-priced districts, offering signing bonuses, moving expenses, and free graduate courses. This same article notes, "One-fourth of new teachers—if they are licensed—are not licensed to teach in the field they are teaching." A similar article by Jeff Taylor (1999) notes, "Most states allow some teachers to enter the classroom without conventional certification. The Department of Education estimates there are about 50,000 teachers nationwide with emergency certification." And despite ardent calls for "highly qualified teachers," in 2006, Lawrence Baines reported that in some states up to 25% of new teachers enter the classroom with alternative certification from nonuniversity certification programs.

8. Bluestein (1995; 2001, chap. 10); Blum (2004, p. 5).

9. Bluestein (1995).

10. One of my favorite jokes came from a student who ran into the room after lunch and frantically asked if I'd heard about the lady who backed into an airplane propeller. "Uh . . . no," I said. "Disaster!" he replied. Although humor is certainly rather subjective, this one got me! There is nothing like being able to laugh with your students.

11. Allen (2005).

12. Visit www.janebluestein.com/forum/easier.html for the full list of the responses I received or to add your own ideas.

5

What to Pack

Your Personal Assets

The greatest gift you can give anyone is your honest self. It's the only unique gift any-one can give. Whatever I did, I would have to be myself, because I believe that is what children respond to. It's a privilege to be trusted by children. And I don't take it lightly.

Fred Rogers, children's television show host[1]

I love working with children and their families and making a difference. . . . Even on my toughest and worst days, I never lose that idealistic hope that all teachers start off with.

Darren Raichart, junior high special education teacher

Young people need teachers, Spirit Whisperers who can teach from the heart. They need people who can say, "The Emperor isn't wearing any clothes," who can stand in the middle of the testing craze and help young people learn the curriculum that the leaders are not giving appropriate attention to.

Chick Moorman, author and educator

So then, do you have what it takes to go the distance? Many new teachers are extremely well prepared when it comes to making materials and planning lessons, and many come to their own classrooms with the assurance of a successful student teaching experience and a strong knowledge base in their content areas. However, these competencies alone are not enough to guarantee that a teacher will survive the first year, much less have a successful career.

So what else will you need? In the course of researching this book, among the questions I considered, researched, and asked contributors were the following: "What makes a great teacher?" "What did you like most about the best teachers you had?" and "What qualities are you looking for when you interview prospective teachers?" What emerged as a result of this exercise was a list of personal assets—traits and characteristics that can improve the odds of a successful teaching career.

Some are painfully obvious and, hopefully, easy to check off. Others are assets you may not have thought about or appreciated as being as valuable as they are, especially in the context of win-win goals. You may find that some of the items on the list are instinctive and somehow just *there,* things you were born with or noticed about yourself at some point; others will have to be learned, built, and developed.

Keep in mind that a lot of people can stand up in front of a room of young people and present information, but only a few will truly engage them, inspire them, and help them redefine their perception of their possibilities and who they are in the world. And becoming a win-win teacher is not just about being successful in your own classroom. It's also about being able to work within a system that will often seem at odds with your educational goals—if not its own.

"We teach who we are," said educator and activist Parker Palmer.[2] So who are you, and do you have the traits of a win-win teacher, assets that will make your work easier, more effective, and more enjoyable?

I care about young people.

As obvious as this asset may be, there are people in the profession who, for whatever reason, have unfortunately lost their ability to enjoy and appreciate their students. There are some who only seem to like some of the kids and don't even try to hide their favoritism (or contempt). A few slip through the cracks with such a strong mistrust and dislike of children that they really would be much better served with a different type of employment. Sure, some have been placed at a grade level or with a particular student population for which they may not be ideally suited, have other stresses going on in their lives, or have simply burned out on the pressures of the job. Nonetheless, you really do not want to join their ranks.

Please consider this asset quite seriously, because teaching is about the connections we make with our students, and learning happens in the context of the relationships we create with them. Elementary guidance counselor Stan Davis shared, "They don't care how much you know until they know how much you care. Connecting and relating come first." Even if you generally do like kids, including the ones deemed "difficult" or "challenging," you will have students who will need more patience, flexibility, persistence, and unconditional acceptance than you can ever imagine. Paul Clements, school psychologist, wrote, "You need to make sure they know you care about them from the first day. You need to make an effort to love the kids who are hard to love." High school guidance counselor Eric Katz advised, "If you don't love kids, you will have a very hard time being a good teacher. Students always know which adults truly care about them and which are only going through the motions."

This asset also assumes a willingness to advocate for the safety, success, and dignity of *all* students. It is, understandably, of primary concern to most administrators interviewing prospective teachers. Middle school principal Mark Fish noted, "I look for teachers who like kids, first and foremost, and can articulate why they want to work with them." Another principal, Iain Riffel, mentioned relationships as a key priority: "Hiring someone who loves kids will see them through the guaranteed tough times in the profession." And others asked me to caution readers, frankly, to "not go into teaching if you dislike children." If you care about your students, they will know.

I am committed to being a nondestructive force in children's lives.

In medicine, doctors take an oath promising to do no harm. We, in education, do not have a tradition of committing to this intention, though well we might. Kids take enough hits, and many come to school defensive or defeated because of previous school experiences, a difficult home life, negative social interactions, or a combination of these and other factors. A classroom environment that mirrors or adds to these stressors only makes it harder for all kids to learn and, in the long run, will make your job harder and more stressful.

"I have worked with some very intelligent teachers who didn't like kids," said one assistant superintendent. "They don't realize the damage that they are doing." But even caring teachers who really like their students can snap on a bad day and say something insulting, demeaning, or just plain nasty. At the end of the day, can you look back and assure yourself that your behavior remained professional and nonhurtful, regardless of what might be considered justifiable provocation?

"This awesome responsibility must be faced with great humbleness and awareness of my own frailty," says the Hippocratic Oath. "Above all, I must not play at God."[3] If you are routinely able to resist hurtful or sarcastic comments to a student, embarrassing a student in any way, or contributing in any way to a student's discouragement, defensiveness, or indifference, you are contributing to creating a classroom environment in which mutual respect and consideration can clear a path for greater learning, even with kids who have historically been hard to engage.

I respect that students have basic needs that must be met before learning can take place.

Somewhere in your teacher training classes, you probably heard something about a hierarchy of human needs, starting with basic physiological needs and progressing through increasingly abstract and complex levels. While many of the most basic needs (like food, shelter, and clothing) will be beyond your immediate control, be aware that there are millions of students for whom these essentials are not a given. Nonetheless, there are other basic, lower-level needs—such as the need for structure, success, autonomy, involvement, a sense of purpose, authenticity, relevance, belonging, dignity, and confidence—that you may well be able to accommodate. Your appreciation for these needs can contribute a great deal to your priorities and the choices you make, particularly with regard to classroom management.

This asset indicates an understanding that these needs occur in a hierarchy, with the more basic needs taking priority over higher-level needs. (Physical discomfort, which can include being hungry, too hot or cold, not fitting in the furniture provided, or having to sit too long, can be incredibly distracting. And students don't get to self-actualize when their concentration is focused on protecting their safety, dignity, or sense of worth.) Because your students need to be neurologically, emotionally, and cognitively available for learning, this asset also supposes a willingness to create an environment to support lower-level needs so that achieving and functioning at higher levels is possible.

I work well with other adults.

Teachers spend the majority of their time with their students, and once you shut your classroom door, you may experience a certain sense of isolation from others in the building. Nonetheless, teachers are also a part of an adult community and it will help if you value these connections as an important part of the education process and culture, one that extends beyond the immediate boundaries of your classroom.

Administrators may appreciate creativity and initiative in their teaching staff, but most are understandably wary of hiring a lone wolf. "I look for teachers who are able to work as a team and who are willing to share ideas," stated principal Reba Lane. Others also want new teachers to be able to become a part of the school community, and many said they look for socially positive people who would be a good match with the students, the community, the school, and the rest of the staff.

Being able to work successfully with other adults also means being accepting and respectful of people who have different teaching styles or approaches from yours. This can be especially hard for new teachers who are excited about the latest strategies and research, especially when they see others not using this information or, worse, practicing ineffective or hurtful teacher behaviors. However, veteran teachers rarely appreciate unsolicited advice or criticism, especially from the new kid on the block, so be prepared to watch and learn from others, even if it's only what *not* to do.

Keep in mind that you will, from time to time, need the help and support of the other adults in your community, including other teachers, teaching assistants, support staff, administrators, central office personnel, custodians, secretarial staff, and parents—whether for securing special services for a student, getting ideas and materials for a lesson, obtaining clearance for a field trip or project, finding out how to work best with a particular child, or getting the lights or heaters in your room repaired. All of these individuals can have a tremendous impact on the quality of your work life. Your ability to build relationships and mutual respect with them is crucial.

I am passionate about teaching.

Think of the teachers you've had whom you would describe as passionate about their work. How did this asset contribute to the impact they had on you as a learner? Passion is one of those hard-to-define, you-know-it-when-you-see-it qualities that add so much to a person's ability to engage and connect with learners. The enthusiasm, excitement, and commitment we generally associate with passion can be quite contagious and inspiring, and it's a quality that ranks high on most administrators' wish lists. "If there's one word that was repeated over and over by principals, it was the word *passion*," stated Gary Hopkins in a report about the qualities administrators seek in new teachers.[4] Contributors agreed. Special education supervisor Berna Levine said, "I look for a spark in their eye, that they really are excited about teaching." And Stephen Vance wrote, "Most of all, I am looking for that passion that is observable in just a short time of talking with that person."

This asset can lend more to your effectiveness than anything you learn from a book. "Of course, knowledge and skill in their subject areas [is important]," said Dot Woodfin, director of her district's character education program. But Woodfin emphasized "a burning passion to help their students succeed" as even more significant in looking at the qualifications of prospective teachers.

This is an asset that's hard to fake. Even young children can tell which teachers are really happy to be there, the ones who really care about the kids and the work they are doing. If you were born to teach, if you get a real buzz from working with young people, if you get excited just talking about your work or your subject area, you know what I'm talking about. If you're not into it, it will show, and it will make for a very long year, for you and your students.

I am positive.

Positivity is such an important asset, and applies to so many aspects of your teaching life, that it is almost impossible to imagine a win-win teacher without this very basic trait. This characteristic can encourage and inspire your students, and can help you stay focused on potential and possibilities, rather than failure, errors, and flaws in the system (or in your students). If nothing else, being a positive person makes you more pleasant and desirable to be around.

Unfortunately, schools tend to be extremely negative places and, even in the best schools, many negatively oriented teaching traditions persist. The challenge will be to not get caught up in these negative patterns—resisting, for example, the urge to gossip or complain about kids, parents, or policies in the hallways or teachers' lounge—or to avoid getting drawn into conflicts and complaints that others want to share with you. And where is your focus when you examine or evaluate your students' work?

If you are not a positive or optimistic person by nature—and incidentally, this tendency can be changed[5]—you can still commit to being positive in how you deal with your students, their parents, and your colleagues. This asset will influence the tone in your classroom, will impact your exchanges with other staff members and your students' parents, and in subtle ways, can affect the climate of the entire school.

I am flexible.

What will you do when something you try simply doesn't work? If a child doesn't understand something, do you have the flexibility and creativity to switch gears and present the concept in a different way? Teaching requires us to wear many different hats and deal with vast differences in student needs and backgrounds. So it should come as no surprise that so many contributors cited flexibility as a high-priority asset for any teacher.

Lindsay Shepheard cited the importance of "knowing that every child and every situation cannot be handled with the textbook approach taught in college prep classes." And Theresa Weidner wrote, "You have to be able to deal with all personality types and make sure your lessons are adaptable for all types of learners." Regardless of your previous experience, every group dynamic is different. What worked last year might not go so smoothly this year. What took twenty minutes in the past might go down in five with a different group.

Michelle Tillapaugh, who has been a part of many interview teams and hiring decisions, commented, "Good teachers can change direction on a dime, think on their feet, adapt to an unannounced assembly, or deal with faulty equipment." Like any teacher, you will need to deal with changes and interruptions—things you can't control and wouldn't ordinarily anticipate. There is great value in learning to expect the unexpected. Count on days when you'll need to shift attention to issues that are not in your lesson plans and put something important off for another day. The greater your flexibility, the fewer headaches you're likely to have when the demand for it arises.

I am organized.

How good are you at managing papers, keeping your classroom neat and organized, and focusing your time on the things that really do need to get done first? Can you find plans and materials when you need them? If you're not an organized person—and I'm hardly the person to be writing about this, although with a lot of work over the years, I have gotten better—daily assignments can become an avalanche.

For the sake of your professionalism, effectiveness, and sanity, you will need to devote time and attention to staying a step ahead of the papers and materials that will accumulate in your room, on your desk, and in your life. This asset will help you avoid wasting time looking for things you need or, worse, losing a student's papers or records.

This is a skill that can develop over time, especially when you start to observe how other teachers keep track of their stuff. But no matter how long you're teaching, there will always be more to do than time to do it, and the better organized you are—or can learn to be—the more time you'll have for the things that are most meaningful and important.

I have a strong work ethic and am willing to put in more hours than are specifically required.

This asset is about dedication and commitment. Although your contract may specify a specific number of hours and school days, are you prepared to devote many, many hours of "your own time" to planning, preparing materials, arranging and rearranging your classroom and materials, grading papers, and staying in touch with parents, for example? I'm talking evenings, weekends, and summers. Especially during your first few years in the profession (or at a new grade level or different subject area), the time you're with your kids is only a fraction of the time required to do your job well. And throughout your career, be prepared to be distracted by meetings, committees, and other duties that may not appear to be directly related to your immediate teaching responsibilities—some of which are important and valuable, all of which come with the territory.

Shepheard values a prospective teacher's work ethic, including "knowing how to set personal performance benchmarks and modeling those for students." Reba Lane said she looks for teachers "who are willing to commit the time to the job" and advised, "the day does not end at 3:15." This is not a job that responds well to cutting corners. As one long-time educator noted, "The teachers who come in late and leave early are usually the first to leave the profession." This is incredibly rewarding work if you're willing to give it the time and dedication it requires—and deserves.

I am knowledgeable about my subject area.

Presumably, you were hired to teach because your grasp of the content you will be teaching exceeds that of your students. But even if you know a particular content area inside and out, you will probably be assigned to teach more than one subject. (This will certainly be true for nearly all elementary teachers, though secondary teachers will have to adjust for different classes even if they teach the same subject to each one.) In fact, there's no guarantee that, as a new teacher, you will even be assigned to the subjects or grade levels for which you've prepared. When you are face to face with a roomful of students, how well do you know your stuff—not just the content, but how best to teach it?

I've heard stories of teachers who have been assigned to classes where they spent the entire year scrambling to stay one step ahead of the students and still managed to do a decent job. (And unfortunately, I've also seen teachers teach from the same lesson plans for decades.[6]) If you've been assigned to a subject or grade level with which you are less familiar, you will have some catching up and possibly a great deal of preparation ahead. This asset also presumes a willingness to continue learning and deepening your understanding of the content you teach by observing other teachers, taking extra classes, and doing whatever it takes to get—and stay—on top of your content.

I am skilled at the art and craft of teaching.

There's a big difference between knowing content and being able to teach it in a way that your students can actually learn it. Riffel looks for what he calls "craftsmanship" when hiring new teachers and considers "the art of their practice in teaching" as a big selling point for new hires. This asset includes your understanding of what it takes for your students to learn, including the cognitive foundation and prerequisite skills your students need to acquire the material you plan to teach. It refers to your ability to get content across to your students, connecting new information in a meaningful way to their cognitive experiences and understanding. Competence in a subject area is not enough, and "covering content" is not even remotely the same as teaching it—much less making it interesting and relevant. (In fact, college chancellor Jo Alice Blondin urges the educators with whom she works to *uncover* content.)

This asset also involves a willingness to appreciate—and reach—a wide range of kids (regardless of their abilities, skill levels, or feelings about school), to teach the way they learn, and to stick with it until they get it. Ray Dagger described the "true progression in teaching" as "becoming the teacher that can teach all students, not just the more intelligent students." Since your students will learn at different rates and in different ways, you'll find that different kids may need different instructional approaches to the same content and that many need to see or hear something more than once before it starts making sense. Are you able (or at least willing to learn) to differentiate instruction and materials to accommodate the learning differences you are certain to encounter? Can you look past defenses and deficiencies and teach to the part of the child that wants to be successful?

This asset assumes an appreciation for the students' need to experience success and the value of helping them perceive themselves as capable of learning. It also requires a sensitivity to—an almost intuitive awareness of—the kind of physical environment, placement, and teaching strategies that will meet these needs, which will vary from one student to the next. Further, this asset assumes an awareness of the overall energy and interest in your classroom and attention to where and how kids need to be engaged. So ask yourself how well you are able to translate your passion and understanding of a particular skill or subject area into inviting, involving, and academically appropriate assignments, projects, materials, and presentations. Because the best lesson in the world isn't worth much if nobody is listening, participating, or learning.

I am willing to address and accommodate nonacademic student needs.

My teacher training program paid some vague attention to the concept of teaching to the "whole child." But although the notion that children have affective and psychomotor needs came up from time to time, everything I was learning seemed to focus exclusively in the cognitive domain. Educator and author Michelle Borba noted that the "biggest surprise for most teachers new to the classroom is they aren't prepared for the breadth of students' emotional needs, and the roles they have to play as teacher [in response to those needs]." Clearly, these roles include attending to nonacademic issues, and teachers who walk into their classrooms thinking that all they will be dealing with is the content in their books and curriculum guides are generally in for a pretty rude awakening.

Many contributors, when asked to reflect on the strengths and weaknesses of their training, echoed Borba's sentiments. One eighth-grade English teacher wrote that she was unprepared "for all of the social and emotional issues that our students face on a daily basis. We talk about Maslow and basic needs being met, but you don't fully understand until you get into the classroom." Julia Frascona commented, "I was ill prepared to effectively deal with mental health issues in my students and their parents." Marti Johnson agreed. "It was the children with all the emotional and behavioral issues that stumped me," she said.

Dagger noted, "Each student arrives for a scheduled class with different baggage." Whether previous experiences at school, problems at home, or stressful social interactions with peers, there are a lot of things that can get in the way of learning. I was astonished at the lack of self-management and self-control in my upper elementary and middle school students. If I hadn't taken the time to help them learn how to choose which of two assignments to do first, get materials they needed (and put them back), or work independently while I worked with other students, my ability to accomplish my instructional goals would have been severely limited. There were also physical and neurological issues, which I needed to learn about and accommodate, that got in the way of my teaching. And I was certainly not alone in needing to address a lack of social competence or friendship skills—and even basic manners—to create a functional win-win classroom. If your picture of working with young people includes attention to these dimensions of the job, you will be way ahead of the curve in your work as an educator.

I am open to feedback, suggestions, and criticism.

There is a certain dysfunction in the teaching profession that supposes that all teachers will not only know what they are doing but also be able to handle just about any situation that arises in their classrooms—effectively, assuredly, and correctly. This perfectionism breeds a tendency toward impression management—an understandable response to the pressure many teachers feel to appear competent and in control. But it's hard to grow and develop your skills if you already know everything, and frankly, you don't. You will make mistakes. Even veterans can misread a situation, make a bad call, or have a lesson bomb.

There are people in your district whose job description includes observing your work and sharing their perceptions and recommendations. Your willingness to hear what they have to say—without becoming argumentative, dismissive, impatient, or defensive—and incorporate their suggestions into your teaching is an asset that was highly valued by nearly every administrator I interviewed. For student-assistance coordinator Sandra Kenyon, "a willingness to learn" ranks high, along with qualities such as enthusiasm, honesty, and responsibility. And while most educators want their colleagues to be confident and self-assured, cockiness and arrogance are not appreciated. As one director of education cautioned, "There is no room for know-it-alls."

Of course, you will need to use your discretion in following advice—not all of it will be sound—and sometimes you will need to follow what seems like bad advice, at least to a certain degree, in order to establish yourself or even keep your job. But if you can keep an open mind and build a trusting relationship with a few established members of the staff, you will probably find much to be learned from their wisdom and experience.

I am resilient.

If you're like most teachers, you will have days when even your most cooperative kids are grumpy and difficult, when the majority fail what you thought was an easy quiz, or when nobody gets your jokes. You will have a parent complain about something you've said or done. Your ideas or enthusiasm will draw a colleague's impatience—or contempt. Your supervisor will walk in on the one day that nobody seems to be listening and walk out telling you that you need to "do better."

These things will happen, and they can suck the life out of you. Good teachers really care about the quality and outcomes of the work they do and take these disappointments to heart. But as Sherry Annee stated, the key is in "using your 'failures' as motivation to design new and better lessons rather than letting [them] paralyze you." Or as one high school English teacher noted, "Learn from your mistakes but don't beat yourself up for missing something or disappointing people."

How long is the stretch between feeling awful (or feeling angry or feeling like a failure) and getting to the place where the experience becomes just another opportunity for learning? When bad things happen—not just in your classroom but anywhere in your life—can you dust yourself off and start fresh the next day? Your ability to take a hit and bounce back will prove to be one of the most valuable assets you can cultivate.

I am willing to spend time reflecting on what I am doing well and how I can improve.

In my work with beginning teachers, I saw individuals become nearly incapacitated by a poorly received lesson or a behavioral situation that got out of control. On the other hand, I also encountered teachers who responded to the same situations by blaming everything from the kids to the weather. I found both types of exchanges particularly frustrating because nowhere in either, at least at the time, was the spirit of "OK, how do I make sure *that* doesn't happen again?"

This asset is about gaining clarity about the quality of your work—including what you're doing *right*, a habit few educational systems actually encourage—and taking time to reflect on what worked and what didn't. It's about the information you receive when you examine your own performance and how you use this information to tweak your lessons, activities, instructions, presentations, and materials.

Win-win teachers make a habit of looking for opportunities to continually evaluate how they're doing—what they're doing well and what they could improve. Charla Bunker described this win-win asset. "It becomes a reflective obsession!" she said. "Every lesson you teach replays over and over in your mind on what went well, what could be changed for next time, and how can you make your best better." This is a great habit to develop if it's not already on your asset list, as the profession deserves the kind of conscious attention that reflective teachers bring to the continued refinement of their craft.

I am curious and strive for continual learning.

This asset is about growing your teaching skills throughout your teaching career and about staying current with research and news about teaching and learning. Several administrators included this asset in their list of the qualities they seek in their staff. Principal Amna Abdullah Hamad Al-Sharqi values "self-development" as well as their understanding of "their role in the educational process." "There are only two kinds of teachers," claimed educator William Purkey, "growing ones and declining ones."[7] Erin Beers agreed: "If you stop learning at any stage of your teaching career, so will your students."

Every day, new information emerges about issues that are relevant to people in the education world. Although the profession builds in very little time and support, if any, for professional development, you will be expected to make time for keeping up with advances, research, and new programs. "Teachers never have a chance to stand still or go stale," cited a report by the National Education Association.[8] Even if you work in a district or state that does not require continual recertification and credit toward advanced degrees, this is a good habit to develop early in your career. An occasional conference, class, or foray into professional literature can help you stay fresh and charged about your work.

Shepheard noted the importance of teachers having a strong "sense of self" in terms of "knowing when it is time to make a change for the sake of the children and themselves." Indeed, some educators recharge their teaching batteries by changing subject areas, grade levels, or even schools every few years. Some stretch their skills with summer or weekend jobs at a tutoring center or community college or by presenting to colleagues at professional conferences. Many of the best teachers I've known who have stayed with the same grade level or subject area year after year, willingly reinvent their approach and develop new lessons and materials each year. Just keeping up with developments in technology—which can be a full-time job in itself—will help keep your teaching current and relevant. Regardless of how far you are willing to step out of your comfort zone, keep in mind that a big part of your job includes continual professional development.

This asset will contribute much to your skills and attitudes about the work you do, not to mention your professional resume.

I am able to work on faith.

"Teaching is the greatest act of optimism," said educator Colleen Wilcox.[9] As many of the teachers I interviewed mentioned, you *will* see the proverbial light go on. You will see a child "get it." You will see improvements in their work and understanding, and you will look back at the end of the year and barely recognize some of the kids who walked in your room the previous September. But most of the time, the results of your efforts will be less obvious, if not totally invisible, occurring gradually, imperceptibly, over time. From time to time, you get to see that you are making a difference. But teaching requires a fair amount of faith in the potential our work has for impacting and influencing our students—without immediate or visible feedback—even when it seems that we aren't getting through.

Author C. S. Lewis said, "The task of the modern educator is not to cut down jungles, but to irrigate deserts."[10] Or to use another metaphor, think of your work as tilling fields and planting seeds that may need a long, long time to germinate. You will need to believe that growth is taking place, even if you can't see it, because things you say, do, or explain today may resonate with a student a year from now. Something they're not getting in your classroom will make sense in another setting or context. In fact, for some students, you will be little more than a place in which to simply *be*—and not get worse. (Remember, we don't get to see what would have happened if we *hadn't* been a part of a child's life.) "The truth is," said Elaine Anderson, "you cannot save every child." But you never know when something you have said or done will have a life-changing impact on a kid, "so you need to be willing to put it on the line for everybody."

This asset also applies to your students' emotional growth and their feelings about school and learning. Bill Funkhouser wrote, "You can pour everything you have into treating [students] respectfully and showing them you care and it won't end up like it does in the movies where they open up and everything is OK. They might still claim to hate you, school, and the whole world." Still, he assured, "Your efforts were not without merit." If immediate and concrete results are important, make sure you have something in your life that will fulfill this need—knitting, carpentry, or cooking, for example—some activity that provides the immediate feedback and reinforcement you may not often experience in your day-to-day work with students.

I respect kids' needs for autonomy, dignity, and power.

Anybody who has ever had a two-year-old can tell you about the very basic and universal need humans have for some sense of control in their lives. When this need is frustrated, that is, when people do not have positive, nonhurtful channels for satisfying this need, we see all sorts of acting out, antisocial, or even criminal behavior. (Think of some of the examples of negative student behavior you have witnessed, and note how often you'll find those students competing for power with an adult, attempting to assert their dominance over another student, trying to prove "you can't make me," or simply struggling to retain some dignity in the face of humiliation or provocation.)

Unfortunately, this topic tends to generate a great deal of all-or-nothing thinking, and adults who enthusiastically agree that kids need structure and limits, love and belonging, success, fun, and worth, for example, get very nervous when the need for power and control comes up. With a few glorious exceptions, most of the resources and information for teachers and parents on discipline emphasize strategies for controlling (and often frankly disempowering) kids—a very win-lose approach.

Because these strategies are generally so ineffective (or seem to work occasionally but at a pretty significant cost), it's not much of a surprise to see "behavior management" at the top of the list of areas in which new teachers feel the least prepared, as well as the list of weaknesses observed by administrators, supervisors, mentors, and veteran staff. Whether or not you are familiar with strategies for creating win-win authority relationships with kids, just being willing to acknowledge that this need exists will allow you to move in that direction.

I am able to forgive.

Kids can say and do incredibly mean, thoughtless things. It's a fair bet that, along the way, some of them will say or do something mean and thoughtless to *you*. They will hate your lessons, say something hurtful to you or their classmates, make fun of what you're wearing, not care about things you value, or have an unreasonably contentious and oppositional response to a perfectly reasonable request. They will, on occasion, make you question your effectiveness, your career choice, and your sanity. How quickly will you be able to let go of whatever resentment and anger you experience in those moments? Will you be able to avoid taking their behavior personally, even when it feels very personal indeed? (And if a parent behaves badly toward you, will you be able to resist the urge to take your resentment out on the child—or the class?)

"You have to be bigger than the behavior that hurts you," advised educational consultant Jenny Mosley. Kids need role models who can deal with an incident, let go, and move on, adults in their lives who can start fresh each day. The classroom is no place for grudges, self-righteousness, or resentment. Your students will test you. They need to know they can mess up and still be accepted and valued, even when their actions and words are not. To what degree are you able to provide this kind of environment for them?

I am capable of controlling my emotions.

Along the same lines as being able to forgive, this asset reflects a high degree of emotional maturity and self-control. By extension, this asset refers to a generally respectful modeling of behavior and interactions with students, regardless of the students' behavior. (The same holds true for dealing with adults.) It does not presume that you will never get angry or frustrated but that, even when apparently justified, you are able to resist allowing your feelings of anger or frustration to insult, belittle, or humiliate a student.[11] It means that you are able to maintain your composure under stress and can attack a problem without attacking a person.[12] It means you are willing to look for alternative ways to teach something instead of demonstrating impatience because the student hasn't learned it yet. And it means that you can resist using sarcasm or similar comments that could be construed as insulting or embarrassing in your interactions with students, especially in front of others.

This is where having a sense of humor will come in handy (and can actually count as a win-win asset on its own). Outbursts and mean-spirited teacher behaviors affect the climate of the class and every student in the room. Kids need adults they admire and respect, adults who can model emotional stability and maturity. This asset includes a willingness to examine your personal hot buttons and to explore nonreactive ways of responding to these triggers. One special education supervisor advised, "Treat each individual with respect and dignity and you will receive rewards tenfold." Perhaps most rewarding, however, is the potential for avoiding additional conflict and stress in your classroom. As one middle school teacher advised, "Never underestimate the power of a child's need to save face."

I practice setting and maintaining good boundaries.

Nobody was talking about boundaries when I was going to school. In all of the materials I've explored regarding discipline, motivation, classroom management, and for that matter, self-care, I haven't seen much about this concept, which makes the understanding and use of boundaries kind of a secret asset. But when it comes to behavior management, motivation, and building student self-management, boundaries offer some of the most powerful tools available. And since these issues are so important—not just to effective teaching but also to the people who will be evaluating your performance—this asset is an extremely important one to develop.

If you are (or get) in the habit of setting good boundaries, you are clearly communicating what you want, letting people know how they can get what *they* want from you, keeping your focus on the positive outcomes or consequences available, and following through to allow these outcomes to occur only when the boundaries have been respected. You are conscious of your own needs and considerate of the needs of others—in other words, you use boundaries to establish your authority in a win-win, mutually respectful power dynamic.

Using boundaries allows you to avoid far more ineffective and destructive (if not flat-out pointless) practices like nagging, threatening, warning, criticizing, complaining, labeling misbehavior, or asking for excuses. If you're already good at setting boundaries, then you are probably experiencing fewer misunderstandings, power struggles, and incidents of opposition or confrontation in your relationships. If this asset does not currently describe you, relax—you're in good company; alternatives will be forthcoming. A simple intention of asking for what you want (as a behavioral replacement for complaining about or describing what you do *not* want) is a huge step in this direction.

I am committed to a strong sense of professionalism in my behavior and appearance.

Each school will have its own version of what it means to be a professional. Culture, history, politics, mission, mandates, and the influence of the surrounding community contribute to the "feel" of any school you will visit. And while that energy may be far more casual in one setting than in another, there are certain aspects of being a professional that are fairly constant throughout the industry.

Many contributors emphasized the importance of what might create a first impression in an interview, or for anyone visiting the school. Marcia Rosen wrote that as a department chair, "First I look for professional attire and bearing. Correct speech and grammar are expected." Likewise, Levine looks for "intelligence, good communication skills—both oral and written" as well as "good grooming and professional appearance." This asset supposes that you represent your school in a way that a supervisor or visitor might consider well educated and professional—not only in how you dress, speak, and behave but also in the spelling, grammar, and clarity of anything you send home.

This asset is also about the way you interact with the rest of the staff, your respect for existing relationships and traditions, your openness to sharing and to asking for help when you need it, and your willingness to contribute to discussions that concern you or your students. It's about your attitude toward your students, your schedule, and your school's policies. It's about how you act in the teachers' lounge. (As one supervisor cautioned, "Whining and self-righteousness aren't professional. You are not the only teacher who cares!") Perhaps most important, this asset reflects a high degree of discretion in terms of what you share and with whom—what your students know about you and what you disclose about them (or their families or other teachers). This is about being authentic with respect for privacy and confidentiality, and within the bounds of what your campus would deem appropriate.

I am passionate about something unrelated to teaching.

If you do your job well, there's a good chance you won't have a whole lot of free time during your first year—at least. So this asset may seem a bit paradoxical, especially in light of the other points on this list that reflect a serious commitment to time and energy around this job. But effective win-win teachers are well rounded and have a degree of balance in their lives. They take time to renew and refresh, and make sure they have something satisfying and fulfilling in their lives *besides* their work.

Diane Callahan advised new teachers to "take time for yourself. Commit a night a week or a weekend a month where there will be *no* school work." Another veteran, Jolene Dockstader, said, "Expect to work hard and don't be afraid of the work, but don't work to the exclusion of home time with family and friends. Take time for yourself. If you burn yourself out the first year, you won't want to come back for a second."

Anissa Emery agreed: "In order to stay healthy and vital, I think it is crucial to maintain outside interests, which provide a rich experience from which to draw while you are dancing as fast as you can, trying to capture those little minds in front of you." Self-care is an important component of win-win teaching, and making sure to devote time to relationships and other interests will help you stay engaged and enthusiastic about your work.

I can see the big picture.

In the day-to-day crush of planning lessons, grading papers, and dealing with student behaviors, it's easy to lose sight of your priorities and sense of purpose. This will be especially true in data-driven districts that exert a great amount of pressure on teachers to get through large amounts of curriculum and raise test scores. Nonetheless, win-win teachers know that academic goals are easier to achieve when they take the time to put certain nonacademic priorities in place first. We sometimes forget that teaching is really about connecting, "a way to touch another's soul," as one music teacher described. Everything else that happens, in terms of learning and growth, starts there. "You are trying to humanize a very dehumanizing system," said school bus driver Andy Quiñones. Although you will feel pressure to jump into the books and stay caught up with what's going on in other classes, this asset asks whether you are willing, for example, to "teach procedures before content and start working on relationships with your students," as retired educator Anna Barsanti advised.[13]

A school's priorities are not always the same as the ones you bring to your classroom. "What we want to see is the child in pursuit of knowledge, and not knowledge in pursuit of the child," said George Bernard Shaw.[14] While I suspect that the mission statements of most states and districts would agree, actual mandates and budgets may suggest the exact opposite. Educator Frank Champine noted, "We can find money to pay for more testing," although "we never seem to come up with the funding to properly create positive learning environments for everyone."[15] This asset also suggests that you will do well to develop a good sense of humor and an appreciation for the absurd. If your need for approval doesn't get in the way, so much the better.[16]

There will be times when your intentions and integrity will come up against job demands, and from one day to the next, you may have some tough choices to make. This asset assumes you know how to pick your battles, that you realize that you don't have to die on every hill. Being able to keep the big picture in mind by focusing on the intentions and goals that brought you to the profession will help. The truth is, as Dennis Littke and Samantha Grabelle contended, "We do some things not so well so that we can do the more important stuff better. It's as simple as that." The question is what you value most, what you believe deserves your time and attention. "Your priorities will be clear to everyone who walks into your school or your classroom," they added.[17] If you are primarily concerned with the climate of your classroom, with the people in it, and with creating a love of learning, it will show.

I can work within the system.

If you're going to get anything done as a teacher, it will help to know how the system works. "Accept the fact that human nature and organizational politics are inseparable," advised author Joel DeLuca.[18] "People do not function in isolation from one another, but are interconnected and interdependent in their lives and in their organizations," claimed authors Patricia Clark White, Thomas R. Harvey, and Lawrence Kemper.[19] "To function effectively in this system of connectedness, we must not only be aware of the strengths and deficits of our own political style, we must also understand how to work with others who have a whole range of styles," they added. Dave Friedli agreed, noting that "beginning teachers can be naive about how things really work and how position, power, and teacher longevity influence decisions that are made in schools." He was one of several contributors who counseled new teachers to "be prepared for the politics that go on in schools."

This asset is about what education professor Victor McGuire described as being able to "think outside the box but work within the system." Likewise, Lyle Hartman, the coordinator of a beginning-teacher support program, advised that it's about learning to play the game, going through channels, and "being smart enough to know who the boss is." "Understand that your first two or three years are essentially a long interview that will determine whether or not you achieve more permanent tenure," he said. Still, Hartman encouraged beginning teachers, "You're a player. Be wise about it." (I once met a first-year teacher who managed to get a districtwide rule overturned after meeting with the superintendent. She went in armed with research and data, knowing that information goes a lot further than emotion in these endeavors.)

This asset requires a certain degree of salesmanship and a willingness to work within existing structures and traditions. It assumes a certain understanding that you may not get what you want or need just because it makes sense or would serve the best interest of the children you teach. It means that, regardless of what you are trying to accomplish or change, you are willing to accept Saul Alinsky's premise that "the basic requirement for the understanding of the politics of change is to recognize the world as it is. We must work with it on its terms if we are to change it to the kind of world we would like it to be."[20]

ACTIVITY

Looking at the assets mentioned in this chapter, rate each one in terms of its relevance using the following scale:

4—*This is true about me most of the time.*

3—*This is true about me some of the time.*

2—*This sounds like me to a small degree (or rarely).*

1—*This doesn't sound like me at all.*

After rating the assets in this chapter, answer the following questions.

1. Which assets represent your greatest strengths?

   a. How do (or might) your strengths contribute to your success in the classroom?

   b. How do these assets help you in other areas of your life?

   c. What other assets do you bring to the classroom that are not included in this list?

2. Which assets represent areas that sound the least like you?

   a. How do (or might) these assets create problems or difficulties for you?

   b. Which of these assets do you believe are the most important or immediately valuable to cultivate?

   c. Identify a potential support or strategy for developing one or more of the assets you believe would be the most beneficial.

3. Which assets are familiar (behaviors or priorities you have seen in schools or heard about in your training)?

4. Which assets are unfamiliar (behaviors or priorities you did not expect, have not seen, or have not heard about in your training)?

5. Which ones are different from what you were taught?

6. What did you learn from reading through this list?

7. What do you plan to do with this information?

Please note that these assets will contribute to the enjoyment and success you experience in your work. If a large number of these assets do not sound like you, read on for strategies that will help you develop the skills and beliefs that will contribute to your success and your enjoyment of your work. I believe that with conscious intention, just about all of these assets can be developed and acquired.

Many of the assets listed will be valued, if not expected, by others in your district. Although some of the assets represent a somewhat nontraditional approach to teaching, they are all very likely to *lead* to outcomes that are valued and expected by your supervisors and colleagues.

NOTES

1. Quote appeared in a tribute in *USA Today* (Bianco, 2003).

2. Quoted in an article by Jeff Sapp (2005, p. 26), "Body, Mind, and Spirit."

3. WGBH (n.d.). Written in 1964 by Louis Lasagna, academic dean of the School of Medicine at Tufts University, and used in many medical schools today.

4. Hopkins (2007, para. 8).

5. Psychologist Martin Seligman (1991) asserted that "pessimists can learn the skills of optimism and permanently improve the quality of their lives" and that the same skills can help optimists when they're experiencing difficulties (p. 207). He claimed that people become more positive by learning to interpret and explain negative events in ways that allow us to continue to believe in our sense of power to make things better. From Seligman (1991, pp. 207–236) and Scott (1999, p. 23).

6. Long after my high school graduation, I went back to the school to visit a couple of my favorite teachers. Walking through the halls, I was stunned to pass by one teacher's room and hear him reading from his outline while the students presumably wrote down what he was reading. Aside from the dubious instructional value of such an exercise, the punch line of the story was the familiarity of the content, which was identical to the outline he had dictated to my class years before. I tried to imagine how he would have justified not having updated this presentation and suspected that the last class this teacher had taken in his subject area had happened years before he had *me* as a student. Be aware, kids can smell a stale presentation a mile away.

7. From a handout by William Purkey (1996), "A Survival Manual for Beginning K–12 Teachers."

8. National Education Association (n.d., para. 18).

9. I've used this quote for years and found a source on the Cybernation Web site (Wilcox, n.d., para. 1).

10. Quoted in Wesley (1998/1999, p. 45).

11. This is not only professionally inappropriate but specifically prohibited by the National Education Association (1975) Code of Ethics, which includes, in "Commitment to the Student," the following items: "4. Shall make reasonable effort to protect the student from conditions harmful to learning or to health and safety" and "5. Shall not intentionally expose the student to embarrassment or disparagement." (From my perspective, this also applies to selecting instructional placement, materials, and strategies appropriate to a student's cognitive, experiential, and learning-style needs, but for the moment, let's focus on the behavioral and emotional implications here.)

12. The ability to maintain composure when confronted with stressful situations is one of eighteen points measured on a teaching dispositions assessment rubric available through the

College of New Jersey (n.d.). This is a trait strongly valued by administrators, parents, and other educators. Weakness in this area will sabotage your efforts at effective instruction and classroom management, and will rarely be tolerated for long.

13. Even if you have no discretion at all about what you teach or when you teach it, the better you can keep these people-first priorities in mind, the better your classes will function and the more enjoyable your job will be.

14. Thanks to the Cybernation Web site (Shaw, n.d.) for this quote.

15. Champine (2004).

16. Most people want to be liked and valued, and you need to function within certain structures and requirements to keep your job. I'm talking about a sense of adequacy and competence that depends on other people's approval. The stronger this need, the more likely you will be to filter every decision you make through your anticipation of their possible reaction. Most of us were raised to be people pleasers, so this tendency is understandable. However, high approval needs will affect your sense of worth and power, as well as your performance in your classroom, and can create a great deal of resentment, self-righteousness, and a sense of victimization. If this seems to be a pattern in your life, please consider finding someone who can help you work through these issues.

17. Littke and Grabelle (2004, p. 191).

18. DeLuca (1999, p. 49).

19. White, Harvey, and Kemper (2007, p. 64).

20. Alinsky (1971, p. 12).

PART II
Survival

I do think new teachers can create win-win situations, even in a broken, win-lose system. The trick is to decide which battles are nonnegotiable while making just enough compromises, or the appearance of compromise, that will keep the guardians of the system off their back.

Eric Katz, author and high school guidance counselor

We believe excellence can be achieved if we care more than others think is wise, risk more than others think is safe, dream more than others think is practical, expect more than others think is possible.

Author unknown[1]

How do you change things that you don't feel are right and, at the same time, take care of the kids in front of you every hour? It's like trying to change a tire while the car is still moving.

Dennis Littke and Samantha Grabelle[2]

If you stay in teaching long enough, you really *will* have seen it all. From colleagues who will give you the shirt off their back to those who are threatened by your enthusiasm, happiness, and success. Kids whose lives will visibly change for the better under your care and those you can never seem to reach.

You'll get the exact classes, grade levels, or subject areas you love and then get assignments far outside your comfort zone. You'll have administrators who appreciate you, who are invested in your success, and who go out of their way to make sure you have everything you need and then find yourself working with someone who seems to sabotage your every move.

Your creativity, initiative, and good instincts will be encouraged and respected in one setting, severely constrained in the next. You'll see projects and programs come and go, some of them educationally sound and others a detriment to good practice and staff morale. (Rarely will any of them be left in place long enough to work.) You'll encounter absurd legislation, needless paperwork, and people who wouldn't last a day teaching in your classroom spouting off about what's wrong with education.

You'll have kids who love learning and want to be there and those who have given up before they ever set foot in your classroom. Kids who could learn from anyone using any approach and kids for whom you will have to explain things six ways from Sunday. Kids behind grade level. Kids who are bored and underchallenged. You'll encounter students who lack skills they need for what you're supposed to teach, and you will have pressure to teach inaccessible content anyway. You'll have kids too emotionally wounded or hungry to learn and some for whom your classroom is a sanctuary, a place where they can engage to distract themselves from fear and pain.

You'll meet parents who will stand behind you and others who will be suspicious of your best intentions, parents who hover, parents who act as though their children are the only ones in your class, and parents you will never see or be able to contact. You'll know teachers who stay at school until midnight and others who are out the door before the last bell has stopped ringing.

In a perfect world, you would have cooperative students who are easy to engage, plenty of resources and supplies, supportive colleagues and administrators, a curriculum that makes sense for the population with whom you are working, and the respect and compensation that your skills and commitment deserve. Lacking these accommodations—and trust me, in the best possible placement you will want for many of these things—there are a few strategies that will enable you to succeed in your professional undertakings, avoid some of the most common stumbling blocks, and retain the drive and commitment that brought you here.

In the meantime, keep in mind this hard truth: You will almost certainly be working in a system that does not want to change. Not surprisingly, many of the resources for beginning teachers that I've encountered contained page after page of suggestions guaranteeing, for better or worse, that new teachers would perpetuate old win-lose traditions, structures, and beliefs. Win-win teachers are about doing things in more positive and effective ways, but there is always the danger that you will succumb to the status quo, start doing what everyone around you is doing, and eventually stop questioning what happened to your ideals.

As one counselor observed, "Teachers today need to incarnate like Che Guevara disguised as Mayberry's Miss Crump."[3] Job status is tentative for at least the first few years,[4] and in most cases, job security will depend on your ability to adopt the values, practices, and priorities of the system—or at least work within your district's guidelines and requirements. If these are not consistent with your own, it will take an exceptionally strong character to hold onto your integrity, not to mention your intentions. So you need to be able to execute win-win practices in such a way that you can get and keep your job. The following chapters will tell you how.

NOTES

1. Quoted in Kathleen Butler's (1997) presentation handouts, "Learning Styles Workshop."

2. Littke and Grabelle (2004, p. 190).

3. Che Guevara was a revolutionary and guerilla leader who lived from 1928 to 1967. Helen Crump was the teacher on *The Andy Griffith Show,* played by Aneta Corsaut, from 1962 to 1968.

4. Tenure requirements and pretenure or provisional certification stretches vary from district to district. Current requirements are subject to changes under proposed tenure reforms.

6

Assume Your Professional Identity

Teaching became easier when I started seeing myself as a teacher and no longer [as] a college student.

Primary teacher

If you want to make the transition from student to teacher a little easier, understand that you have just become what many youngsters revile. The trick is not to let that get to you.

Amy Sutton Mahoney and Christopher Purr[1]

Once you have signed a contract with a district, you have accepted the responsibilities of a teacher. You must behave as a professional and insist that students accept you as a professional. Before long, you will find yourself more comfortable with your status as classroom teacher and will find your niche in the new environment.

Robert L. Wyatt and J. Elaine White[2]

Considering I had wanted to be a teacher from the time I was about three years old, you might have expected my transition to an actual classroom to be less of a shock to my nervous system than it was. While I may have had a good sense of what my new role entailed, there were some real discrepancies between these expectations and the way I had been living my life as a student for the previous four years. Stepping up to the plate required certain skills and self-discipline, at least in certain areas of my life, that I'd managed to avoid until that point.

Even if you were responsible and mature as a college student, you may find that walking into a classroom as a professional requires a degree of conscious attention to things like the opinions you express, the language you use, and the way you present yourself in front of a group of students—aspects of student life that probably had far fewer restrictions or consequences. This transition requires a shift in roles and self-perception, and an adjustment to a world that is nowhere near as insulated or as free as are most college experiences. If you have made that shift easily, and already see yourself as a professional, more power to you. For many of us, however, even with extensive pre-service experience (and perhaps some tutoring or coaching experience as well), some aspects of the teacher side of the teacher-student equation take time to integrate into our actual behavior patterns, much less our self-image, and may be a bit unclear, unfamiliar, or unanticipated initially. While some of these may seem very obvious, many of the new teachers with whom I've worked found themselves a bit unprepared for some of the realities of actually living this role. (And more than a few administrators were concerned about the difficulty some young faculty members had in filling a professional's shoes.) So let's look at some of the considerations you're likely to encounter.

IT'S ABOUT TIME

A big part of what was a rather rude awakening for me was, quite literally, about time. I've always been more of a night owl than a morning person, and one of the things I liked best about college was that I could usually indulge this preference. While I was able to get away with orchestrating my undergraduate career around classes that were available in the afternoons, the schools in which I taught were not nearly as accommodating. When my student teaching assignment began midway through senior year, I suddenly found myself having to leave the house just after 6 a.m. to catch the buses that would connect me with a ride to my school, which was still about an hour away. Although not completely unexpected, this was not a smooth transition for me. Unless I wanted to be absolutely useless the next day, I had to get to sleep just as life around me was getting interesting, and my alarm would go off just as many of the people I knew were heading off to bed (or home). Although their own adult realities were soon to catch up with them, at the time it seemed as though everybody was having a lot more fun than I was.

A fair amount of professionalism has to do with time, whether it's reflected in showing up when you need to be there, turning in plans and reports by the deadlines requested, or being in your classroom any time the students are there. You will never have enough time to get everything done, so learning to make the best use of this precious commodity is essential.

Teaching demands a high degree of focus and attentiveness on a daily basis—not just when the kids are there but also during the hours you'll devote to planning, preparing, and assessing their work. Most people figure out pretty quickly that the job really isn't well suited to certain things that some college students may be able to pull off, be it skipping class or showing up late, hard partying on a school night, or all-nighters to finish a paper or cram for a test. Teaching is physically and emotionally demanding, hard enough to do *with* a rested body and mind. It won't take long for a lack of attention to this very basic need to start showing up in your performance, practice, and patience with your kids. If you're a morning person and have tons of energy, this won't be a big deal. The same is true if you've acclimated to the schedules and routines from previous work experience. For the rest of us, however, learning to adjust our body clocks to a life ruled by buzzers and bells has to move way up on our list of priorities.

STEPPING UP: YOU IN A LEADERSHIP ROLE

Ideally, your students will look to you for leadership and direction. They neither expect nor want you to try to be their peer, and they do need to perceive you as confident in your role. This is another aspect of becoming a win-win teacher. Learning to see ourselves not only as an adult and a professional but also as a responsible authority figure requires a certain amount of perceptual catching up and can be a challenge if we have never thought of ourselves in these terms.

If you are coming to teaching from a leadership position in another career, this transition will likely be easier than for those without that experience.[3] However, many beginning teachers need to make space in their mental pictures of themselves to include the sense of authority that successful teaching requires. This can be especially challenging for secondary professionals who, right out of college, are only a few years older than their charges. One beginning teacher I surveyed expressed the following: "Many times . . . students do not want to take me seriously, mainly because of my age." This individual is in her early twenties and could pass for one of the kids she teaches. "Many students . . . do not want to take instruction from a person who is only a bit older than they are," she continued.

Educator and author William Purkey recommended that new teachers have students call them by their last name and title. "The playing field is not level, and dual relationships are the major source of ethical misconduct," he cautioned.[4] Unless all or most of the adults in your building have their students call them by their first names, use your last name and title. It took a while to get used to people calling me *Ms. Bluestein*, and although the title alone didn't automatically accord me the authority I would have liked, this was the practice at my school, and I do believe it positioned me in a way that made that goal easier to reach. I have heard from many students who were put off by teachers trying to be cool (or look hot), flirting with students, or even mooching food from the kids. Even if you really *are* cool (or hot), acting as though you're hanging out with your peers when you're in your classroom is a sure way to erode your students' respect.

"Remember you are not their friend," advised authors and teachers Amy Sutton Mahoney and Christopher Purr. "If you act too much like a buddy to the kids, which is so tempting because it is fun to be liked, you are setting yourself up for major failure. Even though they like you, they will test your limits; and when you punish them, they will feel betrayed and will no longer trust you. Those kids who adored you and made you feel like the coolest person who ever walked through the door will make your life as miserable as they can."[5] Especially if you work in a high school, you may find it easier to relate to your students than the other staff, particularly if you find a wide age gap between you and the rest of the faculty. But they cautioned, "However uncomfortable you feel in your new role as a faculty member, you must make the transition from student to teacher immediately."[6] Facilitator Marcia Rosen agreed. "Try to understand the kids but don't try to be their friend," she wrote. "Remember, you are a role model. Don't cross the line with kids. If you do, you will not be able to teach effectively."

Keep in mind that an authority role does not preclude friendly and caring interaction. Perhaps understandably, there is a fair amount of black-and-white thinking around authority roles and relationships, and it may be easy to assume that you'll have to choose between being a heavy-handed authoritarian or a permissive pushover. Not true. In a win-win environment, you are very much in charge, but your authority does not depend on disempowering or even controlling your students. You will certainly want to establish a positive classroom climate—after all, you will be spending the next nine or ten months with your students. Constantly having to monitor and manage student behavior won't be much fun for anybody. Being an adult still leaves plenty of space for you to be friendly and human. It can be a fine line sometimes, but you will be no less a leader for laughing with and enjoying the kids you teach.

There are, unfortunately, a number of ways to get this one wrong. One evaluation form for prospective teachers includes, among the skills it identifies in its assessment, the way the teacher interacts with the students. On one end of the continuum, it specifies that the candidate "is very natural in interactions with students and is able to develop mutually respectful relationships and rapport." At the opposite end, the assessment form lists several unacceptable options including being overly friendly and lacking maturity and responsible judgment, being extremely withdrawn and not engaging with students, being overly anxious when interacting with students, or having difficulty maintaining positive rapport with students.[7] This is where having a good mentor and professional role models can really come in handy. If you're not clear on where to draw the line, or aren't sure whether a particular behavior would be considered inappropriate or unprofessional, watch how other teachers behave—or ask. I suspect that in most instances, if something feels questionable, it probably is. Trust your gut, and err on the side of caution.

LOOKING LIKE A TEACHER

In general, there's a big difference between campus casual and the kind of attire that makes you look like a professional educator, even if you're teaching in a pretty relaxed environment. A great deal of identity can be tied up in appearance, and some of us need to modify both before we walk into a classroom (or a job interview). A little discretion and sensitivity to the expectations at your school can help you present your authentic self in the kind of packaging, as it were, that can make successful integration into the profession a whole lot easier. For years, I fought this notion on sheer principle, but the fact is, a part of who people perceive us to be is based on outward appearances, especially when it comes to first impressions—which happen long before our competence and legitimacy are taken for granted, or at least well accepted.[8]

This was another hurdle for me. My college wardrobe—a basic early 1970s T-shirt-and-jeans couture—didn't exactly provide the look that would have presented me as an educator worthy of the title. I needed to *look* like a teacher and not like a college student, not only to be taken seriously in my new work situation but also to help me start thinking of myself as a professional.[9]

Notice how teachers dress where you work or in the schools you visit. In general, choose *conservative* over *cool*, especially early in your career. I have met teachers at conferences and in schools who looked as though they stepped out of a fashion magazine and others who looked like they'd been doing yard work all morning. Technically, this has nothing to do with our ability to do our job, but especially as we're trying to establish ourselves, inspire respect for our authority and teaching skill, and secure tenure in a district, the less people have to get over our appearance, the easier this will be.

If you are especially attached to a more nontraditional appearance, look for a school that will appreciate your uniqueness. They are out there. Working in any system requires a certain degree of sacrifice when it comes to our individuality. This doesn't necessarily mean compromising our authenticity. Keep track of your priorities and your sense of self, and do what you need to do to get in there and perform—and keep—your job.

WHAT MATTERS MOST: WHO YOU ARE IN THE CLASSROOM

Of course your professional identity goes beyond authority roles and appearances. In fact, despite all the emphasis on curriculum and achievement, assessment, and teaching skills, the person you bring to your relationships with the students is far more likely to have an even greater impact. Your sense of purpose and priorities say a lot about who you are, so it pays to be honest with yourself about your core values as an educator. "Everything you do—what you say, your policies, how you treat others—is filtered through your values," wrote Sherry Annee. "Do you believe all children can learn? If you feel as though students can't be trusted, then you will be suspicious of cheating each time a student raises his or her head during a test."

What do you emphasize most in your interactions with your students? What would *they* say is most important to you? Do your students feel safe, valued, and capable of success? On a scale of one to ten, how high would they rate your love of teaching? "Years later what students remember is not the bulletin boards or even those hours you spend preparing those lessons," noted author and educator Michele Borba. "They remember your character." She recommended intentionality in presenting yourself to your students. "Ask yourself at the beginning of each school year what you most want your kids to remember [about] you . . . and then find little natural ways to tune that up. Twenty-five years later they'll come back and thank you," she said.

This is where your individuality, personality, and passions come into play. Anne Morgan noted, "I've always been creative, organized, patient, and a little bit goofy as a person. Teaching Pre-K allows me to incorporate my personality into every aspect of my career." One student related an example from a high school class in which the history teacher would come dressed in costume, animate his storytelling with sound effects, and incorporate jokes into the lesson.[10] My love of travel and geography spilled into the classroom every year, whether it showed up in pen-pal opportunities for my students, cultural activities and guest presentations, or slide shows from my summer vacations.

Introduce yourself to your kids with a display that shares some of your interests. Include copies of photos of you with your family or friends, a picture of your pets, some postcards from your last vacation, a copy of your diploma, a list of your goals (personal or instructional), your favorite books or movies, the sports and teams you like best, or an example or photo of something related to your hobbies.[11] Common sense would suggest that you do not bring in originals or anything of value that can't easily be replaced. And use discretion about what you share about yourself, and when. Once you've connected and built a sense of community with your students, you'll probably feel more comfortable sharing more personal things about yourself, but be aware that it can be dangerously easy to slip into "too much information" territory. Also keep in mind that anything you say, show, or do *will* be repeated, so run these choices through a mental filter that asks, "Will I feel comfortable when another teacher, an administrator, or a parent hears about this?"

How you present yourself to the rest of the faculty matters as well. Lyle Hartman advised, "You need to be wise about professional communication—how you conduct yourself, the way you dress, how you respond to people. If you smirk or roll your eyes, know that you have the right to make this statement but that there are consequences." Christie DeMello added, "This may seem harsh but, know your place in the school. If it's your first year (or even first couple of years), you need to respect the knowledge and experience of those around you. I get really upset with beginning teachers who act like they know everything. It's viewed in our community as disrespectful and is not tolerated."

Likewise, I once observed a first-year teacher who was technically very competent and had a great understanding of instructional processes and materials. Unfortunately, her talents were consistently undermined by inordinate self-deprecating and approval-seeking behaviors with the other faculty. Whether you feel like it or not, you are an adult. Act like one. Legitimate questions and concerns are a sign of commitment; apprehension about something you've never done before is understandable. However, a fragile ego and need for constant reassurance suggest you aren't emotionally equipped for the job. Your best bet is a mix of openness and self-assurance, confidence that doesn't come off as cocky or arrogant. "I know you may feel nervous, but don't let the kids or the parents see you sweat," counseled Gerri-Lynn Nicholls. "You are a professional. You are not going to work to make friends. Don't lose focus. Do not be intimidated by seasoned teachers."

Clearly, teaching demands a certain degree of showmanship. Whether you are tired or discouraged, or stressed about something in your life that has nothing to do with your work, when you walk into your classroom, a competent performance is expected. "You may not be happy when you enter class, but you can always be cheerful," noted Purkey. A director of elementary education advised new teachers to "take an acting course because you have to be *on,* even on bad days." Teacher educator Wendy Marshall agreed: "You're on stage every day." Deal with what's going on in your life, certainly, and also be prepared to shift your focus to your work and your kids when you walk across that threshold, as difficult as that may seem at times.

There will be days when teaching will test every promise you've ever made to yourself, whether it's to avoid losing it with the kids or resist eating every bit of chocolate you can find in the school. You need not only a cool head but also integrity, ideals, and faith in your inner guidance. Who you are, the *self* you bring to your work, will be evident in just about every choice you make.

"Reputation, it has been said, is about who you are when people are watching," wrote columnist Leonard Pitts. "Character is about who you are when there's nobody in the room but you. Both matter, but of the two, character is far and away the more important. The former can induce others to think well of you. But only the latter allows you to think well of yourself."[12] At the end of the day, what have your students learned because of what you brought to their lives, because of the time they spent with *you?*

LIFE IN A FISHBOWL

Here's something else to consider, something that was not a factor when I started teaching. We now live in a world where everything about our lives is far more public than ever before. Online photos and videos that were funny or cute when you were in high school or college can put you at risk for not getting hired or actually losing your job. And anything you say or do—in your classrooms *and* in your private lives—can become grist for the Internet mill in seconds.

"If you go out on Fridays to party, don't do it in the town, city, or county where you teach!" advised one assistant superintendent. A contributor to an online discussion about the ethical aspects of teachers' behavior in their personal lives acknowledged that openly engaging in "inappropriate" behavior in public "is very different from doing it in private. Unfortunately, sometimes things that were done in private end up becoming public."[13]

While perhaps not entirely fair, teachers are, in most communities, held to higher standards of comportment and can come under sharper scrutiny than individuals who aren't responsible for "shaping and molding" the youth of those communities. While many people—including educators, parents, legal advocates, and other community members—defend teachers' rights to live their lives as they choose, school districts are understandably nervous about the potential embarrassment reflected in what they (or some parents) might consider to be inappropriate language, photos, conversations, or behavior on public display. Although perhaps legally defensible, Wyatt and White noted that "from a practical standpoint, parents often expect teachers to forgo their rights if the parents see the teachers as having a negative or threatening influence on their children."[14]

Author Yvonne Gentzler observed, "Professional roles include those qualities that constitute responsible and ethical conduct. Teachers are trusted with a tremendous power to influence the thinking, motivation, and knowledge of their students. It is incumbent on you to consider how your practice, behavior, and actions will impact the lives of your students."[15] As one superintendent asked (referring to material posted online by one of his teachers), "Would you do this in the class in front of your students?" If the answer is no, you probably don't want the material available to anyone with Internet access.[16] Or as another blogger noted, "No one wants to be the teacher . . . on the six o'clock news."[17]

The path gets narrower when you step into your classroom, and even if your youthful exploits aren't plastered all over cyberspace, the possibility of ever running into your students or their parents in public, whether it be at a supermarket, a concert, or a bar, puts you in a fishbowl you may not have experienced prior to becoming a teacher. Even if the behavior isn't illegal or unethical, be prepared to clean up your act if need be—much less any content that might be considered inappropriate on a blog or social network site if, for example, a student or parent (or district administrator, for example) were to come across it. In other words, even if you're still a kid in your head, be prepared to look and act like a professional, not just on the job but anyplace your work life is likely to catch up with you.

PROTECTING YOURSELF

In recent years, cultural changes, technology, and legislation have significantly complicated teachers' lives and made us more vulnerable to legal action than ever before. Where "school law" topics were once reserved for advanced and somewhat esoteric graduate classes, a paper written by Phillip H. Wagner advocated for preservice programs that "prepare potential educators with a working knowledge of the fundamentals of school law."[18] He cited the increase in volume and complexity of school-related legislation as a requirement for teachers "to possess a basic understanding of the laws that impact them and the concerns that frequently arise in education law." He also cautioned that "educators must recognize how their actions can lead to litigation and the impact of legislative and judicial mandates on the teaching profession."[19]

Legal implications will touch just about everything in your teaching life, including such aspects as classroom activities, records and privacy, and ethical behavior. For example, the Family Educational Rights and Privacy Act (FERPA) protects the confidentiality of information related to students' records and who gets to see or hear about students' progress. It also gives parents the right to contest "records which they believe to be inaccurate or misleading."[20] From a practical standpoint, FERPA violations include things like posting students' grades, allowing students access to graded papers or tests other than their own, or sharing any information about students—from personal or contact information to grades and records—with anyone who does not have a "legitimate educational interest" in those students.[21] Wyatt and White elaborated: "The only way information is to be passed from one teacher to the other is in a private area, such as an office, away from other people, especially students. A teacher or administrator should share confidential information only if teachers *need to know* that information in order to be more effective in teaching that particular student."[22] So from the start, be careful to avoid idle chatter with specific and confidential information about your students in the hallway, teachers' lounge, and certainly in your classroom when students are around. If you're not familiar with the legislation behind these cautions, talk to someone in your school who is, and find out how the school handles issues of privacy and confidentiality.

Watch out for assignments that can cross into tricky territory. One of my more embarrassing moments happened when the TV miniseries *Roots* first aired.[23] Nearly all my students were watching the show, but when I assigned an activity asking them to create a family tree, several parents let me know, in no uncertain terms, that this information was none of my business. Oops. I knew other teachers in different communities who had no problems with similar assignments, but this was a sensitive issue with the families of my students.

Wyatt and White recommended advising kids to steer clear of certain topics, things like "illegal activities, very personal religious experiences, politics, and anything hurtful to another person," for example, when brainstorming or journaling.[24] If your students journal, be sure to specify under what conditions you are obligated to break confidentiality. (This might include when they share an intention to hurt someone or themselves, disclosure of illegal or self-destructive behaviors, or if they report that someone is hurting them, for example.) And consider this issue when displaying kids' work. Many teachers make it a habit to get students' permission before displaying their work. At the very least, display work without grades—you can submit grades on a separate paper or feedback form if you plan to display the assignments—or cover the grade when you hang the students' work.

Teachers are probably most vulnerable, however, when a student or parent is unhappy with something the teacher has done, even if the teacher's behavior is reasonable, justifiable, and well documented. An article by Nancy Gibbs related, "The fear of litigation has given rise to the practice of defensive teaching. . . . The number of teachers buying liability insurance has jumped 25% in the past five years."[25] Many students come to school armed with a staggering sense of entitlement, and neither they nor their parents will hesitate to defend the child's behavior or fight to give the kid a break. "Anything you say can and will be used against you by a disgruntled student," warned Mahoney and Purr. "It doesn't matter if you were kidding and everybody in the class that day knew it. They're still your words." Gibbs's article described an example of the kind of defensive teaching that is becoming more and more common. She wrote about a sixth-grade teacher who "does not dare accuse a student of cheating, for instance, without evidence, including eyewitness accounts or a paper trail. When a teacher meets with a student alone, the door always has to be open to avoid any suspicion of inappropriate behavior on the teacher's part."[26]

Clearly, the best defense—besides caution and common sense—is a good relationship with your students and their parents. An attorney and risk-management specialist for teachers, David Wolowitz, observed, "In order to be a successful teacher, probably the single-most important thing is to connect with the students." In our discussion, he mentioned several places a teacher's attempt to connect can cross the line, the importance of maintaining a sensitivity to factors such as the age of the child and the nature of the connection (for instance, through e-mail, social networking sites, or physical contact), and an awareness of how the interaction would be perceived—by parents and by other adults, and by the kids themselves. "People who manage risk well make connections but are alert to the risks," he said. He cited examples of inappropriate self-disclosure, including a teacher who had posted vacation pictures giving kids access to photos in which she was wearing a skimpy bathing suit. Likewise, Wolowitz described the kind of physicality that younger students might perceive as warm and caring but which could come across as inappropriate with older students. "Risk management should not interfere with having a positive, powerful, effective connection that leads to good education, but [should focus instead on] having an awareness of the nature of the connection with its benefits and risks," he added. At the risk of encouraging outright paranoia, do develop an eye for how others are likely to see you, because the acid test for liability is not in your intention, but in how your actual behavior is perceived and interpreted.

ACTIVITY

No matter how ready we are to step into a new role or stage in our lives, the process of catching up to who we are becoming—not to mention adjusting to the demands of this new environment—can take some time. Successfully transitioning from student (college student, that is, as opposed to professional, lifelong-learner student) to teacher can benefit significantly from some deliberate awareness of who we are and how we fit into our new role.

In the following chart, describe the differences in expectations, demands, limitations, and consequences in both your college environment and your professional (teaching) environment in each of the categories listed:

	College	Professional
Schedule and time demands		
Appearance (restrictions or requirements)		
Relationships, dating, sexual orientation, and sexual behavior		
Recreation (activities, behavior, and sobriety)		
Supervision, observation, and restrictions		
Work requirements and deadlines (flexibility)		
Life in the fishbowl		
Consequences for inadequate or incomplete work		
Consequences for lateness or absence		
Consequences for behavioral impropriety		
Other		

1. Which of these differences did you best anticipate?

2. Which of these differences were the most unexpected?

3. Which were easiest for you to adapt to or accommodate?

4. Which have provided the greatest challenge in your transition to becoming a teacher?

ACTIVITY

If you are coming to teaching from any other field (including work experience in afterschool and summer jobs), this new environment may represent some significant changes from the demands and expectations you experienced in previous work situations.

In the following chart, describe the differences between your previous work environment and your professional (teaching) environment in each of the categories listed:

	Previous Job(s)	**Teaching Job**
Schedule and time demands		
Appearance (restrictions or requirements)		
Job responsibilities: including preparation, performance, duties (variety and number), and documentation		
Learning curve		
Autonomy (amount of supervision or direction)		
Professional development (requirements and support received)		
Life in the fishbowl		
Salary and benefits		
Impact on personal life		
Other		

1. Which of these differences did you best anticipate?

2. Which of these differences were the most unexpected?

3. Which were easiest for you to adapt to or accommodate?

4. Which have provided the greatest challenge in your transition to becoming a teacher?

5. Think about jobs in fields other than teaching, perhaps jobs your friends have or other jobs you've had:

   a. What benefits do you expect that employees in other fields enjoy that you also enjoy in teaching?

   b. What benefits do you think they enjoy that will probably not be offered or available to you as a teacher?

   c. What benefits do you expect to enjoy that they will probably not experience in the work that they do?

6. Think about jobs in fields other than teaching, perhaps jobs your friends have or other jobs you've had:

   a. What problems or limitations do you expect that they probably also experience?

   b. What problems or limitations do you think they experience that will probably not be an issue for you as a teacher?

   c. What problems or limitations do you expect to experience that they will probably not encounter in the work that they do?

ACTIVITY

Answer the following questions considering what you bring to your classroom in terms of your personality, values, and self-perception:

1. In what ways do you feel confident and prepared about assuming an authority and leadership role in the classroom? About what do you feel most insecure or anxious?

2. In what ways do you resolve the need to be an adult with the desire to be friendly and caring with your students?

3. In what ways does teaching allow you to express your personality, creativity, and talents?

4. If you meet up with your students twenty years from now, what do you want them to remember about you?

5. If you meet up with your students twenty years from now, what do you want them to remember about the year they spent with you?

ACTIVITY

With regard to the liability issues of concern to teachers, answer the following questions:

1. Identify potential liability issues that were addressed in your training. How did your training prepare you to protect yourself from potential liability as a teacher?

2. Which potential liability issues seem to be priorities for your school or district?

3. Which potential liability issues are of greatest concern to you?

4. What precautions do you currently take to avoid problems in this area?

5. What are your plans for future or improved risk management?

NOTES

1. Mahoney and Purr (2007, p. 3).

2. Wyatt and White (2007, p. 13).

3. Interestingly, the beginning teachers who often have the greatest difficulty with the unique challenges of working in an educational environment are not the young people coming to the profession straight out of college but those who enter the classroom as a second (or third) career after working in other fields. While some make the transition smoothly and successfully, others find it disheartening to discover that strategies that were effective in one work environment do not naturally translate to the classroom. This is true even when transferring from one school or grade level to another, much less from one career to another. I continually encounter dedicated folks who are incredibly perplexed and frustrated by their inability to get their classrooms to function as smoothly as their previous design teams, sales forces, or military units.

4. Purkey (1996). This advice is especially relevant for beginning teachers whose authority, competence, and professional reputation have not been established. Be aware that a title alone does not confer authority. Your behavior and interactions with your students will do that. I have been in several schools, public and private, in which students called teachers and administrators by their first names, and the authority relationships were not compromised, partly because this pattern was accepted and familiar at those sites. Follow the conventions in your school.

5. Mahoney and Purr (2007, p. 86). I once had a first-year teacher for a sculpture class in high school. She gave us each a mound of clay but no actual instructions or requirements, because she was trying to be "real cool with our creativity." Until we actually turned something in. Having her publicly criticize—ridicule was more like it—one project after another burned any trust we had in her, personally and professionally. For my money, this qualified her as one of the worst teachers I ever had. I transferred into another class immediately. It would be another thirty years before I was even tempted to put my hands in clay again.

6. Mahoney and Purr (2007, p. 12).

7. College of New Jersey (n.d.).

8. A 2005 article described a new generation of workers who expect to bring their "campus-casual" habits to the workplace. It cited findings from a survey from that same year by the National Association of Colleges and Employers that found that 49% of employers "said nontraditional attire would have a 'strong influence' on their opinion of a candidate." In a 2002 study, "38% of respondents had such an opinion." Barker and Bailey (2005, pp. D1–D2). Although these surveys reflected a broad (that is, not specifically educational) work environment, it is clear from the feedback I received from administrators and veteran teachers that a professional appearance is a significant factor in hiring (and, I suspect, evaluating) the individuals on their faculty.

9. I'm still more inclined to dress for comfort than "show," but in a work situation, I don't want my students or audiences to be distracted by my appearance.

10. From a story shared by then-high school student Tony Salaz in *Mentors, Masters, and Mrs. MacGregor: Stories of Teachers Making a Difference* (Bluestein, 1995).

11. From several sources, including Wyatt and White (2007, p. 5).

12. Pitts (2002, para. 15).

13. "Ethical Behavior" (2006). Questions of propriety can apply to things you did before you became a teacher, things you did in other jobs, or things you do outside of teaching that are completely unrelated to your work. One article reported on a teacher who was suspended after her students discovered a racy ad she did for a clothing company two years before she started

teaching. The article suggested an overreaction on the part of the school and noted that "it's so over-the-top comical it's hard to believe anyone would read any intentional nastiness into it on the part of [the teacher] or in anyway cast her in a negative light." Nonetheless, the author also admitted, "it would be pretty creepy to see your schoolteacher having simulated sex on a desk." Hall (2008).

14. Wyatt and White (2007, p. 129). While the majority of comments on public blogs and responses to news stories exposing teachers' private lives (which tend to focus on the more sensational and negative examples) support teachers in having a right to privacy, the idea of being a role model for the community is frequently mentioned as being a part of the job. Also keep in mind that the smaller the community, the fewer freedoms you are likely to have about how you live your life—all the more so if you live in the same neighborhoods in which your students and their families live.

15. Gentzler (2005, p. 159).

16. "Teachers Expose Private Lives Online" (2007). In this same article, author Tim Delaney used the example of how the same image or language posted on a billboard along the freeway would be considered offensive.

17. "Ethical Behavior" (2006).

18. Wagner (2007). Wagner noted that the legal issues of greatest concern include child abuse reporting, special education (IDEIA: Individuals With Disabilities Education Improvement Act of 2004) concerns, discipline policies, and federal mandates.

19. Wagner (2007).

20. Family Educational Rights and Privacy Act (FERPA, 2009).

21. "Student Record Confidentiality: FERPA Information" (2009); "Those Who May Have Access to Educational Records" and "Do's and Don'ts" (*FERPA Information Sheet,* n.d.). This latter reference defined *educational interest* as follows: "In accordance with FERPA, a school official has a legitimate educational interest if the official needs to review an educational record in order to fulfill his/her professional responsibility."

22. Wyatt and White (2007, pp. 47–48).

23. *Roots* (n.d.) was based on Alex Haley's work *Roots: The Saga of an American Family* and first aired in 1977.

24. Wyatt and White (2007, p. 31).

25. Gibbs (2005, p. 48). These statistics also appeared in Wagner's (2007) paper.

26. Gibbs (2005, p. 48).

7

Understand Schools in Context

We are living in exponential times.

Karl Fisch, Scott McLeod, and Jeff Brenman[1]

Our students have changed radically. Today's students are no longer the people our educational system was designed to teach.

Marc Prensky, educator and author[2]

It's hard to expect any significant change in the outcome if there is no significant change in the process and sadly, education often seems to favor institutional familiarity and self-preservation over change, especially of the bleeding edge variety.

John MacBeth, retired administrator

To get what we've never had, we must do what we've never done.

Mark Lee, finance professional[3]

A few months ago, I was working with a very bright twenty-five-year-old program manager for one of the seminars I was presenting. At one point in our conversation, she mentioned that for all of the research papers she had written in high school and college, she had used an actual book only once. She didn't understand why the teacher insisted that the students use at least one book for that project. What was the point? Although a voracious reader, she was completely lost in a library, and besides, everything she needed for her papers was available online.

I shouldn't have been surprised. After all, all but my first few books included e-mail surveys and Internet research, and it's been years since my manuscripts went back and forth between my editors and me on actual paper.[4] Things are moving so fast anymore that it's not surprising that so many of us feel like the contributor who complained, "I'm running as fast as I can to not get too far behind!"

So let's talk a little about change and what's happening these days—in the world, with our students, and in our schools, because all of these factors will impact your experience in the classroom and can explain why a lot of what you are expected to do may not work quite as well as it once did.

THE WORLD HAS CHANGED AND SCHOOLS HAVE NOT KEPT UP

In the Middle Ages, change happened so slowly that people had lots of time to contemplate technological, political, and social advances that would affect their lives—if they noticed or considered them at all. That's no longer the case. The same amount of change that used to take hundreds of years to unfold now happens in a matter of weeks.[5] In all likelihood, this pace will continue to accelerate, with no signs of slowing down, much less going back.

Each advance seems to spread faster than the last. It was thirty-eight years before radio reached a market audience of 50 million people. Television hit 50 million after only thirteen years, and the same number of people were using Facebook within two years of its release, with up to 200 million active users worldwide in the following three years.[6] Think of the technologies that have emerged in the past few years and how they have affected our habits, our thinking, and even our vocabularies. (It wasn't that long ago that every student in school would know what you meant when you talked about "winding the window down," "dialing the phone," or "sounding like a broken record.")

In terms of information alone, examples of acceleration boggle the mind. Consider the fact that, according to a 2008 video researched and designed by Karl Fisch, Scott McLeod, and Jeff Brenman, you and I will come across more information in a week's worth of *New York Times* than people in the eighteenth century would encounter in an entire lifetime. This video reported that there currently is "more information generated in one year than in the previous five thousand years." It also noted that "the amount of new technical information is doubling every two years. For students starting a four-year technical degree this means that . . . half of what they learn in their first year of study will be outdated by their third year of study."[7] And it's not just technical information. A 2002 book by Peter Kline announced, "The amount of available information in *all* fields is growing at more than a billion times the rate it was in 1950."[8] In this context, the notion of a "body of knowledge" seems pretty absurd.

A few years ago, Education Secretary Richard Riley predicted that "the top ten in-demand jobs in 2010 didn't exist in 2004."[9] Fisch and friends stated, "We are currently preparing students for jobs that don't yet exist, using technologies that haven't been invented, in order to solve problems we don't even know are problems yet."[10] But *are* we preparing them? In recent decades, educational demands have increased dramatically in the workplace. Authors Kenneth Wilson and Bennett Daviss reported in 1994 that even the least skilled jobs in the new millennia would "require a command of reading, computing, and thinking that was once necessary only for the professions."[11] While an eighth-grade education may have been adequate for many jobs in the past, even a solid high school education won't go far today. Journalist Bob Herbert affirmed, "We are now in a time when a college education is a virtual prerequisite for achieving or maintaining a middle-class lifestyle."[12]

Twenty-first-century jobs increasingly require technological literacy in all fields, as well as the flexibility and commitment to keep up with constant changes and developments in this area. "If we simply train a new generation of students in the math, science and engineering skills in demand today, by the time they graduate, the global economy will have new requirements," wrote educator Michael Bassis. "A formal education that just teaches us to understand today's technology is, in an age of rapid change, just another example of planned obsolescence."[13] Author Thomas Friedman agreed. "What you know today will be out-of-date sooner than you think," he warned.[14]

The rate of change and acceleration can be pretty disorienting. But if you want your head to stop spinning, you need only to go back into a typical school, where things really haven't changed much since the 1700s, when education, in western culture, hit its own market expansion, granting access "to larger numbers of children from increasingly diverse segments of society."[15] This was the time when many of the systems we see in schools were established—which would be fine and dandy except the world into which our current schools deposit our students is radically different from the world in which these protocols came about.

The most recent cultural and economic shifts are described in different terms by different people, but all point in a similar direction. Friedman talked about the world going "flat," with the latest version of globalization connecting individuals in ways that previous transitions once connected countries and companies. The notion of a flat world includes an economic reality in which workers around the world are now in a position to compete for work previously done in more developed nations. As manufacturing jobs have been moving overseas, now information jobs are following a similar trend. "Everywhere you turn, hierarchies are being challenged from below or are transforming themselves from top-down structures into more horizontal and collaborative ones," he wrote.[16] Well, globally perhaps, but hardly the model to which many schools adhere.

In this context, Daniel Pink presented a case for an increasing need of right-brained thinkers in what he called the current *conceptual age.*[17] As we move further from factory-era models, players in the newly emerging economy will be the creators and empathizers, with right-brain strengths such as "forging relationships rather than executing transactions, tackling novel challenges instead of solving routine problems, and synthesizing the big picture rather than analyzing a single component."[18] Friedman concurred with the need for creativity and interpersonal skills. He concluded, "No matter what your profession . . . , you better be good at the touchy-feely service stuff, because anything that can be digitized" is likely to be outsourced.[19]

Win-win teaching requires an appreciation for the context in which schools exist, and win-win teachers strive to keep up with changes occurring in the culture and economy schools serve. Educators Lynne Gerlach and Julia Bird challenged twenty-first-century educators "to move from outside to inside, from provision to learning, from facts to meaning." They also stressed the value of learning to learn, as well as the importance of living intelligently, and being able to manage paradox, live with contradictions and uncertainty, and demonstrate creative resilience within complexity.[20] Unfortunately, these skills—and others, such as social and interactive competence, humor, creativity, ingenuity, imagination, holistic thinking, gut instinct, and emotional climate (each of which gains importance the further we get from left-brain directed models)—tend to be undervalued and marginalized in schools, if not ignored altogether. Back-to-basics is fine as long as the basics are relevant to the needs of the twenty-first-century workplace. Today's economy demands kids with information literacy, as well as good people skills, good communication skills, good networking skills, a knowledge of the global community, an appreciation for cultural diversity, creativity, innovation, the ability to think outside the box, and as one CEO requested, "vision and attitude."[21] John Bickart shared, "I really wish someone had told me that [teaching] is more about changing attitudes than imparting facts." But according to educator and author John Gatto, even in the best schools, "the logic of the school-mind is that it is better to leave school with a tool kit of superficial jargon derived from economics, sociology, natural science, and so on than with one genuine enthusiasm."[22] And authors Claudia Wallis and Sonja Steptoe warn that the way schools are currently configured, "an entire generation of kids will fail to make the grade in the global economy because they can't think their way through abstract problems, work in teams, distinguish good information from bad, or speak a language other than English."[23]

Looking at schools through this lens can be fairly disconcerting. In attempting to prepare children for accelerating change, it hardly makes sense to try to meet future needs with curricula and practices developed to serve the past. But those traditions persist in most schools today. Educator Allan Ilagan agreed, noting that education "is not changing at a rate even close enough to keep up with the need for change." Wallis and Steptoe imagined Rip Van Winkle awakening in the twenty-first century after a hundred years of sleep and being "utterly bewildered by what he sees," that is, until he walks into a schoolroom. Our schools, they claimed, "aren't exactly frozen in time," but they've certainly been outpaced by the rate of change in other areas of our lives. "Kids spend much of the day as their great-grandparents once did: sitting in rows, listening to their teachers lecture, scribbling notes by hand, reading from textbooks that are out of date by the time they are printed," they continued. "A yawning chasm (with an emphasis on yawning) separates the world inside the schoolhouse from the world outside."[24] Educator Sarah Guthrie also commented on the difficulty schools have keeping up. "We don't teach what students need to know in order to succeed in this modern world," she wrote, criticizing current efforts "to teach a set of mostly unnecessary skills to students who are less and less open to outdated, meaningless, inapplicable tasks."

Few educators would deny that the knowledge base is expanding at increasingly unprecedented rates, that there is more and more to know every day. Unfortunately, the response to this phenomenon has been to simply cram more content into each grade level, introducing material to kids at younger and younger ages, developmental appropriateness be damned. Michelle Colbert was surprised to discover, when she returned to teaching after taking off five years to have her children, that the content she had been teaching to first graders was now being taught to kindergarteners. Author Sue Ferguson observed that the term *school readiness* once referred to kids' ability to separate from their parents for a few hours without too much fuss and go to the bathroom by themselves. The same term, she said, now refers to their mastery of early numeracy and literacy skills.[25] And one first-grade teacher related that kindergarten "has gone the way of the little red wagon and mud pies." We no longer give children time to learn how to use a tricycle or wait their turn on the swing. "These were important skills," she added, "vital to success in the grades to come." But current mandates favor worksheets and take-home books as expectations expand at each grade level and leave many of her students behind.[26] While this content acceleration is probably most obvious in the younger grades, I've heard similar stories from a number of secondary educators, including several middle school math teachers bemoaning the fact that they are now pushed to teach content once reserved for ninth-grade algebra classes.

Cranking up the speed on the curricular treadmill is devastating this profession. Cesar Delgado, a beginning preschool teacher, described feeling "left out from the education system, and incompetent before veteran teachers." He described his desire to really connect with his kids from the first day of teaching, "but the overload work, due dates, and lesson plans . . . kill you, leaving no strength to inspire students." It is understandable how dedicated teachers can feel a sense of personal failure for not being able to keep up with unrealistic demands. And truly, the expectations in some settings are pretty wacko. We don't know what kids will need to know in a couple of years. We can never cover it all.

"If all of the standards were taught, schooling would move from a K–12 structure to a K–22 structure," wrote Robin Fogarty.[27] Be aware of the likelihood that you will be expected to teach far more than can reasonably be taught in the time you have with your students. Several of the books for beginning teachers that I reviewed try to help, but I was frankly unnerved by advice to plan content according to the testing schedule, presumably so that you will have presented everything by the test, or to break down your curriculum by month, week, and day to be sure that you get through the books. This may well be the expectation in your school, but don't for a second confuse this approach with actual teaching. Instruction without regard for students' individual needs, experiences, and abilities will surely become a huge source of stress and frustration (and yes, failure) for all concerned.

If we're going to really make education work, we need to start with the kids—who students are, what they know, how they learn, and what makes them tick. We will shift our attention from facts and content to process and passion, and more important, learning how to learn. Bassis wrote about the problem with current reforms being their focus "on what students know, not what they are capable of learning. Knowing is important. But it cannot be an end in and of itself. What we know today will be outmoded tomorrow. . . . It isn't enough just to learn anymore, one must learn how to learn. How to learn without classrooms, without teachers, without textbooks. Learn, in short, how to think and analyze and decide and discover and create. That is the ultimate test of good education."[28]

KIDS ARE NOT WHO THEY USED TO BE

There was an article in the morning paper about thousands of high school students in my state alone who are going for their GEDs (General Equivalency Diplomas) rather than staying through four years until graduation. While students chose this route for a number of reasons, the ones who caught my attention were those who opted for a GED because they were dissatisfied with the instruction they were receiving in school. "I was given facts, and I was meant to memorize them and spit them back out on paper," said one of the students interviewed. "I was never really fond of that kind of learning. My soul was hungry, with nothing to learn."[29]

A few years ago, while researching a book for high school students, I heard similar complaints from kids over and over again. "I'm already not in a good mood knowing that all I have to look forward to is going to a class to learn about dead guys and math formulas that I will never use again," was how one fifteen-year-old described the start of his day. Another contributor lamented, "I wish my school system had encouraged the art of thinking and learning, as opposed to memorizing and regurgitating." One freshman advised readers, "All you have to do is play the teachers' games. Do what you got to do and then get out."[30] The problem is, a lot of students don't have the patience to "do what they got to do," and with something like seven thousand students dropping out of U.S. schools every *day*,[31] it's pretty clear that, somewhere along the line, we are failing to connect with the instructional, curricular, emotional, social, or behavioral needs of the students in our care.

"Students look at school as a place they *have* to go," wrote one high school contributor. "It is not an option. They don't come to learn. They're here because they *have* to be here."[32] Now, certainly there are kids who enjoy school and look forward to being there, but how often do their agendas focus on factors that have little to do with academics? "While learning might be the priority of teachers, students have many other reasons to come to school. For some, socializing, sports, and extracurricular activities are at least as important as learning," reported researcher Robert Blum.[33]

On the other side of this equation, listen to what teachers have to say. The primary concern I hear from school personnel at every grade level focuses on the lack of motivation and increasing indifference they see in their students. And the gap seems to be getting wider as students become less and less dependent on adults to give them information about how the world works and increasingly intolerant of instruction that feels irrelevant and poorly matched to how they learn. At the same time, teachers claim to feel increasingly hamstrung by overwhelming content loads and bureaucratic regulations and requirements.

Many of us are further foiled by the expectations and beliefs we bring to the classroom, especially when our students' abilities, behavior, and commitment don't match up. We come to the profession shaped not only by our desire to teach but also by our experiences as students, our observations of the educators we've encountered, and our personal biases that define concepts of good teaching and how students should behave. "I loved school and I loved learning as a kid," said one contributor. "I never expected the resistance and indifference I found—and this was in an elementary classroom!" Fourth-grade teacher Catherine Nguyen-Ho found that "the children are very needy and often show no effort or desire to learn." Kim Wilson had a similar experience: "How difficult it is when you have students that are not achieving at their potential. I went into teaching thinking that everyone was going to do his or her very best and always try, but there are students [who] need more encouragement, and more support."[34]

Further, our experiences as students don't necessarily correlate to our successes as educators. Elaine Anderson observed, "I really wish somebody had told me college grades would not dictate how great an educator you can become." In fact, some of the teachers who have the hardest time in the classroom are those who were well behaved and high achieving as students—and expect their kids to come to class with the same level of commitment, readiness, and support from home.

The Students We Were Taught to Teach

Traditional policies, materials, and instructional strategies are geared for teaching students who are left-brain dominant, are strong in linguistic and logical-mathematical intelligences, are academically on grade level (not too far ahead or behind), prefer working in a quiet environment, are at their best in the early morning and afternoon, have a limited need for interaction, can handle a highly structured environment (seated in chairs, sitting up straight, without rocking or fidgeting), have low mobility needs, and have a limited need for intake (food, drink, snacks, or gum). We are trained to teach students who are strong in their auditory and visual modalities, have low tactile or kinesthetic modality needs (limited need for touch or movement), and have high verbal skills (able to respond immediately when called on rather than needing time to process quietly, internally, before responding).

We expect eye contact and little talking or movement (although note taking is okay as long as it's in linear, traditional form) from students who are high in adaptability, persistence, and regularity and low in distractibility, intensity, and sensitivity to sound, light, smell, or touch. And we've been taught to gear our lessons toward concrete thinkers who are logical, rational, organized, prompt, and able to follow rules and procedures.[35]

Does this sound like your students? These descriptions match only a small percentage of individuals in the general population. If you teach early childhood, special education, or alternative classes, the percentage will be closer to zero.

Many parents are also frustrated with what's happening in schools, some of them opting to pull their children out of the school system and teach them at home. The trend to homeschool kids has grown in recent years and, as journalist Susan Saulny reported, some parents seek to actually *unschool* their children. This philosophy "is broadly defined by its rejection of the basic foundations of conventional education," with adherents dismissing the type of instruction that would stifle children's natural curiosity and love of learning.[36] Their concerns that schools are not engaging students' interests, integrating content areas, or allowing adequate time to pursue subjects—not to mention issues of physical and emotional safety—are worth noting.[37] The hunger for more personalized curriculum and a sense of community attracts more and more families to magnet schools, charter schools, and private schools committed to these values. And in an era when online classes and resources are becoming increasingly available, the wider the gap between what kids need and what they get in school, the more tempting alternative routes become.

The sad fact is that schools *could* be the kinds of places that teachers, parents, and kids want, but we have some serious catching up to do—starting with the students themselves. Simply looking at young people through the lens of technology reveals a big piece of the explanation for the frustration so many people seem to be feeling. A conference paper by educator Marc Prensky observed that students today are "'native speakers' of the digital language of computers, video games and the Internet." On the other hand, he referred to those "who were not born into the digital world but have, at some later point in our lives, become fascinated by and adopted many or most aspects of the new technology" as *digital immigrants* by comparison.[38]

Of course, there are also those in education who resist information technology altogether, but even those most committed to assimilating into a digital culture face discrepancies in the skills, characteristics, and needs of the *digital natives*. We need teaching strategies that will engage kids who "have spent their entire lives surrounded by and using computers, videogames, digital music players, video cams, cell phones, and all the other toys and tools of the digital age." These students "are used to receiving information really fast. . . . They like to parallel process and multi-task. They prefer their graphics *before* their text rather than the opposite." Clearly, there are serious educational implications when dealing with kids who "grew up on the 'twitch speed' of video games" who "are used to the instantaneity of hypertext, downloaded music, phones in their pockets, a library on their laptops, beamed messages, and instant messaging. They've been networked most or all of their lives," Prensky added. "They have little patience for lectures, step-by-step logic, and 'tell-test' instruction."[39] To those of us who did not grow up with these skills or experiences, the behavior of these students not only looks totally foreign, but is often interpreted as hyperactive, inattentive, or disrespectful.

"The new reality for kids demands that teachers take a close look at the old lesson plans and the other methodology," advised author and consultant Ron Nash. "The content in the average language arts or economics classroom may not have changed substantially over the years, but what is needed to manage process and keep students engaged certainly has."[40] How many policies and decisions in education today are based on the assumption that what worked once will work now? "But that assumption is no longer valid," insisted Prensky. "Today's learners are different."[41] An article by Claudia Wallis agreed, reporting that at the college level, longtime professors have noticed that "kids arrive on campus with a different set of cognitive skills and habits than past generations."[42] She, too, described students who come to school wired with an expertise for multitasking, finding and manipulating information, and analyzing visual data and images. However, instructors are now also dealing with kids who have a low tolerance for quiet and "discomfort with not being stimulated," as well as a frustratingly short attention span, low tolerance for ambiguity, and aversion to complexity.[43]

But if these students learn differently from their predecessors, they certainly are learning nonetheless. Interestingly, many participate in activities on their own that are developing skills that are useful in the workplace. A study of 2,500 video gamers discovered that these kids "are smart, savvy new thinkers who are climbing the corporate ladders using the same problem-solving strategies they used to come out winners in [video] games."[44] Not only do gamers defy the old stereotype of being loners and isolates with few social skills, the research, instead, found them to be well-adjusted people who "interact intensely with others," although "they are more comfortable with communication, education, and training online and need less face-to-face interaction." In the workplace, their talents show up as a willingness to "jump in and try things rather than gathering lots of information, doing lots of analysis and then making the decision."[45] Hence the recommendation that we capitalize on the skills and preferences these kids bring to the table and leverage our instruction accordingly. In response to students' evolving learning preferences, needs, and experiences, some university professors—as well as classroom teachers—use "film, audio clips, and PowerPoint presentations to play to their students' strengths and capture their evanescent attention."[46] As Prensky noted, "There is no reason that a generation that can memorize over 100 [video game] characters with all their characteristics, history, and evolution can't learn the names, populations, capitals, and relationships of . . . 101 nations in the world. It just depends on how it is presented."[47]

While unsettling to some educators, others are responding to this challenge with creative, clever, and engaging strategies. Veteran teacher Lydia Aranda shared, "Students are generally much less motivated than they were when I started teaching nineteen years ago. In light of this, I feel more than ever that acting is a very important skill for a teacher. You have to become more interesting and intriguing than any video game or TV show that consumes most students' waking hours outside of school. You will have to over-dramatize everything, even to the detriment of your reputation as a well-educated proper member of society. You must do things that you thought you'd never be caught dead doing, like singing the spelling words opera-style to your class or putting on a [funny] accent to keep their attention piqued."

Understandably, some educators balk at the degree to which kids interact with technology today, blaming anything that looks like a decline in the current system on these developments. But there have always been educators who resisted advances in technology, whether in complaints about students' dependence on slate at a teachers' conference in 1703, fears expressed at a principals' conference in 1815 that students were getting too dependent on paper, or concerns that ballpoint pens would be "the ruin of education in our country" in 1950.[48] Computers and iPods didn't break the system; they are just a part of the evolution of our culture with which our systems are having a hard time keeping up.

For better or worse, technology is very much a part of our world. By 1991, ninety-eight percent of the schools in the United States had at least one computer; the ratio of computers to students is now one to four.[49] One of my favorite quotes comes from a former principal who likes to remind teachers, "Our job is not to teach the students we used to have, the students we wished we had, or the students we should have. Our job is to teach the students we do have." We can complain about students not fitting in with outdated standards, or we can start looking for ways to build systems that will educate kids in a context that makes sense to them. Make peace with progress. There is no going back.

THE CHALLENGE OF CHANGE

A friend told a story about an experience her son had in fifth grade. His teacher had put the students into groups and posed a question: "If you have a drawerful of an equal number of black socks and white socks in a dark room, how many socks do you have to take out of the drawer to be sure you have two of the same color?" The students were instructed to brainstorm ideas, and after a minute or two, when she asked the students how they would solve this problem, this young man responded, in all earnestness, "Turn on the light."

How often do kids get in trouble for thinking outside the box, for having an opposing opinion, for having a different "right answer"? Although these are exactly the skills that many employers seek, they are still so often discouraged—if not outright punished—in schools. How do we teach kids who will have already sliced through the Gordian knot before we've finished handing out the directions for working with it?[50]

Kids have changed. Our culture has changed. Is it any wonder that so many teachers complain about kids who do not see the importance in following rules, have trouble listening, and—neurological and developmental implications notwithstanding—can't sit still? It's time that our entire concept of educating children changes as well. But look what we're up against.

We've seen the need for right-brain processes increasing for the past few decades, with a greater emphasis on process over product. We recognize that the sheer volume of factual information makes it impossible for anyone to get much depth from a fact-based curriculum. We've known for decades that certain management strategies work better than others for inspiring commitment and cooperation. We've witnessed an enormous acceleration in social, cultural, economic, and technological changes. We have brain research to support developmental and physiological suggestions that have been around for years. And if that weren't enough, the feedback we receive on a daily basis from our students' behavior, attitudes, and achievement should be a reasonable barometer of just what is working and what isn't. So how is it that our schools remain so steadfast in their attachment to linear, measurable, product-oriented approaches to working with children?

Years ago, a colleague at the university came out of a daylong restructuring meeting shaking his head. "All they're doing is moving stuff around. They're stacking stuff in different ways and calling it by different names, but it's still the same old *stuff!*" he said. I'm still seeing old formulas and cheap advice that never worked all that well being recycled and presented in new products and programs that don't work any better. And yet we're surprised when the end result of doing what we've always done is the same. Or worse.

Even if you are one of the digital natives now entering the field, and even if you are very familiar and comfortable with what drives your kids, you may discover that much of the mentoring, supervision, and professional development you receive will do its best to steer you back to existing traditions and in-the-box approaches to challenges you encounter. Regardless of your relationship with technology and how well your classroom is stocked and wired, in all but a few rare cases, you will feel pressure to acculturate to the demands of traditional practices and priorities. If you do, you are not alone.

Resistance to change has always been a trademark of education. Most changes that do occur tend to be superficial—adding smartboards, computers, and wireless networks (if we're lucky), while long-standing hierarchies, win-lose power dynamics, and standardized curriculum stubbornly persist. School handbooks and policy manuals from 2009 look remarkably similar to the ones we were handed in the early 1970s, expanded perhaps to include newer communication systems and references to a wider range of student infractions.

Individually, I see teachers resist change because, for some, new ideas just represent more "stuff" to squeeze into an already overburdened schedule. Others don't trust that they will be supported by their administrators and colleagues, no matter how much research or apparent encouragement is behind the ideas they would like to try. For others, change requires stepping too far outside of their comfort zone. (Even if old strategies aren't working well, there is a certain satisfaction and ease in their familiarity.) And frankly, it will always be easier to complain or reject an idea than to change a well-entrenched—and long-supported—teaching behavior.

This theme played through a great deal of the data I collected from interviews and surveys. One middle school social studies teacher wrote, "New teachers who have just experienced working with new research are often hushed and told to go with the 'old way.'" Veteran kindergarten teacher Anita Scherer reported, "I have been teaching for twenty years. My greatest challenge is battling past old mindsets!" Even with administrative support, she noted, "I can adapt and be successful, but the staff will fight change every step of the way." I hear this resistance in every "yeah, but" response that comes up in seminars and classes (including the ones I conduct as well as the ones I observe or attend). You will need to watch out for these attitudes; they can be toxic and infectious. Columnist Dale Dauten cautioned, "The 'it'll never work' presumption kills not just ideas but the creative impulse."[51]

Jeremy Freedman urged new teachers to continually reinvent themselves. "Don't keep using the same methods if they do not work," he wrote. "I have seen a lot of good teachers go bad. . . . I hear them say things like, 'It worked twenty years ago. It isn't my problem if it doesn't work now.' Good teachers are always trying new things." Even the possibility of increasing student success, engagement, and achievement doesn't always dislodge people from their attachment to old, familiar ways of doing things. Frank Champine, in reporting on the need for differentiating instruction to reach larger numbers of students, described the "old dogs" who were "trained to teach one lesson to the entire class. They would just as soon take a pay cut as develop multiple approaches to content, process, and product, or figure out how to blend whole-class, group, and individual instruction."[52]

Looking at the process of change, it's also easy to understand how hard it can be to get schools to budge. "Really good ideas break a rule," insisted toy developer Reyn Guyer, the inventor of Twister and the Nerf ball.[53] Now filter this quote through the largest segment of a school population, one that includes "planners and organizers," people who prize correctness, loyalty, stability, and the ability to follow rules and procedures, and are most upset when others question authority or don't follow rules, act disrespectfully, come late or unprepared, or don't take things seriously.[54] In a population that attaches such importance to following the chain of command, the notion of breaking rules is sure to elicit a few gasps.

"Change is hard," said Thomas Friedman. "Change is hardest on those caught by surprise. Change is hardest on those who have difficulty changing."[55] For decades, I've been hearing people talk longingly about the "good old days." But even if things really *were* better back in some other time or place, learning to keep our focus grounded in present realities—*and* future possibilities—will serve us far better than idealizing the past.

"If constructive patterns were all that were necessary for creative new ideas, we'd all be creative geniuses," said author Roger Van Oech. "Creative thinking is not only constructive, it's also destructive. Creative thinking involves breaking out of one pattern in order to create a new one."[56] In a world often ruled by black-and-white thinking, this statement is sure to raise a few eyebrows as well. Clearly, we need to go further than just rearranging the "stuff" we've always had, used, and done. Breaking or discarding the least effective (and most destructive) policies will be unavoidable.

One more thing, and it's a big one. We, as a culture, have a hard time focusing on the big picture and wrestling with the multiple dimensions of complex problems. We focus on isolated pieces of big issues—math scores, gum chewing, tardiness, clothing, swearing, even bullying—instead of looking at the multiple dimensions of a school's character and culture. Consequently, we end up with a lot of superficial, quick-fix, short-term, narrowly focused, two-dimensional "solutions" that, in the long run, often create more problems than they solve. Kenneth Hodge, a sixth-grade social studies teacher in his third year of teaching, has already noticed the tendency for schools to use "the latest gimmick of the day to try to improve problems" like student achievement and behavior, regardless of the lack of results.

But what gives me hope—and what has always given me hope—is the fact that there have always been teachers who know what really matters, and who accomplish near miracles on a daily basis, regardless of their political and bureaucratic surroundings. I see people who teach as though test scores don't matter and who manage to coax extraordinary achievement from their students. I see people at the state level who work to incorporate the importance of school climate into policies and goals. I see what Prensky called "future content" (including software, hardware, robotics, nanotechnology, and genomics, as well as the ethics, politics, sociology, languages, and other things that go with them) starting to show up alongside "legacy content" (reading, writing, and arithmetic, along with the rest of our more traditional curriculum).[57] I visit schools that are becoming increasingly brain-friendly, adjusting their curriculum and environment to ensure developmental and neurological appropriateness, and I see research that supports good practice reaching larger segments of the general population—which also needs to be brought up to speed to minimize opposition to necessary changes.

Despite the tenacity of old systems, teaching is actually a fluid and dynamic profession—influenced by, as well as accountable to, changes in the cultural environment it serves. It is also a profession prone to getting locked into rigid, repressive structures, obstructed by competing political agendas, and choked by restrictions and timetables enacted by people who presume expertise on the basis of having once been students. As a beginning teacher, your energy, talents, and perspectives are the lifeblood of the profession. Don't let the system stifle your sense of win-win possibilities. Learn how things work in your school, district, and state, and keep hold of your intentions. "Don't be put off by people who know what is not possible," said author and business leader Paul Hawken. "Do what needs to be done, and check to see if it was impossible only after you are done."[58]

ACTIVITY

Look at the skills described as right-brain directed (skills valued in a conceptual-age classroom):

1. In what ways has your training prepared you to encourage these skills?

2. Which of these skills does your district value or encourage?

3. Which might create problems for you? For your students?

4. Which of these skills do you feel you bring to the classroom?

5. How do you suppose these skills will help (or have helped) you teach effectively?

6. Technology aside, in what ways is your classroom different from the classrooms you sat in as a student? In what ways is it the same?

7. Technology aside, in what ways are the other classes in your school (or other classrooms in which you've worked or other classrooms you've observed) different from the ones familiar to you as a student? In what ways are they the same?

8. What kinds of strategies or activities do you use to help students learn how to learn? What else could you do?

ACTIVITY

Look at the characteristics of digital natives:

1. Which characteristics do you share?

2. Which do you suspect will be a challenge for you?

3. In what ways do your school policies, rules, and practices support their experiences and needs?

4. In what ways do your school policies, rules, and practices conflict with their experiences and needs?

NOTES

1. Fisch, McLeod, and Brenman (2008).

2. Prensky (2001, p. 1).

3. Lee (2008). I found this quote on dozens of Web sites and blog pages. Only one included this attribution, which I found on the BookMarkLee Web site.

4. This is the first book I've written that includes comments posted by Facebook friends.

5. Lungold (2003).

6. Fisch et al. (2008). You can see various version of this content in several formats (video, PDF, Word), additional quotes, and other terrific "Fischbowl Presentations" at http://www.lps.k12.co.us/schools/arapahoe/fisch/fischbowlpresentations.htm.

7. Fisch et al. (2008).

8. Kline (2002, p. xii, emphasis added).

9. Osmar (n.d.); also Fisch et al. (2008). Osmar (n.d.) noted on this Web page, "When I started college in the fall of 2003, Facebook, YouTube, Flickr, Digg, Yelp, and Twitter didn't exist yet. MySpace and Wordpress were brand new."

10. Fisch et al. (2008).

11. Wilson and Daviss (1994, p. 11).

12. Herbert (2006).

13. Bassis (2004, para. 2).

14. Friedman (2007, p. 309).

15. Pulliam and Van Patten's (1995) *History of Education in America, Sixth Edition* (as quoted in Bluestein, 2001, p. 82).

16. Friedman (2007, pp. 1–40, 48).

17. Pink (2005) described the *information age* in terms that are very similar to the ones I've used in my previous works to describe the *industrial age* or *factory era,* and where I stated the need for greater creativity, networking, and nonlinear thinking as a product of the information age (which, certainly compared to the assembly-line thinking of the industrial age, is quite reasonable). Pink took this transition one step further, identifying another transition to a right-brain-directed thinking conceptual age. Similarly, many of the talents and needs he described as necessary for a conceptual-age economy overlap the characteristics of what I have, in previous writings, called the *age of connectedness* (Bluestein, 2001) and what John Naisbitt identified, in 1982, as a "high touch" balance to a "high tech" environment (p. 39). Clearly, the direction is very similar in each of these examples.

18. Pink (2005, pp. 39–40, 49). And not to be totally cynical here, but chances are, as schools (hopefully) start to reckon with the importance of these right-brain talents, you can be sure that somebody will be working very hard on finding ways to measure them!

19. Friedman (2007, p. 15).

20. Gerlach and Bird (2005, p. 3).

21. Bluestein (2001); Wallis and Steptoe (2006, pp. 52–53).

22. Gatto (2005, p. 2).

23. Wallis and Steptoe (2006, p. 52).

24. Wallis and Steptoe (2006, p. 52).

25. Ferguson (2004, p. 32).

26. Jones (2008, para. 7).

27. Fogarty (2007, p. 22).

28. Bassis (2004, para. 3, 5).

29. Rodriguez (2009).

30. Quoted in Bluestein and Katz (2005, p. 11). We heard from many students who described their high school experience in positive terms. However, the issue of boring and irrelevant classes and assignments came up repeatedly.

31. Alliance for Excellent Education (2009). About 1,700 high schools are "dropout factories," where 60% or less of the students who enter as freshmen make it to senior year, according to "One in 10 High Schools Gets an F" (2007). This article noted that "lack of funding is part of the problem: Even though the dropout factories overwhelmingly are in the poorest communities, only about 25% receive the federal assistance for low-income schools that they should be getting" (p. 10). Bob Herbert (2006) reported that minority students are underserved by our current system of education. "Nationally, just two-thirds of all students—and only half of all blacks and Latinos— who enter ninth grade actually graduate with regular diplomas four years later," he wrote. "Far from preparing kids for college, big-city high schools in neighborhoods with large numbers of poor, black and Latino youngsters are just hemorrhaging students." He quotes Harvard Professor Gary Orfield: "Only about a twelfth of the Latino kids and maybe a sixth of the black kids are getting college degrees."

32. Quoted in Bluestein and Katz (2005, p. 12).

33. Blum (2004, p. 13).

34. Even basic assumptions can be challenged. Erin Beers wished someone had told her that she would be teaching sixth-graders how to read. Elementary principal Jacie Bejster Maslyk was surprised to find "that a lot of first-graders are not truly potty-trained! I never imagined that so many kids still wet themselves."

35. Studies show other factors, such as gender, culture, socioeconomic status, appearance, popularity, or membership in highly valued groups or teams, to be relevant to teachers' expectations as well (Bluestein, 2001, chap. 12). These characteristics of "ideal students" have been collected from a number of resources and were also reported in Chapter 13, "How Does Your Garden Grow? More Diversity, More Discrimination," of *Creating Emotionally Safe Schools* (Bluestein, 2001).

36. Saulny (2006, para. 5).

37. Issues addressed in the Family Unschoolers Network (2006) mission statement. The statement concluded, "We believe these aspects of learning are limited by the traditional implementation of a curriculum, and we choose to homeschool as a way to circumvent those limitations" (para. 3). Also Thornton-Cullen and Ryan (2007); Ray (2006).

38. Prensky (2001, para. 5, 6).

39. Prensky (2001, pp. 1–3). In *Generations at School: Building an Age-Friendly Learning Community,* Suzette Lovely and Austin G. Buffum (2007) suggested, "For teachers, presenting the same material in the same fashion in which they may have learned it can lead to a cycle of boredom, especially as schools face such stiff competition for students' attention" (p. xiii).

40. Nash (2009, p. 102).

41. Prensky (2001, p. 3).

42. Wallis (2006, pp. 52–54).

43. Wallis (2006).

44. Gaudiosi (2005, p. 86).

45. Gaudiosi (2005, pp. 86–87). Prensky (2001) reported, "Today's average college grads have spent less than 5,000 hours of their lives reading, but over 10,000 hours playing video games (not to mention 20,000 hours watching TV)" (p. 1).

46. Wallis (2006, p. 54).

47. Prensky (2001, p. 5). Culturally, even the way we use our memory has changed. While we once depended on what author Joshua Foer (2007) referred to as "internal memory," we are now inundated with new information, and very little of it makes its way into memory. We now rely on technology to keep track of the data in our lives. (I noticed this phenomenon the first time I had to look up my own mother's phone number after dumbly staring at a phone that didn't have her on speed dial.) "We've gradually replaced our internal memory with what psychologists refer to as external memory, a vast super-structure of technological crutches that we've invented so that we don't have to store information in our brains" (p. 50), he wrote.

48. Fisch (2007). I remember when the children's program *Sesame Street* first aired in November 1969. I was starting out in college, and by the time I got into my first education classes in college, there were already courses and seminars to help teachers come to terms with what they saw as the competition and take advantage of television programming as an instructional tool.

49. Ansary (2009).

50. Remember the story of Alexander the Great? The legend goes that there was this knot that nobody could untie. Taking on the challenge, Alexander didn't do any better with the usual attempts to untie the thing. So he basically said, "The hell with it," and sliced the knot in half. He not only didn't get detention for his unorthodox approach, but according to the story, he got to be the king of Asia as a reward for his creative thinking. Ha!

51. Dauten (2001). More about self-protection and self-care in later chapters.

52. Champine (2004).

53. Quoted in Dauten (2001).

54. From Bluestein (2001, p. 197), *Creating Emotionally Safe Schools*. This information is based on the Myers-Briggs Personality Inventory as well as the work of David Keirsey ("True Colors," n.d.). This group accounts for 38% of the general population, with about equal numbers of males and females. In high schools, 43% of teachers and 45% of students are in this category; these numbers are even higher among administrators.

55. Friedman (2007, p. 21).

56. Van Oech (2008, p. 47).

57. Prensky (2001).

58. Paul Hawken (2009, para. 6), commencement address to the class of 2009, University of Portland, with reference to the challenge of saving the planet. With thanks to Stephen Haslam for the reference.

8

Learn the System

You don't learn to deal with ethical dilemmas by avoiding them.

Abraham Lincoln[1]

If an idea is truly original, then expect resistance; indeed, welcome it as a measure of originality. Organizations are built for continuity, not creativity.

Dale Dauten, columnist[2]

I wish somebody had told me what the heck all the acronyms meant in each county.

Michelle Colbert, preschool teacher

Imagine this: A new teacher walks into the lounge at lunchtime on the first day of school. She starts to unwrap her sandwich and notices an amused silence from the other teachers in the room. Before she has a chance to inquire into the obvious change in the energy in the room, a veteran teacher walks in, glares at her, and announces, "That has been my seat since I arrived at this school eighteen years ago!"

Becoming a win-win teacher is more than just a skills issue. It's a survival issue. No amount of preservice training can prepare you for every awkward moment, personality, or unwritten rule you will encounter in an actual school setting. Getting to know the system involves an understanding of your school and district culture as well as an ability to function—at least at first—within established and accepted structures.

A beginning teacher's tool kit includes a lot of information and support, both of which you may need to assemble or create on your own. The last thing you want is for your teaching and classroom-management abilities to be undercut by not knowing how the system works. Lyle Hartman advised new teachers to become politically astute: "Some campuses are highly political environments." He suggested that new teachers need to understand the process. "This is the game. This is the way things get done," he said. "Know what's going on." So let's look at what's going on, what you need to know, how to work the system, and how to avoid some of the political obstacles and toxicity that can add unnecessary challenges to your life.

WHAT YOU NEED TO KNOW

Understanding the system, as it were, can range from something as simple as knowing where and how to get supplies to procedures for making a referral for special services for a student. To complicate matters, every school district seems to have its own way of doing things, so that even if you've been teaching or training in one setting, chances are you will need to learn different procedures for your new school. (The good news is that you'll usually only have to do this when you start at a school. Once you have a sense of how your district operates, you'll be able to incorporate new information and changes as they come along.) If you're lucky, you will receive materials that will help, perhaps a checklist or handbook with all the information you'll need, and maybe a new teacher orientation workshop with people from the district explaining things you'll need to know. But that's not always the case, and if you feel as though you've walked into a "sink or swim" situation, you're hardly alone.

"We all need training wheels for the first year, but few of us get them," commented Sandra Kenyon. One article geared to help new educators quoted a veteran teacher remembering the start of her career when she was told, "Here's the key to your room, here's the Xerox machine, here's the books. Now go at it."[3] In an article about why teachers leave, Cynthia Kopkowski acknowledged that new teachers "often encounter an isolated, every-one-for-themselves system vastly different from the collaborative school of education or student teaching environment they just left."[4] In some environments, any attempt you make to collaborate—or otherwise re-create the supportive environment of your teacher training experience—can generate annoyance, resentment, or even suspicion that can further alienate you from the staff with which you're trying to bond. (Of course, if your pre-service experience was negative and competitive, your placement could actually be an improvement.) Either way, a great deal of time and energy during your first year will involve learning about how your facility functions and how to get things done there.

Clearly, you might expect not to know your way around the paperwork and procedures—or even the building, for that matter—if you haven't been introduced to them yet. But many of the "surprises" you might encounter are pretty subtle, and not knowing what to anticipate can account for a great deal of frustration and discouragement. At the end of a recent seminar, I discovered a note left on my table by one of the participants that said, "College fills your head with all these ideals about the perfect Pollyanna classroom. It doesn't prepare you for the real world." For too many teachers, the more challenging aspects of this "real world" can range from not having enough supplies, furniture, or even space to be able to function effectively to hidden job expectations that can eat up a big chunk of your time and energy. Wyatt and White cautioned about the number of additional duties assigned. "You may have to give up part of your lunch or planning period to supervise students who are on the school grounds before or after school," they wrote. "You may have to sponsor a student organization or help another teacher plan and sponsor an activity. Sometimes you are paid for the extra time you spend on these activities, but usually, they are just added to your teaching duties as part of the job."[5]

Know your contract well, and even if extra duties aren't specifically mentioned, be aware that your day will very likely include them. Cindi Allen was one of several contributors who noted that these additional demands made the job more difficult. "As if we don't have enough to fill our time, we have to serve on committees as well," she wrote. "We are expected to take time out to have reading, science, and math nights at school. We have to serve on holiday program committees, character ed, and school improvement teams. The list is endless. We are evaluated on the amount of extracurricular work we do for the school."

Record keeping is another issue. Stacy Harris knew that as a special education teacher, she'd have more paperwork than usual, but she described the expectations as overkill. "I would like to focus on teaching instead of filling out the paperwork," she wrote. This theme runs through many of the correspondences I receive from beginning teachers who feel overwhelmed in their efforts to control what they describe as an avalanche of paper. Computerized records can help, but they are not always available and, in some cases, can actually make things worse.[6] Either way, you'll want to find somebody to show you the kinds of record keeping required by the district and, if possible, offer tips for managing the paper load, including organizing and storing copies of assignments, plans, contacts with parents—e-mails, written correspondences, and dated notes about phone calls or face-to-face meetings—and anything you send home. (Possibly the best advice I ever got involved the importance of keeping good records. Do not underestimate the value of documentation. Nothing says *professional* better than a good paper trail, whether you use it to back up decisions you make about strategies or content, to obtain necessary services or resources for individual students or classes, or protect yourself in case of a dispute with a student, parent, or colleague.)

Make friends with the people in the front office; they are often your best resource for information and procedures. Michelle Mayrose recommended, "Ask the school secretary or bookkeeper for a list of county office personnel and phone numbers" or to otherwise direct you to that information. "Take some time to familiarize yourself with the name of the head of any department you may need to contact: personnel, benefits, your academic department head, payroll, legal counsel, [or] board members." An NEA (National Education Association) article about what new teachers need included "knowledge of what to expect" and "handbooks with succinct, key information" among the things that can help teachers succeed.[7] If you haven't already received the information you need, ask around.

Although your primary concerns will focus on your classroom and your students, keep a big-picture sense of your job in the back of your mind. The specifics of teaching happen in a larger context, so it will help to get a handle on district policies and procedures. Do you have a copy of your subject-area or grade-level curriculum? For a better understanding of context and sequence, see if you can get ahold of the curriculum for previous and subsequent grade levels or for prerequisite courses your students were supposed to have taken before they got to your class. Use your district's calendar of events or mark all relevant dates (and breaks) into your own planning calendar. Take a look at district and state assessment requirements. Find out anything and everything you can to make your teaching life easier or prevent potential problems down the road. What kind of procedures are already in place for contacting and meeting with parents? What will be an issue for the fire marshals when they visit your room?

Veteran Bonnie Milanak offered a number of suggestions for keeping your room organized. She recommended labeling supplies, books, and field-trip items, for example, and keeping a copy of any notes that you (or the office, or anyone else) send home, as well as keeping track of daily homework assignments on a Web site or in a daily homework tracker. You'll need a grade book and lesson-plan book—paper or electronic—and binders or other storage materials for grades, plans, team meetings, faculty meetings, general announcements from the office or administration, personal notes, or referral information, for example. She also suggested keeping a roster of your class every year and labeling class photos. (As someone who was very inconsistent about jotting down the names of my students in the numerous photos I have from my days in the classroom, I can personally attest that years later, when you go back and try to remember the names of your kids, you'll be glad you did.)

Finally, develop a sense of humor and appreciation for the absurd. Michelle Tillapaugh wrote, "I really wish somebody had told me that I would be practicing fire drills for the rest of my life! And then the one time my school actually has a fire, everyone is so consumed with putting it out that no one even pulls the alarm."

Information and Materials Beginning Teachers (May) Need

- Fire drill procedures and assembly points
- Evacuation drills, Homeland Security policies and procedures
- Lockdown procedures, with color-coded cards or other notifications to be displayed in the glass on the classroom door
- Release authorization protocols, with information regarding who is authorized to take students home in regular dismissals as well as in the case of an evacuation
- Monthly book order and in-school book fair information
- Schedules and procedures for indoor and outdoor recess
- Lunch ticket procedures, with strategies for dealing with misplaced or forgotten lunches
- Internet resources for parents and students, including those associated with textbooks or units of study
- Web site protocols for communicating with parents and students, method of use and codes of behavior
- Medical forms and procedures for medicines to be distributed by nurse or designee
- Policies regarding classroom pets or visitations
- Procedures for special requests, such as those regarding chemical sprays or disinfectants, to protect students with allergies or asthma
- List of student and staff birthdays
- Parent-volunteer information, such as contact information, policies, tasks, and activities
- Open house information and resources, including materials and slide show presentations
- Floor plan and seating charts, kept updated as you rearrange your class
- School-sponsored programs, such as food drives for local organizations
- Rubrics for all subjects
- Individual Education Plans (IEPs) for students in gifted or special-need programs
- Any current or educational material relevant to your school, students, or subject areas, including newsletters for the school district, union, or parent-teacher organization
- Organization system for keeping copies of records and student work [8]

NAVIGATING POLITICS AND AGENDAS

Some teachers are content to keep to themselves, concerning themselves with little in the school beyond their own classrooms. You probably don't want to be one of them, especially early in your career, for a number of reasons. For the moment, let's focus on the likelihood that, at some point, you'll probably want to do something with your class that requires the consent, support, or cooperation of some or all of the adults in the building. Regardless of the scope of your plans, the amount of resources you'll need, and the degree to which these objectives will affect others in the school, clearing obstacles to get a go-ahead for something you want to do can require some skill and savvy, an understanding of how things work in your school, and a good sense of who's got your back.

The ease with which your idea is accepted will depend on a number or factors. Pulling off a field trip, for example, will be more difficult if you are the first teacher in the history of the school to propose one than if similar excursions are a regular and accepted component of your school's programs. Or your suggestion for a schoolwide holiday pageant may meet with resistance simply because past performances have always featured students in the fifth-grade classes alone. Involving your students in even a simple research or data-collection project you wish to conduct may require fairly extensive paperwork, permissions, and clearance all the way up the food chain. And funding priorities may be another obstacle, no matter how badly your school could use lab equipment or computer upgrades.

Personality and power dynamics are factors as well. I've met administrators who didn't care what the staff did as long as it didn't ultimately end up as a problem in their office, and others who obstructed really good ideas (or dragged their feet in granting clearance) just because they could. "Brace yourself for the fact that some administrators want to feel like they are in control of everything, including your classroom and how you run it," advised Mayrose. Colleagues can likewise be resistant. Richard Biffle cautioned, "Veteran teachers will be quick to tell you, 'You can't do that. That isn't allowed.' New teachers need to know what they can do regardless of the political climate or restrictions, including the reaction of negative colleagues." Although this is certainly not always the case, be prepared for the possibility that some people on your staff will be rattled by proposals for anything that might look different from what they're doing or have always done.

There are indirect but powerful forces at work from outside the school as well, and many contributors noted the frustration of having to work around obstacles and constraints determined by external political agendas. "Everyone has attended school and is an expert on schooling as they have personally experienced it," noted lifelong educator Jo Ann Freiberg in a presentation on school climate.[9] So be prepared for opinions and judgments that could impact your work. "I really wish somebody had told me that people who have never taught children would be telling me how it should be done!" wrote Stacey Ferguson. "Too many decisions about education are made without regard to the actual classroom." School psychologist Paul Clements likewise bemoaned having to "put up with rules made by politicians who don't know what they are doing."

Plus, there is the system itself. There is a persistent attachment to stasis in most organizations, and this is certainly true in education. "Schools are inherently top-down organizations," said Aaron Trummer. "The entire point of the first few years of teachers' careers is to indoctrinate them to the belief system of the district. If you don't have the beliefs of the organization, the organization does not want you," he added. Not surprisingly, books and resources for beginning teachers offer much guidance and many strategies for fitting in and becoming a part of the system. But there can be a lot of toxicity and bad practice in a school setting, and "fitting in," then, becomes a bit of a double-edged sword. (And by the way, coming in cold and pointing out the district's shortcomings—even if your observations are accurate and reasonable—is a fairly effective way to alienate the entire staff, something you really don't want to do, no matter how *right* you are.)

So where does that leave an idealistic, energetic teacher? As Trummer also noted, "Great teaching comes from developing relationships with the *kids*, not with the system." What kind of skills will you need to work successfully within a system that will do everything it can to make you a part of a status quo? Despite the generally unspoken insistence that your primary loyalties lie with the organization, this need not be an either-or issue. It will, however, require bringing a consciousness—and a conscience—to teaching, rather than simply doing things the way they've always been done. Integrity and enthusiasm will often come up against tradition, and not all policies in schools reflect what research, experience, and a good intuitive hit would suggest is best for kids. A win-win approach considers the needs of the students, the system, and yourself. You'll know you're working in this direction when you see yourself thinking and making decisions in terms of the most basic win-win question of all: "How can we all get what we want?"

Which brings up the issue of politics and how political some school environments can be—something that is rarely addressed in our training and, at least from my own experience and the feedback of many contributors to this book, may come as a bit of a surprise. Hartman acknowledged that teachers have "a tendency to shut the door and keep their world limited to those four walls" and that few of us are prepared for "the amount of political nuance we aren't trained to understand or navigate." In his work, he encourages teachers to become politically active. "You're entitled to advocate for an ethical outcome," he said. But what does that look like?

I remember a conversation with a friend regarding the advantages of entrepreneurship, which given her personal and professional goals, looked like a strong option at the time. Curiously, she responded, "I would never want to be in business for myself. I'm just not willing to crawl over people. I'm not pushy or cutthroat enough to be successful." I thought it fascinating that she would see these characteristics as necessary or that she would see this approach as her only option. I think that this belief is at the heart of most people's distaste for organizational politics. Even the word *politics* carries with it a sleazy kind of energy, and I doubt that many people go into education for its political appeal. Nonetheless, education, and certainly becoming a win-win educator, has its political component. "Yes, there are times I would just like to be left alone to do my job," wrote Mayrose, "but we all have to play the game."

Watch out for the tendency to fall into the all-or-nothing thinking that afflicted my friend. "Working the system" does not necessarily mean manipulation, deceit, excessive ambition, backstabbing, or asserting your own selfish agendas without regard to others' needs. That would be a very win-lose approach, which is what we're trying to avoid. The opposite end of the political continuum is something called ethical influence. This win-win alternative combines an ability to get things done with a high concern for people in the organization *as well as* a concern for the organization or system itself.[10]

There are some genuine advantages to understanding the workings of the system and to knowing, as Victor McGuire mentioned, how to work outside the box and within this system. Master these skills and you're more likely to get away with nontraditional seating, room arrangements, and instructional strategies. You have an edge when it comes to getting approval (and maybe even funding) for special programs or excursions for your students, for a special project or a study you want to run, or for staff development opportunities. You can fast-track acquisitions for resources or repairs your classroom needs. You might even be able to get around rules and requirements that obstruct good instruction and student attention or even, eventually, change or eliminate rules that do not work in the best interest of students.

Political savvy can help you hang onto your passion and creativity, and prevent your feeling defeated and disempowered or impeded and obstructed from reaching your goals. (Once you get into "why bother" or "that won't work" territory, you limit any possibilities that may exist. And incidentally, it will always be easier to adopt this attitude than to advocate for what you and your students need.) So perhaps the most basic strategy in navigating politics and agendas is the belief that it is possible to do so. In many ways, we have to become smarter—and certainly more positive—than the system. Eric Katz wrote, "New teachers will need to know that they can impact change, but a system so entrenched as education will change slowly and only once a critical mass is reached with other teachers who see the value and the need for change." Some new teachers, said one contributor, are "either so compliant they lose themselves or so outspoken they're inappropriate." You don't want to fall into either category. Find that middle ground, a way to have a voice that counts for something. Norman Vincent Peale urged, "Become a possibilitarian. No matter how dark things seem to be or actually are, raise your sights and see possibilities—always see them, for they're always there."[11]

In the meantime—and I know that this may sound strange—it can help to suspend a certain degree of logic when it comes to organizational politics. There are few things more aggravating than being the only one who can see a clear solution to a problem (or that a particular problem actually exists). Certainly an idea that's light on logical reasoning won't get far, but a good, logical argument does not automatically get you what you want, and even the most reasonable, rational, commonsense proposal can disappear in a bureaucratic fog. Authors Patricia Clark White, Thomas R. Harvey, and Lawrence Kemper contended that one of the primary prevailing myths about organizational politics is that "decision making is rational. It's not!"[12] They also cautioned against underestimating the complexity of the political arena. "We assume that if we take a simple and direct strategy, such as just telling people our decisions, that that will do it," they added. "It seldom does."[13] An article on teacher retention noted, "Policy decisions in education are never made solely on the basis of objective information. There are always values that come into play and, in the world of politics, compromises to win support or bow to fiscal constraints."[14] Hartman likewise cautioned, "Things don't progress according to a logical unfolding. Things progress because people have interests, they unfold because they have power—either formal power accorded to them because of the position, or informal power because they are good with people, know how to persuade and influence people." This, by the way, is a good argument for developing the kind of people skills that will endow you with the power of persuasion. If you don't have formal power—and as a beginning teacher it's a fair bet that, within the system, you don't—your ability to connect with people in positive ways will give you a political advantage you may not otherwise enjoy.

It's also a good idea to keep in mind that in education, resources and programs are always subject to the whims of funding, budgets, political priorities, and indeed, the economy in general. "This world is governed by people's interests," Hartman added. "Everyone is vying for a limited number of resources." All this means is that if there's something you want or want to do that will cost the district in some way, your idea has to look more important—and in fact, more beneficial to the organization—than the others in the pile.

Even passion and enthusiasm may not win the day. While it is true that some people will buy on enthusiasm alone, and that little can be sold without enthusiasm, most people need something more, and win-win educators know how to pitch an idea in terms of how it benefits others. Author and organizational specialist Joel DeLuca described the most effective political style as one in which the individuals "believe strongly that progress depends on aligning the personal interests of individuals with each other (team building) and with the interests of the organization." These people also "strongly believe in searching for the win-win solutions in which everyone gains something."[15]

You have a much better chance of getting support for an idea when others can see what's in it for them—and if "what's in it for them" is something they consider important and valuable. Your administrators are more likely to support a talent show if they see it as an opportunity for community involvement, particularly when the show's production will teach various skills and help kids meet district standards or curricular goals. These are stronger selling points than "Main Street School is having one" or "It's something I've always wanted to do" (unless, of course, you've learned that your administration is devoted to competing with the other building or fulfilling your personal goals). Hartman recommended, "Give yourself the authority to enter into the political realm and argue for the things you really believe in. . . . Advocate for your kids, not just to boost your career. Don't think you can advocate on behalf of yourself and think it'll look like you're advocating for the kids." Focusing on concrete probable benefits for as many people as possible provides a tremendous asset for any proposal.[16]

Several contributors mentioned the importance of knowing the people with whom you're working. "You need to know who will stand up for you when things start to go south," said Biffle. McGuire agreed, suggesting the value in creating "your personal board of direction, people who will listen when you talk, people who are not feeling a sense of jealousy or resentment or intimidation toward you." Start, perhaps, by identifying "who needs to be on board," he added. "If you have people who want to sign off on something that's important to you and give you their vote of confidence, everyone else will get on board."

Consider the nature of the people whose support you need. Don't assume that the strategy that gets your attention or influences you will be the one that works on everybody else. This is where knowing other people's agendas, priorities, and political style can really come in handy. Would they buy a car only after comparing all makes and prices, or simply because it's red and goes fast? Will they be more impressed by an idea that can engage a wide range of students, or are they more interested in numeric results? Milanak advised, "Be a listener. You can learn so much by listening—in the office, the faculty rooms, hallways, or corridors." White et al. saw this step as an important part of the process as well. "To build trust, you need to determine how you can fill a need that others may have rather than only looking to them to fill your needs," they wrote. "You can develop your own sensitivity to their needs through observation and good listening skills."[17] Do your homework, and keep in mind that teaching involves a good bit more salesmanship than most of us were led to believe.

Finally, truly win-win teachers rarely fit into settings heavy on traditional approaches to instruction, discipline, and other district policies, although they can accomplish the same stated goals, and often with less drama and distraction, within their own classrooms. "I have chosen to always put my students' best interests ahead of what looks nice to the system," said Katz. "I do not do it in loud or dramatic ways, and I buy enough operating room to work effectively."

There are almost always individuals or groups of individuals, even in the most toxic or repressive system, who quietly go about their day doing what is best for the students, people who know how to work the system, build relationships with colleagues and parents and kids, engage the students against all odds, and avoid drawing much fire in the process. These are the individuals with whom to align yourself, the ones who will best help you survive and indeed thrive, regardless of what's going on around you.

DEALING WITH TOXIC ENVIRONMENTS AND SITUATIONS

There can be so many contradictions in schools that some days feel like you've stepped through the looking glass the minute you walk in the door. You'll know what I mean when you see the most challenging students given to the least experienced teachers, or when the teacher with the least seniority and the fewest resources to fall back on receives a last-minute transfer or new grade-level placement because of unexpected changes in enrollment or district boundaries. You'll puzzle over the lack of congruence you may encounter between the character posters and slogans that decorate the halls of your school and the actual way the adults interact with the kids—or one another. And you may also come to wonder at the discrepancy between the expectations and demands being put on teachers and the lack of support and resources some actually receive.[18]

In really bad cases, political agendas, competition for resources, cliques among the staff, poor leadership, or longtime, preexisting problems can make for a pretty toxic and emotionally unhealthy work environment. Schools can be incredibly negative places for adults and kids,[19] and even one bitter, hostile adult can bring down the morale and emotional climate of an entire school.

I've seen too many people who didn't even bother to hide their distaste, if not outright contempt, for the kids (or colleagues) with whom they worked. To be fair—and this is admittedly a stretch here—some people who are trained in negative environments with a great deal of scarcity thinking honestly believe that this negativity is a necessary part of their job. Indeed, a common bit of advice during my on-the-job training came from established staff who warned me that if I was nice or friendly or laughed with my students, the kids would walk all over me. More than one veteran warned, "Give them an inch and they'll take a mile." It took me a while to discover the lack of truth in this statement, although perhaps in the absence of good boundaries or a more positive model, this may seem like the only alternative.

Sadly, I still see this attitude in schools. I was once visiting a middle school and noticed, as the students were changing classes, a staff member with the incongruous title of Student Support Coordinator standing in the hall, apparently scouting kids she could scold or criticize. One after another, this individual went after everything from a shirt not fully tucked in to a laugh that was a little too loud. (I had to wonder how many students would have thought to intentionally seek this person's "support.") Even little ones aren't immune. In a different district, I was observing a young kindergarten teacher who, for the entire time I was in the classroom, not only didn't smile once but continually barked commands and criticism to the children. I'm still hoping I just caught this teacher on a bad day, because I wouldn't wish that kind of environment on any child for an hour, much less an entire year. Clearly, these are not behaviors that build emotionally safe learning environments, and if you see this kind of behavior in your school, please let it serve as a role model for how *not* to act. (If you see these patterns in your own interactions, let me invite you to please consider other options or to think seriously about changing careers.)

It's this combination of all-or-nothing thinking and scarcity consciousness, both grounded in a zero-sum notion that there is somehow not enough to go around, that contributes to systemic dysfunction and toxicity: "If you win, I lose" or "Either I have power or you do." It is the belief system that most directly opposes—and obstructs—win-win thinking, and it is very, very common in education and in our culture in general. In schools, it limits our approach to discipline and power dynamics to win-lose options and makes it impossible for all students to actually succeed (think bell curve). "We are educated to be critical and judgmental. To be supportive and positive is viewed as being weak," wrote author Anne Wilson Schaef. "Rather than seeing the possibilities within and around us, we see only our limitations and the things we cannot do."[20] Becoming a win-win teacher in this kind of environment can challenge the most positive person on earth! Yet the more we can shift away from scarcity thinking, the greater our sense of power, optimism, and perception of what is possible for our students and ourselves.

The issue of how political and competitive schools can be came up frequently in interviews and contributions to this book. If this is the case in your building, it may be most obvious in discrepancies or preferential treatment you start to notice among certain staff members, seeing that some are more likely than others to get support for programs and proposals, have schedule or grade-level preferences accommodated, get the room or the subjects they want, be supported in conflicts with parents, or get permission to leave early, for example. I once interviewed a teacher who transferred schools because the favoritism got to be more than she could bear. "You never knew who you could talk to and who you couldn't," she said. "Everything would get back to the principal. . . . If you were on her 'good list,' you could do anything."[21]

Several contributors described similar clashes with the higher-ups in their building. Secondary counselor D. Moritz shared, "If a school or administrator wants to get rid of you, they can do it. Even if you don't commit a fireable offense, they can make your life so miserable that you will not want to stay."[22] One elementary teacher described the reason she left her school. "My last principal took a strong dislike to me early in the school year right after she found out I was closing in on my graduate degree. I think she felt threatened by my academic ambitions, like I didn't know my place," she wrote. "Although she could never 'get' me on anything specific, she made the year as difficult for me as possible—ignoring my proposals for field trips, delaying clearance for me to participate in a district-sponsored training seminar until it was too late to go, obstructing petitions for badly needed repairs in my classroom, and even preventing my access to basic supplies, things my kids needed. A challenging job became impossible. I held on until the end of the year, but left the classroom and never went back." I also heard from a high school teacher who had seriously considered leaving the teaching profession twice. "Both times, my frustration was due to administrators and not what was going on in my classroom," she wrote. In the last situation, "I tried to stick it out for four years. When it got to the point that my stomach was clenching every time I parked my car to go to work, I decided that something had to change. I was frustrated with the disorganization, the silly paperwork, and the backbiting atmosphere. I witnessed a great school drop to a mediocre school in a short time period. The teacher turnover rate was appalling."

Poor leadership—what columnist Dale Dauten called "impedership"[23]—often results in the demotivation of motivated people. Notice how frequently good people are rewarded with more work, for example. Corporate trainer Ken Cooper offers a list of ways someone in authority can kill an employee's enthusiasm and commitment, and while his training programs may be designed for a corporate audience, they certainly sounded a lot like some of the complaints I received about superiors who frequently made last-minute demands, devalued the educator's time and personal life, played favorites or accommodated the people who agreed with them, criticized or humiliated staff in public, or didn't give the staff members information they could use to work effectively or improve their performance. Cooper also included blaming the system for what they would not allow, dismissing ideas, ignoring requests, treating people like interruptions, and discouraging talent with comments like "Just do the job," "Don't think," or "We don't need your ideas."[24] Columnist Barry Ray added to the list, which likewise sounded remarkably similar to comments I heard from school personnel. He included among the chief complaints about bad bosses things like getting the silent treatment, not receiving credit for work done, lack of follow-through on promises made, invasion of privacy, negative comments made to other employees or managers, and "blaming others to cover up mistakes or to minimize embarrassment"—bad leadership experienced by educators at all levels in the organization.[25]

By the same token, I also know some extraordinarily *good* administrators at the building and district level who have their hands full with especially challenging staff members. One elementary principal needed several years to undo damage done by what she called "a venomous veteran staff" at the site to which she had been assigned. Her efforts to break up cliques on her staff, weed out the most hostile and negative teachers, and bring the parents back on board eventually created a more positive, cohesive atmosphere. "Anyone who manages a school must be cognizant of the effects that negativity, meanness, inconsistency, lack of caring and disrespect have on a community, which is what a school is," she said.[26]

While it is unlikely that you will be walking into the level of toxicity these individuals described, do be aware that you *are* walking into an existing community, one with history and problems that, while they may have nothing to do with you, can affect your work environment and life. "You must be extremely careful, especially in the first years in a district, to stay out of conflicts that have been brewing before you were hired," cautioned Wyatt and White. "Be suspicious of teachers who befriend you by sharing negative comments about administrators and faculty members. Don't engage in negative conversations with them, and refuse any offers to join with them in their plans to solve the problems. That will spell disaster for your credibility and career."[27]

One veteran middle school teacher included the need to create a "network of supportive teachers that trust you" among her greatest challenges. A high school counselor found an interesting way to cope with negative and suspicious colleagues. "At times I have to put on the serious mask because if I look happy and relaxed at my job some will see it as a sign that I am either not working hard enough or being serious enough, or that I am somehow mocking them," he wrote.

Sometimes the problem is with the policies—not the people. One beginning teacher lost his position to someone with more seniority when his district opened all first-year teacher positions to anyone with more seniority in the district who wanted them. "I had plans for the next year at that school as I had become very fond of my position there and received excellent marks on all of my reviews," he wrote. "It was sad and frustrating to see that no matter how well you perform at a school you can still get dismissed due to some unfortunate rules."

Districts or states that adopt merit-pay policies can run into problems by creating win-lose, even cutthroat, environments. Although ideally every teacher could achieve merit pay and would be similarly incentivized, merit is typically measured comparatively and creates situations in which one teacher's success comes at the expense of another's. An NEA report mentioned, "Merit pay systems force teachers to compete, rather than cooperate. They create a disincentive for teachers to share information and teaching techniques. This is especially true because there is always a limited pool of money for merit pay. Thus, the number-one way teachers learn their craft—learning from their colleagues—is effectively shut down."[28]

Indeed, the perception of a competitive, zero-sum policy can create some pretty bizarre, no-win situations. "Teachers can be incredibly territorial," one high school principal shared. "I tried to institute a program where kids could go to different teachers for help in any subject area where they needed help. But teachers refused to participate because they were afraid that helping other teachers' kids might negatively affect *their* test scores." Eric Katz wrote, "The environment, especially in a high school, is very vested in winners and losers—the football team, the valedictorian, the class president, prom queen, and such. The notion that winning does *not* mean another must lose is almost an alien construct and is nonintuitive to many who dwell in the high school world." (Rest assured that feedback and observations at other levels, including preschool and primary grades, suggests that this kind of thinking is definitely not limited to high school, although it may show itself in different ways.)

Fortunately, in most situations, there are ways to cope and to create the kind of support you need. "In a school, win-lose is not a true and absolute dichotomy," said Katz. "I am not sure that new teachers are able to always see this." Even if you've been blessed with a good placement and a supportive administration and staff, "it is so important to find positive mentors, to have some fun in your work day even if things are not going well, to find something to be grateful about," he added.

Be selective about where you spend your time and the people with whom you connect. Many contributors noted the corrosive effects of being around negative people. Faculty lounges are known for being centers for "complaints and contempt," as one colleague described them. And while this is not always the case, "if the teacher's room is negative, stay out of it," advised Chick Moorman. Middle school teacher Ruthann Young-Cookson concurred. "Avoid the faculty lounges and negative people," she wrote. She also noted the toxic effect of associating with negative people: "Even the most positive people will start looking at things in a negative manner." Nancy Foote agreed: "Don't hang out with negative people or teachers who are just waiting to retire—it's painful and contagious."

Stephen Vance shared, "There are win-lose or lose-lose teachers out there that continually try to pull you in. At first, I was not always apt to just ignore them, but I learned to." Erin Beers also noted, "Negativity can bring anyone down and misery loves company!" Katz elaborated: "New educators need preparation so that they can find a strategy to remain as positive, loving, and nonpunitive as possible, even in an insane environment. They need to be inoculated from the toxicity that will come their way. I see so many who begin with good intentions erode to whiners and shirkers."[29]

Part of this inoculation process will involve the connections you can secure with people who leave you feeling uplifted, encouraged, and empowered. These are the ones who will help prevent you from being corrupted by negativity and despair. "There are all kinds of people working in schools today," wrote Beers. "Most are good-spirited, high energy, and only wanting the best for students. Take guidance and focus from the effective ones! Stay optimistic!" It will also help if you can withstand comments and criticism from others. McGuire advised new teachers to emulate a turtle or a crocodile, someone with a hard shell or thick skin to deal with "crusty colleagues who will 'get' you." Teddy Meckstroth agreed: "You really have to remember to have thick skin."

Of course, if you find yourself frequently clashing with a particular colleague, an administrator, or a group of people on your school's staff, you will need more support than a relatively simple inoculation from negativity. In this case, be sure to document every incident with as many details as possible, including dates, times, locations, conversations, participants, and witnesses. Keep the information clear, nonjudgmental, and as simple as possible. Rather than interpreting someone's actions (or chronicling your personal reaction to it), simply identify the behaviors you observed and any comments made—as objectively and accurately as possible. It may even become necessary, in extreme cases (especially if you don't believe you have the immediate support you need), to record encounters and interactions.

Know where to go for help. If you are fortunate enough to have a trustworthy mentor, administrator, or colleague on your staff, so much the better. Find someone, on- or off-site, who can lead you to the resources you need and do more than just commiserate with you. In high-risk situations, it may be necessary to contact someone at the district level, the legal department, your union offices, or an employee-assistance program for mediation. Barry Ray assured, "No abuse should be taken lightly," especially when it involves physical violence, harassment, or discrimination.[30]

Hopefully, you will never need this kind of intervention or mediation, and in many cases, you can avoid a great deal of toxicity and dysfunction by learning to operate within the system, by being discriminating about the people with whom you spend the most time at work, and by taking care of yourself on and off the job. Learn, if you can, to take something positive from every encounter, including the most negative. "I really wish someone had told me to fully appreciate the people we meet in life—all of them," wrote Kenyon. "The most difficult people and encounters can teach us the greatest lessons."

If you're particularly courageous, examine your contribution to the situation and make a plan to avoid ending up in similar circumstances in the future. In some no-win situations, it does pay to look for greener pastures. I've seen teachers struggle in one setting and thrive in another. However, most of us tend to re-create dramas until we start making some changes in our own behavior, so if you start seeing the same patterns recurring in your life, look for things you can do differently.

Worst-Case Scenarios

A vindictive administrator can introduce an incredible amount of stress into your work life. In interviewing several hundred professionals for this book, I heard stories that would have been unbelievable had I not witnessed or experienced similar events myself over the years. One beginning teacher described a meeting with an upset parent. "To my face, my principal supported me completely," he said. "But as soon as we sat down with the parent, he went all politician on me, smiling and fawning, making me the bad guy. I was completely dumbfounded by his betrayal." Perhaps predictably, this teacher left the school by the end of the year.

It's not uncommon for districts to transfer or reassign a principal rather than dismiss him or her, even when that individual carries a history of grievances—including gross misconduct.[31] Unfortunately, without a great deal of support, retraining, and commitment to change, the dysfunction simply follows the administrator to a new, often unsuspecting building and staff. (I know of one school that lost 50% of its staff the year after a principal had been assigned there. This individual's previous placements had apparently caused similar turmoil and dissent.)

It's hard to concentrate on being an effective teacher when you are devoting so much energy and thought to simply trying to stay safe, protecting yourself when you feel scrutinized and attacked, or fighting for your professional rights or dignity. (Through the years, I've spoken with a few educators involved in grievances or lawsuits with their districts. In each case, the emotional toll was palpable.) A nonsupportive principal, especially one who takes a dislike to you, can make your life miserable. In worst-case scenarios—and I heard about quite a few of these—longevity and dedication do not guarantee protection, nor does distinguished service. In fact, several of the

(Continued)

(Continued)

most troubling stories I heard involved extremely successful and well-liked teachers. In each case, the individual's work went well beyond the classroom, from extensive community service to involvement in professional organizations—a potential factor, many felt, in them drawing as much fire as they did.[32] "Some administrators—principals and often superintendents—do not appreciate attention or honors bestowed on their staff by outside organizations," wrote one contributor. She mentioned teachers in the district who had gained state or national attention for their talents. "They didn't get transferred, but their status as 'preferred' within the district has fallen. Mediocrity is the preferred method of operation in our district," she added. Talented new teachers are rarely a threat to the people in power, but be aware of the possibility that if you're good at what you do and you become well known and respected in the field *and* you have a particularly insecure, win-lose administrator, you could be in for a rough ride.[33]

A twenty-plus-year veteran advised new teachers to be on their guard: "There are misuses of power in education. You don't want to walk around feeling paranoid, but you can't be oblivious to the flaws in the system, or in the people running the show." I heard from several longtime veterans whose principals retaliated for reasonable actions, especially those that went over an administrator's head, for example, seeking support and protection from their union or upper-level administration. Even in well-documented harassment cases, contributors reported that the district's main priority was protecting itself from liability. Settlements often included nondisclosure to protect the district's image, "which left everybody else hung out to dry," as one individual described. "The support we were promised was never there," she added.

Once an educator starts butting heads with an administrator, supporting or even being friends with that person can put you at risk. "There is a culture of coercion and fear to quell teachers from speaking up," said one union representative.[34] In one case, a group of strong tenured teachers kept a toxic principal "mostly in check." But when the core of those teachers retired, a very young, mostly untenured staff remained. As the principal's behavior reportedly became increasingly abusive, "fear of retaliation dissuaded others to come forward and support the people involved," said one educator who eventually left the district. "Once they saw how we were treated, there wasn't a soul who would have risked standing up and getting treated in the same way."

While these extremely toxic situations touch only a small percentage of the teaching workforce, for the individuals targeted, the effects can be profoundly negative and long lasting. One educator, having a job under "a toxic, narcissistic, power-abusing bully," wrote, "I 'rented space in my head' to this man for a very long time, and grieved my identity and lack of closure with the staff, children, and their families for a long time as well." Another wrote, "Despite a terrific track record with the students, staff, and community, it was years before I regained any confidence in my ability to work with anyone in authority."

All this to say that sometimes we run into no-win situations in which the best choice of action is to simply jump ship and look for a placement where you can experience the support and success you deserve. Cut your losses if you have to, but do not allow another person's insecurity, lack of skill, or abusive behavior to destroy your confidence, much less your career.

With regard to the suggestions in the first section of this chapter, "What You Need to Know," answer the following questions:

1. Which resources and information have you received?

2. Who provided them, or where did you find them?

3. Which are available? Do you know where to go for these resources or this information?

4. Identify information and resources you still need.

5. For each item you named in Number 4, identify your plan for obtaining what you need.

ACTIVITY

Setting an Intention: In the chart below, fill in the boxes for each time frame with specific goals you would like to accomplish in each of the categories listed. Be as specific as possible.

	Within the Next Two to Four Weeks	By Winter Break	By the End of the Year
School policies and routines			
School culture and community			
Classroom environment (décor, furniture, and arrangement)			
Materials and resources			
Instructional strategies and routines			
Meeting various student needs (cognitive)			
Meeting various student needs (learning styles)			
Creating a sense of community in your classroom			

	Within the Next Two to Four Weeks	By Winter Break	By the End of the Year
Record keeping and management			
Relationships with staff			
Relationships with administration			
Relationships with students			
Relationships with parents			
Student behavior and self-management			
Other			

ACTIVITY

Select one goal in the previous activity and answer the following questions:

1. How will you know that you have achieved this goal?

2. What are the immediate or long-term benefits of your achieving this goal:
   a. For you, personally or professionally

   b. For your students

   c. For your school

   d. For your community

   e. For your district

   f. Other benefits

3. What kind of resources will you need (material, financial, time, emotional, and so on)?

4. In what ways will the implementation process affect others in your school?

5. Do you need anyone to sign off on this goal? If so, how will you present it to secure clearance?

6. Is the objective of this goal something that has been done in your school before? If not, how will you justify its importance?

7. What types of constraints or resistance might you anticipate?

Repeat with other goals or with the same goal at different points in the year.

ACTIVITY

Schools can be very politically complex places. Consider the following with regard to your ability to navigate school politics and agendas:

1. In what ways would you describe yourself as politically savvy (for example, effective in persuading or influencing others)? How have these skills and assets made you more effective as a teacher?

2. If you do not feel strong in this area, how has it impacted you (or might it impact you) professionally and personally?

3. What do you see as the advantage to being politically *un*involved? Disadvantage?

4. What excuses have you heard yourself use to not become involved in the politics of your school? (Examples: "I don't want to be a bother." "It probably won't work anyway." "There's no money in the budget for this.")

5. Identify any skills you would like to develop that you believe would help you become a more effective "ethical influence" in your school—better able, for example, to get things done, get what you need for your classroom or students, or change things that create problems for you in school that involve other people or policies. Who or what can help you to develop these skills?

ACTIVITY

With regard to the issues presented in the section "Dealing With Toxic Environments and Situations," give an example of toxicity or negativity you've encountered or witnessed in your school or district:

1. Tell how the situation impacted you professionally.

2. How did it affect you personally?

3. Where did you go for help? (Or where can you go for help?)

4. What do you need to do or change to avoid being involved in a similar situation in the future?

NOTES

1. Quoted in DeLuca (1999, p. 33).

2. Dauten (2007a).

3. Quoting teacher Kathy Wiebke (NEA, 2000).

4. Kopkowski (2008, p. 22).

5. Wyatt and White (2007, p. 127).

6. I heard from a number of teachers who had devoted hours to inputting data or learning their district's software, which was, in a couple of cases, then changed to a different system. In one rather extreme instance, an assistant superintendent wrote, one group of the beginning teachers' support team wanted a nearly full-year teaching plan in one format, while the school improvement people wanted plans in a different format (using different software and with different binding). Meanwhile, the district office wanted the plans in a proprietary program that accepted neither of the other formats, with three entirely different sets of requirements for the district Web site people, improvement specialists, and reading coaches.

7. NEA (2000). This article also listed mentoring as one of the most important factors, as well as "administrative support, adequate resources, collaboration and cooperative teaching formats, professional development, tips on instructional techniques and management routines . . . autonomy, participation in decision making, performance feedback, emotional support, observing experienced teachers, [and] discussing their teaching experience with others, both teachers and non-teachers."

8. With hearty thanks to Bonnie Milanak, who sent a long e-mail detailing some of the things new teachers need to know. While her list may not apply to every school or grade level, even a small portion of this list reflects the number of details that can occupy a teacher's attention.

9. Freiberg (2007a).

10. Summarizing ideas in sources including a number of individual contributors; also DeLuca (1999); White, Harvey, and Kemper (2007).

11. Quoted in Naylor (2009a).

12. White et al. (2007, p. 5). They did concede that rational decision making is possible when "resources are plentiful, goals are unambiguous and consistent, and there is no conflict over priorities," a situation that rarely occurs in the realm of education. "Seldom is even one of these conditions present, let alone all three!" they insisted (p. 5).

13. White et al. (2007, p. 6).

14. Allen (2005).

15. DeLuca (1999, p. 19).

16. Adapted from Jane Bluestein (1999a), "Are Your Colleagues Driving You Crazy?" which first appeared in a 1986 edition of *Instructor* magazine.

17. White et al. (2007, p. 9). If you have an opportunity to take a class, attend a seminar, or read up on personality styles, learning styles, or any of the numerous factors that influence how people receive and process information and make decisions, please do so. It's easy to get locked into working from our own styles and priorities and assume others function in similar ways. Learn how to reach a variety of people and you can expand your own ability to work successfully within the organization.

18. I recently spoke in a district where teachers were, in the words of one high-level administrator, "under the gun" to bring up test scores and meet AYP, or Adequate Yearly Progress, requirements.

The stress of the threats and pressure these educators endured was palpable. The irony of being brought in to help teachers create emotionally and academically safe learning environments when the teachers themselves did not feel remotely safe in this district was not lost on me.

19. Elementary-age children will receive, on average, three negative comments for every positive comment they hear. By middle school, the ratio jumps to nine negative comments for every positive communication. And by high school, kids might hear between eleven and seventeen criticisms before they hear anything positive—from adults or peers. I have heard these ratios consistently reported for decades, in workshops I've attended and feedback I've gotten from other educators, writers, and speakers. I have been unsuccessful in numerous attempts to locate the original studies from which these numbers were determined. My faith in their credibility comes from the variety of sources from which I've heard them, the consistency with which they've been reported, anecdotal feedback from adults and kids, and personal experience as well. Clearly, the feedback kids receive is overwhelmingly negative, and it gets worse the older they get and the longer they stay in school. Adapted from Bluestein (2001).

20. Schaef (1987, pp. 78–79).

21. Adapted from Bluestein (2001), *Creating Emotionally Safe Schools*, Chapter 19, "Teacher Safety."

22. I've also heard from several longtime veterans whose administrators punished them for reasonable assertive behaviors, including objecting to policies and decisions that violated contractual specifications and filing well-documented sexual harassment charges.

23. Dauten (2007b).

24. Ken Cooper (2007), presenter in "Impedership vs. Leadership"; also contributions from numerous teachers, counselors, administrators, and other school personnel.

25. Ray (2004). These conditions exist at all levels in education, from the classroom to the district office, and in postsecondary environments as well.

26. Quoted in Bluestein (2001, p. 354).

27. Wyatt and White (2007, p. 124).

28. NEA (n.d.); also Lewis (n.d.).

29. Unfortunately, negativity is a far more powerful force than positivity. In an earlier book, I quoted retired football coach Dave Triplett, who would tell his players, "It only takes one negative person to convert seven people to their negative thinking. But it takes seven positive people to convert one negative." Bluestein (2008, p. 193).

30. Ray (2004). More self-care strategies are available in later chapters in this book.

31. Whether hoping that the principal will behave differently in a different setting or simply wishing to avoid the headaches or potential legal backlash if a dismissal is disputed, many of these individuals somehow remain in the system. I also heard from contributors describing situations in which bad principals were protected by good-old-boy networks and, in one case, where a human relations department would not touch an abusive, incompetent principal who, among other things, rounded out a badly needed gender and ethnic balance at that level of administration.

32. Alverado (2007); also several contributors who wished to remain anonymous.

33. Do *not* let this possibility squelch or discourage any ambitions you may have for growing along your career path. Just know that excellence can be threatening to some people. And keep this in mind so you don't fall into the same trap should you assume a higher-level position in the system.

34. Alverado (2007).

9

Build Your Support Team

Dig the well before you're thirsty. Every day, make sure you put a deposit in the bank of good will. One day you're going to need to make a huge withdrawal. You're going to make a mistake.

Lyle Hartman, coordinator, Beginning-Teacher Support Program

I owe whatever success I've had to following a simple truth which my less successful colleagues seem to ignore. Underneath it all, it's a people business. I'll be effective only to the extent I know and care about the people here.

Scientist, research and development[1]

Parents do not keep their best children at home and send their worst to school. They send the best they have with the expectation that their children will return home much better.

Pearl M. Drain, staffing specialist

I just got off the phone with a director of a small private school. She called to order some resources as a last-ditch attempt to keep a first-year teacher on her staff. The teacher is having a hard time accepting the need to employ approaches different from the ones she's currently using, and while the principal is willing to work with this individual, the sad fact remains that if the teacher continues on the path she's on, the principal will have to let her go.

When I hear from administrators about problems their teachers are experiencing, the issues rarely involve a lack of skill or passion. Instead, they seem to focus more on the teachers' resistance to changing behaviors to become more successful or an inability to work with others to become a part of the team. Successful teaching requires a degree of collaboration, especially right out of the gate, and this includes an openness to suggestions and tips from others.

Anyone who works in the business of educating teachers—whether an instructor at an institution of higher education or at an alternative-certification training center, an independent consultant hired to present staff development programs, or a building- or district-based support person—has heard comments like "That won't work" or, the even more closed, "I tried that" invoked to dismiss suggestions, ideas, or advice. Although perhaps understandable, especially for teachers who feel (or create for themselves) a great deal of pressure to perform to higher expectations than might be appropriate for a beginner, defensiveness and a lack of openness are tremendous obstacles to growth and learning. Teachers, and perhaps especially new teachers, need to feel safe and supported to be able to even hear a new idea without becoming defensive, much less be willing to try a new approach or abandon a current practice that is not working. Building a team of supportive and encouraging colleagues, people you trust and can go to on good and not-so-good days, will very likely be the most important resource in the entire toolbox and, in most cases, will be the key to your longevity in the profession. "There is a bond that forms when you teach with someone," observed Susan Bailey, who values these connections for "the sharing of ideas, putting theory into practice, and reflecting on what went well and what I will change for next time."[2]

Clearly, your primary and most immediate concerns will focus on your students. In fact, you may have days when you find yourself wondering when you last spoke with an adult. But adults are an important part of your teaching life, and even for the most introverted educators, the need for interactive competence goes beyond the world of the classroom. "Don't underestimate the value of being a well-respected and cooperative colleague," advised Sherry Annee. So let's first look at the importance of creating a support team—people you can approach for ideas as well as encouragement. We'll also look at what to look for in a mentor or role model, as well as the kinds of behavior that will have people willing, if not wanting, to be a part of your team.

THE VALUE OF COLLABORATION

Most people who have been in the profession for a while recognize the need for new teachers to feel capable and effective, as well as a conflicting need for help. One professional development director noted, "There's an internal struggle between the need for their colleagues to see them as competent and the fact that there are things they don't know and need people to ask." Many beginning teachers express an overwhelming concern with looking good and keeping up—doing what they believe others expect. And I certainly remember the panic I felt when I discovered that my class was two weeks behind the other fifth grades in a particular subject, the fear that my kids would be lower achieving or noisier than kids in other classes, and the pressure I felt, whether real or imagined, to look like I knew what I was doing.

Professional safety—which is essential to the survival of any beginning teacher—is reflected in the faith that you can make a mistake and receive information, encouragement, and caring guidance without insult, derision, impatience, or disrespect. It is grounded in knowing that there is someone to go to, someone who has your back and wants you to succeed. Jacie Bejster Maslyk acknowledged, "Many new teachers leave the field within the first three years, often because of a lack of support." In her first few years of teaching at a tough, inner-city school, she solved this problem by finding a core group of colleagues and friends at work. "We were able to support one another, venting about problems, struggling with kids or parents, trying to balance teaching and life. It was so important to have those people to lean on." Having started in a similar environment, I can attest to the importance of my fellow intern teachers and the supervisors and professors in our program who got me through the year with the confidence and skill to go on. Maslyk, like dozens of other contributors, advised finding "at least one person at school that can be your support. It will help to make that first year, and those that follow, a lot easier."

Any time you're in unfamiliar territory, your confidence and potential for success can get a tremendous boost from the connections you make with someone a few steps ahead of you. Nearly all resources for beginning teachers emphasize the need for all new teachers to find someone in their school they can trust and lean on for support. Robin Fogarty offered, "Without a doubt, the number one priority for the new teacher is to have a friend in the school, on the premises, visible, available, and accessible, a knowing colleague on staff who is there for the new kid on the block."[3] The number of contributors who offered similar recommendations—individuals at all grade levels, staff positions, and levels of experience—underscores just how crucial it is to start off your career with this intention.

The good news is that, in most settings, veteran staff will *not* expect you to know everything right off the bat. An assistant superintendent wrote to assure readers, "No matter what your building administrators tell you, they were beginning teachers at one time and they made first-year teacher mistakes, too." They also won't expect you to go it alone. In fact, many, if not most, will be more than willing to help, especially if you are open to the information they take the time and effort to share. Many contributors commented on the generosity and willingness of people in this profession to support new members of their community. Behavior specialist Jean Ramirez wrote, "Become friends with the most positive talented teachers in the building and learn from them. Don't be afraid to ask for help. Most teachers are at heart helping, loving people who love nothing more than helping new teachers." Aili Pogust concurred. "Find a good mentor," she wrote. "You do not have to do it alone. Many of us who have learned the intricacies of teaching over time want to share our experiences. Teaching is not a job. It's a calling. And a calling requires mentorship and apprenticeship."

Many people wrote to reassure new teachers that asking for help is appropriate, accepted, and generally encouraged. Tammy Hanna assured, "It is not a sign of weakness if you ask the teacher next door for great ideas on how to present a lesson." Jill Snyderman agreed, "Don't shut your door and try to be independent. That is the death of some beginning teachers. They think they know it all and a problem will arise that will bite them hard and then the veteran teachers will have no sympathy," she wrote. One third-grade teacher likewise warned, "Rather than acting like you know everything there is to know about teaching, swallow your pride and ask people those seemingly hard, silly, puzzling questions. Their answers will come from experience and may encompass wisdom and educational elements you've never thought about." Michelle Tillapaugh agreed: "Don't be afraid to ask lots of questions of the veteran or quality staff around you. They are underappreciated and would welcome the opportunity to share their successes and mistakes. It doesn't show a weakness, but instead a willingness and desire to be better. And let's face it, we can all be better."

I was touched by the number of contributors who admitted how easy it is to blow it from time to time. "Go easy on yourself when you make mistakes, because you will make tons of mistakes," wrote a contributor who teaches high school English. Elementary teacher Wonell Miller shared, "Take all the help you can get. Believe me—right out of college, you need help whether you know it or not." Julia Frascona encouraged, "Hang on tight. Find a teacher or two in your building you can relate to and have real honest chats with. Your learning curve as a new teacher is steep. Don't try to do it all alone."

As most veteran teachers will tell you from their own similar experiences, there will be days when you feel as though nothing you are doing is right: Lessons that looked great on paper fall flat or take a lot less time than you thought, kids are inattentive and uncooperative, or a behavior intervention somehow makes things even worse. These are the times you'll want to have strong connections in place. "Don't suffer alone," advised author and former high school teacher Hal Urban. "Talk about what happened with someone whose insight and judgment you respect. Get reassurance and encouragement, and lessons from that person's experiences with failure."[4]

Don't be afraid to reach out and take some responsibility for what you need. Lydia Aranda noted, "If your colleagues don't share with you voluntarily, ask what they have that you could use for a specific lesson. Most teachers will share, but they are so busy thinking about what they need, that the beginning teacher is neglected." Likewise, if you don't ask, it may appear that you don't want any assistance or advice. April Keck DeGennaro advised, "Ask for help and then when you are no longer a beginner, give back. Don't be afraid to admit that you got it wrong. The key is that you keep asking for help until you get it right. Teachers are the most generous breed. We give anything and everything to each other because we are successful together." And while not all teaching environments will offer this abundance of support, there is an exceptional chance that you can find at least one person in almost any school who will be willing to give you the assistance you need. (If you find it hard to connect with *anyone* on your staff, step back and ask yourself whether others are receiving support and information and, if so, what they might be doing differently. If your school climate is generally positive and encouraging, keep trying. If your environment is so toxic and competitive that you experience negative, useless, or hurtful responses when you ask for help, look at some alternatives online, through a professional organization—especially one for beginning teachers—or through the training program you completed to get into the classroom.)

Seek out a variety of experienced teachers, if possible, including those teaching grade levels or subjects different from yours. High school teacher Mary Edmunds remarked, "I am a science teacher but the social studies teacher down the hall and the special education teacher across from me were my lifelines." Seeing a variety of teaching styles and approaches can help you select strategies and techniques that best match your own personality, what feels best to you. "Observe as many classes as you can," wrote another contributor. "You need time to develop your own style. Take what suits you from as many different teachers as you can."

Fellow teachers can fill in gaps in your preparation, especially if you end up with an assignment to subject areas or grade levels that are different from the ones you trained to teach. When an overflow of third-graders were added to my somewhat light fourth-grade roster, I found myself teaching kids who seemed much younger than the ones I had been teaching for the past few years. Even one grade made a huge difference, and I found myself looking to the primary teachers for much-needed ideas and advice. Similarly, Stephen Vance came to teaching well prepared in terminology, jargon, and theory involved in reading instruction but was caught off guard when it came to the specifics of actually teaching his kids how to read. "By magnetizing myself to other teachers who knew how to teach students how to read, observing what they did, and having conversations about powerful teaching, I learned how to teach," he wrote. Cast a wide net, as help can come from anywhere. Eric Katz urged, "Don't be afraid to speak with a student's counselor or parent to get background information so that you can understand a student in context."

Anyone who has been a part of a school community for a long time will have a sense of the overall climate, the needs and history of the community, and the interpersonal and political dynamics within the school. These individuals, including the office and custodial staff, usually know many of the families in the community and are known there as well, either through personal contact or reputation, or both. They can help you get a better sense of the community you serve, and the cultural, economic, and historical context in which you are teaching—another important piece of the puzzle that will come more easily from collaboration than from attempting to go it alone.

FINDING AN EFFECTIVE MENTOR

One of the biggest mistakes I ever made was trying to copy one of the other teachers at my grade level. She had already been teaching for twenty years when I got there, so I figured she must be good. As it turned out—and I think this is true whenever our behavior lacks congruence with who we really are—none of my kids bought the act. They realized before I did that this teacher's style did not work for me and saw through the lack of authenticity that will always be evident when we're trying to be someone we're not, even when we're convinced that that's who we really should be.[5] Experienced teachers have had years to develop their teaching selves and identify the strategies and styles that work best for them. Different personalities can carry off different approaches successfully, and while trial and error will be a part of this developmental process, you can expect to encounter models, as well as advice, that simply won't resonate with who you are and the teacher you want to become. Maslyk cautioned, "During that first year, many people are going to tell you how they teach a certain subject, manage behavior, deal with parents, [and so on]. Take it all in. Listen to the advice of others, but don't lose sight of what you think is best for kids. Learn as much as you can from those around you, but continue to develop your own repertoire of teaching strategies." Miller likewise shared, "After you see many ways to do something, you can decide what is best for you." First-grade teacher Jill Denson agreed: "Talk to many different veteran and new teachers. Then, follow your heart."

Many schools and districts have programs in place to provide mentors or support providers for you. If not, you will need to take some responsibility for connecting with people who can serve in this role. In fact, it's a good idea to do this even if you have a mentor assigned to you. "Get to know some of your colleagues to determine who you would have a good working relationship with and ask them if they would mind being a resource person for you," advised Michelle Mayrose. These people will be your backup, she noted, in case you find your mentor to be "unhelpful, unavailable, or for any other legitimate reason, not someone you are comfortable with." Pogust also cautioned, "Not all are effective mentors. Find one who knows how to guide you and acknowledge your efforts as you begin this journey."

But where to start? Several contributors suggested qualities to look for in a potential mentor. Roxie Ahlbrecht recommended that you look for "the busiest, most-frazzled teachers you can find. They are that way because they are devoted and accomplished in their craft. They will make time for you. They will help you. They are the ones you want to use as your mentors." Nancy Foote counseled, "Find someone who loves teaching and ask that person to mentor you." Diane Laveglia had similar advice. "I would pick the most enthusiastic, knowledgeable teacher on staff and the one the principal likes best!" Sione Quaass mentioned the importance of trust. "Find a person you can debrief with, who won't gossip, and who understands what it is like to be a teacher," she wrote. Robin Fogarty advised looking for qualities like "a solid knowledge base, a sense of humor, or a manner of working with the students," characteristics you admire, someone who reflects your own core values.[6]

If you look at individuals whose influence and leadership exemplify true quality mentorship, you'll see certain patterns emerge. By definition, mentors have something you want to learn, develop, or emulate. They model behaviors, values, attitudes, performance standards, and even their appearance in a way that has meaning and importance for you. They are good at what they do and are likely to be in a state of continual growth, learning, and renewal themselves. They are driven by motivators and values you respect, and operate with high integrity. They will challenge you and, at the same time, support the fullest expression of your creative potential. They will allow space for you to grow at your own rate and in the direction that is right for you.[7]

While the idea of mentoring has typically emphasized learning new skills and understanding the subtleties of functioning in a new setting or situation, mentors who seem to have the greatest impact are those for whom the relationship is a primary focus. Look for someone who will accept and value you unconditionally. Good mentors believe in you and have faith in your ability to achieve, learn, solve a problem, overcome an obstacle, and grow into your own successful teaching style. They genuinely care about you and want you to succeed; however, they don't have a stake or personal investment in your success and are not personally attached to particular outcomes. They respect the ideas, enthusiasm, and skills you have already developed and appreciate the knowledge you have acquired to get where you are, yet they can also see you beyond where you are now and will help you to do the same, holding a picture of a broader reality for you to grow into.

Effective mentors will sometimes push you beyond your comfort zone, or at least lead you to the edge—but they will take care to avoid overwhelming you. They can hold you to high standards without setting you up to fail. They will not exploit your vulnerability and will see your mistakes only as opportunities for you to learn, rethink, make a new plan, or try again. They will not express impatience or frustration with you or disappointment in you, nor will they look down on you or treat you as an inferior or ever shame, embarrass, or bully you.

Look for people who will encourage you with general expectations (for example, that you fulfill your potential or produce the highest-quality performance you're capable of producing) rather than specific agendas (such as pursuing a particular career goal or resolving a dilemma in a particular way). Good mentors will support your goals and intentions and may help you explore different options or sharpen your focus.

You want people who will be facilitators in your growth—helping, coaching, supporting, and listening—rather than people who wish to "fix" or mold you in a particular fashion. Find individuals who are especially passionate about teaching and who will very likely inspire you to feel the same. By your association with your mentors, your knowledge and beliefs about yourself and the profession will take on new dimensions. Many people I've met who experienced quality mentorship shared discoveries they made about their own capabilities—skills, hidden talents, character strength, or persistence, for example—they never imagined they possessed, as well as possibilities for growth and achievements they never would have otherwise envisioned.

And finally, effective mentors are able to let go. They wish for your success, but they do not need for you to succeed in order to feel competent, successful, or valuable themselves. Nor do they need to keep you small or dependent in any way. They are willing to allow the relationship to change as you grow and will stand beside you as your colleague when you no longer need their guidance in the way you once did—perhaps when you reach out and mentor someone yourself.

Now, I realize that sounds like a lot to ask, but these qualities tend to be the most helpful in any teaching relationship (which you may want to keep in mind when developing your role as a teacher). You deserve the help an effective mentor has to offer. Be aware of how you feel when you're working with anyone on your support team, and keep an eye out for any red flags or gut feelings that suggest that a particular person may not be a good match for you (see "Run for Your Life!"), because the quality of the relationships you have with these individuals can have a tremendous impact on the way you experience your life—and yourself—as an educator.

Signs of a Good Mentor

You know you have a good mentor if . . .

- you are gaining skill, comfort, and confidence in the areas in which you are being mentored.
- you feel safe making a mistake or asking for help.
- you feel *visible*—seen, heard, and appreciated at many levels.
- you perceive that your skills, priorities, personality, talents, wishes, intentions, and perception of reality are valued and respected.
- you are inspired and encouraged in ways that leave you feeling "lit up" and energized (rather than stressed, fearful, exhausted, or self-doubting) when you interact with your mentor.
- you have access to information, resources, guidance, and reassurance as you need them.
- you are growing and learning in healthy ways—not just keeping your mentor off your back or trying to gain approval.
- you feel as though something is being pulled or drawn from you (rather than imposed on you).
- you see yourself realistically but can envision yourself beyond where you are now.
- you feel secure in knowing that your mentor's sense of success, competence, or adequacy does not depend on your inexperience, adulation, or vulnerability.
- your life is changing in positive ways.[8]

Run for Your Life!

A bad mentor can have a significantly *negative* impact on your confidence, growth, morale, and career. Although not always immediately apparent, certain behaviors or characteristics may indicate that your mentor will not give you the support, help, or guidance you deserve and, in fact, can hinder your development in dangerous and long-lasting ways. The following red flags will tell you what to watch out for:

You probably have a bad mentor if . . .

- interactions with your mentor leave you consistently feeling drained, defeated, self-doubting, or overwhelmed. Sometimes even a well-meaning mentor can push too hard. Watch for indications that your mentor doesn't comprehend your intentions or respect your limits or seems to be attempting to satisfy personal needs through you or your efforts.
- your mentor violates your trust in any way. This can include anything from abusive behavior to a breach of confidentiality. Watch for a nagging feeling that you need to protect yourself in this relationship.
- your mentor frequently makes promises and doesn't deliver. I've seen plenty of charming and charismatic individuals more enchanted with the idea of mentoring (or being asked to mentor) than with the actual process, or those arrogant enough to confuse mentorship with mere association.
- your mentor expresses doubt in your ability to succeed. If you sense a lack of faith or indifference from this person, you will not receive the help you need.

(Continued)

(Continued)

- your mentor seems threatened by your success. This problem may not be evident at first. However, as your skills and confidence grow, watch for efforts aimed at discouraging progress you're capable of making, minimizing your growth and accomplishments, withholding acknowledgement or recognition, or deliberately holding you back when you have opportunities to move forward.
- your mentor is competitive with you. This can come out in subtle and not-so-subtle ways, from blatant one-upmanship or put-downs (or "putting you in your place") to backhanded compliments that consistently emphasize former weaknesses or failures. This is someone who needs to be better than you in some way—financially, socially, or professionally, in terms of position, visibility, or acclaim—in order to feel a sense of adequacy or worth.
- your mentor has inappropriate agendas for you or goals for you that are different from your own. Years ago, I had to break off a relationship with a mentor after he became my dissertation adviser. After months of spinning my wheels, it became clear to me that no matter how much work I did, he always seemed to find one more piece of research or task to involve—and often distract—my efforts. I doubt I ever would have finished had I not found someone to support me through the process who was more respectful of the direction I had for this project, as well as my intention to finish it.[9]
- your mentor operates by values or principles that are vastly different from yours. A friend told of being initially attracted to a potential mentor's great and sudden success. Although the mentor seemed to have much to offer, deep down he was driven by insecurity and greed. Although it may be possible to learn from someone with personal values or qualities you neither admire nor wish to emulate without being corrupted by that person's value system, when it comes to choosing a mentor, you might want to look elsewhere.
- your mentor uses (or intends or threatens to use) your talent or work for personal advantage or advancement, especially if you aren't credited for your contribution. I've heard dozens of horror stories of employers, advisers, professors, or supervisors who published (in their own names) or received awards for the work of someone they had mentored. This one is especially hard to spot before it happens, so it might be a good idea to at least clarify expectations beforehand. Especially if you are writing, producing research, or developing a program with someone, do your homework. Research copyright laws and intellectual property rights to protect your work. Hire a lawyer if you have to, or consult legal assistance if it is available through your district.
- your mentor mistreats you in any way. Be careful to neither excuse nor deny abusive behavior, including any attempts to ridicule you, demean you, or treat you dismissively, even if you've made a serious or dumb mistake. No one has the right to presume what you know or "should have known." Responding negatively—with anger, disappointment, impatience, or contempt, for example—to a request for information or to something you did because you were unfamiliar with a policy or procedure is neither supportive nor appropriate. Likewise, be wary of any mentor who fails to value your input, take you seriously, or respect your reality or your version of a particular event or experience.
- your mentor seems to need you more than you need your mentor. A healthy mentoring relationship will always be somewhat reciprocal, but beware of mentors

who are particularly invested in or attached to your choices or your success. This problem will be most evident in situations in which your mentor has difficulty letting go, feels threatened by guidance you get from others, or attempts to undermine your efforts to move on or make different choices from those suggested. It may also come out as disappointment when you don't live up to expectations (expressed or unexpressed) or fulfill a particular agenda. Mentors who even remotely suggest that they are the best—or only—person who can help you, or that you would be nothing without them, definitely do not have your best interests at heart. Cut your losses if you have to, and run as fast as you can. [10]

BUILDING YOUR SUPPORT TEAM

Becoming a win-win teacher includes being able to successfully enter into an established adult community. This process requires a different set of skills from the ones that prepared you to work with your students. I've seen beginning teachers who were really sharp and effective in dealing with their students but who had a hard time establishing themselves professionally or creating solid, trusting relationships with others on the staff. As a result, their work lives ended up being far less satisfying than they could have been.

People in your building will be curious about what you bring to this community, and clearly, certain behaviors and attitudes you exhibit will work to your advantage— whether you need guidance or just want someone to chat with at lunch. In many ways, this process isn't much different from the kinds of things you do to be welcomed and accepted in any social situation. Are you friendly and open, for example? Do you initiate conversations to get to know individuals one by one? Do you participate in school programs and social activities that involve the staff? Do you contribute positively to discussions that concern you? Would others perceive you as respectful of different teaching styles and philosophies? The more of these questions you can answer affirmatively, the more willing your colleagues are likely to be to include you in their world.

What kind of energy do you bring to the office, faculty lounge, and hallways of your school? Being relentlessly or inappropriately chirpy can get on people's nerves, but you really don't want to be a cloud of negativity either. Be aware that certain behaviors add to the toxicity of the climate of your school. Even if things like complaining, gossiping, backstabbing, and triangulating[11] are common in your environment, be careful that you do not participate. These behaviors may feel like a familiar and appropriate bonding technique, but engaging in them will invariably come back to haunt you. "Never speak badly about anyone or thing," warned Laveglia. No matter how upset you are about a student, a parent, or a colleague, detailing incidents publicly—either in front of a large group of uninvolved staff or going to them one by one to complain—will not reflect well on you professionally. (This is where your support system comes in because you *will* need to get things off your chest from time to time. Use discretion about what you share and with whom, whether asking a trusted colleague to simply listen or help you strategize a solution.)

Approach other staff members with a blend of confidence and openness. Even if you're new, you're not there by accident. You've worked hard to get this position, and you're also willing to grow. Start with existing relationships and conventions, respecting what seem to be the acceptable expectations for your particular school when it comes to appearance, language, tone, and the kinds of things you share or discuss.[12] Professional competence and credibility are difficult to appreciate if people can't get past an outrageous appearance or abrasive personality. Yes, bring your personality and personal tastes to add to the texture of the school's social tapestry. Just be aware that it's always easier to push the boundaries once you're an established and respected member of the community than it is to demand that people stretch to accept an unknown, untested, and unproven quantity.

Being socially positive means that you avoid soapboxing, grandstanding, and complaining about the system or school policies, even if everybody else seems to be doing it. While you certainly have a right to your opinions, you are not obliged to impose them on your colleagues. Even if they ask, be cautious. (Are they genuinely interested or simply baiting you? I've seen both.) Outside of your most trusted alliances, it's often wise to go with understated, noncommittal responses. ("I'll have to think about that," is a legitimate way to disengage, especially if you're not sure of your position or how your comments might be received.)

Listen more than you talk. Be careful not to suggest that everyone knows what they're doing except you or that no one cares or works as hard as you do. Both attitudes wear thin quickly, and neither is likely to be true. Offer to share resources or ideas if you want, but be extra cautious in setting up expectations or unexpressed demands. If you give, do so for the sake of giving, and don't take it personally if the other person declines.

In addition to these general recommendations, there are specific groups within the adult community, including the parents of your students, who warrant some special consideration. Let's look at how you can enhance these relationships and gain the maximum support from each.

Mentors and Supportive Colleagues

If people in your school and district are willing to help you, keep in mind that they are committing their time, energy, and resources for your benefit. Any one of them will have plenty of other things to do, so do not take these gifts lightly, for that is exactly what they are. We know what makes a good mentor. Now, let's look at what makes someone worth mentoring.

Of all the comments relevant to this issue, perhaps the most common themes focused on openness and willingness. "My first year of teaching was like my first year of college," Snyderman reported. "I soaked in all the veteran teacher would offer. Coming early and leaving late every day, copying all her files and getting her advice on everything from how to handle a parent to how to write a comment on a report card." When others see that you are using the information and resources they give you, you validate the investment they have made.

The opposite is also true. It's rare that support people would give up on a struggling teacher; however, it's understandable if these individuals start to burn out and back off when they feel like they're pouring water into a leaky bucket. "If I have to decide which new teachers I'm going to help," one veteran admitted, "my first choice would be the ones who show the greatest commitment. I'm not inclined to make much time for the ones who come to me for ideas and then respond to everything I say with 'yeah, but. . . .'" If you're more attached to having a problem or being a victim, it will be obvious when you fail to search for the additional information, create the necessary materials, or try an approach that someone suggested. It won't take long for your lack of follow-through to burn the people who are trying to help.

A number of veteran educators expressed an appreciation for the talents, ideas, and experiences new teachers have to offer and encouraged new teachers to not be afraid of sharing ideas with seasoned teachers, many of whom appreciate a fresh approach. Still others advised proceeding with caution. Bailey was among several contributors who cautioned against being overconfident or cocky. "You need to get the lay of the land and figure out how things work in the school." She advised against being too pushy: "Let the veteran teachers share things with you and do not tell them what to do. After you have had some time in the school you can begin to share more of your ideas with others. This will make your transition into that school smooth." And Snyderman suggests that when people go out of their way to share resources or ideas, invite you to observe them, or simply sit and listen, don't forget to acknowledge them for helping you.[13]

Administrators and Central Office

In a perfect world, every administrator would embody management skills to create structure and safety, people skills to build connections and trust, and leadership abilities that inspire loyalty, commitment, and the best possible performance from every employee. Bruce Hammonds observed, "Being in a good school with a progressive principal is often the secret to future success because it allows you to pick up positive teaching habits that you will be able to build your own teaching philosophy on." I could not agree more, and if you can find such a placement, so much the better. Unfortunately, not all beginning teachers are assigned to such a setting, and frankly, for the years that I was in the classroom, I was just grateful any time I got to work with an administrator who didn't get in my way or make my life more difficult than it already was.

It's long been known that principals set the tone for the school.[14] Although you may be able to exist in your classroom with few encounters with your building administrators, your relationship with them can have a strong and extensive impact on your teaching experiences. A supportive, visionary principal can endow you with the confidence, sense of possibility, and resources to accomplish amazing things in your classroom. On the other hand, regularly having to deal with rigid, controlling, obstructing, or disparaging administrative behavior can erode everything from your faith in your own capabilities to your passion for (or even interest in) the profession. One program coordinator described trying to work in an environment where "the staff is managed like buffaloes and vision is not valued." She likewise related the negative and exhausting impact of "fear and micromanagement" when staff saw "effort and a passion for doing the right thing for kids" repeatedly come up against politics and personal "gotcha" agendas.[15]

Regardless of the administrative behaviors you'll encounter, you'll want to minimize stress and conflict wherever you can and maximize the potential benefit from having administrative support in your workplace. Here's another place to see the value in listening and observing. Do you know who the administrative staff is—in your building and at central office? Are there support personnel assigned specifically to work with beginning teachers? Once you have identified who's available, try to get a sense of your administrators' values and priorities and whether actual behavior truly reflects expressed goals and vision. Notice the degree of supportiveness, flexibility, and interpersonal capabilities they exhibit with various members of the staff. What kinds of help and support are they likely to offer? Where do you think you might run into conflict or opposition? Which individual can you count on to have your back? Who would have the best ideas about how to run your classroom?

"You want to know a secret about principals?" asked one contributor. "We don't like surprises." To be sure, one of the earliest bits of advice I received was to keep the office apprised of any problems or incidents, preferably before they reach the principal through a third party. "Be honest with your support provider," counseled Lyle Hartman. "If you're in trouble, take some responsibility. If you come to me with a problem, you have a friend. If someone else comes to me to tell me you have a problem, you have an enemy. Don't let me have a rude surprise. Your support providers are people who are paid to support you. This is especially true if they have invited you to go to them. Ask for help and be honest about what you need."

If you really want to present yourself as a professional, and increase your odds for a satisfactory resolution, provide documentation of any problem you have. If your school has an incident report form or procedure, start there. Note pertinent details (as objectively as possible[16]), and furnish any supporting materials that will help your principal or any other intermediaries get a better understanding of what occurred. Especially if this has been an ongoing problem, you will want to have a file cataloguing details of related incidents, including what you've tried or done with regard to this situation, the outcomes of your efforts, and copies of any prior notifications you've shared with the office. Keep copies of any communications with the office about potential or existing problems, because if things ever go south, a good paper trail can be a really good friend.

In addition to letting the office know about any conflicts with students, parents, or other staff members, you might want to let them in on any changes you make in your classroom or instructional program—whether you are implementing a new program, for example, or planning something that involves other staff, students in other classrooms, parents, or guest speakers. Consider inviting administrative staff to observe special activities, celebrations, presentations, or events involving the students as well. Also, make sure that the office gets a copy of any communications you send home or outside of the school regarding school business. (And for heaven's sake, run a spell-check on this material. Even better, get a colleague or friend to proofread anything that leaves your room. Every spelling, logic, syntax, or grammatical error will cost you a piece of your professional credibility.)

Stay on top of the details of your professional life—leaving good plans for a substitute, being in your classroom any time the students are there, turning in well-prepared plans or reports on time, and registering complaints or proposals for change with discretion and through the proper channels, for example. And finally, I've met few administrators who appreciate being used as a dumping ground for discipline problems. Recruiting their help for suggestions, guidelines, resources, or support is entirely appropriate. Even if you are working with administrators who are willing to play the heavy (although few relish the opportunity to scold or punish a child for something they did not themselves witness), expecting the office to warehouse, reprimand, or "fix" difficult students is not only unprofessional, but it also suggests an inability to manage your own classroom, not just to the administration but to colleagues, parents, and the students as well.

Depending on the relationship you have with your administrators, the degree to which you feel safe opening yourself to their involvement, and the interest they have indicated in serving as an instructional resource, engage their talents to give you feedback on any aspect of your teaching or classroom management. A good administrator or support provider will not only offer suggestions to fine-tune your approach but will also give you feedback and reinforcement on what you're doing right, or where you're making progress. Lacking this valuable support, secure connections with others on the staff you can trust, and be sure your bases are covered.[17]

Specialists on Board

At some point in your career, you will have students who present challenges that go beyond the strategies you know or the information you have. For some teachers, this need will arise only occasionally—in response, say, to an injury or extended absence or to a family or community crisis. But it's probably safe to say that most teachers find a more regular need for the skills, resources, and perspective of certain adults in the school community. If you are fortunate enough to have a school nurse, social worker, counselor, psychologist, speech and language pathologist, resource specialist, occupational therapist, or other support professionals available in your district, you are blessed with a pool of talent and a fresh pair of eyes to help you better meet the needs of your students or resolve issues you may run into in your work.

Current legislation, including the Individuals with Disabilities Education Act (IDEA), exists to protect the rights of students with a variety of disabilities "by ensuring that everyone receives a free appropriate public education (FAPE), regardless of ability." In addition, the law ensures the necessary services for students with special needs.[18] There are, therefore, specialists available who are trained and licensed in a range of services from diagnosis and documentation of special needs to working with individual students or groups of students in or outside of the classroom on any number of social, emotional, developmental, behavioral, medical, or neurological issues. They can recommend materials and strategies for working with particular students or solving specific problems, offer therapeutic resources and interventions, work directly with or as a liaison to families, and help support students struggling with problems that can affect their behavior and performance in school.

Some districts have site-based personnel as well as itinerant staff, and you may have to dig a bit to find the resources you need. I've been in schools that have many of these individuals in their buildings on a regular basis and others that did not have even a school nurse on site unless one showed up to collect height and weight information on the student population or to run assessments like eye tests (rather than to respond to student illness or injury). Support staff are often available on a squeaky-wheel basis, so it's well worth your time to find out which positions are staffed through the district, what services each can provide, and how to go about engaging their services.

These individuals are a part of your school system (or are contracted through your district) to offer services to students who qualify for their expertise. Like reaching out to mentors and veteran staff, seeking their help is not an admission of failure or inadequacy. The problem arises when teachers expect support personnel to fix the problems they have with these students—or indeed, to fix the students themselves. Be really clear when you request input or help from these individuals that you are doing so in the interest of the student and not just for your own convenience. Provide good documentation of the issues or problems the student is experiencing, whether a particular pattern you've observed over time or some recent event in the child's life that is affecting current behavior or performance. Be sure to indicate what you've done or tried so far and any factors that seem to be a part of patterns you've observed. The more details you can provide, including information about factors like the time of day, the weather, the type of activity, the room environment, or other students involved, the more helpful support staff can be.

Also, affirm your intention to work with this student and your willingness to make adjustments necessary for the student's success. Your flexibility and commitment to accommodating the student's needs will be far more inviting—and far more likely to get you the help you want—than approaching support providers with the hope of getting the child moved out of your room, or with a resistance to changing anything in the classroom or doing anything special for this student. Finally, respect the student's privacy and keep conversations and records confidential.

Classified Support Personnel

The adult community in a school extends beyond the certified staff, and many contributors wrote in to remind readers not to overlook the benefits of a good relationship with paraprofessionals, office staff, translators and community involvement coordinators, security personnel, cafeteria workers, and custodians, for example. "Get along with everyone," advised special education teacher Amy Donner Chait. "Often custodians and secretaries make a big difference in your ability to get things done, sometimes more than the classroom teacher next door." School secretary Janice Carvajal likewise recommended office and custodial staff as "good sources for parent and student information and site information, as well as smoothing out wrinkles that come with being new at a school." Mayrose agreed. "These are the people that have the vast majority of answers and are fantastic resources. They know the true workings of the building and are the [ones to] go to for everything from supplies to getting things fixed in your classroom."

Counselor Barbara Muller-Ackerman advised, "A principal spends a lot of time out of the office. The person who really keeps things running at the school—juggling parents, ordering supplies, deciding who gets an aide and when, for example—is the school secretary," she said, noting that this position now carries "the new and more dignified title of administrative assistant. Time spent building a genuine alliance with the school secretary is repaid many times over, often guaranteeing that you will be taken care of and protected to the best of her ability. This is not a relationship to be discounted in any way. Annoy her, be condescending, disrespect her position in the school hierarchy, and you will pay dearly," she warned. These are the people who can direct you to the appropriate forms, phone numbers, or procedures. As with anyone else on the staff, courtesy and kindness go a long way. In addition to regular pleasantries, Joanne Davidman sometimes takes baked goods as a special thank you to the custodians. Mayrose also noted the importance of treating the classified staff with respect. "Many teachers in a building have a tendency to look down on these people. *Don't!* If you are polite and respectful on a regular basis, they will often bend over backwards to help you."

For many kids, classified staff represent safe adults, and many take an active role in students' lives and school events. Paraprofessionals (sometimes called teaching assistants or teachers' aides) play a direct instructional role and can be the key ingredient in reaching larger numbers of students on an individual basis. They often know the kids as well as the content and can provide the additional instruction, attention, and practice some students need. They have much to offer, so don't be afraid to ask them for information and suggestions.

Carvajal reminded, "Classified staff, such as secretaries, clerks, custodians, security aides, [and] classroom assistants . . . are also professionals. Many of these support staff members have college degrees or may be working toward their teaching credentials. These staff members are your support team! Equal respect of all staff members as professionals goes a long way in creating and maintaining a positive and harmonious work place. In times of need, the support of a classified coworker can make a challenging day successful."

Planning for Substitutes

If you've ever worked as a substitute teacher, you can appreciate how challenging a job it is. Although I've met some people who are perfectly happy working as a sub (often in a very small district or assigned to one or two schools where they know the majority of the kids), most find it rather daunting to walk into unfamiliar territory day after day and work with kids who aren't particularly inclined to make a good impression on someone they may never see again.

You won't always know when you're going to be out. I've known too many teachers who came to school practically on death's doorstep because they hadn't left plans or didn't feel comfortable asking a sub to work with the plans they had. Working when you're sick is a miserable experience, nor is it fair to your students or colleagues. In addition to the likelihood that you'll actually get worse, you also risk exposing others to whatever you've got. (Staying up all night when you're sick to make plans that you run to school in the morning isn't much fun either, so be proactive in preparing for a sub.)

Substitute teachers are a part of your support team. You have a professional obligation to help them have a positive experience in your classroom—not just for their sake but for the sake of your students, your colleagues, and your administrators. You also increase the odds that you won't return to a classroom in disarray, or worse.

Try to keep things as simple as possible—including the instructions you leave. Subs rarely have much time to review the materials you leave for them, so keep the sub folder lean and clean. Minimize changes in routines and activities, if possible, but be careful about asking a sub to conduct specialized programs or routines (such as those that involve things like lab work, instructional conferencing, evaluations, or individualized prescriptions). "Don't expect too much of the substitute," cautioned educator Kurt Schwengel. "While planning the day, you might want to avoid extensive art projects or other high-maintenance lessons."[19] You'll probably have better results with plans that review or reinforce content you've already taught, rather than introducing new or particularly complex content, especially if you're out for only a day or two.

If your school does not require you to prepare emergency plans for a substitute, do so anyway. Keep materials on file in the office, with another teacher, or with your department chair. Knowing that your sub will have access to a folder with the information and materials needed to successfully take over your room will bring you much peace of mind when you can't make it to school. (See "Checklist for a Substitute Folder.")

When you know you'll be out, make sure that your plans are clear and manageable and that materials are accessible. Be sure to have plenty of emergency activities, especially for unexpected absences, for times that your plans might be unclear or too complex to be run by a sub, or for when planned activities run short, leaving everyone with extra time on their hands. Have enough copies of materials for each class, and ideally, include activities that students will enjoy doing, can do independently, and will take up some time. Make sure the location of these materials is included in the sub folder.[20]

Prepare your students for the possibility of an occasional need for a sub. Some teachers shared that they refer to subs as *guest teachers* and assign specific students to help the guest teacher with routines, logistics, technology, or the location of certain materials, for example. Identify student helpers in your emergency sub folder.

Leave a brief welcome note thanking the sub in advance for covering your class, and request a review of how the day went. If your district has a feedback form for substitute teachers, include it in the folder. If not, invite the sub to share what was taught or assigned each period, how much work was completed, how the kids in each class behaved, and what you can do in the future to ensure a positive experience for all concerned.

Checklist for a Substitute Folder

Different schools, subjects, and grade levels will require different types of information to be left for a sub. Below is a sample of items some teachers include in a folder with essential information for a substitute teacher:[21]

- Where to meet students, in the morning or before class, if they do not come directly to class on their own
- Copy of the schedule with plans and materials for each period, including scheduled interruptions (announcements, pull-outs, breaks, recess) or the arrival of another adult to work in the room (with the entire class, a small group, or individual students)

(Continued)

(Continued)

- List of students who go to other classes (where they go and when)
- Procedures, including times and locations, if you accompany students to other classes or if you need to meet them and walk them back to your room
- Procedures for using the hall pass or accommodating needs for bathroom breaks
- Map or explanation of the environment, including location of work centers, storage areas, and equipment
- Up-to-date seating charts for each class
- Instructions and an evacuation map for a fire drill or other emergency
- Schedule of subjects and activities, including materials, books, and teachers' guides
- Special needs of individual students in each class
- Names and locations of helpful staff and resource people, including a nearby colleague
- Names of student helpers or hosts in each class, including who's in charge of technology, who runs errands or messages to another part of the school, and who knows where materials are stored
- Location of emergency lesson plans, extra activities, and time-fillers
- Location of bathrooms (for students and faculty), teachers' lounge, cafeteria, library, or other important places on campus
- Means and procedures for contacting the office or handling an emergency in the classroom (intercom or phone, for example)
- Any other tips or important bits of information[22]

Parents as Allies

There's one other important piece of the support-team puzzle, and interestingly, this group—the students' parents—seems to be most challenging for many teachers.[23] A 2005 article by Nancy Gibbs quoted a recent study that found that "of all the challenges they face, new teachers rank handling parents at the top. . . . Parent management was a bigger struggle than finding enough funding or maintaining discipline or enduring the toils of testing. . . . Even master teachers who love their work call this 'the most treacherous part of their jobs.'"[24] She also noted that while nearly all new teachers agreed that parent involvement was a priority at their school, "only 25% described their experience working with parents as 'very satisfying.'"[25]

Pogust related a story about a parent "who was actually banned from school property because she created such a turmoil in the school community. I truly understood," she wrote. "I've experienced parents hovering unannounced at my door early in the morning waiting to dump their issues. It was harassment, plain and simple. What a horrible way to begin the day, as that encounter sits with you." Although I would agree with elementary teacher Sherri Leeper, who urged new teachers to "try to let negative comments or reactions from parents roll off your back," I know from personal experience how hard it can be to keep a negative encounter with a parent from spoiling your mood, your day, or even your relationship with a student.

A professional development director observed, "This is the biggest hole in teacher prep courses. Parents are more and more educated and more and more involved, and we don't help new teachers learn how to talk to them. How do you handle the helicopter parent, how do you handle the ones who want to sit with their kids all day long, who want their kids in gifted or advanced placement classes? This is a public relations issue and new teachers are not prepared." (I would add that we are no better prepared for parents who are not particularly well educated, or for those of any background whose default relationship with the school is one of mistrust.)

Certainly, the topic of dealing with parents came up over and over in contributors' comments, particularly with regard to feeling unprepared for what they encountered when they started working with young people. "I wish someone had told me that I wouldn't get the parental support I thought I'd get," wrote Linda Keegan. "A lot of criticism from parents was unexpected." A veteran third-grade teacher noted, "I would have liked more training in good ways to deal with parents of varying degrees of involvement, from those you never meet to overbearing parents who think they can waste forty-five minutes of your time over something as silly as the student's lunch, or who try to control how you do things in the classroom." And several administrators weighed in as well, listing "handling and communicating with difficult parents" among the top areas in which beginning teachers are the least prepared and need the most help.

Like it or not, parents are a dominant part of the lives of your students, and they are invariably going to be a part of your professional life as well. Your interactions with parents are as implicit a part of your job as are presenting a lesson, evaluating students' progress, or taking attendance. How you approach your students' parents will influence their attitudes toward and involvement with you, your class, and the school, but be aware that many parents harbor strong feelings that developed long before you walked into the building that, at least for starters, have nothing to do with you personally. "Most of our parents went to this school and a lot of them had bad experiences here," one middle school principal shared. "They don't think the teachers understand the kids or their families, or they think that we look down on them. So if you see parents here, they've usually got a pretty big chip on their shoulder."[26]

Building Bridges

It's not always easy to make decisions that are right for a student when you can anticipate resistance—or worse—from the parents. DeGennaro acknowledged that "sometimes you have to tell a child or a parent a truth they don't want to hear. Sometimes you have to make parents angry and hostile before you can move them, and their child, to a better place. Knowing when to fight the difficult battles is important," she maintained, adding that standing your ground for whatever is truly in the best interest of the student never gets any easier. "It is only palatable when after some time, you hear, 'Thank you for helping me see what was best for my child when I couldn't.' That makes it all worth it. You know then that you *are* a professional and that you have won the respect of your constituents by applying the pedagogy of good teaching even when it isn't popular."

Even if everything is going well, you may be surprised by what Gibbs described as "suspicions born of class and race and personal experience."[27] One of my earliest experiences with a parent brought about a completely unexpected reaction. I called home to report that the student had a big breakthrough in math and was doing really well. I thought the parent would be happy to hear about her son's progress, so imagine my surprise when she replied, "Yeah? What do you want?" She simply stopped hearing me once she realized it was a teacher calling about her son.

We don't have to look far to explain this defensiveness. Too often, interactions with parents are limited to brief hellos on open-house night or requests for their signatures on report cards. (And the older the student is, the scarcer the parents—and parent-involvement programs—tend to be.[28]) How often do parents and teachers silently coexist, knowing one will hear from the other as soon as something is wrong? For parents who are only contacted by someone at school when there is a problem, it's understandable that it might never occur to them that a teacher would be calling to share something positive. Certainly, this was a first for many of the parents I called or contacted with good reports. And not surprisingly, parents are likely to be defensive if they feel that the teacher is talking down to them or criticizing their parenting, or if the teacher tries to come across as caring more about the child than the parents themselves do.

From the parents' perspective, I want to suggest another obstacle, and it's one that is fairly common in teachers' communications with parents. I'm talking about the tendency to report a problem with the expectation that it is up to the parent to correct the situation. Now, we certainly want to keep parents informed, especially in the case of an incident involving their child or an emerging pattern that could have a negative impact on the student's grades, promotion, or graduation. (Few parents appreciate learning about an ongoing problem only after report cards come out, when some significant intervention becomes necessary, or when failure or expulsion, for example, is imminent. These "surprises" reflect a significant failure of communication and lack of professionalism on our part as educators, and it's something you never want to have to explain.) But contacting parents to keep them in the loop is quite different from calling in the hope that the parent will motivate, much less punish, the child or otherwise fix the problem.[29] You are more likely to build positive relationships with parents when you do not depend on them to keep order in your class, engage their children in your instruction, get their children's homework in on time, or otherwise do their children's jobs—or yours. "Good schooling must come before parental support," admonished columnist Jay Matthews, "not the other way around."[30]

Teachers who would characterize the majority of their encounters with parents in negative terms—from indifferent to hostile—may try to avoid dealing with parents at all. But there are some very good reasons to take the exact opposite approach, actively building relationships with parents at all grade levels and encouraging their involvement in their children's learning and in their participation in the school as well. "Parents can be a really big help to you as a teacher," wrote one elementary teacher. Indeed, I often gained insight about what motivated students or what had worked (or had been problems) for other teachers from conversations with their parents. Research strongly supports parental involvement as well, pointing to benefits that include fewer behavioral problems, better academic performance (higher grades and test scores), higher graduation rates, better school attendance, increased motivation, lower rates of suspension, decreased use of drugs and alcohol, and fewer instances of violent behavior when compared to schools with low rates of parent involvement.[31] Even if you're working with kids whose parents have typically avoided contact with the school, or students whose parents have a history of antagonistic relationships with their kids' teachers, there are things you can do to turn these traditions around.[32]

Think about what parents want. In general, if parents see their children coming home excited about what they're doing in school, if they see their children being successfully challenged and making progress, if they perceive that their children are safe (physically, emotionally, socially, and academically), and perhaps most important, if they believe that you genuinely care about their children, the parents are far less likely to meddle, complain, or dispute your recommendations. Once again, we see the benefits of win-win objectives. "When children succeed, their gratified families will be with them all the way," concluded Matthews.[33] In other words, parents win when kids win, and by extension, teachers win as well.

Let's start with the belief that parents have a right to be informed on a regular basis of their children's progress, performance, achievement, and behavior in school, and that they have a right to inquire about the instruction and accommodations provided for their children. Granted, some parents will be less involved than others, but even in the case of parents you never hear from or see, assume that with few exceptions, parents are very much interested in their children's school lives and generally hold academically high aspirations for them. This statement holds true for parents of all social and economic levels, including parents of children often identified as educationally disadvantaged.[34] Mayrose cautioned against assuming that students from low-income families don't care or that their parents don't care. "Often they have the basic needs of food, shelter, and clothing to worry about. Parents often are unsure how to help their kids with school and intimidated to come into the school for a variety of reasons."

The Community: A Hands-On Approach

Many contributors suggested that new teachers, including teachers new to a school or district, get to know the community. This is especially important if your upbringing and experience are culturally and economically different from that of your students or if you work in an unfamiliar area that is culturally and economically diverse. Some teacher-preparation organizations recognize that it is not fair to simply train teachers in "how to teach a certain subject and then send them out," as education professor Alberto Bursztyn related. "Teachers have to understand the community in which they will be working."[35] Assistant professor Wayne Reed (and a colleague of Bursztyn) noted that several of the courses in their program "now include community-based assignments—that is, assignments that help students in the School of Education develop their community knowledge," including one program designed "to help teachers develop their practice in the context of the social and cultural framework of the neighborhood they serve."[36] But not all teachers obtain positions in the area in or near where they trained, and you may find yourself in a neighborhood that is very different from where you did your preservice work. Mayrose suggested getting a map of your district and taking a driving tour of the area within your school's zoning boundaries. She described how seeing some of her students' homes and neighborhoods "was a very eye-opening experience." Whenever practical, seeing where your students live, or where their parents work or shop, can give you a much better sense of the community.[37]

Home visits, when they were possible, gave me a much broader sense of the students with whom I was working and helped me connect with parents in surroundings that were familiar and comfortable for them. Many parents appreciate the time and effort that goes into home visitations and may actually feel more comfortable talking to teachers or asking questions in meetings on their own turf. However, you may encounter some parents who feel that home visits are intrusive and patronizing. While these meetings can help build communication, trust, and parent involvement, going to a child's home requires a great deal of openness and sensitivity. Be aware that, whatever your background, you are certain to have students who come from cultural or religious traditions, family arrangements, or standards of living that are different from those most familiar to you.

I've known teachers who clearly resented the fact that some of their students had bigger allowances than they did or that their students were provided with housing or health care. These feelings are hard to hide. Parent involvement starts with an enormous amount of trust, acceptance, and respect. And while you may encounter parents who come to you with those feelings, assume that the relationships begin with what *you* bring to the equation. If there is any chance that you might be perceived as judgmental, condescending, or shocked (whether or not you actually are), or if a home visit could increase tension between you and the parents (or you and the student), please look at other options, including the possibility of meeting on more neutral territory like a neighborhood coffee shop, eatery, or park.[38]

Talk to veterans about their experiences, and ask the office for any policies or programs already in place. Some schools and districts require home visits early in the school year, especially in the primary grades, and some even offer a stipend for the time teachers invest in this practice. However, others discourage home visitations because of safety or liability issues or reserve the practice for social workers, school resource officers, or home-school liaisons. If you visit a student's home, arrange the time well in advance. Schedule your visit during school or daylight hours, and if possible, plan to go with another person, such as a team teacher, the counselor, a translator, or a paraprofessional. Let the school know where you are going and when you expect to return. Have your school identification with you, although not necessarily immediately visible. (These considerations would also apply to a driving tour of some neighborhoods.)

Connecting With Parents

More commonly, face-to-face contact will occur at school during an open house, a scheduled conference, or a drop-in visit by the parent.[39] There are clear advantages to meeting parents in your classroom, as you have access to records and work samples and can share things you are doing in your room. Many parents enjoy having a visual context for what their children talk about at home, although some feel a little overwhelmed, if not a bit intimidated, meeting teachers in school. (You can help avoid unequal power implications by sitting side-by-side with the parents, at a table or in same-sized chairs or desks, rather than across from them at your desk.) Try to meet as many parents as possible early in the year in an open house or a meeting designed around a general discussion of the curriculum for your class or grade level (during which you can mention any strengths or interests you've noticed in their children). "Start on a positive note," advised author Alain Jehlen, who quoted Jerry Newberry, the head of the NEA Health Information Network, as stating, "Many parents come to a conference highly defensive. Year after year, for 12 or 24 conferences, maybe all they've heard has been bad news. You have to be different: 'I'm here to help your child be successful.'"[40] Ruthann Young-Cookson agreed. "Always have something positive to say about their child. Never end a conversation with parents on a negative note."

If you want to build a foundation of trust, openness, and support with parents, probably the most effective strategy involves regular, positive contact—and this goes for every child, not just the good ones. (If you're working with multiple classes, start with the most challenging.) There are many ways to connect with parents, including electronic options that did not exist until relatively recently. Between or before face-to-face meetings, you can get a lot of mileage with phone calls, e-mails, notes, or reports. Even teachers with large or multiple classes have found efficient ways to maintain contact with families on a regular basis through these avenues. I was amazed at the impact a simple "good note" could have, even with my older middle school kids, and when I started sending weekly reports, I finally had the sense, with the majority of the families, that we were in an actual partnership on behalf of their children's education.[41] Simply too much happens between report card periods to allow parent-teacher contacts to depend entirely on quarterly grades. Even a little effort can go a long way, and it really did not take much to turn around the caution and tentativeness I first experienced.

Use different strategies for different types of information. Newsletters—hard copies, or online versions if the majority of your families have computers and Internet access—are great for sharing information about activities, projects, events, topics, or units involving your students. It's also a great place for offering resources, ideas, and links the family can use to enhance the child's learning or to build parenting skills. One second-grade teacher shared, "I started writing a newsletter every week for the parents to keep them informed. This made them happy when they knew what their kids were doing and it kept them off my back." If your school has a Web site, find out how you can create your own pages to display students' work, reports about what your classes are doing, important dates and upcoming events, or helpful links for parents.[42] Parent involvement tends to improve with contact and quality information. In addition, your visibility and involvement at school activities that parents attend can up your approval rating, whether they see you at plays, games, concerts, or parent-teacher organization meetings.

For more personal and student-specific feedback, consider phone contact, e-mails, text messages, or brief handwritten notes. Young-Cookson suggested phoning parents in the first few days of school to establish a positive rapport. And while this practice may be less common in the upper grades, many contributors working with older students found these contacts worthwhile. "Communication with home, I feel, is number one to a student doing well in the class," wrote one high school English teacher who sees early contact as a way to create win-win situations with parents. "I suggest new teachers connect with the home within the first two weeks. I call them all and send a positive note within that time frame," she wrote. "They love to hear good things about their child [at the] beginning of school." (Phone conferences can also help avert blowups if some conflict occurs between you and a student or between a student and a classmate. Getting your version to the parent before the child does can often prevent serious miscommunications or the anxiety of a parent wondering "why didn't the teacher ever call me about that?")

Regardless of how you make contact, you really don't want your first communication or encounter to be about a problem concerning their child. Keep in mind the primary goal of building positive involvement and support, which develops through the relationships you create, connecting so you can work together in the best interests of the child. Think about the things that make people feel welcome and safe when they're meeting with someone in authority—and yes, you are an authority in their child's life. You want to exhibit the confidence that will invite parents to respect this authority, along with the caring, openness, and capability to confirm that their faith in you is well placed. This is especially important when dealing with angry parents or those whose experiences with their children's teachers have been less than optimal. White, Harvey, and Kemper recommended, "Your body language needs to demonstrate that you are professional, confident, and willing to listen but intolerant of abuse."[43] In other words, as Sandy Goldman advised, "Try to act like you aren't a first-year teacher with the parents."

Protecting Yourself

Decide ahead of time on the boundaries you'll need—not only to take care of yourself at home and respect the needs of the people who live with you but to present the kind of voice, tone, and energy you'll want to recruit any time you communicate with a parent. I've known teachers who had separate e-mail accounts or cell phones exclusively for school use (which they only checked or answered during specific times) and others who considered themselves on call day and night. Some teachers feel quite comfortable giving out their private contact information. Nonetheless, Wyatt and White cautioned, "In a world where technology makes everyone more vulnerable, you may want to consider making calls to parents from school telephones rather than your cell or land line."[44] If you suspect harassment, or think you'll sound inconvenienced or annoyed getting a call from a parent during off hours, screen your calls and if necessary, pull the plug. You are entitled to some recharge time and the occasional distance from work, and parents are entitled to be heard—at a time that works for you. Unless your school has a policy insisting that you take a call from any parent at any time, if you're not in a space where you can be a respectful and receptive listener, you're not likely to handle the call as positively or patiently as you'd like. Let the call go to voice mail and respond at a more convenient time. Finally, you might not want to take potentially upsetting calls right before dinner or bed, or when you won't be able to resolve the problem until you get back to school the next day or after the weekend.

Once again, this is where doing your homework can really pay off. The time you invest in regularly connecting with parents *before* there is a problem will give you a foundation of support and understanding that will very likely generate respect for your time, including your time away from school. These proactive efforts will perhaps pay the greatest benefits when you need to contact parents about a negative pattern or behavior you observe or an incident involving the child. Young-Cookson noted that prior communications to touch base and share information tend to make parents more receptive if you ever need to call on problematic behaviors or poor academic performance. "Never wait until a problem arises to make first contact," she reminded.

Here, too, a paper trail will help. Any time you do need to discuss a problem, the better you can document whatever is going on, the more support you're likely to receive for decisions and recommendations you make (and the better protected you are in case the parent is not as receptive as you might like). "Document everything," wrote one elementary teacher. "Parents need to know if something is happening in the classroom, whether good or bad, so that they aren't shocked when a report card comes home with a failing grade or a negative comment about behavior or any skill. Documentation also covers your butt if something were to happen, or if questions are raised." Jehlen likewise commented, "The solution is concrete evidence."[45]

Also document your contacts with parents, including attempted contacts, missed meetings or no-shows, and any follow-up efforts you've made. Date each record, whether written or recorded, and note the type of the contact (for example, phone call, home visit, note, scheduled conference, or drop-in), who initiated the contact, and the purpose of the contact. Keep copies of letters or notes sent home, as well as e-mails sent and received. Include detailed notes or recordings from meetings, descriptions of incidents, plans for follow-up, or outcomes of contacts. You'll rarely ever regret keeping good records, but you are likely to wish you had if you don't.

In face-to-face meetings, pay attention to subtle nonverbal cues you may be broadcasting. White and colleagues recommended an open, pleasant, and relaxed facial expression. "Make steady eye contact with those who are speaking, even if they are assaulting you. Looking down, to the side, or over their heads suggests that you are guilty, disinterested, or arrogant. People read frowns as disagreement or disapproval."[46] As much as possible, mirror their body posture during this process.

Teachers who have successfully navigated encounters with angry parents recommended giving them a chance to vent. When they slow down, ask them what else is bothering them, they suggested. Try to exhaust their list of complaints. One high school teacher with prior experience in customer service learned to resist the urge to interrupt. "If you cut somebody off in the middle of a rant, they just start over again," she said. (This applies to students, as well, she noted.) White and friends concurred. "Resist the temptation to argue with the speakers or to return the attack with one of your own. Let them vent even if it becomes redundant," they suggested.

Also, consider the value of validating the parents' feelings, even if their concerns are not accurate or reasonable. Countering with a genuinely compassionate and reassuring response (for example, "I can understand your concern," "That's quite disconcerting," or "I can see how that would have upset you.") not only relays your concern for them and your respect for their feelings, but can also defuse some of the stress and upset that may have been festering for a while. White and coauthors suggested that you "listen and respond briefly to correct any misinformation when they are finished. At the end, share your next steps to consider their concerns."[47]

Many contributors mentioned taking notes during conferences, even if you use a voice or video recorder. "Taking notes during the speeches can help you to get through the attacks, stay more objective, and have a record of ideas to follow up on after the meeting," wrote White et al. "It also lets them know that you are taking their ideas seriously."[48] You may want to include another colleague to mediate or help you stay objective, particularly if the parent does not seem to calm down or if you feel threatened in any way.

Tune in to your own emotional state. Avoid the temptation to argue, become defensive, or raise your voice. "Don't talk to a parent—or write—when you're mad," wrote Jehlen, also citing high school English teacher Linda Robb, who advised, "Never ever reply immediately to an angry e-mail. . . . Wait. Do not delay more than 24 hours, but give it time. And then call them instead of writing an answer."[49]

A couple other courtesies to consider: Whenever possible, avoid contacting parents at work, during dinner hours, or after nine o'clock unless you've been advised beforehand that doing so will not be invasive or disruptive. Keep conversations short, professional, and to the point. Avoid discussing other teachers, students, or families, unrelated incidents, or details of your personal life. Likewise, be careful about bringing up your feelings about school policies or expressing personal opinions on other hot-button topics. Be on time for meetings and return calls promptly. And be sure to follow up on any promises you make at the time of your meeting or conversation.

In any conversation with parents, maintain your professionalism. "Remember, no matter how friendly you become with parents, they are *not* your friends," advised Goldman. "You need to remain professional yet friendly with them." Even if discussing a problem or conflict, do your best to keep it positive, emphasizing the child's strengths, skills, and interests, and your commitment to a mutually supportive effort to enhance the child's development and growth. And be prepared for the fact that even parents who are familiar with the concept of win-win in a business context may not think to apply the same thinking when it comes to their children. Instructional support teacher Jamie Kunkle noted that "you have to educate the parents as well as the children" and has found that "parent education is much more difficult." However, simply coming to the table with the intention to work toward win-win solutions in the best interest of the child can eventually break through a great deal of all-or-nothing thinking, as well as a parent's need to be right, affix blame, or win at someone else's expense.

Assume that the parents want to trust you and that they all want their children to have successful and enjoyable experiences with you. Frascona commented, "You are some parents' only hope." She advised looking parents in the eye and reassuring them, offering stories or comments about their children "that show you know and care about them." While you never want to promise something you can't or won't deliver, commit to reasonable, win-win solutions and do your best to end every contact on a positive note.

Benefits of Weekly Progress Reports

- Weekly progress reports assess, on a regular basis, student behaviors that affect learning. They provide feedback that reinforces student behavior and stresses the importance of these behaviors to a student's success in school.[50]
- Progress reports help break the pattern of negative contacts with parents as well as perceptions of teacher-parent contacts as punitive or threatening. They do not require or request intervention from the parent.
- Reports provide ongoing documentation that can protect you in the event of learning or behavior problems, particularly those requiring a referral or intervention. They can help you avoid being placed in the embarrassing situation of having to explain to a parent who wants to know, "Why didn't you tell me before this?"
- Reports can reflect progress in academic performance, behavior, and social and emotional development. They acknowledge small increments of growth and can alert parents to weakness or patterns that may have an impact on their children's learning.
- Weekly contacts assure parents and students of your commitment to the students' success, as well as your commitment to regularly including parents in their children's behavior and progress at school.

ACTIVITY

With regard to becoming an accepted member of your school's adult community, respond to the following questions:

1. What does "fitting in" look like at your school?

   a. In what ways are your personality and energy a good match?

   b. Where do you feel the greatest mismatch or discrepancy?

2. What do you think will be most appreciated about what you bring to your building?

3. What do you think you'll most need to tone down—or turn off (at least initially)?

4. What kind of behaviors or attributes do you believe are expected of you to gain acceptance as a member of your school staff?

5. Have you experienced or witnessed any expectations for you to participate in behaviors you would consider destructive or toxic? How can you avoid getting drawn into these patterns?

6. Identify any steps you intend to take to become a "well-respected and cooperative colleague."

ACTIVITY

For the following activity, consider members of the adult community in your school who could play a valuable role on your support team:

1. In the first column, identify individuals in each category (if possible or available) that you believe would be able to help you in some way. Note that person's availability or schedule.
2. In the second column, identify ways you believe that person could help you. Consider the need for resources and materials; procedural help (how to get things done or acquired); information about students, families, or the community; information about the district policies and priorities; emotional support; or other needs you may have.
3. In the third column, identify the attributes, characteristics, or personal qualities that suggest that this person would be a good member of your support team.

	Name(s) and Availability	Help, Resources, Support, or Information That May Be Available	Attributes or Qualities That Would Make This Person a Good Match for You
District-level support person			
On-site administrator			
Mentor (assigned or selected)			
Other teachers on staff			
Specialists			
Paraprofessionals			
Classified staff			
University support			
Online support			
Other			

ACTIVITY

The following questions look at considerations for working successfully with your principal. (You can also do this activity to explore these considerations with regard to a district-level administrator, your supervisor or mentor, department chair, or any other person who has some authority over you.)

1. Do some teachers seem to get more support (or space) than others? How would you explain this discrepancy?

2. What would you say your principal's greatest priorities or goals for the school are?

3. Where do you get (or think you'll get) the most support?

4. What bugs your principal the most?

    a. What kinds of things are likely to make you a target?

    b. Where do you get (or think you'll get) the greatest resistance, criticism, or opposition?

5. What is the best way to give information to your principal (for example, in a formal meeting, in a handwritten memo, in an e-mail, in a phone call, or in a casual conversation in the hall)?

6. What type of information does your principal want most (for example, extensive information with facts, feelings, and specific details or general information and copies of only important things that go home)?

ACTIVITY

Answer the following with regard to your preparations for a substitute teacher:

1. Describe plans and materials you will need for a substitute. How are these plans different or separate from your regular plans?

2. Which of your routines would you like the sub to carry out? What provisions do you need to make to ensure that these routines continue smoothly in your absence?

3. Which parts of your instructional program do you not intend to assign to a sub? What materials, routines, and plans do you need to provide in their places?

4. Where do you plan to store the sub folder and related materials? Who will know where these materials will be kept?

5. How will you prepare your students for a substitute?

ACTIVITY

Answer these questions in reference to working with parents:

1. How would you characterize the majority of contacts you have had with parents so far?

2. What are your primary ways of communicating with parents about programs, activities, events, curriculum, or information about your class in general (for example, phone calls, home visits, in-school conferences, notes about individual students, newsletters, or Web sites)?

    a. How would you characterize the parents' response to these communications?

    b. In what ways have these communications encouraged or improved parent involvement?

    c. What are your intentions for continuing, improving, or refining your efforts to build parent involvement through these avenues?

3. Using the same examples of means of contact mentioned in Question 2, what are your primary ways of communicating with parents when their children are doing well?

    a. How often do you contact parents about positive student behavior?

    b. How many of your students have had their parents receive positive contacts?

c. How would you characterize the parents' response to these communications?

d. In what ways have these communications encouraged or improved parent involvement?

e. What are your intentions for continuing, improving, or refining your efforts to build parent involvement through these avenues?

4. Using the same examples of means of contact mentioned in Question 2, what are your primary ways of communicating with parents when their children are having a problem (behavioral, social, academic, or other)?

a. How many of these students have had their parents receive positive contacts before you needed to contact them about a problem or concern?

b. What percentage of your total contacts with parents would these positive contacts represent?

c. To what degree have you been able to resist the temptation to ask parents to "talk to the student" about the problem or otherwise intervene on your behalf?

d. How would you characterize the parents' response to these communications?

e. What effect have these communications had on the level or quality of parent involvement?

f. What are your intentions for continuing, improving, or refining your efforts to inform parents about problems or incidents?

5. If you were to post a note on your refrigerator with a reminder of the top three to five behaviors you want to use to build positive relationships with parents, what would you include?

6. If you were to post a note on your refrigerator with a reminder of the top three to five behaviors you want to *avoid* to build positive relationships with parents, what would you include?

NOTES

1. Quoted in DeLuca (1999, p. 90).

2. I agree and have come to appreciate these connections even more over time. I live two thousand miles from most of the people with whom I started teaching, yet the affection and history we share speaks to the bond we forged nearly four decades ago.

3. Fogarty (2007, p. 1).

4. Urban (2002, para. 3).

5. Adapted from Bluestein (2002), *The Beauty of Losing Control*. What initially attracted me to this teacher was the fact that she seemed to be getting results. Her kids were quiet and busy, and I equated that appearance with successful teaching. But it turned out that some of the strategies this teacher used to *get* her kids to be quiet and on task involved teaching behaviors with which I was not remotely comfortable, but which I initially assumed I needed to adopt. I was wrong and have spent the time since looking for more positive win-win options, techniques I did not realize existed at the time. I have also learned that *quiet* is seriously overrated and, as far as appearing to be on task is concerned, that being busy is not the same as being engaged—or learning.

6. Fogarty (2007, p. 2).

7. All qualities listed here were adapted from a more generic article I wrote titled "Secrets of Successful Mentorship" (Bluestein, 2003c).

8. Adapted from Bluestein (2003c).

9. The fact that my original adviser (the person whose work had attracted me to the program in the first place) never spoke to me after I started working with the other individual reaffirmed my suspicion that this person was not a good match for me at this stage of my program or in this capacity. Fortunately, he was not in a position to impede my progress, which is not always the case, although that may be an issue worth considering. If possible, find someone higher up the food chain to watch your back if you need to terminate a relationship with someone who becomes—or turns out to be—toxic for you.

10. Adapted from Bluestein (2003c).

11. Although the term *triangulating* appears in various contexts from mathematics to psychology (with several interpretations in the latter field), I'm referring to the unprofessional and socially destructive practice of getting in the middle of a conflict by going to a third party or going behind the back of the person to whom an issue needs to be addressed instead of attempting to resolve a conflict or get what we want more directly and assertively.

12. Certain topics can provoke heated exchanges and bad feelings. Until you have a sense of the pulse of the campus and the political inclinations of your colleagues, be cautious about some of the topics you broach or opinions you share. By all means, advocate for the rights, needs, and safety of a student, but when it comes to potentially incendiary topics (including sports in some places), spend some time listening and observing to get a sense of the people you're working with and the kinds of things that normally come up in conversation.

13. Thanks to Jill Snyderman for this reminder.

14. Bluestein (2001, p. 361). In one report, educator Wayne K. Hoy (n.d.) referenced a study in which the very definition of school climate was described "in terms of educators' perceptions of the leadership behavior of the principal and interactions among teachers" (para. 3). (Hoy described *climate* as "a general term that refers to the feel, atmosphere, tone, ideology, or milieu of a school," or the personality of a school.) While I would attribute the impact of a wider variety of factors to the climate of a school—including priorities as expressed in instructional or discipline policies, the

needs and demands of the community, the availability of support for biological and neurological requirements, the importance placed on students' social and emotional development, and aspects of the physical environment from the color of the paint to the types of lighting—there's no question as to how crucial the impact of a principal's skills (or lack of skills) can be. This correlation goes back a long way. A study cited in a 1977 resource found that the principal's behavior affects the quality of school climate and classroom communications—for better or worse. Aspy and Roebuck (1977, pp. 39–41). Similarly, there is a trickle-down effect present in the relationship between the way principals treat staff and the way staff treat students. Rogers and Frieberg (1994, p. 5).

15. Quoted in Bluestein (2001, p. 350–351). Not unlike the potentially long-term destructive impact of a negative, hurtful teacher, I've met teachers still bitter and shaken, even years after working with a negative, hurtful administrator. Not surprisingly, conflict with or lack of support from administrators is often cited as a reason for teachers requesting transfers to other schools, moving to different districts, or leaving the profession. "Employees don't leave their job or company," noted Wayne Hochwarter, an associate professor of management. "They leave their boss." Quoted in Barry Ray (2004, para. 2).

16. Try to avoid judgments and subjective descriptions. "The student suddenly started yelling and threw a pencil and book at the wall" generally works better than "The student just went crazy."

17. From Bluestein (2001). "While ideally, all teachers would see the logic and ultimately self-protective value in clearing personal policies and procedures with the office early in the game—if only to help avoid surprises down the road—being able to do so assumes that teachers and administrators see themselves as being on the same side of the fence, committed to finding equitable solutions, and that teachers feel safe opening up to their principals. But in many settings, teachers believe that any attempt to secure support beforehand could come across as an admission of weakness, insecurity, or incompetence and leave them vulnerable to administrative sanctions, criticisms, restrictions, or worse. It's not surprising, then, that many teachers keep themselves as isolated as possible. 'It's easier to beg forgiveness than ask permission,' came up as a personal philosophy more times than I could count" (p. 353).

18. National Resource Center on AD/HD (n.d.); also National Dissemination Center for Children With Disabilities (n.d.); U.S. Department of Education (2004). IDEA identifies fourteen categories under which a child could qualify as one with a disability, particularly if the student's educational performance is adversely affected due to the disability. Support for providing appropriate, individualized instructional services in the least restrictive environment is assured under this law.

19. Schwengel (n.d., para. 2).

20. I cannot overemphasize the importance of leaving good plans and backup activities for a sub, and I speak from firsthand experience. My first substitute job was in a sixth-grade classroom, and the only plans (referring to the more familiar "lesson plans" a sub would normally expect) left for the entire day was a note to "discuss gerunds." I'm not kidding. No materials, no notes, nothing. Although I knew enough to not go in empty-handed, by the end of the day, I had gone through an entire suitcase full of materials I had brought with me—which I'm sure cost far more than what I earned for the day's work. This is *not* how you want a sub to experience your classroom. At the risk of never being hired in the district, I refused to work at that school ever again.

21. Check to see whether your district already has material you can leave for a substitute teacher. Likewise, there are a number of commercially prepared substitute instructions or substitute kits available online and through teacher supply stores. Chances are good, however, that you will need to customize any prepared materials to match the needs of your students, routines, and specific planning requirements.

22. Schwengel (n.d.) mentioned parking, for example, particularly if you're in an environment where street-cleaning schedules would result in the sub getting a ticket.

23. I use the term *parent* to refer to parents, stepparents, grandparents, or any other primary caregivers.

24. Gibbs (2005, p. 42).

25. Gibbs (2005, p. 44).

26. When I started at my last classroom position, I was hired to take over for a beloved institution of a teacher who had retired right before Thanksgiving break. Starting in the middle of a semester is never easy, and in this case, I had some pretty big shoes to fill. I spent the entire year fighting comparisons to the teacher who had left and trying to win over parents who frankly resented the fact that this woman had been replaced. New teachers will always have to make their bones, but if you find yourself in a similar situation, it may take a little more time, faith, work, and excellence to be accepted by staff and community.

27. Gibbs (2005, p. 43).

28. "Parent Involvement in Schools" (n.d.); also Michigan Department of Education (n.d.b), which claimed: "School activities to develop and maintain partnerships with families decline with each grade level, and drop dramatically at the transition to middle grades." In addition, Wyatt and White (2007) noted that "high school teachers complain that the evening is a waste of time: only a handful of parents attend, and these are the parents of the students who already perform at high levels" (p. 119).

29. If we value the idea of teaching students responsibility, it will never be appropriate to call a parent with this expectation. The frequency with which this pattern occurs in home-school relationships probably accounts for much of the antagonism both parents and teachers report. You can make your intentions clear by stating up front that you don't need or expect the parent to do or say anything, that you're calling only to keep the parent up to date. Then you can ask for any ideas that have worked in the past and share how you are handling or planning to handle the issue. Offer to follow up in a day or two.

30. Matthews (2009, para. 7).

31. "Parent Involvement in Schools" (n.d.); also Michigan Department of Education. (n.d.b).

32. Research also points to three major factors in parental involvement in the education of their children, including the parents' beliefs about what is important, necessary, and permissible for them to do with and on behalf of their children; the extent to which they believe that they can positively impact their children's education; and their perceptions that their children and school want them to be involved (Michigan Department of Education, n.d.b). These are factors you can influence through the attitudes, information, and invitations you offer in your interactions with parents.

33. Matthews (2009).

34. Champagne and Goldman (1972). The term *educationally disadvantaged* typically refers to factors such as low family income or growing up in neighborhoods with low graduation rates. Scoring below the 40th percentile is also included in some definitions, as well as any factors that might contribute to children struggling in school or being less likely to achieve than children without similar disadvantages. Although a broad definition (which I would favor) would include children whose learning style or modality profiles do not fit traditional teaching methods, the term typically reflects an economic emphasis.

35. Quoted in Evelyn (2007, p. 23).

36. Quoted in Evelyn (2007, p. 23).

37. I once worked with teachers in a district that had five schools spread out across 180 miles from one end to the other and have been in others that required students to commute close to two hours each way, so taking a driving tour of your students' neighborhoods could, in some

situations, clearly present special challenges. As with any of the suggestions in this book, try the ones that are feasible in terms of your placement, resources, and personality.

38. Bluestein (1989); also Francis (2000); "Teacher Home Visits: Discussion Topics" (2009); input from colleagues and contributors.

39. Several contributors mentioned the benefits of encouraging parent visits and setting up opportunities for parents who have the availability and inclination to volunteer as helpers in the classroom. (Sandy Goldman, however, suggested that the parents help *outside* of the classroom to avoid any misunderstanding or misinterpretation of your behavior, which will be scrutinized when parents observe you working with children.) Again, check with your school about existing programs and policies.

40. Jehlen (2008, p. 30).

41. These notes included a simple checklist of four or five behaviors I wanted the students to exhibit, behaviors that would improve the climate of the classroom and their performance in school. Items varied by class and grade level and changed as students mastered individual skills. Each behavior was stated positively, with the majority identifying skills most of the students exhibited most of the time: "Comes to class prepared." "Completes assignments." "Says 'please' and 'thank you.'" My goal was to send notes home every week with as many skills checked off as possible. These notes only took a few minutes to complete, but they had a surprisingly positive impact on the kids' behavior and always seemed to get back to the parents. I generally did not require that parents sign these notes, yet many came back with the parent's notes of appreciation for my time and care.

42. Consider your district's privacy restrictions before displaying work with students' names, and be sure that all students have a chance to see their work included at various times. If your school does not have a site, or has a site that is not set up to enable individual teachers to create pages, talk to someone at your district about restrictions and requirements for setting up your own site (including privacy, security, and restricted access). Encourage your students to create content, but screen anything that would be included and do the upload yourself once you've vetted what they have created.

43. White et al. (2007, p. 17).

44. Wyatt and White (2007, p. 119).

45. Jehlen (2008, p. 30).

46. White et al. (2007, p. 17).

47. White et al. (2007, p. 17).

48. White et al. (2007, p. 17).

49. Jehlen (2008, p. 30).

50. Objective, observable behaviors are easiest to evaluate and are most effective as reinforcers when stated positively.

PART III
Students

Love the kids you teach. If you don't love them, pray that you can find something about them to love. . . . If they don't feel safe, it will be hard for them to learn anything except fear.

Joani Heavey, music teacher

Show me a school where instructional leaders constantly examine the school's culture and work to transform it into one hospitable to sustained human learning, and I'll show you students who do just fine on those standardized tests.

Roland Barth, education professor[1]

It is easier to build strong children than to repair broken men.

Fredrick Douglas, abolitionist[2]

The things that matter most should never be at the mercy of the things that matter least.

Johann Wolfgang van Goethe, writer and philosopher

When I first started presenting inservice programs and seminars, I created a brochure listing topics I could address. Among several literacy and instructional programs was a presentation called "21st Century Discipline," which focused on strategies to teach students the self-management skills they'd need to function in the new millennium. Between my own training and the work I was doing with beginning teachers at the time, I was well aware of the need for practical and effective ideas in this area, but I really did not appreciate just how well the word *discipline* would market. Perhaps predictably, every call I received requested that particular program. The direction for my career thus charted, from that point on, just about every training and keynote presentation I've done for educators has focused on some aspect of the teacher-student relationship. Whether in a purely discipline-oriented context or one with a slant toward achievement, classroom management, emotionally safe schools, or something as specific as bullying or substance-abuse prevention, it always comes back to how well the students connect with the teacher (and by extension, with one another).

If you were to talk to the people who attend these presentations, you'd find that the majority are dedicated individuals who just want to spend their time teaching but, too often, find themselves occupied with student disruptions and disinterest. I know that some participants come looking for a magic answer to their "What do I do when . . ." questions or for suggestions for bigger and better punishments when their own negative consequences have little effect. Instead, I ask them to back up and look at the big picture, where the behavior of their students—and the way students interact with them, with one another, and with the assignments they give—happens in a bigger picture, that of relationships and the emotional climate of the classroom. I know this is frustrating for some, because frankly, it's more work to build relationships and restructure power dynamics than it is to, say, assign a detention or send a child down to the office. But everything that happens in a classroom happens within this frame of reference, including students' behavior, attitudes, commitment, and academic performance, and unless you want to spend your entire career nagging, chastising, punishing, and dealing with antagonistic student interactions, you'll want to consider the importance of encouraging positive and mutually respectful bonds with and among your kids.

"The quality of teacher-student relationships is the keystone for all other aspects of classroom management," wrote educational researcher Robert Marzano.[3] If your training emphasized this priority, you're already aware that relationships are "job one" for win-win teachers. Unfortunately, for many of us, the concept barely comes up in our training, if it is mentioned at all—and when this is the case, it shows. The emphasis on cognitive development certainly overrode any mention of affective needs in my own coursework, and any reference to issues of relationships and classroom climate lacked practical information I could have put to good use with my students. And be aware that even if you did have training in this area, the political agendas of a school district and the community often tend to marginalize the value of the affective elements in favor of more measurable outcomes. It can be a real challenge to keep our priorities straight in a culture where tradition often leans on clichéd nonsense like "I don't care if my students like me, as long as they respect me" and where the benefits of connectedness are obscured by the public's perception of teaching excellence as reported by test-score rankings in the Sunday paper. But positive relationships with students are essential to the survival of any teacher, and any quest for effective classroom and behavior-management strategies will always start right here.

NOTES

1. Barth (2002).
2. Quoted in Borba (2002).
3. Quoted in Michigan Department of Education (n.d.a, para. 2).

10

Make a
Connection

You are the best thing you have to offer them. They do not take a year of fifth grade from you. They take a year of you *for fifth grade.*

Chick Moorman, author and educator

What a shock it was, being so good at teaching until I actually started doing *it and then finding that so many assumptions were unfounded, so many tricks didn't work, and so many kids didn't care.*

First-year teacher, elementary

It isn't all about the subject. Sometimes, it rarely is about teaching a class. It is about assisting in the raising of a child.

Dave Friedli, high school principal

Talk to successful people in any field, and you're likely to find that they have one thing in common. At some point in their early lives, even if they grew up in difficult circumstances, they had a positive relationship with an understanding adult. Study after study shows that a "caring and supportive relationship with at least one person is a key protective factor [that] helps to inoculate kids against adversity and build resiliency."[1] An article on dropout prevention quoted author Bill Milliken regarding what kids need to be successful and stay in school. Once again, the list includes "a one-on-one relationship with a caring adult." Whether the adult is a parent, relative, coach, mentor, or representative from a spiritual or religious organization, "it all starts with relationships," he said.[2] Researcher Robert Blum agreed: "People connect with people before they connect with institutions."[3] Educator Roland Barth likewise commented, "The nature of the relationships of the adults who inhabit a school has more to do with the character of the school and the accomplishments of its students than any other factor."[4] The significance and potential impact of these connections is inestimable, and thankfully, many teachers intuitively accept the need to provide this kind of availability and support as a generic and unquestioned requirement of the job.

Too often, however, despite decades of research, affective considerations and things like connectedness still end up shoved behind curricular goals. "In general, schools put too much emphasis on cognitive ability when the social and emotional well-being of students also has a powerful effect on achievement," said researcher Christi Bergin.[5] A professional development director shared a familiar quote: "They don't care how much you know until they know how much you care," he said. "But you can't measure how much you care." I have seen evidence of these priorities any time I meet educators who describe their primary goals in terms of "covering content," "getting through the books," or "raising test scores."

When teachers contact me about how to deal with behavior problems or the indifference they see in their students, my first questions try to identify what drives these kids: "What do they like? What are they most passionate about?" In most instances, any response beyond a blank stare tends to simply reiterate the problem the teacher has with the student or elaborates the specifics of the student's misbehavior, neither of which answers the actual question. Author Rebecca Lynn Wilke advised, "Each student that enters your room is carrying an invisible backpack full of experiences, interesting data, language, strengths, weaknesses, cultural nuances, heritages, needs, and desires!"[6] Whether trying to prevent problems in the classroom or working to resolve one that exists, it's always a good idea to note the relevance of examining what these students bring to our classrooms—who they are, what's going on in their lives, and what matters most to them.

So here is some information about the value of connectedness (sometimes referred to as *attachment*), along with some ideas for collecting meaningful and relevant data. Because you can be a fantastic instructor with an inspiring grasp of technology, curricular design, and presentation, but if your students don't feel connected—or if they don't feel safe and trusting in the environment you share with them—your talents will be squandered, assuming you get to use them at all.

DISCONNECTED STUDENTS

We have a great deal of research reflecting a high correlation between teachers' ability to connect with students and positive outcomes ranging from increased learning to lower levels of disruptive behavior. "The extent to which schools create stable, caring, engaging, and welcoming environments is the extent to which all our kids will thrive," wrote Blum. Unfortunately, the apparent scarcity of such environments takes its toll on students' attitudes and behavior in school. "By the time they are in high school, as many as forty to sixty percent of all students—urban, suburban, and rural—are chronically disengaged from school. That disturbing number does not include the young people who have already dropped out," Blum's report concluded.[7] A 2001 report exploring differences between young people who were successfully navigating educational realities and those who were more at risk or disengaged determined that "the most important factors connecting young people to school were linked to relationships—friendships with other students and relationships with teachers that involved mutual respect and responsibility." Perhaps not surprisingly, among the "major concerns cited by young people who were disaffected by school were their relationships with teachers, the way teachers treated them, and teaching methods used." Specific complaints included the students' perception that the teachers did not listen, did not want to be there, or were "arrogant, too busy, not maintaining confidential comments, and in bad moods."[8] Columnist David Brooks wrote, "You ask a kid who has graduated from high school to list the teachers who mattered in his life, and he will reel off names. You ask a kid who dropped out, and he will not even understand the question. Relationships like that are beyond his experience."[9]

Several frontline people shared similar observations. Principal Kathi Walsh mentioned the influence of "our educational systems" on kids who are having a hard time in school, behaviorally and academically. Walsh suggested that these students "are labeled at-risk because they have not developed a meaningful, positive relationship with their teachers." She believes that "kids do not drop out of school because of alcoholic or drug-involved parents, serious illness at home . . . , or any other social discord. The reason kids drop out of schools is because we, the teachers, have not connected." School social worker Debra Sugar agreed: "Schools often fail to adequately fit the students who they are designed to serve. High dropout rates, student violence, behavior problems, student alienation, and substance abuse are all more likely to occur when children feel that they are not valued, that they don't fit in, that there is no place for them."[10]

I've seen students, including young children, go to great lengths to try to convince their teachers that they weren't good in particular subjects or even that they weren't capable of being successful in school in general. Because the brain interprets new experiences in the context of previous ones, students who have had positive, successful, challenging experiences in school will come to you with a set of beliefs and expectations—as well as the behaviors and attitudes driven by these beliefs and expectations—that are very different from those for whom school has represented failure, boredom, humiliation, or social rejection, for example. The significance of the brain's tendency to protect us when we feel threatened underscores the importance of creating an environment in which kids perceive safety and, ideally, the potential for success. In other words, for some students, the experiences in *your* class need to be different from the experiences they may have had in school up to this point—or from what they run into in their other classes, or at home—so that they do not feel the need to rely on the survival repertoire that may well be necessary elsewhere.

Walk down the hall of any school and listen. Feel the energy, tone, and intensity coming out of the rooms you pass, and note the effect these have on your body and mood. Whatever you are feeling out in the hallway, good or bad, it's a sure bet that the impact on kids in the classrooms is even stronger. These are the environments from which students exit happy to be in school, hungry for learning, and secure in their ability to succeed—or defiant, defeated, or numb and indifferent. Pay attention to the nature of your own interactions with your students. To what degree does your behavior with your students reflect your commitment to the primary importance of your relationship with them? (And if this hasn't been a priority for you, are you willing to make it one?) Where are your interpersonal strengths? What needs work? Do your students see you as an advocate? Do your interactions with them build connections or obstacles? Because sadly, not only do many teachers *not* make connecting a priority, but there is also research to indicate that many practice the types of interactions that "retard rather than facilitate learning."[11] Principal Gary Cardwell said, "If a teacher has no understanding of another's feelings, the teacher will most likely be ineffective. When empathy and compassion are present along with intelligence, training, knowledge of subject, creativity . . . the learning environment is enhanced."[12]

Be careful not to underestimate kids' power of perception. Students know who cares about them, and even young children can name the teachers who like kids—as well as those who do not. "You simply cannot have an attitude and keep it a secret," observed Mary Robinson Reynolds and Craig Reynolds. "If you don't like a child, you will not be able to work with that child successfully."[13] It's the children who don't feel valued or safe who tend to concoct the most elaborate defenses and safety nets. But don't for a minute doubt your ability to dislodge old, well-entrenched defenses, even if you only see these kids for forty-five minutes a week. (And by the way, at least one study showed that the number of beginning teachers at a school is *not* a factor in the school's capacity for improving the students' sense of being connected there.[14]) Of course, the longer students have been in school and the more negative experience they have had, the more dismissive or mistrusting they may be of your efforts, and the longer it may take to turn some of these attitudes around. Hang in there. Kids know authenticity and caring when they see it, and it often doesn't take much more than those qualities to get their attention. Even students with a history of chronically bad school experiences may find high levels of understanding, genuineness, and respect difficult to resist for long. I've known a number of fairly hardened young people who would do anything for the teachers they came to like.

Your success starts with where and who the students are when they walk into your classroom, and if you have any intention of starting where they are, it pays to find out what they know and love. "You have to reach them to teach them," observed retired administrator John MacBeth. "[And] it is hard to reach them if you can't keep them connected." Teacher Kim Wilson described how relationships with students can help you find out their interests and capture their attention. "Building strong relationships with students is the key to survival," she wrote. Elaine Anderson affirmed, "Academics cannot happen until you understand the world from which a child comes." Anna Barsanti recognized that in addition to teaching the curriculum, "it is the teacher's responsibility to know the context of each student so that the curriculum resonates with the child, if only a little, to hook him or her to learning."

But many students have a lot more than school on their plate, and their lives will typically include a variety of preoccupations beyond the requirements of your class. Indeed, many young people's lives are crammed with extracurricular activities, jobs, and family responsibilities. Some students are dealing with illness in the family or addiction problems (a family member's or their own), and others are caring for elderly relatives, younger siblings, or their own children. Anissa Emery observed that the students "who function the least well, according to our narrow academic standards, are often the ones who are working as hard as they can to simply keep body and soul together and get through the day."

And it's not just high school kids coping with competing interests, distractions, and life in general. Tuija Fagerlund shared the frustration of "trying to teach the third person singular or the use of the article to a bunch of kids who were all a flutter over some incident on the playground." And preschool teacher Anne Morgan observed, "Students enter the classroom with a huge variety of factors. They woke up late, they didn't eat breakfast, they fought with a sibling that morning, they are feeling sick, they don't know who is picking them up from school, they feel uncomfortable around certain students, and the list could go on and on. This realization has caused me to evaluate all the things I say and the way I act in order to be dependable for my students. I can't control what happens outside of school, but I can provide an environment that makes students feel safe, happy, and comfortable enough to share their thinking, their learning, and their life with me."

THE VALUE OF CONNECTEDNESS

To some extent, the necessity of positive relationships with students is so obvious and instinctive to the very nature of teaching that it's hard to imagine that anyone would object. But other priorities can distract teachers, too, and just in case you're concerned about when you'll actually get to all that curriculum you have to get through, let me assure you that these goals are not mutually exclusive. In fact, caring and respectful relationships with kids will very likely free up time you might otherwise spend dealing with resistance, indifference, and various other off-task behaviors so you can do just that. This isn't something to squeeze into an already overfull schedule. It's the foundation you build for the entire year. Or as Jo Ann Freiberg counseled, "Dealing with relationship issues is not just 'more stuff on your plate.' This *is* your plate."[15]

Your relationship with your students is the vehicle through which all other goals are achieved. "My biggest problem with beginning teachers almost always comes down to classroom management," said one principal. "And the ones who come in thinking that all they have to do is present what's in the book are the ones with the most management problems." Indeed, teachers with good interpersonal skills are high on most principals' wish lists. "The most important quality I look for in a new teacher is the ability to build trust with students," wrote district administrator David Steinberg. "When interviewing a teacher candidate I try to imagine the teacher in the classroom and I ask myself the question: Will students raise their hands and ask this teacher a question when they don't understand something? For students to take that risk, they have to feel that they have a relationship with the teacher built on respect and trust." Similarly, principal Mary Ellen Imbo looks for interpersonal skills "that will connect with the student. This connection, this caring attitude, motivates learners to learn." She asks teachers, "What do you do to make students successful?" and will disqualify candidates who respond with a strictly curricular answer.[16] In fact, in one article on what principals are looking for when they hire teachers, the majority focused on the teacher's ability to bond with kids. Middle school principal Steven Podd looks for what he calls "Kid Magnets," noting that "once a student really connects emotionally to the teacher, then the rest will follow."[17] And vice principal Paul McCarty stated that if a teacher has compassion for children, "the rest can be learned with time."[18]

Certainly, the opportunity to connect with young people is a driving force drawing many people to the job. "The underlying reasons I was attracted to teaching remain constant—to guide, to reach, to serve young people," said Barsanti. "It is crucial to explore beyond information, to reach the moral centre, to challenge all of the intelligences. To provide a place where students are willing to take risks, to recognize their gifts, to follow their passion." Teddy Meckstroth noted that the relationships he builds with his students "really make teaching worthwhile."

Do you see your purpose beyond the immediate and obvious instructional duties? Sherry Annee observed, "The most powerful and influential aspect of learning is the teacher-student relationship. Students will thrive in an environment where they are trusted, respected, empowered, and feel safe." Research, observation, and experience would agree. "Simply put, when we create more personalized educational environments, students respond and do better," Blum declared. "Teachers report and research confirms that connected students pay better attention, stay focused, are motivated to do more than required, and tend to have higher grades and test scores. . . . Whatever curriculum is in place will be more effective when students feel connected to school."[19]

Academic benefits aside, the arguments in favor of positive teacher-student relationships are pretty compelling. Freiberg reflected, "Research shows a strong association between what we're calling school connectedness and every risk factor you can imagine."[20] An article by columnist Eric Nagourney stated, "It is fairly well established that students who feel the most connected to school exhibit the fewest behavior problems, like truancy, violence, and drug use."[21] Blum also reported that "strong scientific evidence demonstrates that increased student connection to school decreases absenteeism, fighting, bullying, and vandalism, while promoting educational motivation, classroom engagement, academic performance, school attendance, and completion rates."[22]

And in case you're still not sold, strong relationships between teachers and kids is by far the most valuable ingredient in behavior management—more effective than any rules, threat of punishment, or parent intervention. In fact, one study "indicated that school connectedness seemed to outweigh even feelings of attachment to family in preventing behavior problems."[23] Educator and consultant Gail Dusa wrote, "When there is a bond, the kids will amaze their teachers with their dedication and performance. Attendance will be near one hundred percent. Discipline problems are rare. The kids begin to monitor one another. And teaching becomes so much fun!" Validating the need for commitment and strong interpersonal skills, Dusa cautioned, "The teacher must be worthy of respect, a good role model. Not perfect. Just human. If the kids sense the teacher is just there to put in the hours and collect a paycheck, watch out! Their sense of justice will call for them to bury such teachers, and they will do their best."

In addition to fewer discipline problems, increased student cooperation, and higher levels of academic engagement and performance, teachers who have made an effort to become more positive, accepting, encouraging, and respectful of the students in their classes report increased enjoyment and less stress on the job.[24] Further, these connections will buy you some goodwill from students when you don't have the flexibility to accommodate them or when you're just having a bad day. "If I'm upset, I'll tell the class to tread lightly for the hour," shared one contributor. "Because I've built a good rapport with my high school kids, they immediately calm down. By the end of the hour, I'm usually laughing at someone's stupid joke."

CONNECTING WITH KIDS

So how do dedicated teachers keep their priorities straight, especially in data-driven environments and content-heavy classes? Although the pressure to barrel through curriculum may be intense, "studies show that effectiveness is determined by how well teachers establish relationship with students, not how well they deliver content," reported one professional development director. "Establish a culture of safety and trust in the classroom *and then* introduce content." Many contributors suggested starting off the year with the intention—and time—to connect with kids. Sandra Kenyon noted, "The first week of school is the time to get to know the students, find out about what they know, what they are like, and what they need." Preschool teacher Ginny Luther reported that her first priority involved creating a sense of community with her class. Even at a young age, she found that students could be more successful academically once the relationships, trust, and cohesion were in place to support learning. "No matter what the deadlines are for academic progress, none will be made if the kids don't have a sense of belonging, acceptance, or safety in their classroom."[25]

Another teacher sets time aside on the first day for exercises to build respect between the teacher and students, believing that this sets the stage for a year in which "the students will then do anything for you." A contributor who teaches technology reported, "I take the IEPs for my classes and put them in the bottom drawer so I know where they are at the end of the year. Then I spend the first two weeks establishing a relationship with each student. I then worry about teaching the subject." A high school assistant principal advised, "Don't worry about the worksheets and content the first week. Focus on getting to know the kids, and building those relationships. Mix work with socialization so you can figure out what makes kids tick and let them know you like them. I've worked elementary, middle, and high, and this is true for all kids."

Be prepared for a certain amount of black-and-white thinking around this issue, although this isn't an either-or situation at all. Of course it's important to get into the books and establish the routines your kids will need to function in your class, but let's make these demands in the context of community. "Rigor and relationship go hand in hand," wrote Moorman. "Asking for rigor without relationship is spitting into the wind."

This process doesn't have to be complicated or time consuming, and even the most complex data-collection exercises will only be a tiny blip in the course of an entire school-year calendar. Any information you have about your students gives you leverage in creating lessons that tie in with their interests and their lives. Years ago, a colleague finally managed to break through one student's aversion to reading when she responded to his excitement about seeing *Jaws* by bringing in some books about sharks. A unit on letter writing went nowhere until the middle school teacher brought in a pile of teen magazines with addresses of fan clubs for her students' favorite actors and musicians. Similarly, a brief greeting and exchange at the door each period or at the start of your day will, for some students, be the best contact they have with a caring, supportive, and present adult all day. Sixth-grade teacher Ashley Ferris wrote, "For some kids, you are their rock, the constant in their life. You might be the only person who cares about them and wants them to succeed." Fagerlund likewise mentioned, "You never know. You might be the only adult a child can really trust, so be there for them." Indeed, as Julia Frascona wrote, "You are some kids' only hope."

Many contributors swear by the dividends this investment can pay, especially with the kids who seem shy, belligerent, and generally difficult. ("Even the most annoying student has some trait you can find to connect with," Sandy Goldman assured.) Sixth-grade teacher Ashley Ferris advised, "Get to know all your students, build that trust, and show them you care. Once you do that, your students will love you and respect you. They will care what you say and want to learn." Wyatt and White recommended talking to kids between classes, speaking to them in the halls, and attending sports events and other extracurricular programs. "If you let them know that your interest in them goes beyond their names and a few interesting facts, they will begin to respond to you in positive ways."[26] Even students will back up these claims. "A lot of it goes down by the demeanor in which they teach. If they respect the students, the students will respect them," said one high school student. "I find that the teacher affects the course just as much as the course affects the students."[27]

And flying in the face of anyone who continues to suggest that if you enjoy your students, they'll walk all over you, please let me encourage you to have fun—with your work and with them. Wilson wrote, "If you aren't having fun then the students won't have fun." And yes, that matters. Even Aristotle had this one figured out when he proclaimed, "There's no learning without laughter."[28] Balancing routine and structure with surprise and pleasure helps sustain your students' attention, can reduce stress that gets in the way of learning, and will stave off boredom and apathy—for them and for you as well. The brain loves laughter, and joyful learning is the stuff that lasts.

One final bit of advice: Be patient. Your kids may test you, especially if they've been hurt by previous attachments to their teachers. (One high school principal warned that older kids are often unwilling to allow themselves to invest in connecting with new teachers before the educators have established their commitment and credibility by simply making it through the year.) But even the best defenses aren't likely to stand up to relentless caring and faith. One third-grade teacher confirmed, "The smallest thing you do or say can impact a child." To illustrate, author Jeff Sapp shared a story about a teacher who took time every day at lunch to have a glass of orange juice with a student, sharing "a special time beyond any classroom project or lesson." When asked what lessons the student would take with him when he left the school, the student responded, "Relationships are what I'll take with me. An appreciation of community."[29]

BEYOND THE GRADE BOOK

Most of what you learn about your students will come from the interactions you have with them. Your own intention to connect—and to listen—will go a long way. Kids can share a remarkable amount of information in a very short comment, and their energy and body language can convey even more than words to anyone who is truly paying attention. [30]

"Really listen to your students," wrote curriculum consultant Phyllis O'Brien. "You don't have to always agree with their reasoning, but they will know if you are listening." If you are even a little bit good at listening, you're way ahead of the curve. Feedback from children from a wide range of backgrounds and situations consistently points to a hunger to be heard—along with a significant shortage of people willing or able to simply listen.[31] In a national survey of teens, 40% of young people between the ages of twelve and seventeen gave adults a below-average grade in listening. Said one eighteen-year-old, "If adults would just listen, they could make a big difference in young people's lives."[32] Consultant Jenny Mosley summed up this important means of connection. "The main point for me about emotional safety has to do with people being heard and valued. In schools you cannot leave listening to chance," she said.[33]

There will be times when you may also want to use some slightly more formal data-collection instruments and processes to learn about your students' interests, experiences, work habits, or what's going on in their lives. "Developing a student profile helps to provide a deeper understanding of an individual's unique interests, styles, and abilities," noted educators Elaine Hansen and Velma Corbett. "By gathering information from a variety of sources, teachers and school-based teams are in a better position to make educational decisions that will enhance the student's development."[34] While some of these approaches can help you get specific information about individual students, others will help you make sure that you connect with all of your students, including the ones whose primary survival strategies include staying as far under the radar as possible and who are especially easy to miss.

Regardless of the strategy, instrument, or approach you use, the important part is in *using* the information you receive—after all, that is the entire point of data collection. Whether acknowledging an interest that was expressed during a conversation or instruction, or considering the students' comments in planning, selecting materials, or arranging the physical environment of the classroom, every reference you make to what you've learned about your students reflects a great deal of respect for and attention to the information they have shared. Their feedback will tell you about strengths you can build on and gaps you may need to fill. In addition, every time you can bridge something new or unfamiliar to something real and tangible for your students, they are much more likely to assign significance and permanence to the content.

There are dozens of ways to get information about your students and different aspects of their lives and behaviors.[35] Let's look at three of the most common and simple processes you can use to expand your sense of the individuals with whom you are working and gain information you can use in teaching and connecting with them.

Interest Inventories

Interest inventories offer a systematic means of discovering all sorts of things about your students that can help you understand what occupies their time and attention in and out of school. Many teachers use these inventories at the start of school, although others wait until they have established enough of an atmosphere of trust to get kids to share reliably.[36] The type and administration of your interest inventories will depend on the information you would like to obtain as well as the age and reading abilities of your students and the size of your class or classes. While there are commercially made and online inventories available, most of the teachers I've met create their own instruments based on their own needs and intentions as well as the students with whom they're working.

Generally speaking, most interest inventories take the form of a fill-in survey, a questionnaire, or a checklist for students to complete. Fill-in surveys provide the student with the beginning of a sentence such as "The last book I read was ___," "My favorite food is ___," or "The thing I liked most about my other teachers is ___." Questionnaires ask for similar information, but as questions, with space to respond: "What was the last book you read?" or "What is your favorite food?" This format works well for students with the reading and writing skills to answer the questions, or when used to interview students, where the interviewer records the students' answers.[37]

The checklist provides a series of questions with specific options for students to check: "yes or no" or "true or false," or a Likert scale with options like "yes, sometimes, or no," "many times, once or twice, or never," or the classic five-point range from "strongly agree" to "strongly disagree." Questions can explore any aspect of students' lives, including things like whether they have library cards, where they've traveled, the types of books or TV shows they like, personal qualities they see in themselves or like in others, or the kinds of electronics they have in their bedrooms. Although this information can be gathered with more open-ended formats, the checklist limits the options from which students can select their preferences (unless an "other" option with blank space is available). While this type of survey allows for more systematic analysis of trends and a better grasp of the range of interests or experiences for a group, you might gain a deeper sense of individual students from responses to fill-in inventories.

I've seen all three formats used successfully with students at all grade levels, although teachers of younger children generally benefit from reading the inventory to the class or group, or interviewing individual students and recording their answers. And I've found students can be quite candid, articulate, and forthcoming when they believe that their disclosures will be noticed and respected.

Student Survey

If you want to get a sense of what your students' school experiences have been like, here are a few survey questions that can reveal a great deal of information. I have had a number of teachers use this survey and share their kids' responses. You may be quite surprised by the answers you receive, but if you're committed to finding out what's really important (and really disturbing or hurtful) to your students, questions like these can generate some rather eye-opening responses:

1. My favorite teachers are the ones who

2. The teachers I dislike (or am most uncomfortable around) are the ones who

3. I wish more teachers would

4. I wish some teachers would stop

5. The best thing a teacher ever said or did to me was

6. The worst thing a teacher ever said or did to me was

7. If I were a teacher, I would

8. If I were to change this school, I would

9. Other comments or suggestions

Journals

My love of journaling started with a little pink diary in sixth grade and has continued on a fairly consistent basis ever since. Although much of my ramblings are fairly mundane, the journaling I've done over the years has allowed expression for everything from venting about unpleasant situations to finding solutions to knotty problems, and probably saving my sanity along the way. So I'm a pretty easy sell when it comes to using journals in the classroom, and I've been delighted to see the number of teachers using this fabulous vehicle for expression at all grade levels.

There are any number of ways to use journals in school. Gary Hopkins reported, "Some teachers check journal writing and work on polishing skills; others use journals as the one 'uncorrected' form of writing that students produce. Some teachers provide prompts to help students begin their writing. Others leave decisions about the direction and flow of student journals up to the students."[38] Either way, the potential benefits to the students are prodigious. "Journaling encourages children to be observers of the world, to be reflective of their experiences, and of course, to become expressive writers," wrote English teacher Day Penaflor. "A journal can become an invaluable tool for the emergent writer, one that provides a safe place for privacy, creativity, and individuality."[39] Secondary education guide Melissa Kelly noted that journal writing offers students opportunities to "sort out experiences, solve problems, and consider varying perspectives; examine relationships with others and the world; reflect on personal values, goals, and ideals; summarize ideas, experience, and opinions before and after instruction; witness . . . academic and personal growth by reading past entries."[40]

Journals are valuable teaching tools regardless of the subject you teach, and some teachers have noticed improvements in skills even when the entries were not corrected for spelling or grammar.[41] But whether corrected or left alone, prompted or open to a student's discretion, and regardless of any other benefits to the kids themselves, journals are wonderful ways to connect with and learn about students. They'll offer you insights into their feelings and experiences, give you information about how students learn, and even provide feedback about your teaching to help you tweak lessons and instructional techniques. Journals give kids a chance to speculate, analyze, report, and simply express what's on their mind. One fourth-grade teacher noted, "Journal writing enables me to develop a personal relationship with each of my students. I respond to the journal entries every day, so we have sort of an ongoing dialogue." And an eighth-grade teacher shared, "I've learned a lot about my quieter kids through reading their journals."[42] Former teacher Claude Thau would have students write about what they would like their life to be like in thirty years. "From these exercises, I would hope to gain insight into the students. Are they dreamers? Are they narrowly focused into a life with little hope? I'd hope to leverage these insights into understanding, positive and encouraging comments which could help me to build trust." He noted that he would follow up with "some one-on-one private discussions with them to probe further and encourage them to push the envelope of their thoughts."

There are plenty of books and online resources to get you started, but you probably don't need more than a blank notebook for each student, a safe place to store them, and a clear sense of your intentions. Think about why you'd want to have your kids journal and how you would like to use them. Decide whether journaling will be a regular part of each class or each week or whether the journals will be available as needed. Will they go home with the students or stay in your room (or otherwise in your possession)? Can they draw or scrapbook in their journals as well as write?

For many journalers, myself included, we're writing more than just words. Sharing our thoughts can be an expression of our deepest self, exposing our souls. The process and the content deserve the respect we reserve for something sacred. Although you will want to be sure that no one sees the journals but you, some educators recommend advising students to be careful about what they share, or request that certain topics remain off-limits. Promise confidentiality, but stipulate any conditions under which you would be morally or legally obligated to share something a student has written. Be aware that some students will ask for help in a journal in a way that would be impossible for them to do face to face, and others may write some fairly intense entries or use especially strong language, whether to test you or because they trust you enough to share these deepest thoughts. If this will be a problem for you, let the kids know up front or select another vehicle for learning about your students.

Anecdotal Records

When I was teaching, I had baskets or small tubs in various strategic places around the room, each with scraps of paper that I would use throughout the course of the day to annotate students' behaviors, interactions, or conversations.[43] These notes, or anecdotal records, proved invaluable, not only in helping me get a better sense of the kids in the class but also in backing up recommendations for special services and interventions and decisions I made about content, placement, or accommodations for individual children.

Anecdotal records provide a systematic, ongoing journal of student behavior that will continue to round out your ideas of who your students really are. Unlike interest inventories, in which the information is supplied exclusively by the students, these records are teacher-made, based on observations *of* the students and your interactions with them. Anecdotal record keeping allows you to sharpen your attention and get a more dimensional sense of each student. The practice also reduces the likelihood that you will forget significant details of events, patterns, and behaviors that can impact a child's learning. These records contribute to effective, professional data keeping, lending credibility to reporting, referring, evaluating, and planning with concrete examples of patterns in student behavior.

"Anecdotes capture the richness and complexity of the moment as children interact with one another and with materials," noted one online article. "These records of child behavior and learning accumulated over time enhance the teacher's understanding of the individual child as patterns or profiles begin to emerge. Behavior change can be tracked and documented, and placed in the child's portfolio resulting in suggestions for future observations, curriculum planning, and student or parent conferences."[44] This article described the notation as "an account of an event in a child's day. The record of this event can be detailed or brief. These short reports describe, in a factual way, the incident, its context, and what was said or done by the participant(s). In most cases, anecdotes focus on very simple, everyday interactions among children, children and adults, as well as children and materials in the environment."[45]

The primary value in using anecdotal records is in how the process can help you gain a clearer sense of how students function in the classroom. Data collection and analysis can provide a concrete reality check, validating the existence of a problem and providing details to give you some perspective on the frequency and extent to which the problem occurs. (By the same token, you may discover, over time, that what had seemed to be a significant issue either has improved, stopped, or may not have been as problematic as you had originally thought.) You can use this strategy to record students' modality and attending preferences, chronicle their ability to perform certain learning tasks, or describe their behavior during some classroom activity, including their independent work habits, behavior in groups, ability to take care of materials, completion of assignment, or attention during a video, for example. You may also want to document evidence of special needs, especially if you see patterns in which the student is distracted from work, interfering with someone else's work, unable to do some task, or unchallenged by regular assignments. Anecdotal records can also be useful in documenting resistance to a particular activity or class or documenting conflicts in which a student is involved. This information will be especially useful any time you need to consult with parents or outside resources on behalf of the child.

It's probably a good idea to note the date, time, location, subject or activity, grouping or organization, individuals present or otherwise involved, and any other relevant information related to your observation. As with any documentation, be sure that your observations are "accurate, objective, and specific" and that they don't "make assumptions or use subjective or ambiguous words." Keep records short and clear, and avoid elaborating on or interpreting what you see.[46] Be sure to look over your notes from time to time, particularly those that suggest or require follow-up. (Anecdotal records can paint a very concrete picture of a student's progress, which might otherwise go unnoticed.) Go for a variety of behaviors, positive and negative, particularly if it's a behavior to which you need to respond in some way. Finally, please do not use this process as a punishment or a way to get evidence to use against the kids. The value of these records is in their ability to help you gain insights into how you can better teach, motivate, and accommodate each student. As always, treat this data with the same level of confidentiality you would ascribe to any other student record.

ACTIVITY

Interest Inventories

If you have constructed an interest inventory to use with your students (or used an existing inventory or one commercially available), answer the following questions:

1. Which format did you select (fill-in, checklist, some combination, or other), and why?

2. What was your purpose in administering the inventory?

3. Did the inventory help you achieve this goal?

4. Did you administer the inventory to all your students or just selected individuals or groups? Was this a good call? How so?

5. How might you administer the inventory differently in the future?

6. What changes would you make in the content if you were to give this inventory again?

7. What changes might you make in the format or design of future inventories?

8. What was the overall response of the students to the inventory?

9. What did you learn about your class as a whole?

10. What are some of the significant findings about the individuals in the class?

11. How will the results of this activity affect your planning, content selection, and expectations?

12. How will this activity help in understanding, diagnosing, and providing for the needs of individuals in your class?

Student Journals

Use the following questions to plan and evaluate your use of journals in the classroom:

1. What is your primary purpose in using journals with your students?

2. Are other teachers in the school using journals? (Or is there a history of teachers using journals with kids in school?) If so, what has their experience been like? What recommendations do they have to help you?

3. Describe how, how often, and when you intend to use journals.

4. What materials and resources will you need?

5. Where will you store the journals? How will you protect the students' privacy?

6. What types of structure will you offer in terms of requirements (written, drawn, or other)?

7. What type of feedback will you offer?

8. In what ways will you structure the content (using a theme, concept, or word to get them started, for example), or will the content be open-ended, based on what the students want to share?

9. Are there any limits you feel you need to set regarding content or language? If so, what are they?

10. To what degree are the students' privacy and confidentiality protected? Under what conditions would you feel the need to break confidentiality?

11. Once you have been using journals for a while, describe how they have helped you get to know and connect with your students.

12. Describe any growth you have seen in your students' skills, expression, behavior, or maturity, for example. In what ways, if any, have you tied journal activities into your curriculum?

13. Would you recommend using journals to other teachers? Explain.

14. If you plan to use journals next year, how will you change your management, structure, materials, or approach?

ACTIVITY

Anecdotal Records

Use the following questions to plan and evaluate your anecdotal record-keeping system:

1. What type of system do you propose to design and implement?

2. What materials will you need? Where will these materials be kept?

3. Which students do you plan to observe? How frequently do you plan to observe each one?

4. How will you check to be sure you are observing all of your students? (If you are working with a large number of students, how will you keep track of the quieter or more "invisible" kids in the group or groups you have decided to include in this process?)

5. Where and how will you store your notations? What additional materials, if any, will you need for storage?

6. What type of information do you intend to record? How do you intend to use this information?

7. Once you've been using your system for a few weeks, tell how the management has been working.

8. What changes have you made in your system during the time you have been using it?

9. How frequently are you making anecdotal-record entries

    a. during the day or week?

    b. for each student?

10. What types of information have you been recording?

11. What patterns, if any, have you observed

     a. with particular individuals?

     b. with the class or classes in general?

     c. with your observation and record-keeping skills and habits?

12. In what ways have you followed up on or used the information you have recorded?

13. What impact has your observing and recording had on

     a. your perceptions of the students?

     b. your interactions with the students?

     c. your teaching behavior (in terms of planning, responding, meeting various student needs)?

NOTES

1. Bluestein (2001, p. 99).

2. Talevich (2007, pp. 18–20).

3. Blum (2004, p. 4).

4. Thank you to Dave Friedli for sharing this quote.

5. Quoted in Michelle Pais (2009, para. 6).

6. Wilke (2003, p. 49).

7. Blum (2004, p. 4).

8. Australian Centre for Equity through Education and Australian Youth Research Centre (2001, p. 7). This report also noted a correlation between students identified as at risk and family problems, including not getting along with parents because of "family breakdown, physical, sexual and mental abuse, drug use and behavior problems" in the sample studied.

9. Brooks (2009, para. 4).

10. Sugar (2000). A list of "things that make school suck" included comments like "adults who don't treat you with respect; adults who act impatient, annoyed, or disgusted with you; adults who ignore you or don't take you seriously; teachers who favor some students over others; unpredictable, inconsistent or explosive teacher behavior; not being recognized or acknowledged for positive behavior, achievement, effort, cooperation, etc.; and not being supported or protected by adults when they see other students or adults mistreating you in any way." Bluestein and Katz (2005). This list was compiled from comments contributed by over 2,000 high school students and graduates, including responses to specific questions about what they liked most and least about school. The list also included comments about class and instruction, rules and rigidity, and other students.

11. Aspy and Roebuck (1977).

12. Quoted in Hopkins (2007, para. 6).

13. Reynolds and Reynolds (2008).

14. Blum, McNeely, and Rinehart (2002, p. 13).

15. Freiberg (2007a).

16. Quoted in Hopkins (2007, para. 33–35).

17. Quoted in Hopkins (2007, para. 19).

18. Quoted in Hopkins (2007, para. 26, 27).

19. Blum (2004, pp. 4, 16); also noted in Aspy and Roebuck (1977).

20. Freiberg (2007a). Freiberg identified five measures of connectedness: "I feel close to people at this school," "I'm happy to be at this school," "I feel like I'm part of this school," "The teachers at this school treat me fairly," and "I feel safe at this school." Students who strongly agree with these statements would likewise exhibit many of the benefits connectedness has to offer.

21. Nagourney (2000, para. 1).

22. Blum (2004, p. 1).

23. Nagourney (2000, para. 7).

24. Bluestein (2001).

25. Bluestein (2001, p. 100). Creating a sense of community in your classroom can work just as well as formal programs designed to support kids who feel the most alienated and disconnected. Schaps and Solomon (1991).

26. Wyatt and White (2007, p. 31).

27. Quoted in Pais (2009, para. 18, 20).

28. Thanks to Jenny Mosley (2005), presenter at a conference for the Centre for Child Mental Health, London.

29. Quoted in Sapp (2005, p. 29).

30. By *energy*, I'm referring more to an emotional state than a level of activity or vitality. It's how you just know someone is feeling something without their saying a word, and it's important for people working with children to attune to some of the nonverbal cues they present. I have heard too often and from far too many students (and adults recalling their days as students), incredulous that no one ever seemed to notice or acknowledge their pain or anxiety. It's also important that kids, especially those in pain, have someone, a safe adult, with whom they feel comfortable enough to approach when they need an ear or a little extra support.

31. Bluestein (1995, 2001); also Bluestein and Katz (2005). Comments from students referenced a tendency for adults to notice the superficial (absenteeism, drop in grades, or obvious changes in appearance or weight, for example) and, in place of actual listening, a far more common tendency to respond with criticism, lectures, unsolicited advice, directives, unwanted scrutiny, or some remark suggesting that the students' concerns were not taken seriously.

32. Markway (2004).

33. Bluestein (2001).

34. "The Learner: Interests" (2001).

35. In addition to making audio and video recordings (which can also give you valuable insights into your own behaviors, body language, tone of voice, and other factors of interactions you might not otherwise notice), there are instruments for identifying patterns of social interaction (and isolation) as well as processes for tracking time on (or off) task, for example.

36. Once again, be sensitive about the population with whom you're working. The entire point of data collection is to help in connecting, planning, and motivating. If it feels invasive or too personal, you risk creating cynicism, suspicion, or hostility, and if you suspect the responses you get back reflect a lack of trust, back off the data collection until your relationships are a little more solid, and use other ways to connect with your students to make that happen. And if your students invest time and trust in disclosing information about themselves that is never referenced or used, they're not likely to have much faith in subsequent requests.

37. Usually a teacher, counselor, or paraprofessional, although some teachers have had parents or older students interview kids and record answers. Check your school's privacy policies to see whether they would apply here.

38. Hopkins (2008, para. 1).

39. Penaflor (2004, para. 1).

40. Kelly (n.d., para. 2).

41. Hopkins (2008).

42. Hopkins (2008).

43. I've also seen teachers keep paper, index cards, or sticky notes for this purpose in a pocket or small notebook, which they carried with them. Some of my primary teachers preferred to make a 3 × 5 card for each student and put them, in alphabetical order, on a clip ring, which they either kept in a pocket or hung on a string around their neck.

44. University of Utah, Department of Family and Consumer Studies (n.d., para. 4).

45. University of Utah, Department of Family and Consumer Studies (n.d., para. 1).

46. University of Utah, Department of Family and Consumer Studies (n.d., para. 19). This article suggested asking yourself whether you are recording an event "in such a way that anyone viewing the same scene would write it in the exact same way" and recommended avoiding the use of "ambiguous or suggestive words" such as "crowded, chaotic, wild, messy, sloppy, too many, or roughhousing," as well as "words that convey assumption," like "intelligent, annoyed, anger, provoked, happiness, rude, bored, aggressive, self-esteem, out of control, uninvolved, boisterous, enthusiastic, or ill-mannered."

11

Avoid Win-Lose Power Strategies

I possess tremendous power to make a child's life miserable or joyous. I can be a tool of torture or an instrument of inspiration. I can humiliate or humor, hurt or heal. In all situations, it is my response that decides whether a crisis will be escalated or de-escalated, and a child humanized or de-humanized.

Haim Ginott[1]

It is incongruous to expect children to be respectful when you are not respectful in your attitude toward them.

Mary Robinson Reynolds and Craig Reynolds[2]

We look forward to the time when the Power of Love will replace the Love of Power. Then will our world know the blessings of Peace.

William E. Gladstone[3]

You know when it takes three strong adults to remove a six-year-old from the classroom, something is wrong. This happened during my first week of student teaching in a first-grade class (which followed a successful and enjoyable stint in a sixth-grade class with students who, frankly, made much more sense to me). Whatever set this child off, I have no idea. I just remember that he was beyond anything anyone could do to calm him down. Teaching and learning had become impossible, and he had become a danger to himself and the other students. Out of the classroom, he settled a bit, but getting him there was another story.[4]

This is the kind of situation that throws everybody into survival mode—not exactly where we do our finest work. None of us in education enjoys encounters like these, and anyone who spends much time functioning in survival mode won't last long in the profession. There will always be factors in children's lives you won't know about or be able to control—conditions and events that impact them before they even walk into your room. So it's critical to create the structures, connections, and relationships to prevent these dramas from happening—or at least to reduce the frequency and intensity of incidents that occur.

BEHAVIOR MANAGEMENT AND TEACHER PREPARATION

If there is a particular arena in which a win-win approach will reap the most profound benefits, it is in the area of discipline, or what is often referred to as classroom management or behavior management. You would think, since this aspect of teaching is such a fundamental prerequisite to actual instruction and learning (which frankly won't happen in the absence of cooperative and attentive student behavior), that teacher-training programs would place a great premium on helping prospective teachers develop these skills. Yet the opposite seems to be true.

Of all the areas teachers identify as the ones in which they receive the least useful information and preparation, behavior management consistently tops the list. "The greatest area of need for new teachers is classroom management," wrote Mary Vaglica, an elementary assistant principal, mentor, and supervisor. "Teachers are never fully prepared for discipline issues that occur, [or for] managing the classroom so that students can work independently, and so the teacher can work with small groups." Former principal Lulu Lopez agreed. When asked what she saw as the greatest need for the beginning teachers she has observed in her forty-two years in education, she replied without a second's hesitation, "Behavior management." Few teachers would disagree. Over and over, contributors protested the lack of preparation for the realities they experienced in their classrooms. "I really wish somebody had told me that classroom management is your single biggest battle," said Darren Raichart. "Some people do tell you that in college, but then they spend most of your classes teaching you other things." Holly Davis shared, "I wish my education classes had dealt more with classroom management. I love my subject so finding new ways to teach and grow is easy, but there are still students who defy my most tried-and-true management strategies."

Wherever you work, you can count on having students who lack the self-management, social-interaction capabilities, and the learning behaviors that would otherwise free up your time for actual teaching. Unfortunately, the majority of resources that would attempt to help you deal with these shortcomings tend to be presented in outdated, ineffective, and very win-lose terms. And absent more positive alternatives, these are the strategies we tend to perpetuate because they're familiar and they're there. (And they are generally familiar to administrators and parents as well.) When they don't work, the strategies get repackaged or renamed, but in essence, we keep doing the same things over and over, even when they don't work, even when they make things worse.

Let's step back a bit and get some perspective on how we got to this place. "In previous generations within our lifetime, the values taught by the home, the school, and the media were basically in harmony," wrote author and educator Marvin Marshall. "The values taught outside the home were supportive of values in the home. Needless to say, that is not the situation today."[5] A few decades ago, the most serious complaints about students' behavior listed children who talked out, chewed gum, or ran in the hall. Subsequent generations of teachers have had to contend with these annoyances in addition to fighting, gang activity, and "problems of weapons, substance abuse, and violent assaults against other students and school staff."[6]

I can understand the hunger for the good old days, along with the discipline strategies that may have been effective in our recent and distant past. But many teachers have found that tried-and-true methods no longer hold the clout or effectiveness they once did.

Some still clamor for the harsh penalties of the past, arguing for more of the strategies they idealize from their days as students—or from wistful stories they've heard—only invoked bigger and harder, and with the absurd notion that anything to the contrary is soft and permissive.

But nostalgia seldom accounts for the frequent failures—or the academic and emotional cost—of draconian authority, and it's easy to forget that there have always been opponents to the kind of strict discipline that many in and out of the profession would celebrate.[7] The problem seems to stem from the challenge in finding any win-win middle ground. "At some point in the history of education," wrote educators William Purkey and David Aspy, "a myth developed that education has to be either humane or effective, but that it is impossible to be both. The sad part about this myth is that it has been accepted as reality even though there is a wealth of data to refute it."[8] There is still a fair amount of black-and-white thinking regarding what is necessary to teach children to be civilized members of a school community and society in general, including an assumption that allowing students autonomy will undermine adult authority, or the equally stubborn notion that we have to hurt, criticize, embarrass, or otherwise discomfort students in some way in order to change their behavior. Despite efforts to address this issue in teacher-training and inservice programs, too many offerings are presented in this all-or-nothing, authoritarian context, capitalizing on the fear of kids being completely out of control unless the appropriate sanctions and penalties are in place. But far too many of these approaches are anachronistic and inappropriate to win-win intentions, and considering changes in the student population and culture in general, it's not surprising to hear how many teachers find these strategies to be ineffective and, in some cases, to actually create more problems than they solve.

We have some pretty big hurdles to clear if we're going to get past old win-lose mindsets, much less the discipline traditions still being recommended, used, and supported. I'm going to ask you to take the hard road here and reject the formulas, packages, and quick-fix approaches, as attractive and well supported as they may seem, in favor of developing relationships, questioning assumptions and traditions, and putting your faith in process over product. And rather than worrying about what to do when a student does something disruptive or inappropriate, let's look at what we can do to prevent these problems before they occur. Be assured that by creating a win-win community in your classroom, it is possible to minimize, if not eliminate, the discipline problems that happen when students are competing with adults for power, as well as those fermented in the students' social environment. Win-win solutions give us an open window or side-door access when the main entrance is blocked. But first let's take a look at some of the traditions that are cluttering our path.

OUR MOST BELOVED (AND PERSISTENT) WIN-LOSE TRADITIONS

Think about all the things that can impact students' behavior and attention—how a lesson is being taught, their interest in the subject, the relevance of the content, a comment or look from another student in the hall or on the playground, something that happened at home or in the community, how much sleep or nutrition they had before they came to school, the physical aspects of the classroom (furniture, lighting, arrangement, temperature, and even the color of the walls), the degree to which their biological needs (for movement, water, and bathroom breaks) are being met, or even the weather. Factor in teacher personalities and class dynamics, and it's understandable that any child might exhibit behaviors we deem undesirable, at least occasionally.

Dealing with student behaviors, whether quietly inattentive or disorderly and disruptive, has been one of the greatest challenges for teachers throughout history. Clearly, some responses are more effective than others, not just in their effect on subsequent student behaviors, but also on the climate of the class, their impact on other students, and their ability to support win-win objectives.

Let's look at some of the most common behavior-management strategies and assumptions you're likely to encounter and do some quick and dirty myth busting, examining why these approaches will run anywhere from pointless to counterproductive, often with a side of needless complication and hidden dangers.[9] You'll find constructive, win-win ideas in the following chapter, but get acquainted with these traditions first, because depending on where you're teaching, there's a good chance that you *will* encounter them and they will be held up as recommended protocols, which will add to the enticement to use them. But don't be fooled by familiarity, and know that these are the discipline approaches that have been adding stress to teachers' and students' lives forever. Don't say I didn't warn you.

Control

There's this overt expectation that teachers be in control of their classrooms, which many educators interpret to mean being in control of their students. Assuming that this were even possible, consider the innate need we *all* have for some autonomy and control in our lives. This is the need that makes even the most cooperative of us resentful and resistant to being pushed around or having others try to control us. For this reason, competition for control can turn into a rather ugly win-lose (or no-win) battle of wills. While the first grab for autonomy surfaces around age two, as kids get older, their ability and resources to prove "you can't make me" can get rather sophisticated and effective. If you can resist the urge to seek ways to out-power these students (and "win" at their expense), there are some side-door approaches that will allow them the autonomy they want within the limits you need. In other words, instead of looking for a better way to make them lose, let's start asking the magic, win-win question, "How can we all get what we want?"

"All modern experimental work points to how important for good health is the perception that an individual is in charge of his own destiny," reported researcher Michael S. Gazzaniga, reporting that efforts to undermine people's sense of power and control in their lives can lead to a great deal of stress, along with all kinds of compensating behaviors, or what some might call "acting out." (This can occur whether people are actually being controlled or whether they simply believe that they are unable to impact their own lives.)[10] But all-or-nothing thinking leads back to the win-lose notion that either we are in charge or *they* are. So before I go any further, please let me assure you that a win-win approach to power dynamics *is still an authority relationship*. You are still the boss and you still get to be in charge. You just accomplish this goal without needing to disempower anyone, and as a by-product, you get to avoid so many of the power struggles and other problems that tend to plague adults using authoritarian, win-lose power dynamics. (See "Negative Outcomes of Win-Lose Authority Relationships.")

This model is so common that many of us step up to the plate without even questioning the assumption that this is how we're supposed to be. John Taylor Gatto shared the disciplinary mindset so common in schools. "By stars and red checks, smiles and frowns, prizes, honors, and disgraces, I teach kids to surrender their will to the predestined chain of command," he wrote. "Rights may be granted or withheld by any authority without appeal, because rights do not exist inside a school—not even the right of free speech, as the Supreme Court has ruled—unless school authorities say they do. As a schoolteacher, I intervene in many personal decisions, issuing a pass for those I deem legitimate and initiating a disciplinary confrontation for behavior that threatens my control."[11]

This kind of thinking would explain the tendency for schools and teachers to micromanage the minutiae of students' lives, from how they sit to what they wear, from when they can talk to how they can manage their biological needs for movement, hydration, or a bathroom break. And it would also explain the beliefs that drive much of the policing and punishing many teachers fear they need to adopt to keep the class from going to hell in a handbasket. But the more we try to monitor and control, the more kids have to fight against and the less their incentive to assume personal responsibility for their behavior or develop the self-control we say we desire. (And by the way, discipline programs that rely on surveillance cameras, metal detectors, and a police presence have an intensely negative impact on school climate and have also been shown to negatively affect graduation rates and rates of suspension.[12])

This approach also has a human cost and will invariably get in the way of learning for many students. Middle school teacher Bill Funkhouser shared, "It is almost painful to reflect on who I used to be. I was so caught up in getting students to obey that I lost sight of the humanity of this profession. I was overpowering them—rather than being flexible, understanding, and compassionate." Similarly, an offhand comment by one of his students made high school teacher John Keydash realize how much of his classroom management depended on fear. "It took awhile to learn that what I thought was the superlative of teacher management technique was only half there because I lacked the connection [with my students]," he wrote. "I needed to be understanding and caring but at the same time keep students responsible and accountable. I did not want to manage learning because my students were afraid of me." Besides, a well-controlled classroom is not the same as an actual self-managing one, and I've known teachers whose seemingly well-behaved kids went wild the moment the adults left the room or turned their back.

"How much superior an education based on free action and personal responsibility is to one relying on outward authority," proposed Albert Einstein.[13] And consider Ralph Nader's contention that "the function of leadership is to produce more leaders, not more followers."[14] If we're concerned about building independence and self-management, keep in mind that controlling kids does not grace them with the skills or the confidence to control themselves when no adults are around. There are many effective alternatives to establish the structure your kids will need to function successfully and cooperatively that put far less stress on your management system—and your nervous system as well.

Negative Outcomes of Win-Lose Authority Relationships

Win-lose power struggles are stressful for everyone in the room and especially frustrating, time-consuming, and exhausting for teachers. In addition, attempts to control kids can naturally trigger unwanted student reactions—whether defiance, resistance, shutting down, or giving up. Control reinforces dependence and helplessness and can erode confidence kids need to function and make decisions in the absence of adult guidance. Even apparently desirable compliant behavior presents its dangers in the difficulty these students have when it comes to resisting peer pressure or making decisions in their own best interest. (Compliant students often make decisions based on what they believe would gain someone's approval or protect against someone else's anger, rejection, humiliation, or abandonment. Or they do what they're told, so they can avoid any responsibility for the outcomes of their choices, which are always "somebody else's fault.") Let's help kids learn how to think, anticipate outcomes, and make positive choices, rather than continuing to insist that they simply do as they're told.

Coercion and Punishment

It's almost instinctive, with the upbringing and school experiences most people have had, to assume that something bad *has* to happen to children who have done something wrong, refused to do something they were asked to do, or addressed an adult in a tone deemed oppositional or disrespectful, for example. This pattern consistently shows up in school and district discipline codes, which invariably include a list of rules and violations, each with escalating penalties for infractions.

A little tangent here: You're going to hear these penalties or punishments referred to as "consequences," probably with an argument about them being logical in the context of the misbehavior. But logical or not, I'm betting that the consequence listed will be negative, rendering it punitive—in nature, energy, and intent. Even discipline codes and student manuals that attempt to include a positive focus by listing desirable behaviors still tend to rely heavily on the parts that admonish, "and here's what will happen if you *don't* do this." I understand the political need for these documents. I'm just asking us to quit expecting them to achieve the goals that relationships, structure, opportunities for decision making, positive outcomes, good follow-through, clear directions, and other win-win strategies can accomplish.

Back up and ask, "What's the point of these discipline codes?" What you'll most likely hear is a desire for respectful, cooperative student behavior.[15] But how effective is the fear of punishment when it comes to actually motivating positive behavior? "The object of punishment is prevention from evil," argued education reformer Horace Mann. "It never can be made impulsive to good."[16] The problem with depending on a hierarchy of increasingly negative consequences is that it relies on students' fear of punishment and often requires increasingly harsh outcomes to generate responses from students, which, incidentally, aren't always positive, especially when kids get to the point where they figure they don't have much left to lose. Marvin Marshall noted that "a prime reason—both for teachers leaving the profession and the concern for discipline—is the clinging to coercive approaches as a strategy for motivating students to behave appropriately. If coercion were effective in reducing inappropriate behavior, discipline problems in schools would be a footnote in history."[17]

And what if the student doesn't care? I've seen kids deliberately act up to get thrown out of a class they didn't like or dismiss detention as little more than a chance to get their homework done before they left school.[18] I've met kids with so many hours assigned to afterschool punishments that they would have been in their twenties before their entire sentence was served. And I've even observed little ones who shrug off a name on the board, a missed recess, or a call home. Now what? Are you willing to risk depending on a strategy that paints students into an adversarial corner and can easily escalate or backfire? "When students are not afraid, punishment loses its efficacy," Marshall added.[19]

Besides, it won't take long before you start to notice that it's nearly always the same kids whose names end up on the board or on detention slips, a testament to just how ineffective these classic sanctions are.[20] And if you imagine that a stronger punishment, like tossing a kid out on the street for really bad behavior, will teach cooperation, think again. Here's a little note about the human costs of disciplining by suspension and expulsion, courtesy of Jo Ann Freiberg, education consultant. "Nationally the rate of suspension and expulsion has doubled since the 1970s," she reported, the majority of them for "non-dangerous behaviors." She asks that we keep in mind that while kids are not in school, they are not able to benefit from a potential connection with their teachers, are not receiving academic instruction, and do not benefit from an intervention to ameliorate the behavior in question. Not surprisingly, increased suspension and expulsion correlates with lower test scores and an increased likelihood of these students engaging in risky behavior, dropping out, and becoming entangled in the justice system.[21] Not exactly the positive outcomes we say we're shooting for. And as far as promoting connectedness goes, harsh, restrictive school policies have the opposite effect, as reflected in a high prevalence of disconnected students at those sites.[22]

But even in the face of the well-documented failure and expense of a punitive approach, watch how hard it is to let go of these strategies. I've had avowed converts to a win-win philosophy who still insist on pulling colored warning cards or writing the names on the board—just in case. OK, so they're not there yet. But at some point, I will gently invite them to get off the fence and focus on more positive approaches. When they defend their strategies with a tired cliché about life being tough, I'll share a quote from author Carolyn Kenmore to point out the possibility of a totally different way to think about their authority relationships with students: "If you can learn from hard knocks, you can also learn from soft touches."[23]

Rules, Rules, and More Rules

There is so much mythology around the power of rules that it's easy to start believing that you won't need much else to establish your authority in the classroom. Rules are sacred cows in education that nobody seems to question much, possibly because to do so would suggest chaos and anarchy. Take note, though, that I'm not recommending a lack of structure, which we all need to function and feel safe. But the idea that we can counter misbehavior by making rules—much less that a lack of cooperation is rooted in a lack of *enough* rules—is utter nonsense.

"You cannot make rules based on the exception," said Littke and Grabelle.[24] Nonetheless, I see this tendency over and over again, adding new rules to discipline handbooks any time a student does something an adult doesn't like. Afraid of leaving any stone unturned, some lists include so many details about what kids shouldn't do, say, wear, or bring to school that the rules lose their meaning. (When I was working on a book for high school students, one of my favorite quotes came from a kid who urged, "Get rid of the stupid little rules. Whoever wrote in the handbook that we shouldn't bring ninja stars and swords to school is a moron."[25] Can you imagine this individual taking the rules—or the adults in that school—very seriously?)

I've noticed, too, that the number of rules in a classroom or school tends to correlate highly with the number of behavior problems there. Go figure. The problem is that while rules can provide a starting point for determining the kind of structure you want, they don't actually *inspire* kids to be cooperative and civilized. Besides, emphasize rules and you send a subtle message that your priority is policing and enforcing. Mahoney and Purr advised against starting off the year by "standing in front of the class and reading rules and regulations. This . . . gives the wrong impression. Kids don't want a list of all the things they are not allowed to do. You will look too authoritative and inflexible."[26]

Students behave because it pays off, not because there is a rule somewhere telling them to do so. They behave because in a caring, mutually respectful, win-win classroom, that's just how people act. (Sure, some will test the limits, and some will cooperate so they don't get in trouble, which is a payoff too—though generally the weakest enticement of the lot. Most will find the positive outcomes far more attractive.) I'm always touched by how willing some young people are to take responsibility for their own behavior when we give them a little credit and a bit of breathing room. I've seen students manage themselves quite effectively in classrooms in which the one and *only* rule instructed kids that they could do whatever they wanted as long as it didn't interfere with anyone's teaching or learning.[27]

So by all means, post the rules if you are required to do so. Just don't expect the list to do a thing besides protect the district and maybe impress some people who visit your classroom.[28] (And don't forget, because of the way the brain works, your kids will stop noticing it's even there after a couple of days.) I've never seen students restrain themselves from outbursts, disruptions, or other misbehaviors simply because the list of rules on the wall caught their eye before they had a chance to act out. The list may give you an artificial sense of power—after all, you've got something to point to when a child misbehaves—but the list will not make kids be good.

Consistency and Rigidity

I've never understood the importance my training accorded to consistency, perhaps because I never completely understood what people meant when they advised us to "be consistent." Over the years, I've come to suspect that they were hinting at the need to do what we say we're going to do, which for my money speaks more to the need for good follow-through than consistency. There is a difference, especially in terms of behavioral guidelines and motivation.

Although rules are often invoked in the name of fairness, the fact is, there is little uniformity in which rules are enforced from one classroom to another, or even from one child to another.[29] And the rules themselves can be a bit of a problem, because sometimes there just isn't enough time for students to get to their locker or stop at the bathroom between classes, sometimes they forget to silence their phone, and sometimes the dog does eat their homework. Am I suggesting that we start asking for excuses or become even more arbitrary? Of course not. However, I will argue for some flexibility *built into* the structure we create—before the problems or exceptions arise—and for the willingness to reconsider rules that don't support what actually works.

I recently received an e-mail from a middle school teacher who, among the accommodations he was willing to offer his students, allowed them to wear hats in class. Only a few students took advantage of the privilege—some due to light sensitivities, others perhaps to make a statement of personal style or comfort. Although the offer worked very well as a motivator for a couple of students and did not cause any particular problem in or out of the classroom, the superintendent decided to pull the plug. "The funny thing is, one student in particular, probably our toughest in terms of behavior, was an angel for the two weeks that he was permitted to wear a hat. Did all of his work, stayed focused. We really thought he turned a corner," he wrote. "Then, when [the superintendent] told us to enforce the no-hat rule, his behavior began to spiral out of control. Now, he hasn't done one assignment in a week, and gets kicked out of class probably two out of five classes per day." Here was a child "determined to do anything to not lose the privilege," who now had no incentive to do what anyone wanted.

Rather than get into a discussion of hats or no hats, the point here is that some kids require precious little to get them on board, and flat-out denying the things that work best for them (and their teachers) ends up, as it did here, in a no-win outcome. I've heard dozens of stories like this where, in stunning examples of what journalists Jerry Adler and Karen Springen called "a tremendous victory for bureaucracy over common sense,"[30] a no-drug policy is invoked to suspend a high school girl with Midol in her purse, a middle school boy is expelled for possession of a weapon he found and turned into the office, and a five-year-old is suspended for a day for wearing a fireman costume that included a plastic ax. Is it any wonder kids sometimes have a hard time reckoning with adult authority, much less respecting it?

Some of the most common "yeah, but" questions I get in my seminars refer to dealing with a crisis situation, particularly one in which a student goes over the edge. (Our win-lose programming can be pretty strong. Some people are willing to put only so much faith in the power of prevention, win-win power dynamics, and solid relationships with kids—your ace in the hole, by the way, when the rare crisis occurs in a win-win classroom.) So I looked at the literature and programs I could find and talked to a number of counselors and crisis intervention specialists, and I discovered a hodgepodge of advice: *Talk softly. Be loud and authoritative. Use humor. Avoid humor. Use physical proximity. Don't get too close. Send the child out of the room. Keep the child in the room, but send everyone else out to a predetermined location.* In other words, any strategy can work sometimes and so can its complete opposite. In addition, any strategy can backfire and make things worse. There are factors at work beyond what you can know or see, and most often, you're making a split-second judgment call, because different kids and different situations will call for different approaches. Trying to rely on a formulaic response can actually create more problems than it solves.

Let's pick our battles very carefully. There will be days when things the students do bother you a lot more than they normally might, so you will need to ask for certain behaviors you might not ordinarily require. And there will be rules that would have you bust kids for things you might never notice and don't care about, and rules that obstruct the very things that might help your students focus, attend, and self-manage.[31] There is no one way to respond to every student, every behavior, or every situation.

If you want to find a good use for consistency, commit yourself to being consistent in terms of following through on the conditions for positive outcomes you allow, modeling your behavior to reflect the way you would like your students to act, and holding on to your long-range goals and win-win ideals. Consistency can get dangerously close to rigidity, and artificially imposed uniformity is rarely practicable. Understand the limitations of both, and instead shoot for a mix of good judgment and common sense.

Negative Verbal Responses

A friend recently related a story of riding her bike past a school and hearing teachers yelling at kids from one end of the building to the other. "I'm sure glad I don't have a child at that school," she said. If you're familiar with this phenomenon, I'm sure you can appreciate what it's like for the students who have to spend so much of their lives in such an environment.

As with our attachment to punishment, there are still many adults who believe that kids won't behave or develop properly without the familiar verbal responses like scolding, criticizing, lecturing, preaching, or moralizing or that students won't take teachers seriously unless they are speaking in a loud, angry voice. In fact, these kinds of teacher behavior are so common that few question their value and appropriateness. But as one contributor noted, "Kids get numb to the sound of our voice, especially when we're intent on making them wrong. Teach the behavior you want," she said. "Don't talk it to death." Another teacher shared what she found to be a valuable piece of advice: "Say less, mean more!"

I've known teachers who recorded their interactions with students and were surprised to discover the frequency with which they were prone to communicating in negative, critical, sarcastic, or just plain *loud* ways. Pay attention to your words and your tone. When kids get a wrong answer, do you show them how to get it right or give them the correct response—without referring to their study habits, personality, or what they should have learned by now? To what degree can you resist taking a child's behavior personally? Is your feedback more long-winded than it needs to be? How often do you lose it with your students, yelling or shaming when they aren't doing what you want?

"It's not the children's emotions that teachers and staff need to manage—it's their own," wrote educator Stephen Haslam.[32] I'm not talking about the rare slip on an especially bad day. (In win-win relationships, kids will cut teachers a remarkable amount of slack for human errors.) I'm referring to patterns of verbal assaults that are rationalized with their prevalence, perpetuated by the assumption that negative feedback is necessary, and justified as an appropriate reaction to a child's behavior.[33] While there may be well-documented historical precedents for disregarding a child's dignity, these interactions can have a profoundly negative and corrosive effect on young people—the ones being attacked as well as those witnessing and hearing the interactions. Too often, the results of criticism, particularly when it attacks the character or worth of the child, tend toward a shallow, impermanent form of self-protection, with by-products like perfectionism, low confidence, and a sense of inadequacy.[34] What kids learn from shame, fear, or self-hatred is hardly what most of us want as our legacy.

"Students will always remember teachers who humiliate them, and those memories will be filled with anger and resentment," wrote Wyatt and White. "Students will also remember teachers who treated them with respect."[35] Aside from the potential for provoking even stronger or more disconnected student behaviors and attitudes, violating students' dignity and emotional safety is among the discipline strategies prohibited by the National Education Association (NEA) Code of Ethics.[36] If you want to assess the language and behaviors you use with your students, you might want to reflect on incidents by asking yourself the following questions offered by educator Bryan Cichy: "Would I have felt comfortable intervening in the same way if my colleagues had been watching? If the child's parent(s) had been watching? Did my intervention increase the child's chances of success in the long term? Would I have wanted to receive the same intervention from my superior?"[37] Anything other than an enthusiastic *yes* to all of the above will signal a need to consider other, more positive approaches to verbal interactions with your students.

Other Common Strategies (and Bad Ideas)

There are a few other patterns you're likely to observe or be encouraged to use. If you've already added any of these practices to your repertoire, please be aware of the drawbacks and limitations of each. Positive alternatives will follow.

Labeling Students

Don't put much stock in labels other teachers use to describe your students. While it may be impossible to avoid hearing that Mabel is a brain, Jackie is a slob, Monique is a pest, or Robin is pure trouble, you can refuse to allow someone else's perceptions and experiences to shape your students' chances for success in *your* room. Clear your thoughts of expectations based on gossip and give each student a fair start with a clean slate. Even positive labels are limiting and presumptuous and can impose a great deal of pressure on students. Resist the inclination to reduce a child to a simple, two-dimensional description. And using a negative, derogatory, or demeaning label to describe a student is never appropriate, whether to a colleague or a parent or to a student's face.[38]

Labeling Misbehavior

Notice how skilled some adults are at naming undesirable student behaviors, which you'll hear reflected in comments like "That's inappropriate" or "You're being disrespectful." It's hard to see the point of vague and empty criticism other than making students wrong—hardly a constructive teacher behavior. There's nothing instructive in these statements, no useful information about the desirable behaviors we'd prefer. Keep coming back to intentions to build cooperation and self-management, and use the time and energy it takes to describe a misbehavior to ask for what you want instead.

Relying on Other Adults to Deal With Student Misbehavior

This is yet another practice with plenty of history and precedents behind it. But watch out for the temptation to call parents to have them deal with a misbehaving child, or to send kids to the office or request special services, either to punish or rehabilitate misbehaving students or to get a child removed from your classroom (especially for more trivial offenses). Previous chapters have addressed more productive ways to work with administrators, support staff, and parents. Even if this is an accepted practice in your school and community, asking others to take responsibility for discipline matters reflects very poorly on you as a leader in your classroom and as a professional in general.

Expectations

You're likely to get a good bit of advice to have high expectations, and you will probably be assured that children rise to the expectations we set for them. Unfortunately, expectations, like rules, reflect the commitment of and importance to the adults who express them. They will not generate cooperation unless students also see the value in what is expected and are likewise committed—which is unlikely to happen simply because adults *expect* it of them. Don't confuse expectations with faith in kids, with a belief in their abilities, or with high-quality criteria for work assigned. There are ways to entice commitment from them. But unless they are desperate for your conditional approval (which, in itself, has some serious negative implications), simply expressing an expectation is not among them.

Failure to Follow Through

Two of the most common things teachers do to sabotage their authority reflect a lack of follow-through on previously set limits or boundaries. The first is giving warnings when a particular contingency has been breached. If you have allowed students to work together, for example, on the condition that they do so without interrupting the work anybody else is doing, yourself included, the moment they become noisy or disruptive, they lose the privilege. Warning them confirms that they don't need to respect the conditions you have set. (Pulling a series of color-coded warning cards or writing names on the board with check marks for subsequent infractions is simply an institutionalized, packaged version of the same warning process.) The second involves asking for excuses or explanations when they have misbehaved, broken an agreement, or failed to complete an assignment, for example, which suggests that they can talk their way out of the requirements you set. There are ways to build flexibility into your structures so you'll never have to use warnings or ask for excuses, and if you want to be taken seriously, avoid both of these traps.

Withholding Credit or Advancement

Of course, students need to do the work to receive credit.[39] However, allowing students' behavior to influence grading, eligibility, placement, promotion, or graduation is petty and unprofessional. These practices are also prohibited by the NEA Code of Ethics. This isn't about effort or lack of effort, or about the quality of students' work or their understanding of the concepts being taught. It's about remaining as neutral as possible in evaluating a student's work—especially on a subjective assignment like an essay, for example. If you are feeling angry at a student (or a student's parent) and think it might sway your assessment of that student's work, put it on the bottom of the pile or save it for a later time after you've had a chance to cool down. The same thing goes if you're in a generally negative space about other things going on in your life. Wait until you're in a place where you can see and appreciate the positive evidence of their efforts.

Telling Students How Their Behavior Makes You Feel

This is another popular strategy that just won't go away, so don't be surprised to hear people recommend statements like "When you forget your assignment, I feel frustrated and disappointed" or "I get angry when it's so noisy in here" to keep your kids in line. Your students are not responsible for your emotional well-being, and you really do not want to put them in that position, if only for the possibility that they simply may not care enough for this approach to work. (Wouldn't you prefer that students return library books so they can get a new one rather than having them do so to avoid your anger and disappointment or to gain your conditional approval?) People rationalize using these statements as a means of teaching empathy, but the responses I have witnessed tend more toward stress, resentment, or indifference instead. Caretaking has its costs, so even if this does seem to work, it's a strategy you really want to avoid. There are ways to build empathy and compassion for others—as well as ways to motivate cooperation and respect—without burdening anyone with the job of keeping you happy.[40]

Praise

You'll probably hear that praise is the go-to strategy for motivating and reinforcing positive behavior, but there are a slew of problems here as well. First of all, praising kids to *motivate* them is a misuse of a reinforcer, which only works *after* a behavior has appeared.[41] Second, praise is misused again when it attempts to distract a child from a problem, discount a problem a child is having, or make a child feel better. Finally, even used as a reinforcer after the fact, praise tends to reflect a personal judgment, approval contingent on certain behavioral choices students have made. Spontaneous, random, and genuine expressions of affection and appreciation are fine—assuming there's no agenda or conditionality attached. But if you want to build responsibility and reinforce positive choices, go for the more neutral acknowledgment in a recognition statement that does not rely on your reaction. (See the next chapter, "Create a Win-Win Classroom.")

Projection

If you've ever heard someone tell a child "You must be proud" or "You should be thankful," you've witnessed examples of adults projecting their feelings and values onto the child. This strategy is usually fairly innocuous, and more presumptuous than dangerous, although I've seen it used to deliberately attempt to reinforce something the teacher wanted the child to continue doing. The problem is that something like "You must be happy" presumes students feel a certain way, although the experience may hold an entirely different meaning or value to them. As an alternative, you can share your observations ("You're obviously excited about this" or "You seem pleased"), ask students how they feel, or simply recognize the accomplishment ("You worked very hard on this!").[42]

Tokens

This idea has also been around for a long time, referring to a reinforcement system that uses some tangible reward—a sticker, ticket, chip, gold star, piece of candy, or other items to which a student attaches value—to acknowledge the performance of a desired behavior. Even in the 1970s, research revealed that this strategy was often overused and was discouraged as not necessarily the most effective reinforcement strategy in the long run.[43] However, those of us desperate enough to try it soon discovered that it was hard to avoid being arbitrary in how we ended up distributing the tokens, that the system was unwieldy and time-consuming, and that after a while, the classic "token inflation" would indeed rear its ugly head—in my case, when kids started asking whether they were getting tickets for going to lunch. While I know teachers who indulge their students' enjoyment of stickers (especially the scratch-and-sniff variety, and yes, this includes high school kids), the ones who do it successfully tend to do it infrequently and uniformly, say, for every student who turns in a particular assignment or project. Nonetheless, look to desirable activities and privileges kids can earn for more motivational leverage.

Physical Punishment

It's pretty sad that we still need to address this topic at this point in our history and social evolution, but as of late summer 2009, there were still twenty states in the United States that permit children to be paddled in school.[44] I'd like to think that it goes without saying that there is no place for physical punishment in a win-win classroom, regardless of the apparent justification. Although often touted as a last resort, there is far too much evidence of the practice invoked as a first response, often to trivial infractions. Research speaks to a wide range of negative outcomes of corporal punishment—not just for the children being hit but for their classmates and the climate of the school, too—including a tendency to make behavior even worse. Again, think in terms of the honorable intentions schools profess and consider the insanity, much less hypocrisy, of using physical punishment to teach things like respect, self-control, or nonviolence. Hitting children makes us look weak, ineffective, unskilled, and unprofessional. Even if your school condones this practice, don't. If you cannot teach without hitting children, you do not have the skills you need to be allowed in the classroom with them. There are better ways.[45]

Attitudinal Obstacles

OK, so these aren't strategies as much as stumbling blocks. Attitudinal obstacles tend to show up in a couple different ways. One is a resistance to having to motivate kids in the first place. I still hear people insist that students should want to learn for the love of learning and that the satisfaction gained from new knowledge and personal growth should be motivation and reinforcement enough. While few people would argue with the desire for such evidence of self-actualization, you may have to stretch a bit to entice some of your students, especially those who have yet to experience the joys of successfully exploring a school subject they just loved.

There is no such thing as unmotivated behavior—for kids or for adults—and few people are willing to put in time and effort if nothing good comes of it, whether the outcome or payoff is pleasure, satisfaction, achievement, a grade, or a paycheck. (I haven't met many teachers who profess an eagerness to teach exclusively for the love of teaching. And few kids are likely to get excited about work they perceive as boring, irrelevant, or impossible to do.) Clearly, some outcomes are more effective than others, and in case you're worried about the idea that you're bribing a student any time you offer a positive outcome, keep in mind that the threat of punishment or a teacher's angry tirade is just as much a bribe as a chance to work on an enrichment activity, move on to the next book, or work with a partner.

The second obstacle is evident in the mindset that resists the need to differentiate how we motivate or reinforce different students. It's easy to fall back on old standbys like "If I let one do it, I have to let them all do it," but the truth is there will always be students who couldn't care less about whatever *it* is and would just as soon have a chance to work on an art project, work at a computer, or do their assignments sitting on the floor as, say, run an errand, work in a group, or have the rest of the period off to visit the media center or start in on their homework. Different kids, different strategies, and it's the creative and attentive teachers who best connect what they want to what their individual students want.

Finally, there is the obstacle that comes up any time you block an idea or talk yourself out of doing something you think might work with your kids for fear of repercussions. Absolutely proceed with caution when it comes to a strategy or accommodation that's never been tried successfully in your school, or when you approach an administrator or department chair for something that is generally discouraged in your setting. But know that just because it may seem easier to assume "we can't do that" than it is to make a case for what you want to do, in many cases, you can pull off more than you think you can. Many of the strategies involved in becoming a win-win teacher are, as you can see, somewhat outside the traditions practiced in some settings. If you have people rushing to support you in these endeavors—and some teachers do—all the better. But if you find yourself feeling boxed in by restrictions and obstacles, start small and do what you need to do to avoid drawing fire to yourself. Many of these ideas (for example, how you talk to students or your willingness to connect with them) have no impact on others and will happen, for the most part, behind closed doors with little risk of putting your job on the line. Resist the status quo, especially when it includes practices that hurt kids and make things more difficult for you, and don't let yourself be paralyzed by other people's limited thinking. Question tradition, and if you choose a particular strategy or approach, do it consciously, not just because that's what everybody else is doing or because that's the way it's always been done. Your ideas won't always work the way you want or get the support you'd like, but within the walls of your classroom and the relationships you create with your students, keep looking for the most win-win options possible. (See the next chapter, "Create a Win-Win Classroom," for additional positive alternatives.)

ACTIVITY

1. Which of the ineffective classroom-management strategies mentioned in this chapter were familiar to you from your training?

2. Which of the strategies have you observed in your school?

3. Which of the strategies have you tried yourself?

4. Which do you think will be the hardest to avoid or stop using? (Read the next chapter, "Create a Win-Win Classroom," for some additional effective alternatives.)

NOTES

1. Quoted in Quimby (2003, para. 3).

2. Reynolds and Reynolds (2008, para. 1).

3. Quoted in Naylor (2009).

4. This child's brief school history included several learning problems and a fairly extensive behavioral pathology, including some disturbing self-harming behaviors. I have met very few individuals who presented this range and intensity of dysfunction at this age, and few who benefited more from making a connection with a safe adult in the classroom, a process that ended up being more remedial than any cognitive or punitive intervention attempted. Thank you to my friend and former editor Matthew Diener for jogging my memory and for the suggestion to kick this chapter off with this story.

5. Marshall (n.d.).

6. "School Violence: The History of School Discipline" (1998, para. 1).

7. Education professor Jonathan Zimmerman (2007) wrote that strict discipline has been under fire since "the very birth of the common school system in the 1830s" and that objections have come "from a host of different Americans. The most prominent champion of common schools, Horace Mann, warned teachers against excessive force and the suppression of students' natural inclinations. To reformers like John Dewey, schools based on strict discipline—and its pedagogical companion, rote memorization—could never give citizens the skills they needed to govern themselves. Instead of fostering mindless obedience, then, schools needed to teach children how to make up their own minds—that is, how to reason, deliberate and rule on complex political questions" (para. 7).

8. Purkey and Aspy (1988, p. 47).

9. To explore these issues in greater detail, please check out *The Win-Win Classroom* (Bluestein, 2008) and *Creating Emotionally Safe Schools* (Bluestein, 2001).

10. Gazzaniga (1988, p. 205). The sense of power or the ability to impact situations affecting your life also has implications for your body and physical health. In an article on the impact of stress on coronary health, Anne Underwood (2005) reported, "People respond differently to high-pressure work situation. The key to whether it produces a coronary seems to be whether you have a sense of control over life, or live at the mercy of circumstances and superiors" (p. 51).

11. Gatto (2005, p. 6).

12. "NYCLU, Annenberg Institute Release Report on Successful and Safe NYC Schools That Say No to Aggressive Police Tactics" (2009). This report studied the impact of aggressive controlling approaches in schools with high-risk populations. The studies affirmed that "there are effective, real-world alternatives to making schools feel like jails" (para. 4) and, quoting Tara Bahl, data and research analyst for the Annenberg Institute for School Reform, determined that "the successful schools' policies and practices emphasize the students' dignity, their desire to learn, and their capacity for responsible decision making. They have created a culture where positive educational outcomes are common and expected and they've put students on the path toward graduation" (para. 10). The report concluded, "These punitive measures contribute to the school to prison pipeline, a system of local, state and federal education and public safety policies that pushes students out of school and into the criminal justice system. The pipeline disproportionately affects youth of color and youth with disabilities" (para. 15).

13. Isaacson (2007, p. 26).

14. From the BrainyQuote Web site: http://www.brainyquote.com/quotes/authors/r/ralph_nader.html.

15. Liability issues are almost never mentioned, though if we're going to be honest here, they probably drive the need for things like discipline codes and posting rules (with or without the negative consequences) throughout the school or in student handbooks as much as any other concern expressed.

16. Mann (n.d., para. 9).

17. Marshall (2001, p. 49).

18. Please do not hear this as an argument for denying kids a chance to at least do their homework in detention. I've never known detention to work as a discipline strategy and will always vote for more sensible ways to shape kids' behavior, but this is at least a decent use of the time.

19. Marshall (2001, p. 49).

20. With regard to detention, Marvin Marshall (2001) noted, "Students who are assigned to detention and fail to serve it are punished with more detention. . . . In the hundreds of seminars I have conducted around the world, teachers who use detention rarely suggest that it is effective in changing behavior. If detention were effective, the same students would not be consistently assigned to it" (p. 48). To support Marshall's comments, a teacher in one of my seminars sent me a copy of her district's tardiness policy. The "consequences for excessive tardies" included escalating punishments: one afternoon of detention for the first through fourth unexcused tardy, two detentions for the fifth through eighth incident, three for nine to twelve tardies, and four for thirteen through sixteen late arrivals to class. The list concluded with the following warning: "Failure to stay for afterschool detention will result in out-of-school suspension." If this policy is the only incentive for kids to get to class on time, clearly something isn't working. In addition, I'm trying to imagine the record keeping for policies like these, and really have to wonder what this district is trying to accomplish.

21. Freiberg (2007c).

22. Blum et al. (2002, p. 12).

23. Kenmore (n.d., para. 2).

24. Littke and Grabelle (2004, p. 44).

25. Bluestein and Katz (2005, p. 15).

26. Mahoney and Purr (2007, pp. 24, 36). Instead, they suggested, "spend the time doing something to get to know their names and personalities" and allow "limited, structured time to catch up with each other."

27. If you think about it, this single rule is actually quite restrictive, and even preschool kids can get their heads around its meaning. You will want to have specific instructions on how to use certain equipment, or which behaviors will allow kids to continue working on a specific task, but the simpler your rules and limits, the more effective they tend to be.

28. Note that most people generally want the school to do more than manage children's behavior. An editorial requesting that schools stress moral learning in place of listing rules quoted one adult as saying, "Am I the only parent who wants her children to learn to reason rather than memorize a set of behavioral rules?" (Blumenfeld, 1996).

29. Teachers tend to favor students who are more affluent or dress well, as well as kids with superior athletic or academic skills. Likewise, research indicates that minority students are more likely to receive harsher and more frequent penalties for the same misbehaviors observed in nonminority students. Bluestein (2001).

30. Adler and Springen (1999).

31. Teachers report the greatest opposition from colleagues and administrators when they attempt to meet individual learning needs with neurologically appropriate accommodations,

especially if they are working with administrators who insist that students uniformly sit quietly and still. They also report greater success with the support of counselors, occupational therapists, and often parents. Likewise, some have made strides by starting with small and nondisruptive interventions, and by demonstrating (and documenting) the positive impact of these accommodations with improved student behavior and academic performance.

32. Haslam (2001).

33. This type of teacher behavior is often a sign of burnout or extreme stress and may not even be related to the kids themselves. When you find yourself taking things out on your students or feeling contempt for them or the job, please consider asking for help to sort out whatever is going on in your life or to develop better coping mechanisms. (See the next section, "Part IV: Self," for more on self-care.)

34. How often have you met high-achieving individuals who are terrified of making a mistake and see only flaws in their finest accomplishments? How many adults do you know who believe they're "no good at drawing (or math or writing, for example)," or who lack faith in their appearance or social skills because of some reckless comment addressed to them years earlier?

35. Wyatt and White (2007, pp. 53–54).

36. These behaviors include attempts to threaten emotional safety by humiliating, expressing contempt, condemning or attacking students' behavior or attitude, condemning or attacking their values, violating dignity or self-worth, criticizing, shaming, engaging in verbal or emotional violence, yelling, intimidating, threatening, using sarcasm, controlling, manipulating, punishing, employing conditional approval or love, or using the threat of emotional abandonment. National Education Association (1975).

37. Cichy (2008).

38. Note the difference between describing a behavior ("You worked hard on this" or "Your handwriting has really improved") and describing a student ("You're so smart, or neat, or good"). Likewise, rather than labeling needy kids as pests, give them a time you'll be available or assign them to a partner. If they get the answers wrong, explaining the skill again or in a different way will teach them the skill far more effectively than impatience, criticism, or any label that suggests that they are lacking in intelligence or worth.

39. Hopefully, you will be assigning work that they can do successfully so that they perceive this to be possible.

40. Students motivated by the need to please, gain approval, or avoid someone's reactions often have a really hard time making decisions in their own best interests. For more information on this topic, there is a free article on my Web site (www.janebluestein.com/articles/whatswrong .html): "What's Wrong with 'I-Messages.'"

41. This is more common in primary classrooms, where you'll often hear things like "I like the way Susie is sitting" to try to get others in the class to sit quietly. As an alternative, try tying your request to an outcome that does not depend on your students' need for your conditional approval, that is, for you to like them, too. Be aware that even young kids can tell when you're just saying something nice to get them to do what you want.

42. Adapted from Bluestein (2008).

43. Osborn and Osborn (1977, p. 38).

44. Thanks to Jordan Riak and Parents and Teachers Against Violence in Education (http://nospank.net).

45. For more research and information on this topic, there is an excerpt from *Creating Emotionally Safe Schools* (Bluestein, 2001), "Spare the Rod," on my Web site (www.janebluestein .com/articles/no_paddling.html).

12

Create a Win-Win Classroom

Pick your worst students, the ones whose behavior brings you to the edge. Investigate their personal background. You'll wonder why their behavior is so good.

Mel Alper, retired high school history teacher

It takes a strategy for inclusion to counteract human fears and shortcomings.

Mike Smith, president, Alliance for Student Activities[1]

Kindness is a language which the deaf can hear and the blind can see.

Mark Twain, author and humorist[2]

It's always the little things that stand out: A counselor pulling a student aside in the hallway to ask about a sibling or a parent or to wish him good luck in the game on Saturday. The teacher laughing with a student over a cheeky comment without thinking to punish the disruption. The teaching assistant calling a fidgety child up next to her chair to show him something interesting before his behavior became problematic to the kids around him. The teacher who defused a potential incident by agreeing that an upset child had every reason to be bothered by what had just happened to her.

Time after time, I see examples of educators who, whether through instinct or deliberate intention, quietly defy negative traditions and establish more positive patterns of interaction, often turning toxic environments into safe, inviting, and productive ones. I talk to principals committed to creating caring communities, superintendents who emphasize connectedness over more measurable priorities, and teachers and counselors who will try almost anything to engage a resistant, defensive, or defeated child. So there are plenty of examples of positivity out there.

Unfortunately, I also encounter plenty of cynicism in people who, seeing positivity through their all-or-nothing filter, imagine it to represent a loosey-goosey classroom without limits or sanctions, a place where kids can do whatever they want. This is the kind of thinking that's also behind the assumption that focusing on the positive means accepting—even condoning—the negative. If these concerns are nagging at you, I understand, so let me state unequivocally that permissiveness is definitely not the way to go. But as with so many other aspects of this profession, there is a win-win middle ground between permissive and authoritarian methods—both of these being win-lose approaches, by the way.

A positive focus does not interfere with your ability to set limits, request different behaviors, withdraw privileges, or intervene in potentially dangerous or destructive situations when necessary. It simply allows you to do so without shaming or attacking your students, without making them wrong, without violating their dignity, and without creating a whole lot of stress for anyone, yourself included. Positivity reflects a shift in the traditional authority role to one that emphasizes community and cooperation, a structure in which negative student behavior—from disengaged to destructive—is far less likely to be an issue. If you would allow me to mangle a couple of metaphors, let me assure you that just because you're not ruling the roost with an iron fist, you are still running the show. But in this case the responsibility rests with the players.

Having looked at some of the ineffective and destructive strategies most often used in school in the previous chapter, now let's look at the positive alternatives we can use in their place. Any one of these will contribute to your efforts to build a win-win classroom, and in the case of the list that follows, more is absolutely better.

RELATIONSHIPS

There's a reason I devoted an entire chapter to connecting with students, and at the risk of beating this topic to death, I cannot overstate the importance of the relationships you establish with your kids. Whatever else you do in your classroom starts and ends here. "A classroom without a heartfelt connection to a teacher and to the other students is quite comparable to a minimum security prison, [where] the teacher maintains discipline through threat and punishment, and if you listen, the kids will often make that comparison," wrote Gail Dusa. Instead, she suggested, "love is the only teacher. When love, kindness, compassion, and connectedness are present, there are seldom discipline problems, and those that arise can be facilitated with love, kindness, compassion, and empathy." However, since we don't have many models for win-win authority relationships, it may take a while to discover a comfortable line between *friendly* and *friend* or between *bossy* and *boss*, although the other tools in this list will help you do just that.

An authoritarian approach puts a great deal of stress on relationships and is costly and exhausting. A director of professional development noted, "If you lead with fear you'll get little respect. If you lead with respect you'll have little fear." Bill Funkhouser shared an example of something that worked for him after he developed a more compassionate approach to dealing with his classes. "I have a student who doesn't do his homework and who struggles in the class. Last year he would have had several detentions and a failing grade. I would have forced him to come in to do his homework and we would have been in a power struggle," he wrote. "This year I purchased several school supplies for him and have always had a kind word for him. I recently found out he is actually homeless and that he and his dad are living in a cheap motel. Recently he has started spending his break time in my class, by his own choosing, doing his math homework. He also drew me some pictures on binder paper that he wanted me to have. It breaks my heart to think of all the opportunities I have missed for this type of relationship with students."

It may be hard to resist a more negative, reactive path. It is, after all, familiar, may be fairly automatic, and will probably receive support and acceptance in your school community. But make the shift toward win-win objectives and make relationships a primary goal, and you may well discover the only path to engaging some of your more resistant, disruptive, and defeated students. And considering how much more pleasant this will be for you, there really is no excuse for not making these connections a priority.

Report Card for My Teacher

Want to know how you're doing? Just ask! Most students love to give teachers feedback, and considering how insightful they can be, it's really a shame we don't ask them more often than we do. (You do not need to ask for names to get some good reinforcement for things you're doing that are working for them or for ideas about ways you can tweak your teaching, changes you can make in your classroom, or choices you might be able to start offering.) A few sample questions you might consider asking follow:

1. What do you like most about being in this class?
2. What do I do that you appreciate most? Or what do I do that helps you most?
3. What can I do to make your experience in this class better?
4. What do you wish we would study in here?
5. What do you wish you could do in here to make your learning even better?
6. How would that help?
7. What in my behavior makes you feel valued and welcome in this class?
8. What in my behavior makes you feel safe in this class?
9. If there were one thing you could change about the way I teach, what would it be?
10. If there were one thing you could change about this class, what would it be?
11. If there were one thing you could change about this room, what would it be?
12. Other comments or feedback:

STRUCTURE AND ROUTINES

If you want to devote the majority of your time to teaching, your students will need to be able to function independently and nondisruptively, especially when you are working with individuals or small groups.[3] It's a fair bet that the more time you spend with any group of students in a day, the more routines they'll have to master, but even five-year-olds can quickly learn where to put their papers, how to work in centers, and how to clean up their work spaces and put materials away.

Some of the most effective teachers I know have what they call sponge or fill-in activities, something for students to do the minute they walk into the classroom to get them focused and on task. Whether a question-of-the-day or word-of-the-day, a puzzle or problem to solve, a journaling activity, or some other brief, structured assignment, it's a good idea to have kids get used to the idea that they immediately start working when they come in your room. Alternatively, I've worked with kids who got into the habit of pulling their folders as soon as they came in the room and start working on their individual prescriptions or assignments.

And as far as assignments go, overplan! Even after you've been teaching a while, you'll have lessons that run short or activities that take less time than you anticipated. "Always plan for more than you think you can accomplish," said Diane Callahan. "Don't have a lot of down time—that's when kids create trouble. Keep them busy." It's always easier to carry plans over to another day than to teach with your eye on the clock, fretting about stretching your plans out until the bell rings.

Although I'm a huge fan of offering choices, you might want to minimize the need for students to make a lot of decisions until they learn these routines. It's also not a bad idea to assume that you may have to help them develop decision-making skills and other responsible learning behaviors during the year, regardless of how old they are. (In fact, I've found that the older my students were and the longer they'd been in school, the more thoroughly lost they were when required to make choices or self-manage when they weren't being told what to do.) Start small if necessary and increase options as confidence and skills grow. It's always easier to increase complexity and choices than to increase structure and limits. The environment, organization, and limits of the first few weeks will not necessarily reflect what will be happening in the room later in the year. Keep your long-term goals in mind. Remember that even if the students do not have many opportunities for decision making or movement right off the bat, they will have an easier time at it once they have a framework of familiarity from which to work.

FLEXIBILITY AND FAIRNESS

A seminar participant shared an interesting illustration of the difference between treating students equally and equitably, something she learned from a teacher she interviewed for a job. The prospective teacher explained, "Equal means the same. Equitable means giving what is needed. If an aloe plant and an astilbe plant are treated equally, they both may die. If they are treated equitably, given what each needs to grow, they may both flourish." I honestly don't know much about the difference in the care of these two plants, but I wanted to use this quote exactly as it was related to me. I'm taking this teacher at her word, and even without a deep understanding of the horticultural reference, I believe the point to be quite clear. (Impressed by this explanation, the committee hired the teacher being interviewed, she said.)

Flexibility is what brings common sense to the structure you provide, the choices you offer, and your approach to instruction and discipline. "I found that what worked for one child didn't work for the next," wrote Michelle Erickson. "I have discovered it is a mix of everything and that one style won't work for everyone." I rarely had kids question why different students or groups had different assignments and accommodations or were required to do different amounts of work. If asked, a simple explanation almost always sufficed: "Because we're all different, and everyone here gets to succeed." Even young kids can understand the concept of equitable, even if they don't know the word for it, and when the word *fair* is explained as *equally appropriately challenged*, colleagues and parents can be far more accepting of a differentiated approach.

Flexibility will allow you to build a safety net into a boundary or requirement—before there is a problem—and can grant you a great deal of reasonableness without compromising your follow-through in any way. For example, to respect the fact that everybody has a bad night, I've known win-win teachers to build in an allowance to give kids the occasional break they need to still get homework in within specified limits. Allowing a twenty-four-hour grace period for assignments, requiring 95% of the homework, or providing students with a "Get Out of Jail Free" card to exchange for a lost or forgotten assignment, for example, also relieves you of the burden of asking for excuses or having to make a determination on the validity of a child's alibi.

CHOICES

Ask teachers to construct a wish list of desirable student behaviors, and you'll probably see items that point to increased responsibility and self-management. Few teachers mind filling cognitive gaps, yet building independence and learning skills often appears to be an annoying abuse of instructional time. Nonetheless, this investment has a huge potential payoff, as the more self-managing your students become, the more instructional time you'll create in the long run. "If you want a behavior, you have to teach a behavior," admonished Chick Moorman. No question. Unfortunately, I was unaware of how many of these behaviors I would have to teach.

Like many beginning teachers, perhaps, I started my teaching career with a lot of assumptions about what my students could handle when left to their own devices, only to find some of them completely overwhelmed when faced with even the simplest choices, such as which of two assignments to do first. These were eleven- and twelve-year-old students, many with significant responsibilities at home, and many already facing decisions about things like smoking cigarettes, getting high, or engaging in sexual activity. As I discovered the degree to which choices were being made for them at school, however, I could better understand why so many didn't even try to take on this responsibility by the time they got to my class. The more control teachers exerted, the less the kids bothered to try to control themselves, much less assume control of their learning.

Research by Martin Seligman on learned helplessness found that "human motivation to initiate responses is . . . undermined by a lack of control over one's surroundings."[4] But exhibiting helplessness and shutting down are not the only ways kids respond to being so restricted, which is why offering choices is such a great argument as a strategy for minimizing power struggles. In addition, when kids don't have opportunities to make choices, their ability to make sound, constructive decisions is impaired, a deficiency that can affect their lives long after they've left your classroom.[5]

Offering choices is by far the easiest way to bridge the need for structure and the need for power and autonomy that all humans have, and is one of the most effective vehicles for establishing a win-win power dynamic at your disposal. An article by Michael Brockman and Stephen Russell advised, "Research has repeatedly demonstrated that youth development programs are successful in promoting positive behavior and preventing problem behavior" when these programs help young people learn a variety of skills, including decision making and problem solving.[6] In a way, this is so basic to learning and managing a classroom that it's hard to imagine any program that does not persuade teachers to offer students structured choices and encourage decision making. Yet I've noticed a disturbing trend, meeting beginning teachers lately who had been specifically discouraged, either in their training programs or by their cooperating teachers or colleagues, from doing just that. Again, I suspect the culprit to be black-and-white thinking suggesting that giving choices will undermine teacher authority, when in actuality, the exact opposite is true.

Start small, asking students to select which of two assignments to do first, to identify a topic from a list to research, or to choose ten out of fifteen problems. If necessary, set a time limit or deadline for deciding. As students develop more expertise and confidence, expand the limits of the choices you offer and include their input and preferences to whatever degree you can. Make sure you don't have an agenda for the choices they make and that all the options you offer are equally acceptable. These are great ways to assert your authority while respecting your students' desire for some control in their lives. Start including them in decisions that affect their time in your classroom and see if you don't notice a significant increase in your students' willingness to get on board.

ASKING FOR WHAT YOU WANT

Although it may not be immediately obvious to your students why you're insisting that they wear goggles in lab, reshelve reference books in a certain order, put the lids back on the paste jars, or head their papers in a certain way, there are generally good reasons for asking students to follow certain protocols regarding the tasks we assign or the materials they use.[7] As with so many other aspects of our work, there are more effective ways to ask for the behaviors we want than the ones most familiar and most commonly used. Unfortunately, there is a certain cultural conditioning that somehow equates asking for what we want with undesirable character traits like aggressiveness, selfishness, or pushiness. So a lot of people grow up resorting to unpleasant alternatives like giving commands, manipulation, whining, tantrums, coy helplessness, or the threat that their seething resentment will erupt in anger, abandonment, or some other hurtful impulse—patterns that have been modeled for them or have seemed to work for them in the past. (If this sounds familiar, it may take some deliberate thought and intention to switch to more positive behaviors. It's hard to give up behaviors that we come to rely on, even when they cause more pain than good, but change starts with an awareness of the patterns we develop, so start noticing the ways you normally try to get what you want.)

Sometimes, simply giving kids enough credit for understanding a reasonable explanation, one that goes beyond the authoritarian "because I said so," will inspire a surprisingly cooperative response. For example, consider the respect and commonsense grounds for cooperation in statements like "Please put the books back in alphabetical order so they'll be easier to find next time" or "If you put the lid back on the paste, it won't be dried out when you want to use it again." Notice that the reasons for the requested behavior are clearly stated and are presented in terms of positive outcomes with regard to the individual, the group, the environment, or the item in question, rather than being stated as an accusation, a decree, or moral issue. (Compare the previous examples to "If you don't put the lid back on the paste, you won't be allowed to use it again" or "I told you to put these lids on" or even "Put the lids on the paste for me, please." And notice that I've left out examples of personal attacks or expressions of disgust or disappointment.) Think of the real reasons you want your students to do what you're asking, and share the justification in the requests you make.

Likewise, watch the way most adults structure contingencies, statements in which we connect a potential outcome with a requirement or request, and see how often we express these statements as threats, focusing on the negative outcome. Although one of the simplest win-win strategies involves simply shifting from a threat to a promise—that is, a contingency emphasizing the *positive* consequences of cooperation—years of negative patterns make it far more likely that we would automatically warn kids that we're not going to write that letter of recommendation if we don't have at least two weeks' notice instead of happily offering to write the letter as long as we've got at least fourteen days' advance. It doesn't sound like much, but the shift is energetically powerful, respects kids' intelligence and autonomy, and—so long as our follow-through is solid—puts a whole lot of responsibility on the kids.

Even in terms of simple imperatives, we always have two ways of asking for the behavior we want. Consider asking positively, telling students what you want rather than emphasizing what you don't want. Try "Please walk in the hall" instead of "Don't run." Punishing a child for name-calling or swearing teaches a very different lesson from what they learn when you respond with a comment like "We don't say that word in here," which is often all the situation requires. Further, a request is far less likely than criticism or commands to provoke defensiveness or opposition, and it's far easier to internalize, increasing the likelihood of the student maintaining and repeating the positive behavior without instruction or threats from the teacher.

POSITIVE CONSEQUENCES

Over the years, one of the biggest challenges I have faced in my work involves selling the importance of switching our emphasis from negative consequences to positive outcomes. This shouldn't come as a surprise, I suppose. In most instances, even the word *consequence* signals something negative or punitive, leaving little room for the reality that, in any contingency, *positive consequences* are almost always available as well. Nearly all discipline programs emphasize the negative outcomes, although there are some clear benefits to stressing positive outcomes—what the kids get or get to do when they do what you ask. I've talked about the drawbacks of depending on punishments, or the threat of negative consequences, as well as positive ways to ask for what you want, so hopefully this particular pump is primed.

One of the nice things about thinking in terms of positive outcomes you can offer is that it allows you to require certain behaviors or a certain amount of work from the students in order for them to earn, or continue to enjoy, these benefits. In a culture in which far too many kids are growing up with an unnerving sense of entitlement and without limits or accountability, this is not a bad thing. And it's easier to get kids to respect limits and buy into a sense of accountability when offered outcomes they perceive as positive and meaningful.

This is where the whole bribery argument comes up, so once again, let me remind you that there is no such thing as unmotivated behavior. It really comes down to whether we're going to use positive bribes—including work-related options and earned advances—in place of the negative ones on which we currently depend. We connect desired behavior to consequences one way or the other, so why not focus on the good stuff? Because frankly, a reward-orientated classroom that emphasizes the payoff for cooperation—rather than punishment for noncompliance—is not only a cornerstone of win-win classrooms, but it's also a lot easier to manage and, generally, a whole lot more pleasant for all concerned. It doesn't take long for even the most cynical, well-defended students to start seeing your class as a place where "good things happen *when* . . . ." And therein lies the incentive to come to class on time, put things back when they're done with them, or stay quiet while you're reading the story.

Once you get comfortable with the idea of positive consequences, it's time to start thinking about what you can offer. This is where those interest inventories and conversations will come in handy. (If you're noticing a slightly holographic quality to the content of this book, you're right. Everything overlaps and interrelates with everything else, which is why it's so important to maintain a big-picture perspective in a win-win context for everything you do in your classroom.) Shifting your focus to positive outcomes could be as simple as saving a few minutes at the end of each class, or day, for an enrichment activity, story or short video, or time to start on a homework assignment—with teacher nearby to answer questions or offer help as needed. Positive outcomes could also include opportunities to work as a peer helper with other students, design projects based on certain criteria, or use certain equipment or accommodations to satisfy personal learning-style preferences—as long as the privilege is earned and practiced within clearly defined limits. And keep in mind that simply being able to make certain decisions about content, sequence, presentation, or where they want to work, for example, offers a host of positive consequences and, in many cases, will be all you need to engage some, if not most or all, of your students.

Even in cases when students fail to earn a privilege—or lose a privilege because they aren't working within previously prescribed limits—a punitive or shaming response is not necessary. Sallie Chaffin, a professional development project coordinator, suggested that "all class behavior plans should be positive. Students should be able to earn back privileges according to their behavior." And in a win-win classroom, struggling students will presumably have lots of opportunities to refine the behaviors and strategies necessary for gaining access to these positive outcomes until they eventually get it right.

FOLLOWING THROUGH

If you've ever been concerned that your students don't seem to take you quite as seriously as you'd like, take a look at how often you follow through on your boundaries. Have you ever said, "I'm only going to say this once," and then found yourself repeating the same thing again and again? Do you ever back down and make a privilege available even though your kids haven't done what you've asked? Do your students know they can get what they want if they bug you enough or have a good enough excuse for not doing what they were asked to do?

Following through communicates that you mean what you say. Developing this habit will take courage and commitment, especially when students don't do what you've asked. That's when good, consistent follow-through matters most. It means you withhold positive outcomes until students fulfill the requirements to earn them and you withdraw positive outcomes when students fail to maintain the behaviors required for their continued enjoyment. Some kids take a while to figure this out, especially if they're used to having people tell them what to do (whether they comply or refuse), if they've been conditioned to believe they simply can't influence their lives, or if they haven't developed constructive and respectful ways of getting or asking for what they want. Even if they become angry when they don't get their way—something you'll see less and less frequently as they get a handle on how this system works—you still don't have to react, blow up, or attack. You do, however, have to hold your ground. There's a certain degree of safety and security for kids who know they can count on their teachers to mean—and do—what they say.

Use nonattacking language like "This isn't working," which suggests that there is a flaw in the students' choices or commitment, not a flaw in the students themselves. Be specific in asking for what you want, whether it's returning to their seats, putting the materials away, or working on a certain activity in place of continuing what they had been doing (or what you had been doing with them). Reassure with a sentence like "Let's try again tomorrow (or later or next time)."[8] There is no punishment, no negative consequence—other than the absence or unavailability of the privilege or positive consequence until their behavior changes. It's a great, caring, and respectful way to help children learn how to make their choices work for everyone concerned. So keep the door open and continue to offer the privileges, day after day if necessary, until they figure out what they need to do to get what they want. (Note that this is also where you'll appreciate the value of having a variety of privileges, accommodations, and other positive outcomes available.)

It can be very uncomfortable to withhold or withdraw privileges until behavior improves, and I can understand the desire to protect kids from the negative outcomes of their behavior—in this case, lack of access to the positive outcomes. But as soon as you delay your follow-through by, say, giving warnings, making excuses for your students, or encouraging them to give you excuses, you reinforce the idea that you don't deserve to be taken seriously. Respecting your own boundaries is a prerequisite to generating respect from others. Besides, if you let kids cross the line and continue to enjoy privileges that require behavior they are not exhibiting, it's a fair bet that at some point you are going to snap and respond in ways that are decidedly *not* win-win.

GOOD DIRECTIONS

Perhaps the discipline problems that are easiest to prevent are the ones that occur when kids aren't clear on what they're supposed to do. As simple and obvious as this may seem, it only takes a few minutes to anticipate what your kids may not understand to prevent problems and off-task behavior that can emerge when kids don't know how to use certain tools or equipment (including basic supplies like rulers or staplers), are fuzzy about the steps in an activity, are not sure where to put things away or where to turn in work, or, especially with young kids and English language learners, don't understand colloquialisms we take for granted like "pick up the floor" or "scrape off your feet." Of course, this is one teaching skill that improves with experience, but even veterans keep a sense of "what could go wrong" or "what might I need to explain" in the back of their mind as they make their plans.

Another simple, practical hint: Because many of your students will not be primary auditory learners, unless you want to spend the period repeating your directions over and over, write them down—on the board or on a task card or prescription, for example—for each group, each center, or even each child. And get them used to referring to the written instructions, or asking one another for help, so you're free to do other things. Young learners are also helped by pictures, illustrations, or photos used, for example, to label storage areas for classroom supplies and materials.

RECOGNITION AND POSITIVE FEEDBACK

Now here's an alternative to praise that makes sense *and* works as well, not just as a reinforcer that increases the likelihood that kids will repeat desirable behaviors, but as a way to help kids see the connection between their actions and the outcomes of those actions—that is, their ability to impact their lives in positive ways. Where praise often offers nonspecific acknowledgement of the value of the child ("You're so good") or of the teacher's emotional response to the child's behavior ("I'm so happy you remembered your book"), a *recognition* statement focuses on the *behavior,* and stresses the positive outcome or benefit to the child: "You remembered your library book. Now you can take another one home." "Alright! You got this report finished on time. Now you can play this weekend." "You got your centers all cleaned up. Now you can go outside (or go to lunch or hear the story)."

Recognition statements first describe the behavior, without judging it or attaching it to the worth of the child, and follow with the positive outcome or results. They do not preclude personal comments or genuine expressions of affection, appreciation, happiness, or pride. They do, however, allow us to eliminate the dependence on our feelings and reactions—so often expressed as conditional approval—in order to encourage continued cooperation. (Appreciating a child's help or gift is not the same as approving of his or her behavior.) Nor does recognition preclude simple acknowledgments of students' efforts, progress, or achievements—important bits of feedback and encouragement—or letting them know you care.

Our culture tends toward a habit of noticing the negative, and if you think about practices related to evaluating a student's performance, you'll notice the degree to which our attention to errors, flaws, and omissions outweighs acknowledgment of brilliance and effort, much less simple correct answers. But don't discount the power of positive feedback—not just to kids but to their parents as well. A little encouragement and an emphasis on what your students are doing right can go a long way in your efforts to engage them, keep them on task, invite them to take risks, and keep trying when they don't get it right the first time. It may take a certain degree of mindfulness (and perhaps a recording device) to start noticing the patterns in your own feedback offerings, as well as some conscious effort to shift your attention to more positive aspects of your students' work and behavior. But this is, ultimately, a simple way to shift the energy in your classroom and in your interactions with your kids.

KEEPING A COOL HEAD

One of the most powerful teaching tools you have available to you is in the responses you exhibit to stressful situations and to uncooperative student behavior in particular. Some kids have an amazingly intuitive ability for getting teachers off task, distracting from a lesson, and generally getting under a grown-up's skin. Your commitment to win-win practices will continually show your students that these adaptive behaviors are simply not necessary, at least in your classroom. Imagine how much they can learn from instances in which you aren't hooked into the negative behaviors most familiar to them. Remember, for some students, negative attention is still attention, and some are so used to such strong reactions from the adults they have known that anything short of explosive on your end may even be interpreted as indifference. Hang in there. These are the kids most in need of caring guidance and noninvasive correction. Stan Davis found it helpful to acknowledge, "I can welcome each kid every day when I remember that this might be the day that this child changes." Don't give up before your persistence and commitment have a chance to work.

Besides, in any interchange with a student, we really do have choices about how we respond. "Situations do not cause us to feel what we feel," observed Stephen Haslam. "The situation is a catalyst. It is a fact, it is neutral. It doesn't become good or bad, right or wrong until we have had a thought about it, until we have made a judgment."[9] Now, anyone who has slipped over the edge into reactions of which we are not particularly proud knows that the thinking and judging process happens fairly instantaneously. In fact, any time the brain perceives something to be a threat—whether to our authority, dignity, or physical well-being, for example—the more emotional part of the brain automatically kicks in and takes over. What results from this process generally isn't very pretty and would hardly fall in the category of win-win intentions. So unless you're actually in a situation in which someone's safety or survival is at stake, take a breath and allow yourself a chance to think of a nonreactive, nonhurtful way to respond.

Imagine how your day would go if you didn't take your students' comments or behavior personally, even when they are personal—and hurtful, too. Again, this is a choice, and sometimes just knowing it's a legitimate option is assurance enough to seek other alternatives. Consider negative student behaviors in the context of survival, their perception of what they believe they need to do to protect themselves in a school setting. Whether they are trying to lower your expectations of them, push you away emotionally so they don't get hurt, get revenge for a perceived slight, or just look cool in front of their friends, understanding that some kids act out because they feel that this is the way to get by in an often hostile world will make it easier to get past kids' off-putting survival behaviors and deal with them calmly, rationally, and successfully. This gives you a great deal of freedom, not only to model the respectful and understanding behavior you want your students to develop, but also to keep your blood pressure and sanity intact.

Know your needs and limitations, and keep in mind that these can change from day to day, or class to class. Anticipate as well as possible and let kids know where you draw the line, especially if the line is in a different place from where they expect it to be. If a student mouths off to you, or speaks to you in a tone you don't like, watch the inclination to label the behavior as aggressive, disrespectful, or inappropriate, or to make the student wrong, much less punish the child. Try asking for what you want or validating the reality of the student's experience instead. Back off and give the kid a chance to cool off and regroup, and make yourself available when the student is able to share on your terms.

First-grade teacher Jill Denson advised, "Never raise your voice to any child for any reason." This isn't what you want to model, and besides, kids get numb to yelling pretty quickly. Nonetheless, any anger and annoyance in your voice will succeed in raising the overall stress level in the environment. In addition, a raised voice can instantly trigger survival responses in the students—defensiveness or aggressiveness, anxiety, shutting down, or slipping into some other "fight, flight, or freeze" response—whether they are the ones being targeted by your anger or impatience or simply on the sidelines picking up on the energy in the room. No matter how justified you feel at the moment, think really hard about what comes out of your mouth, before you say something that will destroy all your hard work to connect with your kids. Comments that include name calling, public labeling, humiliation, ridicule, and contempt are especially damaging. "Think, think, think!" warned Eric Katz. "Something once said can never be taken back."

We simply have to be more mature than the students. Reynolds and Reynolds reminded, "To transform the emotions of an undesirable situation, you must first decide that you are going to manage your impulse to abandon, avoid, diminish, or punish to make your point."[10] And if you blow it, please take the time to acknowledge your thoughtlessness and apologize. Kids need models for responsibly owning up to an indiscretion *without* any excuses or justification, and where better than in your classroom to learn the maturity in a sincerely expressed comment like "Whoa. That was inappropriate. I'm really sorry"?

If you leave school upset about a student, shift your thoughts to what you might do to work more effectively with that individual, and work hard to let go any residual bad feelings you're carrying by the next day. "Don't hold a grudge," Chaffin reminded. "Each day is a new beginning. Each day, all students start off fresh." Once again, a commitment to a positive focus will help. Katz recommended developing the ability to "separate your feeling about a student's behavior from your feelings about the student. If you can find a positive attribute in your most challenging student, you are well on the way to being a successful teacher." Clearly, problems that arise will be excellent opportunities for you to model and encourage win-win solutions and problem-solving techniques, but only if you can stay grounded and coolheaded.

It's Only Disrespect if I Think It's Disrespect

Attitudes are in the eye (and ear) of the beholder. Like taking things personally—or not—we have options when it comes to responding to how kids talk to us. Some students, especially those with a history of antagonistic relationships with teachers, may need some time to realize that those defenses simply aren't necessary in their interactions with you. (If you think about it, attempting to alienate someone who professes to care is a very clever defense indeed.) Some alternatives to labeling or punishing objectionable attitudes or comments follow:

- Validate the student's experience: "Sounds like you've had a hard time with this subject in the past." "This is a challenging concept. Hang with me. We can do this."
- Agree with the student: "No kidding." "Yeah, this really is a long chapter." "Sounds like you've already got a lot of work this weekend."
- Ask for a different behavior: "Let's try that again without the yelling, please." "OK, say that again, only use the tone of voice I use when I talk to you."
- Defer discussion: "Good point. Let's talk about that after we get the seatwork started." "I want to hear your concerns about that. Let's get through this activity and then we can talk."
- Use the child's objections (or potential objections) to leverage cooperation: "There really are a lot of problems on this page. Why don't you just pick ten of them." "We'll have some time at the end of the period for you [to do something that you want to do] if we can get this done in time."

Sometimes it just helps to know that it's OK to not react or get upset. If you don't take every little thing as a challenge, you'll finish your day in a much better frame of mind.

Watch your body language, too. A smile and nod can unravel dedicated attempts to test or provoke. And modeling respect and enjoying your students is far more satisfying and effective than making them wrong. You're not telling them that disrespectful behavior—if you even choose to call it that—is acceptable. You're simply letting them know there are other, more effective, and yes, more respectful ways of expressing oneself in this class.

OFFERING EMOTIONAL SUPPORT

One of the oddest bits of advice I've ever received came, during my first year, from a veteran teacher who suggested that I could eliminate some of my behavior problems if I would simply tell my students to "leave their emotions at the door." Whether I realized the neurological impossibility of such a request at the time, I *was* aware that I had not gone into teaching to spend my day with a room full of automatons. (In fact, the longest periods were always the ones spent with groups who didn't get my jokes.) But frankly, there were days when emotions seemed to be the only thing happening in my room. Surely there was a middle ground for dealing with feelings, too.

From the brain's point of view, we now know how important emotions actually *are* to learning. Bring enjoyment and fun to the classroom, for example, and you promote the emotional readiness and openness kids need to receive and integrate new information. Emotional engagement also increases the probability of long-term retention of content presented in such an environment. Educator Robert Sylwester wrote, "We know emotion is very important to the educative process because it drives attention, which drives learning and memory."[11]

But historically, the emphasis on the cognitive aspects of learning has been so overwhelming that some teachers still believe that if we could just separate kids' emotions from their thinking, we would be able to teach without all those pesky dramas and issues that pop up in the classroom. "There are those who believe that schools should focus only on the acquisition of knowledge or that we expect too much from schools," reported Robert Blum. "However, current research across disciplines shows that non-academic aspects of school are also significant contributors to both school and student success."[12] Haslam acknowledged the desire "to focus on the curriculum at hand." But, he noted, "whether or not we believe that emotions are appropriate in the schools, the fact is they are experienced and expressed there in the widest ranges possible."[13] Mahoney and Purr agreed: "Like it or not, kids will be bringing much more than their homework into your classroom so be prepared."[14]

There's a lot going on in kids' lives that has nothing to do with our lesson plans and curricular deadlines. Many come to school preoccupied by the stress of a recent breakup, a fight with a friend, a threat in the hallway, or the impact of a family crisis or loss. For some, your class will be a welcome distraction, although others may simply be too anxious, angry, depressed, or frightened for anything you say or do to register—no matter how dazzling and developmentally appropriate your lessons are. Oftentimes, adult attitudes, expectations, and responses only make things worse. "A prevailing cultural assumption" equates intelligence and responsibility with the ability to suppress emotions, observed Haslam.[15] But suppressed emotions have a nasty way of coming out in all sorts of disruptive, antisocial, and self-destructive ways. Columnist Anne Underwood wrote, "Emotional states affect behavior. . . . Negative emotions can have direct effects . . . by provoking the stress response of the classic fight-or-flight mechanism."[16]

The fact is, "learning is an emotional and social process," wrote Gerlach and Bird. "The emotional health of the child makes the child available for learning" and likewise "enables them to go through failure and see struggle, confusion, and frustration as a 'normal' learning process."[17] Debra Sugar similarly confirmed, "Children require proficiency in certain personal and social skills in order to acquire the cognitive and technical skills that schools are charged with teaching them."[18] Dot Woodfin, a character education program director, argued for a more comprehensive approach to teaching. "I think we are doing a great injustice to the youth of today by not balancing the academics with the social and emotional skills, which I feel are critical to their success in life," she wrote.

Like it or not, this is not an either-or discussion. Although no one would recommend that you abandon your lesson plans to deal exclusively with your students' emotional issues, pretending they don't exist isn't the way to go either. While there may be no *off* switch for emotions, there are ways of handling emotional situations that come up in the classroom, as well as ways of building the kinds of aptitudes that contribute to your students' emotional intelligence.[19] Following are some of the things you can do when a child is in crisis, or when feelings would otherwise get in the way of learning.

Paying Attention

You don't need a psychiatrist's license to pick up on emotional subtleties your students exhibit, nor should they need to be hysterical to indicate that something is troubling them. Attention also refers to being clued into the nonverbal signals you get when your kids don't understand something, are having a hard time staying focused, or are preoccupied by something besides the lesson or activity. Your attention to your kids, and to the energy in the classroom, will tell you when you need to shift gears, take a brain break, move to a different part of the room, or address whatever *has* their attention. I've interviewed thousands of kids and adults about their experiences as students, and among the disturbing reports from people who were astonished that no one seemed to notice that they were in so much pain, was one tribute from an eighteen-year-old. "Some teachers have this, like, built-in radar," she wrote. "They really pay attention to their students, and notice when something is going on. I love the ones who listen, and who let you know they're there if you need them." Does this sound like you? Most kids just want to know that you're available—physically present and mentally tuned in, that your door is open if they need to talk. And if they trust you enough to share, take it as a huge compliment, and honor their trust with the respect it deserves.

Listening

Truly a lost art in today's culture of acceleration and busyness, lending an ear to a child in distress is one of the greatest gifts a teacher can offer. Unfortunately, kids' timing isn't always the greatest, which is why you'll want to validate their need to be heard and offer a time you'll be available. Even very young children can wait until "the big hand is on the three," for example, and I've known teens who got through a tough day knowing a caring adult would be there for them after the last bell rang.

Effective listening means more than just hearing words (although for some adults, that alone would be a big improvement). It means taking in the information entrusted to you without interrupting, showing impatience or rushing the child, asking trivial or distracting questions, making assumptions, jumping to conclusions, minimizing or fixing the problem, discounting their concerns, cheering them up, telling them what we think they should do, topping their story with your own problem, or using their problems as an excuse to promote your own agendas—common nonsupportive ways adults respond to kids.[20] A tall order, indeed. If you must talk, use your voice to encourage them to continue or tell you more, to assure them that you're with them, and to validate the reality of their experience.

Validating

A preschool teacher once shared a story about a problem she was having with one of her own children who would wake her up in the middle of the night, frightened of the monster in his bedroom. After a number of unsuccessful attempts to reassure him that there was no such thing, she finally conceded to his reality and admitted, "Yes, monsters can be scary," after which they collaborated on a strategy to keep the monsters out of his room—in this case, creating some "monster spray" the child could use any time he felt afraid. The fact that the monsters quickly stopped being a problem is almost beside the point. What really struck me was this rare and underutilized strategy of simply agreeing with what the child is feeling at the moment.

I've seen children demonstrate enormous shifts in their emotional states, often quickly letting go of intense feelings when an adult validated their experience with a statement like "Of course you're angry. She broke your toy," "It hurts when people call us names," or "Yes, breaking up can be incredibly painful." Even validating desires and preferences you can't accommodate reflects a win-win kind of respect for what the student wants: "I know you wish you didn't have to go to that class" or "I know you'd rather do this report as a video."

Here again, you won't find many models, because in fact, most of the models we have for responding to children's emotions are dismissive, critical, or somehow invasive and controlling. Entitle children to their reality, even if it wouldn't bother you or doesn't make much sense, and recognize that the same obstacles that get in the way of good listening apply here, too.

ENCOURAGING PROBLEM SOLVING

I've deliberately separated this section from the previous information on emotional supportiveness because helping kids through emotional experiences is a different process from supporting them in finding solutions to their problems. In fact, these two processes even involve different parts of the brain, something I'm sure you've discovered if you've ever tried to resolve a dilemma or do a simple cognitive task when you were too angry or stressed to "think straight."

Notice how quickly adults will jump in and give advice whenever students are having problems, or try to direct upset students to finding solutions before the kids can even access the more rational and logical parts of the brain they need for such tasks. I understand the attractiveness of the apparent expedience of telling a child, "Just play with somebody else" or "Well, finish it in study hall." But we can't honestly talk about building responsibility and self-management and then, in the same breath, turn around and tell kids how to solve their problems. And as far as emotionally supportive responses go, it's hard to hear a directive like this and not feel dismissed, or worse.

If you're thinking that giving advice is a part of the job, you're not alone. However, let me suggest an alternative. First of all, if the child is emotionally wound up, go back to the previous section for reminders on listening, validating, and generally holding a space for the child to have the feelings without being criticized or judged. This is not the time to suggest or brainstorm or propose solutions.

However, in the absence of strong feelings, if a child is having any sort of problem, rather than presenting a solution, giving advice, or flat-out issuing a command, *ask questions* instead. Questions afford you a tool to help guide the child through the process of analyzing a situation, considering options, anticipating outcomes, and brainstorming alternatives—all important skills involved in becoming a good decision maker. They allow you to facilitate rather than solve or rescue, and they show a remarkable trust in a child's intelligence. With the right approach—and the right questions—I've seen kids as young as three figure out what they were going to do about something all by themselves, and develop a considerable amount of confidence and independence when it came to making constructive choices when adults weren't around telling them what to do.[21]

If you find students resistant to answering questions, leave the door open and invite them to come and talk to you after they've had a chance to think about it. Be aware that some kids (and adults, too) will see your refusal to tell them what to do as betrayal and abandonment, although nothing could be further from the truth. And some will object to being guided to taking responsibility for solving their own problems because they then can't be victims of advice that doesn't work out. Be patient. Because ultimately, you'll want kids to be able to ask themselves questions to solve their own problems when no adult is there to tell them what to do.

BUILDING COMMUNITY

We've all heard the statistics: Thousands of students stay home from school each day because of threats of violence, harassment, and aggression from peers.[22] Teachers consistently complain of having to deal with disruptions and distractions brewed in rumor and interaction—in the hallways, on the playgrounds, in off-campus hangouts, and increasingly, online.[23] The impact of social violence on students—including teasing, exclusion, scapegoating, malicious gossip, and verbal and physical aggression—as well as a common lack of effective coping skills or psychological strength to deflect these attacks, makes teaching a challenge and learning nearly impossible.

"Students must be free from fear and able to fully devote their cognitive and emotional abilities towards their learning endeavors," wrote Michele Borba.[24] That is, kids simply cannot learn when their brains are consumed with threat and stress. Nonetheless, cognitive priorities here too will suggest that you bury your head in curriculum guides and testing schedules, relegating responsibility for addressing social issues outside the school's purview. But we've seen far too many headlines to forget what can happen when we ignore this pain, dismiss these issues, or participate in a culture of meanness by tolerating it when it happens right in front of us.

In a win-win classroom, teachers recognize the importance of the social environment and the impact a sense of community can have on learning and student behavior and attitudes. They pay attention to how kids treat one another and know they have the power to make a difference. While win-win teachers may have to contend with the political expediency of security measures, they understand the limitations of what Jo Ann Freiberg referred to as "Band-Aid approaches to school safety," particularly in the absence of any attention to more positive efforts to improve school climate.[25] And win-win teachers know that if they've already taken some of the strategies mentioned in this book to heart, they're well on their way to reducing many of the problems that occur when kids aren't respectful and tolerant with one another.

Willingness

It would be hard to argue with people who have noticed what Michele Borba described as a "steady rise of impulsivity, depression, suicide, violence, peer cruelty, and substance abuse" or the "growing rise in disrespect for authority, incivility, and vulgarity, and cheating and dishonesty."[26] But despite evidence of the truth in such social commentary, don't for a second imagine yourself helpless to present other options for your students. The good news is that schools can make things better when they try, and even programs targeted to a specific problem can have positive outcomes far beyond the original intention. A report by Robert Hahn concluded that "school-based programs for the prevention of violence are effective for all school levels, and different intervention strategies are all effective. Programs have other effects beyond those on violent or aggressive behavior, including reduced truancy and improvements in school achievement, 'problem behavior,' activity levels, attention problems, social skills, and internalizing problems such as anxiety and depression."[27] Leadership training programs have had similarly broad results. Although leadership was once "solely considered an innate tendency," contributor Mike Smith asserted, "leaders are not born, they're made. Leadership can be learned and taught." And these skills happen in the context of the community you create in your classroom.[28]

Borba quoted Lonnie Athens, a professor of criminal justice, saying, "Although the community cannot guarantee a good family to every child, it can guarantee them a good school, and a good school can go a long way in making up for a bad family."[29] You are, for many of your students, the best game in town, one of few opportunities for them to see an alternative to win-lose patterns so familiar in the media, in their families, and among their peers. But nobody learns win-win strategies in a vacuum, so be prepared to address your attention to their social behaviors and know that your time will be well spent.

Advocacy

You don't necessarily need formal programs or lesson plans for building social skills, although they certainly exist. Some of the most powerful lessons you teach will come from your own modeling—how you interact with students and other adults, as well as your reaction to incidents between kids that you observe or overhear. If you act as an advocate and speak up any time you hear examples of bias, insult, or general meanness, you model behaviors that give kids permission, as well as the language, to do the same. Unfortunately, in many instances, you are very much in the minority. Research points to infrequent intervention on the part of adults and reveals that the majority of incidents of social, verbal, and physical discrimination and violence are either ignored, accepted, or denied—that is, when adults admit an awareness that these incidents are actually happening. Even worse, there are widespread reports of adults using similarly discriminatory words themselves (including homophobic, racial, and ethnically offensive terms) or laughing when they overhear kids use them.[30]

"The most dangerous deadly weapons in our schools each and every day are words," said Freiberg. "That's where it starts and that's where we can manage it." She cited research that indicates 90% of the school community hears putdowns, slurs, and degrading language on a daily basis. Now granted, for a lot of kids, this language is used so casually and regularly in their worlds that some may not even realize how powerful and hurtful these words can be. But even if their intentions are not particularly malicious, someone has to speak on behalf of sanity, because language is powerful, can be hurtful regardless of intent, and the majority of time, adults just let it slide. "Unless school personnel interrupt degrading comments, challenge the biased assumptions, and educate students about differences, we are likely to see perpetuation of bullying behaviors, harassment, and intimidation," Freiberg admonished.[31] We need to teach kids to stand up for tolerance and respect when they see violations occur. Martin Luther King Jr. once said, "In the end, we will remember not the words of our enemies, but the silence of our friends."[32] While aggressive kids and their targets tend to figure prominently in research, school policies, and intervention programs, let's not forget the power a group of bystanders can bring to a potential incident, as well as the overall climate of the school.

A simple sentence like "We don't say that here" or "Please don't use that word around me" sends a strong message without attacking or judging anyone. Repeat as necessary.

Even if they only see it as a standard of behavior for your room alone, you have introduced a reality that requires the conscious, deliberate use of respectful language and opened the possibility of this mindfulness extending beyond your classroom.

Two more comments about the power of language. Freiberg recommends focusing on *meanness* instead of using the word *bully*. "Labels matter. 'Bully' or 'bullying' is a negatively charged word. No student wants to be called a bully, no parent will claim that his or her child is a bully, and no school happily admits that there is any bullying in that school. This reality stems not from the fact that certain *behaviors* have been experienced, but rather because of the connotation of the concept itself."[33] People are much more likely to be willing to address a problem with students being *mean* than they are to accept the need to deal with a bullying problem. Furthermore, an approach using this language frees you to address minor social infractions and inconsideration before these give way to more serious incidents.

Likewise, I much prefer the word *target* to *victim* when talking about kids on the receiving end of meanness, exclusion, or discrimination. Although many people use the words interchangeably, the word *victim* suggests a sense of abiding powerlessness that is not present in the word *target*—which implies a greater potential for control of the situation, including options and assertive ways out.

Building Tolerance and Friendship Skills

Anyone who dismisses the nastiness some children experience as acceptable rites of passage needs to appreciate the impact that exclusion, rejection, and other forms of attack can have. "When we feel rebuffed or left out, the brain activates a site for registering physical pain," reported Daniel Goleman.[34] School connectedness includes aspects of social acceptance and feeling welcome in school. But Robert Blum, Clea McNeely, and Peggy Rinehart discovered that "nationally, four percent of students reported that they had no friends. There were socially isolated students in every school studied."[35] In addition to being vulnerable to all the negative outcomes associated with disconnectedness from school, Katz believed that isolated students, the kids who lack the protection of social allies, often appear the easiest and "safest" ones for more aggressive kids to target.

Behaviors do not change on their own, however, and kids don't pick up many prosocial behaviors on the streets. Fortunately, some school personnel are beginning to address the need to build friendship skills and social intelligence in their interactions with kids, if not in the curriculum directly.[36] The process doesn't have to be complicated or formal and, in most instances, will simply be built into the way you run your classroom. For example, anything you do to accommodate your students' power needs in positive ways (such as offering choices, soliciting and using their input in your plans, or providing accommodations for individual learning styles) significantly reduces the need for them to get power needs met at the expense of others. In other words, few kids need to hurt or disempower other kids to experience a sense of autonomy and control when those needs are being met constructively in other areas of their lives.

For a strategy worth its weight in gold, find opportunities for your students to help other students through a peer-helping, mentoring, or tutoring program. We can teach tolerance and respect by giving kids opportunities to work with others toward some shared goal. Some of my most challenging students ended up being some of the most effective, mature, and responsible mentors in a program that assigned upper elementary volunteers to help out in the kindergarten.[37] Stay attentive, continue to remind kids about "how we act, talk, and treat one another in here," accommodate power needs, and offer activities where all kids can be helpful and competent, and in short order, there's a good chance that you'll start noticing significant and positive changes in the social culture of your class.

INSTRUCTIONAL ISSUES THAT IMPACT BEHAVIOR

Imagine this: You're a student who is well acquainted with the bottom rungs of the academic ladder and doesn't believe that you have any shot at success. You can't understand the lesson, which incidentally is targeted to your weakest modalities and makes no sense to your nervous system. How would you behave? Even young kids have figured out that it's better to look bad than dumb.

Increase student success and you decrease behavior problems. Gear your lessons and activities to a variety of learning styles and you decrease behavior problems. Because in addition to the students' sense of autonomy, connectedness, structure, and emotional safety, the need for success and competence figures strongly in influencing their behavior. This is why discipline programs that are built on reacting or responding to misbehaviors have never had much long-term success. If you want kids' behavior to change, you have to go back and change the situations in which those behaviors develop and occur and accommodate the needs that are not being satisfied in more positive ways.

This strategy will be most challenging to subject-matter specialists who are used to presenting a specific lesson to an entire group of people at once. But regardless of how much a particular subject or activity apparently lends itself to this type of instruction, you're likely to find that in any group of students, the range of experiences, backgrounds, and skills can make for some pretty extreme variations in the degree to which a whole-group lesson is received. Plus, instruction is a great place to connect with kids. So it pays to find out who your students are and what they know. "Don't assume they've got the basics," advised veteran teacher Roberta Braverman. "I pretest everybody when they come into my classroom and use the results to gauge what I need to teach them." Teaching without any preassessment or simply according to curricular mandates or district schedules completely ignores the individuals you're supposedly trying to reach. So does "standing in front of students and having a conversation with the blackboard,"[38] as one friend described some of the classes he'd had in school. Kids know which teachers are willing to start where the students are, those who will work with the kids in any way that will effectively lead everyone to success. And they know the ones who are just going through the motions. Connect content to students or don't bother to teach it. In fact, if all you want to do is cover content, you don't actually need kids.

Another consideration: Watch how easy it is to project your own learning styles and preferences onto your students and make assumptions about how they learn. I certainly did. As a high visual-spatial learner, I kept trying to *show* things to kids who were overloading with too much visual information and just wanted me to *tell* them what they needed to know. At the very least, get in the habit of presenting information in more than one way—reading word problems that are on the assignment sheet or projecting illustrations and text from a story you're reading, for example. And keep in mind that many learners, myself included, can pay much sharper attention when tactile or kinesthetic needs are met. Learning-style preferences also require us to address verbal ability, sensitivity to light or noise or fragrances, need for movement, temperature, and seating, for example, as well as your pacing, voice modulation, and movement around the classroom, as all can have an impact on kids' ability to take in and process information.

If your training did not include instruction in differentiated, individualized, or prescriptive instruction, or at least in how to run small groups, and if it did not address the variety of ways different students learn and process information, for your own sanity—and your students' success—find a class, a book, a mentor, or teachers you can observe to master this valuable skill.

ACTIVITY

1. List responsible learning behaviors you have observed in your classroom.

2. What decisions are available to your students on a daily basis?

3. What other opportunities have you provided to encourage the development of responsible student behavior?

4. In what ways do the students handle those opportunities successfully?

5. In what ways do they experience difficulty?

6. What decisions do you feel your students should ideally be able to make in your classroom? Which responsible learning behaviors would you like to see exhibited (or exhibited more consistently)?

ACTIVITY

Let's work on asking for what you want. Identify three behaviors you want students to exhibit:

1. Complete the following sentences to create examples that communicate the reasoning behind your requests.

   a. Please _____

      so that _____.

   b. Please _____

      so that _____.

   c. Please _____

      so that _____.

2. Aside from the obvious benefits to you, why is it important that students cooperate with these requests?

ACTIVITY

1. What are some threats you have used, been tempted to use, or overheard? Write the negative statement in the space marked *Threat* ("If you don't . . . I'll/you won't . . ."), and then revise it to focus on a positive consequence in the following space marked *Promise* ("As soon as/As long as/If you do . . . you can . . .").

   a. Threat: _____

      Promise: _____

   b. Threat: _____

      Promise: _____

   c. Threat: _____

      Promise: _____

2. To what degree have you been able to use promises (motivating with an emphasis on the positive outcomes) instead of threats (emphasis on the negative consequences)?

3. To what degree has the use of contingency management been successful? In which instances has it worked best?

4. Which contingencies seem to be the most motivating?

5. What else do you think your students would like that you would be willing to offer?

ACTIVITY

1. Of the positive and effective strategies mentioned in this section, which were familiar to you from your training?

2. Which of the strategies have you observed in your school?

3. Which of the strategies have you tried yourself?

4. A win-win approach to teaching includes behavior-management strategies that address more than students' behavior, attitudes, and language. In addition to addressing their need for autonomy and dignity, as well as structure and routine, we're also looking at the impact of the social environment, the need for emotional safety and support, the need for academic challenge and success, and the importance of being taught in a way that makes sense to their bodies and brains. How is this approach similar to other discipline programs or instruction you've encountered? How is it different?

5. A win-win approach to discipline and behavior management focuses on prevention rather than reacting to negative student behaviors or infractions with punishments or negative consequences. How is this approach similar to other discipline programs or instruction you've encountered? How is it different?

6. Which of the strategies suggested in this section are you using (or have you tried)?

7. In general, you do not need whole-school buy-in or external support to use any of these win-win strategies. Nonetheless, of the strategies listed, which do you see getting the greatest support and acceptance from your colleagues? Your administrators? Your mentor or support team? The parents?

8. Of the strategies listed, which do you see generating the greatest resistance from your colleagues? Your administrators? Your mentor or support team? The parents?

9. Of the strategies listed, which do you feel is a good place to start (or the next skill to build into your own repertoire of skills)?

10. Identify one thing you can do in the next few days to pull your approach to discipline and behavior management more in line with your win-win intentions.

NOTES

1. Smith (2007b, p. 1).

2. Twain (n.d.). Available from a number of sources, including the GoodReads Web site (www.goodreads.com/quotes/show/18058).

3. And you *will* want to work with individuals or groups. High school students can only stay focused for about fifteen to eighteen minutes at a time. The younger the child, the shorter the attention span—roughly one minute for every year of age. So you want to diversify the way you teach and the kind of activities you assign during the day, the block, or even single forty- to forty-five-minute class periods, allowing movement and interaction to keep students engaged. Although most elementary teachers commonly rely on a variety of instructional approaches (including teaching small groups, individual conferencing, and having students work independently—either alone, in pairs, or in small groups on their own), more and more secondary teachers are coming to realize the value of these strategies and are working to get away from an emphasis on whole-group assignments, especially lectures. Bluestein (2008); Kaufeldt (2005); Nash (2009).

4. "Learned Helplessness" (2001, para. 1).

5. It doesn't help that the more rational, less impulsive, and less emotional parts of the brain don't typically develop until early adulthood, but the experiences kids have during adolescence help to hardwire their brains for later in life—another reason it's so important to provide opportunities to develop decision-making capabilities, with all the skills necessary to accomplish this goal, while they are in school. "Adolescent Brain Development" (2002).

6. Brockman and Russell (n.d., para. 5).

7. This is especially true with younger children, although it can apply to anyone who is doing a task or working with certain equipment for the first time.

8. Watch the impulse to come back with a familiar *gotcha* jab like "Well, you should have thought of that earlier!" (For more of these "magic sentences," visit www.janebluestein.com/handouts/magic.html)

9. Haslam (2001). Authority on natural medicine Michael T. Murray (2007) reported, "It is not the stressor that determines the response; instead, it is the individual's internal reaction, which then triggers the response. This internal reaction is highly individualized and holds the real key to the effect of stress."

10. Reynolds and Reynolds (2008).

11. Sylwester (1995, p. 72). A 1956 essay by Rachel Carson (as quoted in Carson, 2007) noted, "Once the emotions have been aroused—a sense of the beautiful, the excitement of the new and the unknown, a feeling of sympathy, pity, admiration or love—then we wish for knowledge about the subject of our emotional response. Once found it has lasting meaning. It is more important to pave the way for the child to want to know than to put him on a diet of facts he is not ready to assimilate."

12. Blum (2004, p. 2).

13. Haslam (2001). "Even as far back as ancient Greece, convention elevated the cognitive and rational over the emotional, with proponents like Piaget, Freud and Kant urging the development of cognitive skills in isolation from emotional development." Greenspan (1997 p. 2).

14. Mahoney and Purr (2007, p. 7).

15. Haslam (2001).

16. Underwood (2005).

17. Gerlach and Bird (2005, pp. 3, 14). This reference includes a statement from their presentation at the Centre for Child Mental Health Conference on emotional health in schools.

18. Sugar (2000).

19. Some of these include skills like "being able to motivate oneself and persist in the face of frustrations, to control impulse and delay gratification, to regulate one's moods and keep distress from swamping the ability to think, [and] to empathize and to hope." Goleman (1995, p. 34). Once again, the quality of the emotional climate of the classroom and your relationships with the students will help create an environment that supports the development of these aptitudes.

20. Adapted from Bluestein, *Creating Emotionally Safe Schools* (2001); also *The Win-Win Classroom* (2008); *Parents, Teens, and Boundaries* (1993).

21. Bluestein (2003a). For examples of questions that will help build students' decision-making skills, visit http://www.janebluestein.com/handouts/questions.html

22. The number 160,000 was quoted in numerous resources in the late 1990s and early 2000s, though current research suggests that this statistic was stable through 2009. Albow (2009); Bluestein (2001); Cody (2007); Sugar (2000). Looking from another angle, Debra Sugar (2000) cited a study that indicated "over twenty percent of school children are frightened through much of the school day and bullying occurs every seven minutes."

23. Cody (2007) defined *cyberbullying* as "the use of technology, such as cell phones and the Internet, to harass or humiliate another person or group of people. The number of children on the Web is also increasing. Eighty percent of students in grades 5–8 are online at least one hour per week" (para. 2). Also, a slide show on the home page of the WiredKids Web site (www.stop-cyberbullying.org) offers specific examples of cyberbullying, including setting up Web pages to vote for the fattest or most unpopular kid, stealing a password and locking the child out of his or her own account, posing as someone else and spreading rumors, pretending to be someone the child knows, sending anonymous death threats, sending hundreds of text messages to run up a phone bill, posting mean things on the child's Web site guest book, posting provocative information about the child on hate sites or pedophile sites, spreading hateful messages (anonymous or signed), and hacking into a child's computer to steal information, send viruses, or post false reports to the child's Internet service provider (costing the child his or her account). Aftab and Wired Safety Group (n.d.)

24. Borba (2002, p. 3).

25. Freiberg (2007c). Freiberg included using security devices such as surveillance cameras, metal detectors, ID tags, clear or netted book bags, locker restrictions, and profiling software among her examples. She affirmed that this approach leads to students' perceptions that they are unsafe in the school, that the school is a repressive environment, that the school is a hostile environment, that students are basically prisoners in the school, and that there is good reason to be fearful while at school.

26. Borba (2001). This conference handout, "Building Moral Intelligence: Our Last, Best Hope," is an excerpt from Borba's 2001 book *Building Moral Intelligence: The Seven Essential Virtues That Teach Kids to Do the Right Thing.*

27. Hahn et al. (2007).

28. Smith (2007a, p. 1).

29. Borba (2002, p. 2).

30. Bluestein (2001); also Freiberg (2007c).

31. Freiberg (2007c). Freiberg cited research by the Surgeon General in which "only fourteen percent reported that someone intervened always or most of the time with homophobic language use. Only twenty-seven percent reported that someone intervened always or most of the time with

racially or ethnically offensive language use." Debra Sugar (2000) commented, "When teachers ignore homophobic comments, turn the other cheek to racist jokes, or surreptitiously smile when a student is being teased, they are teaching values." Let's pay attention to how people in our environment treat one another and be sure that the values we communicate in our responses to hurtful language are the ones we really want to teach. Bluestein (2001).

32. Aftab and Wired Safety Group (n.d.).

33. Freiberg (2007b, p. 3). Freiberg suggested asking parents or guardians "if they are purposely raising a bully and no one will answer *yes*. Ask any child if he or she is a bully and the result is the same. However, if you survey the same group of adults and inquire if their children are ever *mean* to anyone else (call someone a name, make fun of someone, laugh at another person, or tell someone they can't sit with or play with someone), honest affirmative admissions are common. The very same [children who say] they don't 'bully' will admit that the very same behavior was 'mean' and 'not nice.' *Everyone* is mean from time to time. For some reason, owning up to being 'mean' is perceived to be more descriptive and neutral and far less threatening than describing the very same person or act as being 'bullying.' Bullying carries heavy negative emotional baggage; *mean* does not. . . . Educators would do themselves a great service if in *practice* these words were treated as other offensive and inappropriate language" (pp. 6–7).

34. Goleman (2006, p. 13).

35. Blum et al. (2002).

36. Goleman (2006, p. 10). *Social intelligence* is "the aptitude that makes us smart in our relationships. Empathy and social skills are the two main ingredients of social intelligence. This includes being able to read a situation to know how to make a good impression and being able to sense another's feelings and intentions" (p. 10).

37. Bluestein (1980).

38. Or smartboard or overhead or computer. You get my drift.

PART IV
Self

The value of persistence comes not from stubbornly clinging to the past. It comes from a vision of the future that's so compelling you would give almost anything to make it real.

Steve Pavlina, personal development blogger[1]

The most unrealistic person in the world is the cynic, not the dreamer. Hope only makes sense when it doesn't make sense to be hopeful.

Paul Hawken, author and business leader[2]

The deepest craving of human nature is the need to be appreciated.

William James, psychologist and philosopher[3]

But enough about the kids—and the system, and the parents, and your colleagues. Let's talk about you!

You have probably discovered that teaching is more than a career choice. It's more of a lifestyle, for some of us, the very fabric of our lives, integrated into everything we do. It's a richly rewarding experience, and a demanding one as well. If all we did was plan and perform, the job would be exhausting enough. When we do it right, we're almost constantly on our toes, learning and growing, constantly adjusting to changes in the student population, curriculum, policies, and emerging research and best practices as well. So we need to be sure to have some balance and a fair amount of support in our lives.[4]

This section offers a vision for continual growth and some possibilities for directions your growth—and career—may take. And it looks at some of the ways you can take care of yourself—socially, emotionally, and physically—so that your life's work does not become your entire life.

NOTES

1. From Pavlina (2005, para. 27).

2. Hawken (2009). With thanks to Stephen Haslam for the reference.

3. Quoted in Naylor (2009b).

4. Lydia Aranda was one of several contributors who advised, "If at all possible, marry another teacher, so that your spouse will understand what you are going through!" For another perspective, I will admit that there were times I was glad to come home to someone who was *not* a part of the profession. Oh, he still gets an earful on a regular basis, and I also maintain a rather large network of educators on whom I rely when I need current information, a reality check, or just a place to vent (without tormenting my spouse), but sometimes, it's just nice to hear about a day that is quite different from my own.

13

Grow Your Career

Learning from a teacher who has stopped learning is like drinking from a stagnant pond.

Thomas Becket, principal[1]

Great teachers are not only focused on helping their students become their personal best, but they understand that they have to work on becoming their personal best as well.

James Burns, author and educator[2]

I always said that in my first year I was unaware and in my second year of teaching I was fully aware that I was unaware. That is truly an important change of perspective to becoming a teacher, leader, and a lifelong learner.

Third-grade teacher

Having worked as a liaison between the university and the local school district, I appreciate the importance of collaboration between the two. And I can also attest to hard feelings that come up in any locale when current trends and best practices taught at the university are marginalized or ignored in the schools while the concerns of the schools and realities in the actual classroom are not taken seriously at the university.[3]

I received a large number of responses regarding the degree to which teachers felt prepared to enter a classroom and work with kids. While there are indeed cutting-edge programs in both school systems and universities, in general, many of the comments from contributors expressed a mismatch between their training and classroom experiences, wide differences in priorities between the university and the school district, and an overall failure of either entity to communicate the enormity and complexity of the job.

Several contributors expressed concern at the discrepancy between training programs that were hands on, research based, and brain friendly and school systems that did not support—or actively dismissed or discouraged—the skills they had been taught. Even training provided by the district is not always supported in practice. "My kids stayed on task longer and behaved better when I changed the lighting and let them sit where they wanted," said one middle school teacher who was subsequently reprimanded for these accommodations, which in fact had been recommended at a learning-styles seminar his school had recently required him to attend.

Others felt that their training emphasized the wrong things. "I knew my grammar and my vocabulary. I could also translate from Old English and Middle English and could recite John Donne and Andrew Marvell any time of day," wrote Tuija Fagerlund, who found that neither her content expertise nor her talent at making "brilliant lesson plans" prepared her to deal with the "learning difficulties, behavior problems, kids from broken homes, or dysfunctional families" she encountered. Aili Pogust related, "When I learn content or pedagogy, I have it down cold. However, my first year, I felt tremendously inadequate because I just had no idea how to go about teaching a subject. No clue. The methods courses I was required to take were not practical. The college and the school systems just were not collaborating."

In many cases, it just came down to a lack of practice and practical experience. One contributor wrote, "I would have liked to have been in a classroom longer before I started one on my own." Marti Johnson reported, "College students may go their entire educational career and never be in a classroom or see a group of students." She also noted that special education teachers just starting out "may never have an experience with emotionally, mentally, or physically handicapped children." And many districts saddled with teacher shortages, under the gun to hire "anyone with a degree and a pulse," as one administrator described it, end up with people getting their certification—and experience—on the fly.

Wyatt and White noted, "No amount of theory-based education classes can prepare you for the multiple problems and realities you will face, often on a daily basis."[4] Many contributors agreed. "When you graduate and get your diploma, that's when you can officially start learning to be a teacher," advised Fagerlund. Mary Edmunds shared a similar perception: "I really wish somebody had told me that my teacher education will not really start until I step into the classroom on that first day," she wrote. Joel Black described his college courses as "useless" and recommended focusing on developing expertise in your content rather than trying to learn to teach from education classes. "The reality of teaching is *much* different than teacher training," said Cheryl Converse-Rath. "So different, in fact, that I think most of the teacher training courses really need to be tossed."

I was troubled by the number of people who described their training in similar terms, whether they entered the profession through traditional coursework or alternative certification programs.[5] Because there are some fabulous training programs out there. I suspect that, to a certain extent, this problem may represent a bit of a chicken-and-egg situation: You need a certain amount of experience (which beginning teachers generally do not have) for new ideas to make sense in terms of practical application, and you need to actually implement a lot of practical ideas to make your experience rewarding and successful.[6]

All this to say that if you walked into your classroom feeling confident and prepared, that's wonderful. Anything short of these conditions, however, and I'll ask you to do what you'd surely wish for your students—that is, to take responsibility for getting the education, information, ideas, and materials you need right now. Beg, borrow, and steal ideas. Ask, explore, read, observe. Melissa Albright shared, "I kept a camera in my school bag and took pictures of other teachers' bulletin boards [or] projects. Any extra copies on the copier that looked great, I copied or took. I still do this after nineteen years of teaching!"

You never know what you'll hear in a class or a video, and in many cases, it could be something you encountered earlier in your training that now has a place to land. Even *bad* classes, programs, or resources with which you fundamentally disagree, have something to offer, even if it's only a chance to think harder about a particular topic or strengthen your position. Learn how to work the system and how to gain support for strategies you think would work.[7] Learn, and never stop learning, because what works today may not work tomorrow, even with the same students or subject matter. And learn because the process is such an incredible journey, and as far your career is concerned, you never know where the next class or book or seminar can take you.

GROWING WHAT YOU KNOW

In a way, getting your degree is the easy part. Whatever grade level or subject area you teach, and regardless of your preparation, your development as a professional is an ongoing commitment. "The degree and certificates do not make a teacher," affirmed Charla Bunker. "Self reflection, the belief that all students deserve the opportunity to actively engage in learning, and most importantly being a lifelong member of a learning community is what makes great teachers." Bunker also noted, "I have fifty credits beyond my master's degree, National Board Certification, and numerous awards, and still am one of the first to sign up for professional development when the opportunity presents itself. The more I learn, the better I become."

You may not be immediately interested in an advanced degree or specialized certification, but don't think you're off the hook. "I used to think that eventually, I'd master the practice and just show up for the show. Unfortunately, that isn't how it works," wrote Roxie Ahlbrecht. "The more you teach, the more you realize how unprepared you really are. I am an avid reader and any down time is spent planning a new lesson or figuring out what to do next with a challenging student."

A good bit of teaching is trial and error. Now and then, I get a question in a seminar that shows me I'm not explaining something clearly enough or that the example I'm using isn't relevant to the audience I'm addressing, and this can be in the middle of a presentation I've done hundreds of times and on a topic I know inside and out. In part, our professional development is about being willing to constantly evaluate and refine the work we do. David Friedli observed, "Teachers find what works and does not work, and if they pay attention (some don't) and are willing to adapt (some aren't), they eventually eliminate the things that didn't work well or got them in trouble and rely on the best practices. Early in a teaching career, it's OK to do some vast experimentation of methodology—find out what tools in the instructional tool box work, and which ones don't." Or as Marvin Marshall suggested, "Implement now; perfect later."[8]

Title I coordinator Marlene Berman advised, "If you're beginning a teaching career be prepared to be a continuous learner." Albright concurred: "Each group of children is different, children learn in different ways, and curriculum changes. Don't give up. Keep trying and adapting your techniques. Continue to get all the professional development you can." We need to model being lifelong learners for our students, and many of us make sure to let them know about classes we are taking, whether in education or some other area of interest, whenever possible and appropriate.[9]

Teachers most vulnerable to leaving the profession are the ones who, for whatever reason, are the most unwilling to admit a mistake and the least open to doing things differently. It's easy to blame the equipment, the system, the students, their parents, and last years' teachers. I know. I've done it. But bad days don't make you a bad person. They don't even make you a bad teacher. It's just learning, and a responsible educator will *use* this information to get better. "Even during those stressful and frustrating times . . . you will learn something and grow from that experience," assured Erin Beers.

The more willing you are to try new things and change what isn't working, the more likely your shot at success and longevity. This not only protects your students (and the profession) from your going stale, it also staves off boredom, burnout, and bitterness. "The most important quality for maintaining a long, productive, and satisfying career is openness," wrote David Steinberg. "So much changes over time. There is a tendency to stay narrow, to use techniques that worked before. And there is considerable research that says that we, as teachers, tend to get even narrower over time. But the teachers who retain their energy and maintain their momentum are those who stay open to learning new strategies, new understandings, new beliefs, new conceptions of their subjects, new ways of looking at students and their development, and new ways of even thinking about the goals of education. Because all of these things change over time, we have to stay open to the possibilities. This doesn't mean we were wrong in how we used to teach, but it does mean that we have to continue to be flexible in our thinking." Roberta Braverman noted that "some philosophies work better on paper than they do in the classroom" and that many teachers start out shaped by what they were taught in their training, only to find their philosophy and strategies don't always hold up in actual practice, or that their district is using a different approach with a different philosophical orientation. She described teaching as a tapestry, where each idea becomes a thread in the approach you develop throughout your career. "You don't have to totally abandon what you were taught," she said. "Learn to blend what you were taught with what you find works best."

REFLECTION

Perspective is a wonderful thing. It's what allows us to step back and recognize progress, growth, and accomplishments. It gives us the realization that certain problems are no longer problems, that we're handling certain situations more gracefully and effectively, that we've cleared hurdles we may even have forgotten we had. It helps us notice things we don't see on a day-to-day basis, and it's what can help us hang in when we're tempted to give up and walk away. "During the first year of teaching, most experiences are new and so it's difficult to know how to best handle certain situations," Sherry Annee related. "A reflective and effective teacher learns from these experiences and values them." Of course if you're smart, you'll continue to do this throughout your career.

Reflecting on your day is a great tool for professional and personal development that can provide you with this gift of perspective, and it's a great habit to cultivate early in your career. As so many contributors noted, you are going to have good days and bad, lessons that sparkle and some that flop, ideas that work beautifully and activities that fail because of a simple step you forgot to consider. We all do. But the best teachers are the ones who spend some time going over successes and failures and learning from both.

"At the end of the first day, spend some time reflecting on how your classes went. This is an excellent habit to establish early in your career," Rebecca Lynn Wilke advised. "Ask yourself what made the events and activities successful. Was there anything that didn't go according to plan? How would you improve upon the lesson? Was there a way to respond to the situation more efficiently or effectively? Were there things that you didn't accomplish that you should add to tomorrow's lesson plans? Don't get discouraged if things didn't start out perfectly—they rarely do, even for those who've spent years in the classroom. In fact, many teachers will tell you that their best lessons came after failures."[10]

This process is so important that a written journal is regularly required in many intern programs for beginning teachers. Although some teachers do fine simply thinking about what they did and mentally planning the changes they'll make, most of us reap the greatest benefit from taking the time to actually write out our thoughts. For one thing, there are so many details to track that, for most of us, specific ideas and flashes of brilliance can all too easily get lost in the shuffle. Write them down. You'll constantly be getting insights about how you want to do things differently, things you want to add, or sequences you want to change. Do you really want to leave it all to chance that you'll recall them when you need to? Even if you simply jot down an idea in a notebook or on a sticky note, your brain will appreciate the visual and kinesthetic cues and will be more likely to recall the idea, whether or not you ever consult your notes again. You can also say the idea out loud for auditory reinforcement or record your idea to voice mail or to an application that will convert the recording to a written record or e-mail.

"Good teachers constantly reflect on their teaching and management styles. They are constantly learning and evolving to become better teachers," observed one contributor. Many shared that they keep a file specifically for things to do over the summer or ideas for the following year. First-grade teacher Jennifer Burkholder shared, "I have a file with lists of things I need to do before school starts." And Michelle Mayrose wrote that since she started teaching, she ends every year with a list of what she wants to do differently "to make the next year even better."

In addition to jotting notes, many of us find that committing time and thought to journaling actually gives our brain access to a process for sorting out feelings, working through problems, and discovering solutions we might not otherwise find. Journaling can provide evidence of patterns—good and bad—in your teaching behavior and interpersonal skills, sort of a mirror to reinforce strengths and a shortcut to identifying goals to set and changes to make, things that could otherwise take years to notice. Phyllis O'Brien also noted that "doing self-evaluations on all aspects of your teaching" and "reflecting on all that went really well and all that you would do differently" will help you "adjust expectations and objectives." She advised that this process of reflection "must be a part of your teaching in all the years to come." Besides, journaling leaves a pretty amazing souvenir from that year's teaching experience. And as far as perspective goes, my interns were always surprised and delighted to go back around the middle of the year to the pages they had written during their first few weeks to see how far they'd come.

Weekly Reflection Form for week ending _____

New ideas, materials, or strategies implemented:

What went well or improved in your classroom?

What was a problem or did not go well?

How can you remedy what you've described above?

Other goals for next week:

Evidence of growth:

Comments:

OPPORTUNITIES AND NEXT STEPS (WHEN YOU'RE READY)

It was one of *those* birthdays. For whatever reason, I was thinking about my career and my life, realizing that while my work in the classroom was challenging and satisfying, I was feeling a little understimulated intellectually. I decided to sign up for a class at the university, give myself a chance to be around people and ideas that would challenge me in a way that my elementary kids couldn't. I also realized that if I ever wanted to do anything beyond what I was currently doing, it wouldn't hurt to expand my training and knowledge of the field.

To enroll in the classes that interested me most, it turned out that I'd have to enroll in a degree program. Although that hadn't been my initial intention, something happened the first time I saw *PhD* next to my name, even though it was just on the paperwork, indicating the post-master's program in which I'd enrolled. It wasn't long before I'd earned all the credits required and the opportunity to finish and actually earn the degree presented itself.[11]

There's a saying that's been in our family for as long as I can remember: "A doctor can sell apples, but the apple seller can't be a doctor." Whether or not I ever used the degree, I liked the idea of keeping my options open. Before the ink was even dry on my graduate diploma, I was invited to run a graduate program for beginning teachers, and my degree and classroom experience provided the exact qualifications I needed to ultimately get the job. My work at the university opened other doors, and in the ensuing years, I have found myself on a rather exciting journey, one that turned out to be very different from anything I'd ever anticipated when I started training to become a classroom teacher. So you never know.

"For me, teaching is above all, the best way of learning and growing as a human being," wrote Veronica de Andres. "My classrooms have changed. Now it can be big audiences, but still the feeling is the same—the same sense of purpose and fulfillment, the feeling that I am making a small or big contribution to make this world a better place." In fact, many of the contributors to this book have expanded their teaching, finding opportunities as authors and consultants, for example, whether they are still in the classroom or not. All have paid their dues, building success on their classroom-teaching experience. "The skills learned in teaching have taken me around the world and enabled me to do what I do as a professional speaker," reported Glenn Capelli.

Whether you ever leave the classroom or not, keep growing your career, because five or ten years down the road you may be itching for a different type of challenge, and the field of education has plenty to offer. (If you aspire to work outside the classroom, be prepared to spend time on the inside first, especially if you're thinking about training other teachers. The degree may work as far as getting people's attention, but your credibility will come from the realities you can relate from your work in the trenches.) Diane Laveglia shared, "The field of education has afforded me many opportunities outside of the classroom." Laveglia has worked at the State Department of Education as the writing facilitator for the state test, in three different schools as a resource teacher, as a principal, and at central office as the staff development specialist. "I did not realize going into the profession that there were so many different positions outside of the [classroom]," she said.

It's not always about a degree or certificate. I know people who have amassed enough coursework credit to complete several advanced degrees but who were more interested in the learning and stimulation these courses provided than with the credit, degree, or even pay raise they offered. If you do decide to pursue an additional endorsement, National Board Certification, or an advanced degree, there are a number of ways you can go. Consider finances, family obligations and other time demands, as well as your own stamina. Internship programs that offer a master's degree can be pretty intense, but they typically offer more support than just doing your first year on your own and it's a good way to get a graduate degree. Black suggested staying in school all the way to the final degree or specialization you desire before entering the classroom. "What is another year and another loan in the long run?" Since you may not know where you want to head professionally until you've spent some time in the classroom, consider summer classes or weekend seminars. Evening classes can also be manageable. A class here, a class there, and before you know it, you're closing in on another degree or certification. The time is going to pass whether you're building your resume or not.

Karen Fernandez suggested checking Web sites for summer programs, including free workshops, seminars, and classes,[12] which "will not only help you earn some extra money in the form of a stipend but help you get graduate credits to move on the salary scale. And move over on that salary scale as quickly as you can—you won't regret it!" Go to conferences when you can—national and international programs, if possible. There are dozens listed online for every subject or area of interest. If you can't get to a college or university, take a class online. Join a professional organization—there are plenty to choose from. Subscribe to at least one professional magazine, print or electronic, and make a point to read relevant and interesting content on a regular basis. "It is so easy for a teacher to become trapped within the walls of her classroom and have no concept of the big picture and how her job fits into the profession as a whole," wrote Wyatt and White. They recommended becoming affiliated with larger professional organizations to examine your own experiences in the context of what other educators are seeing and experiencing.[13]

There are other ways to challenge yourself. Change grade levels or take on a multi-grade classroom—you already have several grade levels and ability levels in any class you teach anyhow and these configurations can be a blast to work with[14]—or change subject areas or take on a class or two you haven't taught yet. Stephen Vance offered, "Read books and articles often. Take advantage of professional development opportunities that are out there. This is how you will quickly build capacity in so many different areas." Annee added, "Join a professional organization and attend at least one conference or workshop each year. Not only will you learn new ideas, but you will be energized by spending time with equally enthusiastic and passionate educators."

And talk to people who are doing what you see yourself doing one day. During my first year in the classroom, one of my professors told me that he envisioned me starting my own school. At the time, I was still struggling to get through a day without a physical fight breaking out and thought he was out of his mind. But he could see me beyond where I was at the time—something I didn't have the perspective to pull off—and his comment planted a seed. Although my guidance and interests led me in different directions, I have to wonder if his offhand comment didn't subliminally point me on the path my career ultimately took.

ACTIVITY

Develop a Competency-Based Resume

Capelli wrote, "Teachers need to know just how talented they are in juggling all the eclectic things that good teachers juggle. To teach well you need a good mix of creative, analytical, practical, and emotional smarts. Good foundations in such things enable you to tackle most things in life." Think of all the skills you have developed that allow you to run your classroom—day-to-day competencies you may take for granted.

Include personal, interpersonal, and instructional skills. Consider your competencies in the areas of instruction, assessment and evaluation, group management, motivation, behavior and discipline, curriculum and material development, organization, and the use of technology. Reflect on what you do to create meaning for students, support students' social and emotional development, recognize and support diverse student needs, encourage problem solving, accommodate diverse learning styles and modality preferences, increase your knowledge of subject matter, be a reflective practitioner, participate in the larger education community, pursue health and mental well-being, and work with colleagues, families, and support resource personnel.[15]

ACTIVITY

It's never too early to start thinking about your future. Although your energies will certainly be focused on developing experience and expertise in your classroom activities and skills, look ahead to what you might like to be doing down the road. Whether you continue your work in the classroom (at your current grade level or subject area or doing something different) or working in some other capacity as an educator, think of how you can grow your career a little at a time:

1. Where do you see yourself professionally in five years? Ten? Twenty? What type of professional experiences would you like to have amassed during that time?

2. Describe any professional ambitions or goals you currently have or think you may have over the next few years. Dream big and think in terms of the following:
   a. Possible jobs or positions you'd like to hold in the system, for example, in your district, State Department of Education, or university system
   b. Degrees or credentials you might like to pursue
   c. Creative ventures such as developing curriculum or products, writing for professional journals, writing textbooks or other projects, or consulting
   d. Taking your teaching skills into other professions or work areas

3. Beyond experience, what skills do you need to develop or what goals do you need to accomplish to position you to reach these goals?

4. Regardless of your long-term professional goals, what are you willing to do to "grow what you know" right now? Identify three things you'd like to do during this school year from the list below:

   a. Take a class at the local college or university (identify the class or the topic you'd like to pursue)

   b. Take a class online (identify the class or the topic you'd like to pursue)

   c. Take a class at an out-of-town college or university (identify the class or the topic you'd like to pursue)

   d. Sign up for a seminar offered privately or through the district (identify the program or the topic you'd like to pursue)

   e. Begin or continue work on National Board Certification (identify where, when, and how)

   f. Read a book to advance your understanding of a topic relevant to your career (identify the book, author, or topic)

   g. Subscribe to a professional magazine or online journal (identify the resource)

   h. Join a professional organization

   i. Apply for a special program or job at your school or in your district[16] (identify)

   j. Run for office in your school, professional organization, or union (identify)

5. Identify the supports and resources (material, personnel, emotional, or otherwise) that can help you expand your career.

NOTES

1. Quoted in Hopkins (2007).

2. Burns (2009).

3. In this sense, I am referring to universities, colleges, and any other organization that undertakes the training and preparation of new teachers.

4. Wyatt and White (2007).

5. Approximately 59,000 teachers came to the profession through alternative certification routes in 2006, up from 39,000 in 2004. While trends in nontraditional certification routes include rigorous screening processes, field-based programs, coursework or equivalent experiences in professional education studies, work with mentors and other support personnel, and high performance standards, there is, nonetheless, the sense from some of the individuals with whom I've worked that many had not spent adequate time in the classroom before being on their own regardless of the certification route they pursued. National Center for Education Information (2007).

6. I once spent a summer preparing recent college graduates to teach in some of the nation's most challenging school districts. These were bright, dedicated individuals, the tops in their classes, and though none was an education major, they had dedicated themselves to a year or two of working with kids identified as disadvantaged. However, they had no interest in my discipline class—no questions, no doubts, no reason to listen to anything I might have to offer—until the next day, when they returned from their first day in some of the toughest schools in the state, far more ready for what I had to offer. Their behavior and attitudes the previous day simply reflected their lack of context, or frame of reference, for anything I was attempting to share.

7. I've had several individuals tell me they got clearance to bring in accommodations that might otherwise be discouraged or to try approaches that were unfamiliar to the school when they asked for a specific trial period, presented documented data from observations or student surveys, and included solid research to support their request. Others had success when they recruited the support of the school counselor or occupational therapist, for example, or had the backing of the students' parents.

8. Marshall (2001, p. 152).

9. My kids' favorites were when I took cooking classes and shared some of the treats I was learning to make. One year, on a challenge from one of my students, I ended up taking violin lessons with them. Despite a pretty solid music background, I'm not great with strings. (This wasn't the first time I'd tried.) However, I think there was some great value in my kids seeing me struggle with the same things they were trying to learn. And it was an honor to squeak along with them in the concert at the end of the year.

10. Wilke (2003, p. 63).

11. Don't be scared off by the idea of a dissertation. Yes, if you do a decent job, it's a good bit of work, but if you've ever researched a term paper and run any kind of study, it's not much different. Best recommendation: Get a good adviser and recruit good people for your committee—not just the "big names on campus," unless they're people who you know will encourage and support you every step of the way. (Nobody except maybe alumni will ever ask you who was on your committee.) Watch out for people who live to create hurdles and extra work, who might cause you any self-doubt, or who are not seriously invested in your finishing and getting your degree.

12. Google "free classes for teachers," and you'll find pages of sites with opportunities for grants, travel, and programs in specific subject areas. One site (http://freeclassesforteachers .blogspot.com/), on the day I checked it out, offered some incredible opportunities, including programs in history, physics, and social studies with programs through NASA and C-SPAN, plus a Fulbright in Japan.

13. Wyatt and White (2007, p. 132).

14. I loved working with split-grade or multiage classes. The potential for building community and taking advantage of peer helping is terrific, and as long as you're teaching kids according to need and ability, it's not any harder than teaching a group of kids all born in roughly the same year.

15. With thanks to the University of Pittsburgh doctoral program, which required a competency contract as a part of the program requirements, as well as the Interstate New Teacher Assessment and Support Consortium (INTASC) Special Education Sub-Committee, "Model Standards for Licensing General and Special Education Teachers of Students With Disabilities: A Resource for State Dialogue" (INTASC, 2001, pp. 10–39). Their ten competencies are available on the INTASC Web site (http://serge.ccsso.org/pdf/standards.pdf). Few tasks have given me as great an appreciation for the skills I was developing and using on a regular basis or how far I'd come since I'd begun my work in the classroom.

16. For example, writing curriculum, running an afterschool program, chairing a committee, writing a grant, or any other pursuit, paid or not, that could broaden your experience, utilize your talents, and eventually advance your career.

14

Take Care of Yourself

Your life will only make sense when you don't need other people to confirm that it does. The greatest understanding you can have about yourself and others is that no one will ever understand you completely.

Betty Haas, educational consultant[1]

Finish each day and be done with it. You have done what you could. Some blunders and absurdities no doubt crept in, forget them as soon as you can. Tomorrow is a new day, you shall begin it well and serenely.

Ralph Waldo Emerson, author and philosopher[2]

Hang in there. What you do really makes a difference in the lives of children. You are making the world a better place.

Carrie Balent, guidance counselor

At the end of practically every presentation or seminar, I include a section on self-care. Whether the topic is discipline, classroom climate, emotional safety, or achievement, the issue of self-care gets a nod because, without this ingredient, all other skills and talents will eventually be compromised. To a certain extent, the system depends on people's willingness to self-sacrifice, often making impossible demands on teachers' time, energy, and goodwill. And although many educators are willing to work longer and harder than is healthy or sane, Karen Fernandez warned, "Teachers need to stand up for themselves and say no to unreasonable demands without fear of hurting their students, because ultimately, what hurts students is an overworked, burned out, and possibly resentful adult."

I think most of us are better at giving this advice than following it, but several contributors did mention the importance of having good boundaries around the time you put in at work. Jennifer Burkholder "learned to say no to helping too much around the school. My first year I took on tutoring, coaching, and moderating the school government. I should have put more focus on learning the curriculum," she said. First-grade teacher Joanne Peters recommended, "Give yourself a schedule of how long you will stay Monday through Friday and how much time you will devote to the profession on the weekends." Michelle Erickson echoed her advice: "Don't worry about the work at the end of the day. It will be there tomorrow. Take care of the things that need to be done, but remember to take time for yourself. Set a time to leave and actually leave at that time." And Phyllis O'Brien warned, "Be careful not to allow the job to take over your entire life. It is a tough balancing act and difficult not to allow teaching to be all-consuming."

So let's wrap up our journey together with a few words about taking care of yourself on the job—whether dealing with challenging colleagues, managing self-expectations, keeping your body healthy, or looking for balance. We can only give as good as we've got, so let's keep what we've got really good.

FEELING THE HEAT

Our professional self-concept can be rather fragile at times. If most of our experiences with authority figures have been critical or negative, we have years of practice judging ourselves against other people's standards and reactions. If approval from others is a high priority, we become extremely vulnerable to the coworker who doesn't sanction our methods, the parents who would rather have their kids in another teacher's class, or the colleagues who always seem to be weeks ahead on their paperwork. Learning to hear, respect, and operate from our own internal guidance, vision, or priorities promises a great deal of freedom; however, it requires a certain amount of faith in what drives us, as well as a commitment to internal congruence to enable us to stand our ground.[3] This can take some time to develop, so be patient.

"It seems as if others, especially other teachers, have certain expectations of new teachers and if you cannot live up to them, you feel like a failure. I know I felt incompetent and a failure at everything I seem to do," wrote Catherine Nguyen-Ho. "It may have been because I have very high expectations for myself." Another contributor wrote that she wished she had known that she would never be perfect. "If I had stopped beating up on myself as a teacher earlier, I would have felt better about my progress and improvement, realizing that this would be an ongoing process."

Many contributors shared similar feelings, and many others wrote to encourage new teachers to set kinder, gentler expectations for themselves. "I hope that teachers starting out don't feel like they have all the answers or even that they understand all the questions," said Sandra Kenyon. One high school English teacher wrote, "Above all else, go easy on yourself. You will screw up constantly in your first year. After you get through the first year your confidence level will significantly increase. One year of teaching is a *huge* learning experience, unlike anything else out there. You will gain tremendous insight every day." And Melody Aldrich advised, "Patience—with yourself and with your students. Also, you absolutely must be able to laugh at yourself and find pleasure in those kids."

New teachers, like most dedicated professionals, tend to be harsh self-critics, although veterans do have the advantage of having survived a lesson that bombed, a test everyone failed, a discipline strategy that only made things worse, a cranky parent, or a visit from a supervisor on a day that everything went wrong. Josh Moberg was one of several who recommended not taking yourself too seriously. Michelle Colbert agreed, wishing someone had told her that it is OK to make mistakes and laugh about it. "I was so hard on myself the first go around. Now after already teaching, I do laugh about how I should have been enjoying that first year and that experience not stressing." Kenyon wrote, "Be willing to look silly once in awhile and let go of past mistakes."

There's a lot to take in at first, and someone will always be a few steps ahead of you (and probably someone else a few steps behind). Despite what some policies or media reports might suggest, teaching isn't a competitive sport. Yes, other teachers may be ahead because they know the material and have learned efficient ways to get it across. But they may also be further along because they skip over parts you choose to teach or don't bother responding to students' questions or misunderstandings. What matters is your own sense of integrity and intention, especially in terms of what students need, as well as your willingness to continue to refine the work you do. "Remember it's a marathon, not a sprint," wrote Jen Buttars, sharing her special tip for beginning teachers. "Don't go too fast out of the gate, and pace yourself. Think big, start small, go slow." Peters advised, "Don't feel like you have to have it all together. Discuss strengths as well as weaknesses in your teaching with others who have been through the trenches. Follow the manuals . . . the first year. Don't try to reinvent things just yet." And Mahoney and Purr assured, "Look at it this way: If you make it to Halloween, you're probably doing a pretty good job. Until then, just be yourself, think things through carefully, ask for help, and try to have a little fun while you're at it."[4]

And make peace with the possibility of running into somebody's disapproval now and again, because you can be the best teacher in the world and somebody will still manage to find fault with something you said or did. It doesn't make much sense trying to please everybody. Jolene Dockstader related, "I really wish somebody had told me that I wouldn't be liked by everyone and that I would make mistakes. I want to be perfect all the time and I want to be liked by my students and their parents, but that just isn't always possible. My teaching style and personality have not and will not mesh with all students' learning styles and personalities. I just do the best I can and try not to take things too personally."

There's always a bit of stress in starting anything new, but tune in to what you're feeling, because stress can pile up without your even realizing it.[5] "Know that you will be frustrated often. Discuss those frustrations with an experienced teacher, counselor, administrator, or other mentor so that you do not wind up taking them out on the students," counselor Eric Katz advised. "Don't be afraid to ask for help. Your college training will not prepare you for everything. That is OK as long as you can ask for help. Be gentle with yourself and do not set unrealistic expectations. This is a setup for frustration and burnout." Remember, you're in this for the long haul. Give yourself the time—and support—you need to become the teacher you want to become.

Take Charge of Your Life and Actively Live Each Day

By Richard J. Avdoian[6]

- Don't let the opinions of others define your belief in yourself.
- Assume less. Ask for what you need from others.
- Don't let internal fears and self-doubts keep you stuck.
- Stress in life is simply a challenge to your creative ability to live.
- Don't let the criticism from others derail you from your dreams.
- Stay in a positive range of emotions.
- Spend the necessary time and money to get healthy and stay healthy.

(Continued)

(Continued)

- Stop whining and take action.
- Life is a journey; retirement is only one port—not a destination.
- Remember that only a person with your permission can sabotage your day.
- If you do not change your daily routines, you cannot change your life.
- Don't focus on being better than others; focus your energy on being different.
- The longer you relive your misfortunes, the more power they have to harm you.
- It is best to live and err than to be stuck and have done nothing at all.
- Stress is an everyday fact of life. Identify the sources, learn to take control, and cope with it.
- Have a passion for life and live it with enthusiasm.
- Seek opportunities to fail. Selecting only those situations you know you will succeed at will limit what you will explore.
- Never leave home without taking along your sense of humor and appreciation for life.
- Understand no situation or condition is permanent.
- Are you actively in charge of your life? If not, take charge.
- Being happy lies in your ability to seek, find, and gather happiness from common, everyday events.
- Seek opportunities to laugh and do it often.
- Don't let the fears of others keep you from living life.
- Parents gave you life but you are the pilot of your life. Set your own course.
- If people make you mad, you are a willing puppet and they are the puppeteers.
- Accept your weaknesses and be humble of your strengths.

YOUR HEALTH, YOUR BODY, AND STRESS

You've heard it in every airplane safety briefing: If the oxygen masks come down and you're with someone who needs assistance, *put your own mask on first*. These instructions run so counter to the more familiar messages to take care of others that the first time I heard this speech, I was sure the flight attendant had gotten it wrong. But this directive offers great words to live by, on or off the plane, whether or not you're in an emergency situation.

Taking care of your body and health isn't just about how you feel. It also has implications for how well you can function. "Make sure you take care of yourself—teaching is hard!" said Cheryl Converse-Rath. "You need to be a whole, energized person to give the best to your students." Authors David Aspy and Flora Roebuck reported on studies that found teachers' physical fitness and health to be a factor in "their ability to employ interpersonal skills in a sustained manner" throughout the school day. Although all participants studied started at the same level of effectiveness, the performance of teachers in the "low fitness group" deteriorated significantly about halfway through the five-hour day.[7] Add stress and tiredness to the equation and it won't take long for coping skills to deteriorate as well. "The best advice I can share is to take care of your health and maintain balance," Lulu Lopez wrote. "You may be exposed to things you are not used to and if you neglect the physical side, it will affect you and your students adversely."

During the first few weeks of school this year, I noticed numerous posts by teachers on social networking sites complaining about how exhausted they were and, in several instances, specifically about how much their feet hurt! (One of the more practical responses to the survey question asking for special tips for beginning teachers came from a contributor who advised, "Wear comfortable shoes.") Not surprisingly, staying healthy in school is a significant challenge for a lot of teachers, especially those new to the setting. Not to gross you out, but a report on germs in work environments found that "schools are the most germ-filled workplaces. . . . Researchers found that phones, desks, and keyboards used by teachers harbor up to 20 times more bacteria per square inch than those in other workplaces. . . . The study found 400 times more bacteria on a desktop than on a toilet seat." The report recommended that you "clean your desktop, keyboard, mouse, and phone daily. Use a disinfectant and a paper towel, or a disposable wipe. Avoid water fountains; viruses and bacteria love the moist, spit-laden environment."[8]

I never thought my instructional duties would include teaching upper elementary and middle school students how to sneeze, but no immune system can stand up to a roomful of kids who haven't learned proper coughing and sneezing protocols. Even so, my body was never so susceptible to colds as when I was in the classroom, and much of the time, it seemed I was fighting one bug or another. "Do stay home when you are sick," Davidman recommended. "You get better quicker and keep your germs to yourself." She also noted that "you will get sicker the first year than you probably have been in your life. Schools are full of germs. Keep [disinfectant] wipes in your room and have the kids clean their desks often. Keep a bottle of [hand sanitizer] on your desk and use it often." Carol Dinsdale agreed: "Your health is so important! You need to be on a good multivitamin daily, especially if you are new and haven't built up a resistance to all the germs in schools."[9]

Other factors that can contribute to illness include stress and poor coping mechanisms. Any time the demands in your life strain your "adaptive capacity," you run into "both psychological as well as biological changes that could place a person at risk for illness." Therefore, if you're under a great deal of stress and your coping mechanisms aren't helping (or are making things worse), the germs you run into in school will have a greater impact on your immune system than if you're engaging in positive ways to deal with the stress you encounter.[10]

Michael T. Murray, an authority on natural medicine, urged positive and effective ways of managing stress, including "techniques to calm the mind and promote a positive mental attitude, following a healthy lifestyle including regular physical exercise, eating a healthful diet, [and] utilizing key dietary and botanical supplements."[11] Even something as simple as staying organized can help keep some of the usual stress at bay. Develop a manageable system to stay on top of the paper load, contact information, student records, and all your classroom materials related to particular activities or units, *before* things get out of control. You'll make yourself crazy if you have to spend a lot of time looking for things. Trust me on this. Besides, it's hard to teach—and learn—in a cluttered, disorderly classroom. And get some sleep. For some of us, going to bed at a reasonable hour can feel forced and unnatural, but it won't take long for a lack of good, sound, restful sleep to start showing up in your work. Record the movie, pass up the party, and if you have to, finish grading those papers the next day, but give your body the chance to recharge that sleep offers.

Attitude also has a lot to do with how you handle stress. "People often take for granted how much a positive mental attitude affects their behavior and those around them and its impact in a classroom," observed middle school teacher Keith Redhead. "I refuse to become one of the bitter and negative teachers that so many of us have had." Educator Hal Urban included the ability to maintain a positive mental attitude among the characteristics that happy and successful people share.[12] This is the state of mind that will help you recover from setbacks, dust yourself off, and come back with your confidence and determination intact. Darren Raichart urged, "Don't ever give up! Not all teachers have bad first years, but if you do, stick with it." And as many contributors advised, pace yourself. "Perseverance is not a long race," said Walter Elliot. "It is many short races, one after another."[13]

It's also hard to maintain a positive attitude if you're constantly feeling disappointed and disempowered. One of the most potent inoculations against stress is the sense of personal power behind the knowledge and confidence that you can change the things that are not working in your life. Teaching is likely to bring up all sorts of things for anyone. To a certain extent, experience and skill will resolve many of these matters. But don't be surprised if you find yourself stumbling over unresolved issues from time to time, especially those involving power, adequacy, worth, or deservingness. If you find yourself feeling depressed, stuck, or victimized, or feel powerless to set boundaries or say no, please talk to someone or find a group that can help you explore alternative belief systems and behavior patterns. This is especially important if you find yourself coping with outlets that are harmful or self-destructive.

Also consider keeping a journal as a positive way to manage stress. Whether privately expressing strong feelings (in ways that won't hurt anyone or come back to haunt you) or working through problems, journaling can help you get rid of a lot of toxicity you don't want to carry around in your body by giving you a way to leave it on the page, as it were.[14] Besides, "writing in a journal is not just a way to keep track of daily life—it actually can make you happier, more successful, even healthier," reported Kathleen Adams, founder of the Center for Journal Therapy. Adams reported on a study that "found that writing about stressful experiences in a journal relieves stress and thus increases the body's immune response, reducing the impact of chronic conditions, such as rheumatoid arthritis and asthma."[15] And be sure to acknowledge positive experiences so that your journals can validate growth, healing, progress, and achievement as well.[16]

And since journaling doesn't entirely satisfy the body's need for exercise, make time to move. Even a short walk can reduce stress, clear your head, and help you focus. "People who exercise regularly are much less likely to suffer from fatigue and depression," wrote Murray. "Tension, depression, feelings of inadequacy, and worries diminish greatly with regular exercise. In fact, exercise alone has been demonstrated to have tremendous effects in terms of improving mood and the ability to handle stressful life situations."[17] A report by Michael Craig Miller confirmed, "Regular exercise improves your mood, decreases anxiety, improves sleep, improves resilience in the face of stress, and raises self-esteem."[18] (Movement is also a critical component of learning and will help you sustain your focus and concentration, so be sure to take brain breaks when you've been studying or grading papers for more than twenty to thirty minutes.[19])

One other piece of this equation involves the amount of negativity you allow into your life. "There is increasing evidence that there is not an illness known to science that is not affected by our thoughts and feelings and that our attitudes can play a significant role in our ability both to recover from disease and to maintain positive health," wrote authors Gerald Jampolsky and Diane Cirincione.[20] You may find it necessary to make a conscious effort to minimize your contact with negative, toxic people (including coworkers and even relatives), as well as your exposure to negative and toxic energy and information. Seek out upbeat, inspiring, and positive input from books, lectures, tapes, movies, or TV shows. Quit watching the news, especially before bed, if it leaves you feeling anxious and depressed. Watch the quality of your expectations and carefully monitor your tendency toward cynicism or feelings of victimization. Look for the positive in everything. "Life is not about waiting for the storms to pass," shared Mike Smith. "It's about learning how to dance in the rain."[21] Develop a willingness to quit taking life so personally and learn to see with your heart instead of your eyes (or grade book). Because in the dramas of daily living, a positive focus can be hard to hold onto. But making a deliberate effort to stay positive has implications for your mental health, your physical well-being, and the quality of your relationships, all of which can make the challenges of dealing with your life—and the people in it—a lot easier to face.[22]

Recommendations for Reducing Tension and Stress

By Richard J. Avdoian[23]

Avoid the urge to be Superman and Superwoman. Some people get into a state of anxiety because they think they are not achieving as much or as fast as they should. They try for perfection in every facet of their life. Do not insist on excellence in everything; accept average in some.

Give yourself permission to say "No," and do so often. Heart patients and Type A personalities tend to be "Yes" people and find their life consumed with commitments and obligations. Time for yourself to reenergize is not only important but necessary to live a healthy life.

Enjoy the experience. Pursue one activity or task at a time. Typically people who are uptight commonly dwell on the "mass of work" confronting them, develop anxiety, and respond negatively both physically and mentally. It is defeating to take on more than you can handle. Instead, take a few moments to prioritize and begin first working on the most urgent task.

During the workday, take a time-out or make a diversion every fifty minutes or so. Consider doing less taxing/demanding tasks, slowing the pace temporarily, or taking a brief mental vacation to help reduce tension during work.

Learn to effectively juggle work and recreation. Schedule time for recreation and leisure activities to relax your mind and be playful.

Be aware of your body and mind—what makes you tense, reactive, and uptight. Identify your personal common daily sources of stress in your life, such as perfectionism, traffic, employee conflicts, argumentative customers, high level of expectations, etc.

Exercise is a healthful way to cope with stress of daily living. When you're angry or upset, consider blowing off steam physically by exercising, walking, swimming, or running.

Talk out and process your fears and concerns. Sharing fears and concerns with someone you trust and respect can help add clarity and minimize tension and stress. Another person may give you insight into the source and offer positive solutions.

Learn to accept what you cannot change. It beats getting annoyed and anxious. If you cannot change the event or situation, then change your attitude.

Avoid self-medication. There are many nonprescription aids available that can mask the symptoms associated with stress but they do not help you to learn to cope effectively with the stress itself.

Get sufficient rest. Oversleeping can lessen your ability to deal with stress by making you increasingly restless. The lack of sleep can also affect your ability to deal with stress by making you more irritable. Most people need between six to eight hours of sleep every night.

Stay away from negative people, situations, and topics of conversation that typically upset you or make you angry, tense, or anxious.

SEEKING BALANCE

OK, before I send you off on your journey, let me throw out a few final words about maintaining balance in your life. I don't know many people who are particularly good at this, and in fact, your humble author probably has no right to be writing about this at all. But if you'd like some tidbits I've picked up and don't mind my sharing this information from a do-as-I-say place (rather than asking you to do as I actually do), read on. Seeking balance is a good goal for us all to keep in the back of our mind.

"If I am not living a healthy, abundant and balanced life then I cannot help my students to do the same with their own lives. I cannot give from an empty cup," related high school teacher William DeJean.[24] Using a similar metaphor, educator and consultant Jenny Mosley advised regularly visiting five different types of "wells" or sources—places to restock on energy, perspective, and balance. She included the "cognitive well," at which you become more resourceful by reading books, watching plays or films, or debating ideas, for example. The "emotional well" builds resiliency by taking time for fun, friendships, and time with family. Your senses and imagination are at the heart of the "creative well," which helps memory. And the "physical well" builds readiness through exercise, relaxation, nutrition, and sleep. Finally, the "spiritual well" is about "renewing your sense of wonder and awe" to become more reflective.[25]

The key here is to diversify, to make sure your life includes people, activities, and reflection beyond your life at school. "If you ran before teaching, keep running," said Davidman. "Make time for fun, friends, and family." One middle school teacher allowed a great deal of focus during the first year but advised, "Once you are grounded, begin to expand your role outside the classroom in what ignites your passion—maybe athletics, music, drama, yearbook, technology, school trips. If you do what you love, the students will equally become passionate." Interviews with principals hiring new teachers revealed a desire for adding well-rounded individuals to the staff. Many want people whose lives include "involvement and interest in outside activities." Middle school principal Stephen Podd looks for "people who are involved with kids outside of the school setting, especially music groups, theater, and sports."[26] Anything you do that enriches your life, whether reading, traveling, learning a language, playing a sport, or pursuing a hobby or special interest, will add a great deal to what you bring to the classroom.

Another part of staying in balance comes from your relationships with others. Relationships are important. Be sure to keep them high up on your priority list. Positive connections with people you value and enjoy are more than just fun. There are health benefits here as well. A report on stress and illness shows social support to have protective capabilities, potentially reducing the amount of stress we experience as well as our susceptibility to illness.[27] "The people whom we love the most are biological allies," reported Daniel Goleman. "Being with them boosts the secretion of brain chemicals like oxytocin,[28] which calms distress and lowers levels of cortisol, a stress hormone that weakens the immune system."[29] Authors Don Childre and Howard Martin agreed: "Positive emotions such as happiness, appreciation, compassion, care, and love improve hormonal balance and immune system response."[30]

This could explain the overwhelming importance of connectedness. We've seen it in the research on students, and it's equally crucial for teachers. Don't be shy about expressing your appreciation for your kids and your colleagues, as well as the other people in your life. "Don't be afraid to care about others and show it," encouraged Kenyon. Urban likewise urged, "Don't just look for the good in people, *tell* them about it. Make a point of affirming at least two people every day."[31] It doesn't matter if it comes back immediately.

Keep shining it on, especially with your students. If you hit a brick wall with an adult (on or off campus), lovingly move on to someone else. Preventative medicine specialist Dean Ornish reported, "Connections with other people affect not only the quality of our lives but also our survival." Ornish cited "a strong sense of connection and community" as a critical factor in a person's health. "I'm not aware of any other factor in medicine—not diet, not smoking, not exercise, not genetics, not drugs, not surgery—that has a greater impact on our quality of life, incidence of illness and premature death," he wrote. "Instead of viewing the time we spend with friends and family as luxuries, we can see that these relationships are among the most powerful determinants of our well-being and survival. We are hardwired to help each other. Science is documenting the healing values of love, intimacy, community, compassion, forgiveness, altruism and service—values that are part of almost all spiritual traditions as well as many secular ones."[32]

The other aspects of balance I want to mention are more internal. The first has to do with patience and faith. Years ago when my husband was working in construction, I used to marvel at the fact that, at the end of the day, he could look at the results of his work and see that he had accomplished something. We in education rarely get to see such immediate, concrete evidence of the work we do. Oh, it shows in little ways, a smile here, a breakthrough there, and after you've been around for a while, a student who comes back to say "Thanks." But as far as being able to witness your influence on a day-to-day basis, it's not quite as clear as construction work. And this is where patience and faith come in. "Your impact is on a time delay," said Andy Quiñones. "You don't have to witness it for it to be real." Another contributor shared, "If I make a difference in one kids' life, my work has value, and I'm internally at peace. That makes me of greater value to the kids. You have to have some faith that what you're doing is making a difference." And Reynolds and Reynolds assured, "There are times when we think our actions have not made a significant difference—and that can be disheartening. Remember always that you receive the instant you give, and in that, you can trust you made a difference in someone's life because you felt it in your own."[33]

In the meantime, devote some time to something that does yield tangible results. Knit, cook, garden, paint, sew, remodel a room, clean out a closet, fix something. Anything. The progress you can see and the immediate satisfaction you can gain will provide some balance to the work you are doing in the classroom—a process that certainly yields results, but for the most part, far more subtly and over time. One veteran teacher suggested that you "hold on to those special moments, comments from students, and parents. I keep a 'Happy' folder in my email with positive emails that I revisit from time to time." I have a box with cards, notes, and gifts I received from my students and their parents more than thirty years ago that has survived numerous moves and cleaning frenzies. I don't come across them very often, but I like knowing they're there.

And finally, take a moment to appreciate the good in your life. Gratitude is one of the best antidotes imaginable for worry, frustration, negativity, and stress. Make a deliberate effort every day to look for reasons to be grateful—from the conveniences and resources that are so easy to take for granted to the people whose efforts add so much to your life, especially the ones working quietly behind the scenes to create the benefits you enjoy in your life, the ones you might never meet. Acknowledge the magic and synchronicity that come in the form of inspiration and coincidence. Validate your wisdom and creativity. Celebrate the pleasures of giving as well as receiving. And give a bit of thanks for silver linings in lessons learned.[34] "As you sit around your home or watch TV, what if you focused your heart and mind to notice the many blessings in your life and dwell less on the irritations? Such a shift can bring emotional balance to your life in a beautiful way," advised authors Joel Levey and Michelle Levey.[35] And as Roxie Ahlbrecht noted, "The road you take may not be the easy road, but it is the right road. Count your blessings in the lives you touch and impact each day."

So let me close by wishing you great happiness and success in what I hope will be a long and satisfying journey. Enjoy your travel companions and all that you learn along the way. Know that you are shaping the future of the world in each heart and life you touch. And don't forget to write.[36]

The Paradoxical Commandments

By Kent M. Keith[37]

1. People are illogical, unreasonable, and self-centered. **Love them anyway.**

2. If you do good, people will accuse you of selfish ulterior motives. **Do good anyway.**

3. If you are successful, you will win false friends and true enemies. **Succeed anyway.**

4. The good you do today will be forgotten tomorrow. **Do good anyway.**

5. Honesty and frankness make you vulnerable. **Be honest and frank anyway.**

6. The biggest men and women with the biggest ideas can be shot down by the smallest men and women with the smallest minds. **Think big anyway.**

7. People favor underdogs but follow only top dogs. **Fight for a few underdogs anyway.**

8. What you spend years building may be destroyed overnight. **Build anyway.**

9. People really need help but may attack you if you do help them. **Help people anyway.**

10. Give the world the best you have and you'll get kicked in the teeth. **Give the world the best you have anyway.**

ACTIVITY

Which of the following sound like you? Rate each item using the following scale:

1—*Rarely or never*

2—*Sometimes*

3—*Often or usually*

1. I put a great deal of pressure on myself.

2. I feel really bad when I make a mistake or have a bad day.

3. I feel like other people are judging me.

4. I feel competitive with other teachers, especially other beginners.

5. I feel a great deal of stress about my job.

6. I don't feel as though I have anyone to talk to about questions or problems I have regarding my work.

7. I feel very vulnerable to people's opinions of me.

8. I often feel weak or extremely tired.

9. I often feel sick or physically run down.

10. I don't seem to have any time for anything besides my job.

11. Some of the stress-relievers and coping mechanisms I use are not very healthy. (Consider eating—too much, not enough, or not the right foods—alcohol, nicotine, shopping, working, or the use of any other substance or behavior that could possibly or eventually put me at risk or cause problems.)

12. I don't seem to have any balance in my life.

Total up your scores. Your scores will probably be higher now than after you've been at this for a while, but if you marked a lot of these items as "often or usually," please consider seeking help from a reliable and trustworthy mentor, through your employee-assistance program (should one be available through your district), or a counselor. Also look around for online groups or lists for beginning teachers.

Every contributor to this book would probably agree that we want you to enjoy your work and feel excited and energized about what you do. And we would probably all tell you that if it feels like too much to handle, we've all been there. Please reach out. You do not have to do this alone.

ACTIVITY

Make a plan! Identify a goal for each of Mosley's five "wells" for restoration and renewal.

	In the Coming Week	**Within the Next Three Months**	**By the End of the Year**
Cognitive			
Emotional			
Creative			
Physical			
Spiritual			

Check back after a few weeks and answer the following:

1. Which of the wells has been easiest for you to get to?

2. Which has been the hardest?

3. Which of the activities you've completed seemed to benefit you most?

4. Which of the activities you've completed in the past few weeks included things you were doing before you started teaching (or things you've been doing all along)?

5. Which would you like to become a regular part of your daily practice?

6. Is there anything else you're doing that you'd like to add, to update the information you put in the chart a few weeks ago?

NOTES

1. Haas (n.d.).

2. Quoted in Naylor (2009a).

3. From Bluestein (2006), *Dealing With Difficult Colleagues.*

4. Mahoney and Purr (2007, p. 21).

5. The better you are tuned into internal cues, the better your resistance to the negative impact of stress on your physical health. One study showed that people who were the least tuned in to their reactions to stressful life events and who failed to take corrective actions experienced lowered body resistance over time and increased susceptibility to physical illness. "Persons scoring highly on feelings of internal control, commitment, and challenge have been found to be less likely to become ill subsequent to life events than persons low on those three dimensions" (Suls & Fletcher, 1985).

6. Richard J. Avdoian (1996b). Reprinted with permission (www.richardavdoian.com).

7. Aspy and Roebuck (1977), citing studies from the 1970s conducted by the National Consortium for Humanizing Education.

8. "Is your desk a bacteria cafeteria?" (2006, p. 22).

9. Dinsdale also recommended supplements at the first sign of a cold or scratchy throat. Obviously, you'll want to talk to your health care provider about ways you can support your immune system. Do not underestimate how demanding the job is or how willing your students will be to share anything they've got.

10. Despues (1999).

11. Murray (2007). Murray added, "In addition to negative coping patterns (overeating, uncontrolled emotional outbursts, feelings of helplessness, having a cocktail or a beer, or smoking a cigarette, for example), ineffectively diffusing stress, and failure to employ techniques that promote the relaxation response (activation of parasympathetic nervous system designed for repair, maintenance, and restoration of the body), the other primary lifestyle issues that greatly add to reducing a person's ability to deal with stress are poor time management, relationship issues, lack of physical exercise, and poor sleeping habits."

12. Urban (2002). Urban also included being able to bring out the best in others, setting goals, working hard, bouncing back from failure, and being honest among the six characteristics that the happiest, most successful people share. He also said that these are "characteristics that anyone can develop."

13. Walter Elliot, quoted in the video *212°: The Extra Degree* (Parker & Anderson, 2009).

14. Although I know people who do their journaling at a keyboard, either in a private document or in an online blog, I personally need a pen in my hand for this process to work best for me. Could be force of habit, could be kinesthetic inclinations. (I'm actually rather obsessive about having the right kind of pen and writing on the paper that has a certain feel.) I keep a blog and find the keyboard experience satisfying, but I can reach down a bit deeper and say things in a journal that have no business in a blog. It's a very different experience and process for me, but do whatever works for you.

15. Adams (2008, pp. 13–14).

16. Adams (2008) cautioned that "people who write only about difficult life circumstances in their journals sometimes find that the process makes them feel worse."

17. Murray (2007). Michael Craig Miller (2007) added, "Exercise increases nerve cells in the hippocampus which can help relieve—and may also prevent—depression" (p. 49).

18. Miller (2007, p. 48).

19. And build brain breaks for your kids to move, stretch, or talk, for example, every ten to fifteen minutes, to maintain attention and alertness. This is especially important in schools that have limited or eliminated recess and physical education, as more and more schools trend toward cutting time for nonacademic activities. Pytel (2006); Schoellkopf (2008). For more information on creating a brain-friendly classroom, check out Carla Hannaford (2005), *Smart Moves: Why Learning Is Not All in Your Head*; Martha Kaufeldt (2005), *Teachers, Change Your Bait! Brain-Compatible Differentiated Instruction*; Robin Fogarty (2001), *Brain Compatible Classrooms*; Eric Jensen, *Brain-Based Learning* (1996) and *Brain Compatible Strategies* (1997); Sharon Promislow (1999), *Making the Brain Body Connection*; David Sousa (2006), *How the Brain Learns*; Mary Sue Williams and Sherry Shellenberger (1996), *How Does Your Engine Run?* And be sure to visit the Brain Gym International Web site (www.braingym.org) as well as the Edu-Kinesthetics Web site (www.braingym.com).

20. Jampolsky and Cirincione (1993, p. 59).

21. Thank you to Mike Smith for the quote. He included it in an e-mail, attributing it to the world's most famous author: Anonymous.

22. Excerpted and adapted from Jane Bluestein (1997/2003b), "Positively Positive."

23. Richard J. Avdoian (1996a). Reprinted with permission (www.richardavdoian.com).

24. Quoted in Sapp (2005, p. 27).

25. Mosley (2005).

26. Quoted in Hopkins (2007).

27. Despues (1999).

28. Oxytocin is a hormone and neurotransmitter produced primarily in the hypothalamus. Probably best known for its role in childbirth and breastfeeding, oxytocin is "the reason why we form all sorts of deep connections not only with our children, but with our partners, friends and even our pets." Additionally related to touch and bonding, the release of oxytocin—for example, from feelings of love and affection, appreciation, gratitude, emotional connections with others, even petting an animal—can reduce fear and stress and promote positive health benefits. This information is primarily from "Oxytocin: The Real Love Drug" (n.d.) and "The Big 'O' Isn't Orgasm: Oxytocin, the Cuddle Hormone" (Robinson & Wilson, 2004).

29. Goleman (2006, p. 13).

30. Childre and Martin (1999, p. 23).

31. Urban (2002).

32. Ornish (2005, p. 56).

33. Reynolds and Reynolds (2008).

34. Bluestein, Lawrence, and Sanchez (2008). Personally, I find great benefit in noting the things I'm grateful for in my journal, although I have also, from time to time, kept a separate notebook *just* for this task. It's a great way to end the day and a very good habit for shifting out of a negative, anxious, or stressed-out state of mind.

35. Levey and Levey (1998, pp. 119–120).

36. Readers can contact me through my Web site: www.janebluestein.com.

37. The Paradoxical Commandments are reprinted by permission of the author. Copyright © Kent M. Keith 1968, renewed 2001. I have seen numerous versions of this list (with the main point being to care and do your best regardless of the outcome) incorrectly attributed to a number of different authors. My thanks to editorial assistant Allison Scott for tracking down Kent M. Keith, and to Dr. Keith for his permission to include this wonderful piece in this book.

Acknowledgments

I consider myself extremely fortunate to know and work with teachers all over the world. As soon as I started working on this book, I began contacting other educators for their ideas and guidance. I created a survey to solicit tips, observations, and reflections from a wide variety of people in this field.[1] In addition, I contacted certain individuals to discuss specific issues or topics in which each had a particular expertise. I also noted comments expressed during seminars, conferences, book signings, and other events at which I was able to interact directly with people currently in the trenches.

As a result, the content and tone of this book have been significantly impacted by the voices and experiences of hundreds of individuals in the teaching profession. The contributors listed below represent grade levels from preschool through high school and range from preservice teachers to veterans and retirees with decades in the field. I spoke to and heard from classroom teachers, paraprofessionals, counselors, office staff, bus drivers, supervisors, central office personnel, superintendents, consultants and authors, and people from state departments of education. Some of the contributors are longtime friends and colleagues; others I know only from our correspondence regarding this endeavor. The content also includes conversations with people I met briefly and whose names I never caught (or don't remember) as well as comments offered in anonymous notes left for me at the end of a seminar or in program evaluations.

Although I was not able to include the valuable input offered by all of the people who provided material for my consideration, I am immensely grateful to each contributor who took the time to talk with me, complete the survey, or otherwise provide suggestions, perspectives, and material that influenced the scope, direction, and feel of my writing on this project. All of the individuals whose comments were used in this book have been referenced by name and position, unless they requested that their contributions be used anonymously.

This book reflects the experiences, opinions, and observations of educators across five continents; however, I have elected to not name their location or school—in part to avoid drawing unwanted attention to the facilities in which they work but mainly to preserve the universality of their experiences.

Micki Agresta

Roxie Ahlbrecht

Melissa Albright

Melody L. Aldrich

Rita Alfaro

Cindi Allen

Mel Alper

Cheryl Alton

Amna Abdullah Hamad Al-Sharqi

Elaine Anderson

Sherry L. Annee

Lydia Aranda

Wendy Aschenbach

Richard Avdoian

Susan M. Bailey

Susan Baker

Carrie Balent

Anna Barsanti	Paul Darnell	Jo Ann Freiberg
Larraine Bates	Joanne Davidman	Dave Friedli
Ken Bauer	Holly Davis	Bill Funkhouser
Erin Beers	Stan Davis	Don Garrett
Marlene Berman	Veronica de Andres	Jason Gehrke
John Bickart	April Keck DeGennaro	Sandy Goldman
Richard Biffle	Cesar Delgado	Sarah Guthrie
Joel Black	Christie DeMello	Chris G. Hall
Jo Alice Blondin	Linda Denes	Bruce Hammonds
Scott Bohyer	Jill Denson	Tammy Hanna
Stephen Bongiovi	Amy DesChane	Stacy Harris
Michele Borba	Valerie Dickerson	Lyle Hartman
Roberta Braverman	Carol Dinsdale	Joani Heavey
Charla Bunker	Jolene Dockstader	Tihonia Hinton
Marcia Burke	Pearl M. Drain	Kenneth Hodge
Jennifer Burkholder	Gail Dusa	Celine Holloway
Carol Burns	Lesley Dyck	Allan Ilagan
Jen Buttars	Mary K. Edmunds	Mark Ita
Diane L. Callahan	Beth Edwards	Cindy Jaeger
Glenn Capelli	Anissa Emery	Marti Johnson
Maryann Caprioli	Michelle Erickson	Janet Jones
Janice Carvajal	Suzanne Faas	Marcella Jones
Sallie Chaffin	Tuija Fagerlund	Eric Katz
Amy Donner Chait	Stacey Ferguson	Linda Keegan
Brian Cichy	Karen L. Fernandez	Sandra Kenyon
Paul Clements	Ashley Ferris	John Keydash
Michelle Colbert	Julie Finley	Seta Khajarian
Lynn Collins	Mark Fish	Jeff Kirsch
Cheryl Converse-Rath	Eric Flowers	Jamie Kunkle
Jason Cushner	Nancy Foote	Marilyn Lane
Annette Dake	Mandy Frantti	Reba Lane
Ray Dagger	Julia Frascona	Diane Laveglia
Sharon D'Andrea	Jeremy Freedman	Sherri Leeper

Berna Levine	Jessica Pace	Missy Stephens
Lulu Lopez	Roxanna Peña	Debra Sugar
Monica Lopez	Joanne Peters	Olivia Sutton
John MacBeth	Aili Pogust	Claude Thau
Marvin Marshall	Dave Pruim	Michelle Tillapaugh
Wendy Marshall	Sione Quaass	Joshua Torres
Jacie Bejster Maslyk	Andy Quiñones	Shelly Traver
Michelle Mayrose	Darren Raichart	Aaron Trummer
David McAndrew	Jean Ramirez	Jillian Tsoukalas
Jason McCord	Keith Redhead	Mary Vaglica
A. J. McCree	Iain Riffel	Stephen Vance
Victor McGuire	Richard Roberts	Katie Wachtel
Teddy Meckstroth	Lois Romm	Kathi Walsh
Bonnie Milanak	Marcia Rosen	Theresa Weidner
Wonell Miller	Adrian Schaefer	Chris Weitschat
Josh Moberg	Sherry Schafer	Kerisa Wiley
Chick Moorman	Anita Scherer	Amy Williams
Anne Morgan	Gail Scott	Kim Wilson
D. Moritz	Edward Shafer	David Wolowitz
Jenny Mosley	Melissa Shepard	Dot Woodfin
Barbara Muller-Ackerman	Lindsay Shepheard	Eric Wright
Catherine Nguyen-Ho	Mike Smith	Ruthann Young-Cookson
Gerri-Lynn Nicholls	Jill Snyderman	Beth Zelfer
Phyllis O'Brien	David Steinberg	Ales Zitnik

    In addition, I would like to thank Rhea Alper, Hamidah Bahashwan, Leslie Blake, Kathryn Butterfield, Lisa Cramer, Marilyn Davidman, Sherri Davidman, Matthew Diener, Gregg Edwards, Bernardo Gallegos, Jason Gehrke, Susannah Grover, Stephen Haslam, Marcella Jones, Marvin Marshall, Cathy Mellor, Kaye Mentley, Evelyn Mercur, Mary Ellen Rodgers, Kristi Skovgaard, Linda Sorenson, Debra Sugar, and Keith Ward for their part in helping me collect data for this book, either by circulating the survey and connecting me with some exceptionally talented and insightful educators or by sending materials, ideas, and resources.

    Huge thanks to the folks at Corwin: Lesley Blake, Phyllis Cappello, Michael Dubowe, Allison Scott, Cassandra Seibel, and especially Hudson Perigo—an indispensible sounding board who helped me throughout this process to shape the direction, content, and tone of this book. And while I may never get over my various grammatical shortcomings, with copy editors like Cindy Long, my grasp of the conventions of this language continues to show signs of improvement. I particularly appreciate her attention to details and errors I simply don't see, no matter how many times I go through the manuscript on my own.

A very special bit of gratitude to Simone Albert, Rhea Alper, Tanya Baker-McCue, Judie Bennett, Leslie Bihn, Pam Colberg, Lynn Collins, Kate Dixon, Val Ford, Jo Ann Freiberg, Sandy Heimerl, Dodi and Kendra Karp, Linda Karr, Lolly Kersey, Judy Lawrence, Lynne Marcus, Ida Mazzoni, Jo Ann Schaefer, and Linda Sorenson for their continued friendship and support throughout the process of creating this book.

I also want to add a heartfelt thank you to my dog. Shadow wasn't much use when it came to bouncing ideas off him (not that that ever stopped me), but he hung with me through the end of this project and was fantastic for breaking my writers' block when I just needed to step away from the computer and go for a walk. I enjoyed the comfort and pleasure of his companionship throughout the writing and editorial process—right up to the end of his long, well-lived, and well-loved life.

And as always, an extra-special thank you to my husband, Jerry Tereszkiewicz, for enduring yet another two years of books, papers, and printouts all over the house, for picking up a whole lot of slack while I was working on this book, and for being a part of my life since I started my teaching career.

NOTE

1. Visit www.janebluestein.com/forum/survey_08.html to view the survey questions used to solicit responses for this book.

References

2008 Forest Sangha calendar. (2007). Chennai, India: Aruna.

Adams, K. (2008, August 15). The amazing benefits of journaling. *Bottom Line Personal,* 13–14.

Adler, J., & Springen, K. (1999, May 3). How to fight back. *Newsweek.* Available from www .newsweek.com/id/88189

Adolescent brain development. (2002). Available from www.actforyouth.net/documents/may02fact sheetadolbraindev.pdf

Aftab, P., & Wired Safety Group. (n.d.). *Stop cyberbullying.* Available from www.stopcyberbullying .org

Albow, K. (2009, April 8). *Bullied to death.* Available from http://health.blogs.foxnews.com/ 2009/04/08/bullied-to-death/

Alinsky, S. D. (1971). *Rules for radicals: A pragmatic primer for realistic radicals.* New York: Vintage Books.

Allen, M. B. (2005). *Eight questions on teacher recruitment and retention: What does the research say?* (Education Commission of the States Teaching Quality Research Report). Available from www.ecs.org/html/educationissues/TeachingQuality/TRRreport/report/introduction.asp

Alliance for Excellent Education. (2009). *High school dropouts in America* [Fact sheet]. Available from www.all4ed.org/files/GraduationRates_FactSheet.pdf

Alverado, F. (2007, November 7). *Good teacher, bad principal.* Available from www.miaminewtimes .com/2007-11-08/news/good-teacher-bad-principal/

Ansary, T. (2009). *Computers in school: Are we there yet?* Retrieved from http://encarta.msn.com

Aristotle. (n.d.). In *Wisdom quotes.* Available from www.wisdomquotes.com/002493.html

Aspy, D. N., & Roebuck, F. N. (1977). *Kids don't learn from people they don't like.* Amherst, MA: Human Resource Development Press.

Australian Centre for Equity through Education & Australian Youth Research Centre. (2001). *Building relationships: Making education work. A report on the perspectives of young people.* Available from www.dest.gov.au/NR/rdonlyres/8F647C50-0465-46A9-9D1D-C5662342A846/1534/ buildingrelationships.pdf

Avdoian, R. (1996a). *Recommendations for reducing tension and stress* [Conference handout].

Avdoian, R. (1996b). *Take charge of your life and actively live each day* [Conference handout].

Baines, L. (2006, December 1). Deconstructing teacher certification. *Phi Delta Kappan, 88*(4), 326–328.

Barker, O., & Bailey, S. (2005, August 15). Going toe-to-toe on office etiquette. *USA Today,* pp. D1–D2.

Barth, R. (2002, May). The culture builder. *Educational Leadership, 59*(8), 6–11. Available from http:// course1.winona.edu/lgray/el601/articles/Barth_Culture.html

Bassis, M. (2004, March 22). *Students must learn how to learn.* Available from www.deseretnews .com/article/1,5143,595050795,00.html

Bianco, R. (2003, February 28). Children lose a quiet, honest friend. *USA Today.*

Bluestein, J. (1980). *Developing responsible learning behaviors through peer interaction.* Unpublished doctoral dissertation, University of Pittsburgh, Pittsburgh, PA.

Bluestein, J. (1989). *Being a successful teacher.* Torrance, CA: Fearon Teacher Aids.

Bluestein, J. (1993). *Parents, teens, and boundaries: How to draw the line.* Deerfield Beach, FL: Health Communications.

Bluestein, J. (1995). *Mentors, masters, and Mrs. MacGregor: Stories of teachers making a difference.* Deerfield Beach, FL: Health Communications.

Bluestein, J. (1999a). *Are your colleagues driving you crazy?* Albuquerque, NM: Instructional Support Services. (Original work published 1986)

Bluestein, J. (1999b). Foreword. In E. Wright, *Why I teach* (pp. vii–viii). Rocklin, CA: Prima.

Bluestein, J. (2001). *Creating emotionally safe schools.* Deerfield Beach, FL: Health Communications.

Bluestein, J. (2002). *The beauty of losing control.* Albuquerque, NM: Instructional Support Services.

Bluestein, J. (2003a). *Ask—Don't tell!* Albuquerque, NM: Instructional Support Services.

Bluestein, J. (2003b). *Positively positive.* Albuquerque, NM: Instructional Support Services. (Original work published 1997)

Bluestein, J. (2003c). *Secrets of successful mentorship.* Albuquerque, NM: Instructional Support Services.

Bluestein, J. (2006). *Dealing with difficult colleagues.* Albuquerque, NM: Instructional Support Services.

Bluestein, J. (2008). *The win-win classroom.* Thousand Oaks, CA: Corwin.

Bluestein, J., & Katz, E. (2005). *High school's not forever.* Deerfield Beach, FL: Health Communications.

Bluestein, J., Lawrence, J., & Sanchez, S. J. (2008). *Magic, miracles, and synchronicity.* Albuquerque, NM: Instructional Support Services.

Blum, R. W. (2004). School connectedness: Improving students' lives. *Journal of School Health.* Available from www.k12.wa.us/OperationMilitaryKids/pubdocs/SchoolConnectedness.PDF

Blum, R. W., McNeely, C., & Rinehart, P. M. (2002). *Improving the odds: The untapped power of schools to improve the health of teens.* Minneapolis: University of Minnesota, Center for Adolescent Health and Development.

Blumenfeld, B. (1996, October 2). Moral education not rote learning [Letter to the editor]. *Albuquerque Journal,* p. A11.

Borba, M. (2001). *Building moral intelligence: Our last, best hope.* (Reprinted from *Building moral intelligence: The seven essential virtues that teach kids to do the right thing,* by M. Borba, 2001, San Francisco: Jossey-Bass)

Borba, M. (2002, February 13). *Preventing school violence.* Paper prepared for the California State Senate, Committee on Education.

Brockman, M. S., & Russell, S. T. (n.d.). *Decision-making/reasoning skills.* Available from http://cals-cf.calsnet.arizona.edu/fcs/bpy/content.cfm?content=decision_making

Brooks, D. (2009, March 12). No picnic for me either. *New York Times.* Available from www.nytimes.com/2009/03/13/opinion/13brooks.html

Burns, J. (2009, March 20). *100 Everyday strategies to help teachers and students become their personal best.* Available from http://behavioral-management.com/?p=623

Butler, K. (1997, October). *Learning styles workshop* [Conference handout].

Carson, R. (2007, April/May). Keeping alive the sense of wonder. *National Wildlife,* 14.

Chaika, G. (2000, March 27). The teacher shortage: Apply, please! *Education World.* Available from www.educationworld.com/a_admin/admin/admin155.shtml

Champagne, D. W., & Goldman, R. M. (1972). *Teaching parents teaching.* Norwalk, CT: Appleton-Century-Crofts.

Champine, F. (2004, July 28). Teachers should be given tools to excel in diverse classrooms. *Philadelphia Inquirer.*

Childre, D., & Martin, H. (with Beech, D.). (1999). *The heartmath solution.* New York: HarperCollins.

Cichy, B. (2008, February). *Functional behavior assessment on-the-fly.* Paper presented at Minnesota Council for Exceptional Children conference, Duluth, MN.

CNN. (2003, January 29). *Report: Teacher retention biggest school woe.* Retrieved from www.cnn.com/2003/EDUCATION/01/29/teacher.shortage.ap/

Cody, N. (2007, August 21). *The new "face" of bullies.* Available from www.princetonol.com/back_to_school/polArticles.cfm?doc_id=998

College of New Jersey. (n.d.). *Teacher candidate assessment program: Dispositions rubric.* Available from www.tcnj.edu/~educat/dean.html

Cooper, K. (presenter). (2007). *Impedership vs. leadership* [Video file]. Available from www.ej4.com/

Dauten, D. (2001, August 16). The corporate curmudgeon. *Albuquerque Journal.*

Dauten, D. (2007a, April 19). Ethics: Your half of the job is 60 percent. *Albuquerque Journal,* p. 10.

Dauten, D. (2007b, May 31). People don't leave jobs—They leave jerks. *Albuquerque Journal*, p. 10.

DeLuca, J. R. (1999). *Political savvy: Systematic approaches to leadership behind-the-scenes*. Berwyn, PA: Evergreen Business Group.

Despues, D. (1999). *Stress and illness*. Available from www.csun.edu/~vcpsy00h/students/illness.htm

Economic Policy Institute. (2004). *Teacher pay lags compared to comparable professions, national study finds*. Available from www.weac.org/news_and_publications/education_news/2004-2005/teacherpay.aspx

Edutopia staff. (2007). *Readers' Survey 2007: Amount you spend out of pocket each year on classroom supplies*. Available from www.edutopia.org/amount-you-spend-out-pocket-each-year-classroom-supplies-2007

Ethical behavior? (2006, July 28). Message posted to www.proteacher.net/discussions/showthread.php?t=14277

Evelyn, J. (2007, Fall). Creating a new kind of teacher. *Brooklyn College Magazine*, 22–25.

Family Educational Rights and Privacy Act. (2009). Available from www.ed.gov/policy/gen/guid/fpco/ferpa/index.html

Family Unschoolers Network. (2006, December 11). Available from http://unschooling.org

Ferguson, S. (2004, November 22). Stressed out! *MacLean's*, 31–38.

FERPA information sheet. (n.d.). Available from http://hawk.huntingdon.edu/FERPA/fsinfo.HTML

Fisch, K. (2007, February 20). *What if?* [PowerPoint slides and Video file]. Available from http://thefischbowl.blogspot.com/2006/09/what-if.html

Fisch, K., McLeod, S., & Brenman, J. (2008, November 16). *Did you know* [Video file]. Video posted to www.youtube.com/watch?v=Mmz5qYbKsvM

Foer, J. (2007, November). Remember this. *National Geographic*, 32–55.

Fogarty, R. (2001). *Brain compatible classrooms* [Conference handout]. (Reprinted from *Brain compatible classrooms*, by R. Fogarty, 2001, Arlington Heights, IL: SkyLight Training)

Fogarty, R. (2007). *10 Things new teachers need to succeed*. Thousand Oaks, CA: Corwin.

Francis, R. (2000, June 14). Home-grown students: Program bridges gap between school and home. *Education World*. Available from www.educationworld.com/a_admin/admin/admin174.shtml

Freiberg, J. A. (2007a, August 24). *Building a positive school climate* [Video file]. Presentation to the Shelton Public Schools, Shelton, CT.

Freiberg, J. A. (2007b, October 13). *"Bully" is a four letter word: Understanding the concept to manage the territory*. Paper presented to the New England Philosophy of Education Society.

Freiberg, J. A. (2007c). *Improving school climate to diminish bullying behaviors: Creating "climates of respect"* [PowerPoint slides].

Friedman, T. L. (2007). *The world is flat* (Release 3.0). New York: Picador.

Gatto, J. T. (2005). *Dumbing us down: The hidden curriculum of compulsory schooling*. Gabriola Island, British Columbia, Canada: New Society.

Gaudiosi, J. (2005, September). Gamers aren't weirdos! *Sky Magazine*, 86–87.

Gazzaniga, M. S. (1988). *Mind matters*. Boston: Houghton Mifflin.

Gentzler, Y. (2005). *A new teacher's guide to best practices*. Thousand Oaks, CA: Corwin.

Gerlach, L., & Bird, J. (2005, September). *Feel the difference: Learning in an emotionally competent school*. Paper presented at the Centre for Child Mental Health conference on emotional health in schools, London.

Gibbs, N. (2005, February 21). Parents behaving badly. *Time*, 40–49.

Goleman, D. (1995). *Emotional intelligence*. New York: Bantam Books.

Goleman, D. (2006, September 3). Can you raise your social IQ? *Parade*, 10–13.

Greenspan, S. I. (with Benderly, B. L.). (1997). *The growth of the mind*. Reading, MA: Addison-Wesley.

Haas, B. A. (n.d.). Fundamentals for healthy self-esteem. In *Full esteem ahead: Munchies for the heart and soul* [Conference handout].

Hahn, R., Fuqua-Whitley, D., Wethington, H., Lowy, J., Liberman, A., Crosby, A., et al. (2007). *The effectiveness of universal school-based programs for the prevention of violent and aggressive behavior.*

A report on recommendations of the Task Force on Community Preventive Services. Available from www.cdc.gov/mmwr/preview/mmwrhtml/rr5607a1.htm

Hall, S. (2008, January 17). Teacher suspended after students see her in racy ad. *Adrants Newsletter*. Available from www.adrants.com/2008/01/teacher-suspended-after-students-see-her.php# more

Hannaford, C. (2005). *Smart moves: Why learning is not all in your head* (2nd ed.). Salt Lake City, UT: Great River Books.

Haslam, S. (2001, September). *Emotions are a fact of life* [Conference handout].

Hawken, P. (2009, May 3). *Commencement address to the class of 2009, University of Portland, OR*. Available from http://heartlandcircle.blogs.com/circle/2009/05/paul-hawken-commence ment-address-unv-of-portland.html

Herbert, B. (2006, January 30). The lost children. *New York Times*. Available from http:// freedemocracy.blogspot.com/2006/01/bob-herbert-lost-children.html

Hopkins, G. (2007, May 25). What qualities do principals look for in a new teacher? *Education World*. Available from www.educationworld.com/a_admin/admin/admin071.shtml

Hopkins, G. (2008, May 8). Journal writing every day: Teachers say it really works! *Education World*. Available from www.education-world.com/a_curr/curr144.shtml

Hoy, W. K. (n.d.). *Measuring school climate, school climate and outcomes, issues trends and controversies*. Available from http://education.stateuniversity.com/pages/2392/School-Climate.html

Huxley, A. (n.d.). In *Thinkexist: Aldous Huxley quotes*. Available from http://thinkexist.com/quotation/experience_is_not_what_happens_to_you-it_is_what/145524.html

Inman, D., & Marlow, L. (2004). *Teacher retention: Why do beginning teachers remain in the profession?* Available from http://findarticles.com/p/articles/mi_qa3673/is_4_124/ai_n29117808/?tag =content;col1

Interstate New Teacher Assessment and Support Consortium (INTASC) Special Education Sub-Committee. (2001). *Model standards for licensing general and special education teachers of students with disabilities: A resource for state dialogue*. Available from http://serge.ccsso.org/pdf/standards.pdf

Is your desk a bacteria cafeteria? (2006, June 4). *USA Weekend*, p. 22.

Isaacson, W. (2007). *Einstein*. New York: Simon & Schuster.

Jampolsky, G. G., & Cirincione, D. V. (1993). *Change your mind, change your life*. New York: Bantam Books.

Jehlen, A. (2008, February). How can you deal with angry parents? *NEA Today*, 30–31.

Jensen, E. (1996). *Brain-based learning*. San Diego, CA: Brain Store.

Jensen, E. (1997). *Brain compatible strategies*. San Diego, CA: Brain Store.

Jones, M. (2008). *Children have to grow up too fast*. Available from www.edutopia.org/childhoods-end-accountability-forces-children-grow-up-too-fast

Kantrowitz, B., & Wingert, P. (2000, October 2). Teachers wanted. *Newsweek*, 37–42.

Kaufeldt, M. (2005). *Teachers, change your bait! Brain-compatible differentiated instruction*. Norwalk, CT: Crown.

Keirsey, D. (n.d.). True colors. Available from www.truecolors.org/about.htm

Kelly, M. (n.d.). *Journals in the classroom*. Available from http://712educators.about.com/cs/writ ingresources/a/journals.htm

Kenmore, C. (n.d.). In *Motivation quotes*. Available from www.famousquotesandauthors.com/authors/carolyn_kenmore_quotes.html

Kline, P. (2002). *Why America's children can't think: Creating independent minds for the 21st century*. Makawao, HI: Inner Ocean.

Kopkowski, C. (2008, February). Why they leave. *NEA Today*, 21–25.

Lantieri, L., & Patti, J. (1996). *Waging peace in our schools*. Boston: Beacon Press.

Learned helplessness. (2001). Available from http://findarticles.com/p/articles/mi_g2602/is_0003/ai_2602000349/

The learner: Interests. (2001). Available from www.saskschools.ca/curr_content/adapthandbook/learner/interest.html

Lee, M. (2008, April 2). *BookMarkLee*. Available from www.bookmarklee.co.uk/2008/04/02/to-get-what-weve-never-had-we-must-do-what-weve-never-done/

Levey, J., & Levey, M. (1998). *Living in balance.* Berkeley, CA: Conari Press.

Lewis, B. (n.d.). *Pros and cons of merit pay for teachers: Should teachers be rewarded for performance like everyone else?* Available from http://k6educators.about.com/od/assessmentandtesting/a/meritypay.htm

Littke, D., & Grabelle, S. (2004). *The big picture: Education is everyone's business.* Alexandria, VA: Association for Supervision and Curriculum Development.

Lovely, S., & Buffum, A. G. (2007). *Generations at school: Building an age-friendly learning community.* Thousand Oaks, CA: Corwin.

Lungold, I. X. (2003, September 6). *Secrets of the Mayan calendar unveiled.* Lecture at Okanagan University College, Vernon, British Columbia, Canada.

Mahoney, A. S., & Purr, C. (2007). *Untenured, uncensored.* Lanham, MD: Rowman & Littlefield.

Mann, H. (n.d.). In *Famous quotes and authors: Punishments quotes.* Available from www.famousquotesandauthors.com/topics/punishment_quotes.html

Markway, R. A. (2004, June 24). Report says parents not listening enough. *Albuquerque Journal.*

Marshall, M. (n.d.). *The social development program: Ensuring social responsibility* [Conference handout].

Marshall, M. (2001). *Discipline without stress, punishments, or rewards: How teachers and parents promote responsibility and learning.* Los Alamitos, CA: Piper Press.

Mary Parker Follett Foundation. (n.d.). *Mary Parker Follett.* Available from www.follettfoundation.org/mpf.htm

Matthews, J. (2009, March 29). Teach the kids, and the parents will follow. *Washington Post.* Available from www.washingtonpost.com/wp-dyn/content/article/2009/03/27/AR2009032700958.html

Michigan Department of Education. (n.d.a). *Strengthening teacher-student relationships.* Available from www.michigan.gov/documents/3-3_107241_7.pdf

Michigan Department of Education. (n.d.b). *What research says about parent involvement in children's education in relation to academic achievement.* Available from www.michigan.gov/documents/Final_Parent_Involvement_Fact_Sheet_14732_7.pdf

Mikkelson, B., & Mikkelson, D. (2007, July 9). *1872 rules for teachers.* Available from www.snopes.com/language/document/1872rule.asp

Miller, M. C. (2007, March 26). Exercise is a state of mind. *Newsweek.* Available from http://www.newsweek.com/id/35841

Mosley, J. (2005, May). *Visiting the wells.* Paper presented at the Centre for Child Mental Health conference, Understanding and Improving Children's Behaviour: To Impact Learning, London. (Reprinted from *Turn your school round,* by J. Mosley, 1993, Cambridge, England: LDA)

Murray, M. T. (2007, June). Stress-relax: The effective nutritional system for a calmer life. *Vitamin Cottage.*

Nagourney, E. (2000, November 14). *Behavior: Stopping school trouble before it starts.* Available from http://www.nytimes.com/2000/11/14/science/14SCHO.html

Naisbitt, J. (1982). *Megatrends.* New York: Warner Books.

Nash, R. (2009). *The active classroom.* Thousand Oaks, CA: Corwin.

National Center for Education Information. (2007). *Overview of alternative routes to teacher certification.* Available from www.teach-now.org/overview.cfm

National Center for Education Statistics. (n.d.). *Special analysis 2005: Mobility in the teacher workforce.* Available from http://nces.ed.gov/programs/coe/2005/analysis/sa02.asp

National Dissemination Center for Children with Disabilities. (n.d.). *Categories of disability under IDEA law.* Available from www.nichcy.org/Disabilities/Categories/Pages/Default.aspx

National Education Association. (n.d.). *Myths and facts about educator pay.* Available from www.nea.org/home/12661.htm

National Education Association. (1975). *Code of ethics.* Retrieved from www.nea.org/home/30442.htm

National Education Association. (2000). What do new teachers need? Thirteen things to keep in mind. In *A better beginning: Helping new teachers survive and thrive.* Available from http://fape-online.org/NEA-Teacher-Quality-A-Better-Beginning-Helping-new-teachers-survive-and-thrive.htm

National Resource Center on AD/HD. (n.d.). *IDEA (The Individuals with Disabilities Education Act)*. Available from www.help4adhd.org/education/rights/idea

Naylor, A. (2009a, February 28). *3 Keys to personal accountability and creating a better life*. Available from www.huffingtonpost.com/anne-naylor/3-keys-to-personal-accoun_b_169736.html

Naylor, A. (2009b, February 14). *5 ways to turn on the power of your love*. Available from www.huffingtonpost.com/anne-naylor/5-ways-to-turn-on-the-pow_b_166619.html

NYCLU, Annenberg Institute release report on successful and safe NYC schools that say no to aggressive police tactics. (2009). Available from www.nyclu.org/node/2501

One in 10 high schools gets an F. (2007, December 16). *Parade*, 10.

Ornish, D. (2005, October 3). Love is real medicine. *Newsweek*, 56.

Osborn, D. K., & Osborn, J. D. (1977). *Discipline and classroom management*. Athens, GA: Education Associates.

Osmar, A. (n.d.). *Richard Riley: "The top 10 in-demand jobs in 2010 may not have existed in 2004."* Available from http://thecreativecareer.com/2008/10/24/richard-riley-the-top-10-in-demand-jobs-in-2010-may-not-have-existed-in-2004/

Oxytocin: The real love drug. (n.d.). Available from www.antiaging-systems.com/a2z/oxytocin.htm

Pais, M. (2009, July 8). *Study: Positive teacher-student relationships necessary to raising achievement*. Available from www.columbiamissourian.com/stories/2009/07/08/positive-relationships-teachers-influence-student-success/

Parental involvement in schools. (n.d.). Available from www.childtrendsdatabank.org/archivepgs/39.htm

Parker, S., & Anderson, M. (2009). *212°: The extra degree* [Video file]. Available from www.212movie.com/

Pastore, R. (2005). *Principles of teaching: Rules for teachers*. Available from http://teacherworld.com/potrules.html

Pavlina, S. (2005, June 10). *Self-discipline: Persistence*. Available from www.stevepavlina.com/blog/2005/06/self-discipline-persistence/

Penaflor, D. (2004). *Journaling: A perfect way to enhance your child's literary skills*. Available from http://kids.creativity-portal.com/d/articles/journaling.child.shtml

Pink, D. H. (2005). *A whole new mind: Why right-brainers will rule the future*. New York: Riverhead Books.

Pitts, L., Jr. (2002, June 21). Your kid's going to pay for cheating—Eventually. *Jewish World Review*. Available from www.jewishworldreview.com/0602/pitts062102.asp

Prensky, M. (2001). *Digital natives, digital immigrants*. Available from www.marcprensky.com/writing/Prensky%20-%20Digital%20Natives,%20Digital%20Immigrants%20-%20Part1.pdf

Promislow, S. (1999). *Making the brain body connection*. West Vancouver, British Columbia, Canada: Kinetic.

Pulliam, J. D., & Van Patten, J. (1995). *History of education in America* (6th ed.). Englewood Cliffs, NJ: Prentice Hall.

Purkey, W. (1996). A survival manual for beginning K–12 teachers. In W. Purkey & J. Novak, *Inviting school success*. New York: Wadsworth.

Purkey, W. W., & Aspy, D. N. (1988, February). The mental health of students: Nobody minds? Nobody cares? *Person-Centered Review, 3*(1), 41–49.

Pytel, B. (2006). *Recess becoming obsolete*. Available from http://educationalissues.suite101.com/article.cfm/recess_becoming_obsolete

Quimby, D. (2003, May). Overworked and under-appreciated: A tribute to teachers. *Teachers.net Gazette*. Available from http://teachers.net/gazette/MAY03/quimby.html

Ray, B. (2004, December 12). Who's afraid of the big bad boss? *FSU News*. Retrieved from www.fsu.edu/news/2006/12/04/bad.boss/

Ray, B. D. (2006). *Research facts on homeschooling*. Available from www.nheri.org/content/view/199/

Reynolds, M. R., & Reynolds, C. (2008). *The power of connection* [Video file]. Available from www.connectionmovie.com/

Robinson, M., & Wilson, G. (2004). *The big "O" isn't orgasm: Oxytocin, the cuddle hormone.* Available from http://cuddleparty.com/articles/oxytocin.cfm

Rodriguez, J. C. (2009, June 16). Fast-track diplomas. *Albuquerque Journal.*

Rogers, C., & Frieberg, H. J. (1994). *Freedom to learn.* New York: Macmillan.

Romper Room. (n.d.). In *Wikipedia: The free encyclopedia.* Available from http://en.wikipedia.org/wiki/Romper_Room

Roots. (n.d.). In *Wikipedia: The free encyclopedia.* Available from http://en.wikipedia.org/wiki/Roots_(TV_miniseries)

Sapp, J. (2005, Spring). Body, mind, and spirit. *Teaching Tolerance, 27,* 24–29.

Saulny, S. (2006, November 26). More choosing to "unschool." *New York Times.* Available from http://articles.sun-sentinel.com/2006-11-26/news/0611260042_1_settings-and-teacher-led-school-type-settings-hayden-billings

Schaef, A. W. (1987). *When society becomes an addict.* New York: Harper & Row.

Schaps, E., & Solomon, D. (1991, February). Schools and classrooms as caring communities. *Educational Leadership, 48*(5), 38–42.

Schoellkopf, A. (2008, March 18). Need for more instruction hours taking a toll on school recess. *Albuquerque Journal.*

School violence: The history of school discipline. (1998). Available from http://law.jrank.org/pages/12094/School-Violence-history-school-discipline.html

Schwengel, K. (n.d.). *How to make a sub plan for a substitute teacher.* Available from www.ehow.com/how_2188091_sub-plan-substitute-teacher.html

Scott, R. O. (1999, Spring/Summer). It's called optimism. *Spirituality and Health,* 22–25.

Seligman, M. E. P. (1991). *Learned optimism.* New York: Alfred A. Knopf.

Shaw, G. B. (n.d.). In *Cybernation: Teachers and teaching.* Available from www.cybernation.com/quotationcenter/quoteshow.php?type=author&id=8193&page=5

Skirble, R. (2008, March 20). *Fifty percent of new teachers quit profession within five years.* Available from www1.voanews.com/english/news/a-13-2008-02-26-voa34-66636217.html?textmode=1

Smith, M. (2007a, December). The benefits of student leadership programs. *Advocate,* 1–3.

Smith, M. (2007b, November). Solving the leadership dilemma. *In Brief, 1*(2), 1–3.

Sousa, D. (2006). *How the brain learns.* Thousand Oaks, CA: Corwin.

Student record confidentiality: FERPA information. (2009). Available from www.griffintech.edu/administration/FERPAGTC.htm

Sugar, D. (2000, Spring). *How public education is failing our children and what school social workers can do about it.* Unpublished manuscript, University of New Mexico, Albuquerque.

Suls, J., & Fletcher, B. (1985). Self-attention, life stress, and illness: A prospective study. *Psychosomatic Medicine, 4*(5), 469–481. Available from www.psychosomaticmedicine.org/cgi/reprint/47/5/469.pdf

Sylwester, R. (1995). *A celebration of neurons.* Alexandria, VA: Association for Supervision and Curriculum Development.

Talevich, T. (2007, October). Stopping the dropout epidemic: How we can keep kids in schools and build a better future. *Costco Connection,* 18–20.

Taylor, J. (1999). *Certified success: Teachers with "emergency" credentials seem to teach kids just fine.* Available from http://findarticles.com/p/articles/mi_m1568/is_5_31/ai_56640750

Teacher home visits. (2009, July). Available from https://public-groups.nea.org/discussion/topic/show/207725?ssot=1

Teachers expose private lives online. (2007, November). Retrieved from www.kpho.com/news/14705236/detail.html

Teaching Handwork. (2008, September 6). *Life was different 100 years ago.* Message posted to http://teachinghandwork.blogspot.com/2008/09/in-1915-life-was-different.html

Thornton-Cullen, J., & Ryan, T. (2007, May 2). *Home schooling.* Available from http://tiger.towson.edu/~jthorn6/research/paper.htm

Twain, M. (n.d.). In *Goodreads quotable quotes.* Available from www.goodreads.com/quotes/show/18058

Underwood, A. (2005, October 3). *The good heart. Newsweek,* 49–55.

University of Utah, Department of Family and Consumer Studies. (n.d.). *Anecdotal records.* Available from www.fcs.utah.edu/info/cfdc/2610/anecdotal_records.doc

Urban, H. (2002, January 15). *Success secrets of Ben Franklin, Albert Einstein, and other greats.* Available from http://bottomlinesecrets.com/article.html?article_ id=33279&ea=jblue@twrol .com&sid=H070102S4B

U.S. Department of Education. (2004). *Building the legacy: IDEA 2004.* Available from http://idea.ed.gov/

Van Oech, R. (2008). *A whack on the side of the head: How you can be more creative.* New York: Grand Central.

Wagner, P. H. (2007). *An evaluation of the legal literacy of educators and the implications for teacher preparation programs.* Available from www.educationlaw.org/2007%20Conference/Papers/A7Wagner.pdf? PHPSESSID=31584003be141e853c2f7007129eb326

Wallis, C. (2006, March 27). The multitasking generation. *Time,* 48–55.

Wallis, C. (2008, February 25). How to make great teachers. *Time,* 28–34.

Wallis, C., & Steptoe, S. (2006, December 18). How to bring our schools out of the 20th century. *Time,* 50–56.

Wallwork, L. W., & Male, S. (2008, July 6). Fixing our schools. *Parade,* 10.

Wesley, D. C. (1998/1999, December/January). Believing in our students. *Educational Leadership, 56*(4), 45.

WGBH. (n.d.). *The Hippocratic oath: Modern version.* Available from www.pbs.org/wgbh/nova/doctors/oath_modern.html

White, P. C., Harvey, T. R., & Kemper, L. (2007). *The politically intelligent leader.* Lanham, MD: Rowman & Littlefield.

Wilcox, C. (n.d.). In *Cybernation: Teachers and teaching.* Available from www.cybernation.com/quotationcenter/quoteshow.php?id=35548

Wilke, R. L. (2003). *The first days of class.* Thousand Oaks, CA: Corwin.

Williams, M. S., & Shellenberger, S. (1996). *How does your engine run?* Albuquerque, NM: Therapy Works.

Wilson, K. G., & Daviss, B. (1994). *Redesigning education.* New York: Henry Holt.

Win-win games. (n.d.). In *Wikipedia online encyclopedia.* Available from http://en .wikipedia.org/wiki/Win-win

Win-win strategy. (n.d.). In *Wikipedia online encyclopedia.* Available from http://en.wikipedia.org/wiki/Win-win_strategy

Wyatt, R. L., & White, J. E. (2007). *Making your first year a success* (2nd ed.). Thousand Oaks, CA: Corwin.

Zimmerman, J. (2007, July 1). Justice Thomas got it wrong: Goal of schools isn't discipline. *St. Paul Pioneer Press.*

Index

CORWIN

A SAGE Company

The Corwin logo—a raven striding across an open book—represents the union of courage and learning. Corwin is committed to improving education for all learners by publishing books and other professional development resources for those serving the field of PreK–12 education. By providing practical, hands-on materials, Corwin continues to carry out the promise of its motto: **"Helping Educators Do Their Work Better."**